The Freedom Movement's Lost Legacy

THE FREEDOM MOVEMENT'S LOST LEGACY

BLACK ABOLITIONISM SINCE EMANCIPATION

KEITH P. GRIFFLER

UNIVERSITY PRESS OF KENTUCKY

Scholarly publisher for the Commonwealth,
serving Bellarmine University, Berea College, Centre
College of Kentucky, Eastern Kentucky University,
The Filson Historical Society, Georgetown College,
Kentucky Historical Society, Kentucky State University,
Morehead State University, Murray State University,
Northern Kentucky University, Spalding University,
Transylvania University, University of Kentucky,
University of Louisville, University of Pikeville,
and Western Kentucky University.
All rights reserved.

Editorial and Sales Offices: The University Press of Kentucky
663 South Limestone Street, Lexington, Kentucky 40508-4008
www.kentuckypress.com

Library of Congress Cataloging-in-Publication Data

Names: Griffler, Keith P., author.
Title: The freedom movement's lost legacy : black abolitionism since
    emancipation / Keith P. Griffler.
Description: Lexington, Kentucky : University Press of Kentucky, 2023. |
    Includes index.
Identifiers: LCCN 2022051965 | ISBN 9780813197289 (hardcover) |
    ISBN 9780813197302 (pdf) | ISBN 9780813197319 (epub)
Subjects: LCSH: Antislavery movements—History—20th century. |
    Slavery—History—20th century. | Anti-racism—History—20th century. |
    African American abolitionists—20th century.
Classification: LCC HT867 .G754 2023 | DDC 326/.80904—dc23/eng/20221205
LC record available at https://lccn.loc.gov/2022051965

Contents

Preface

From antebellum abolitionism to the civil rights movement to Black Lives Matter (BLM), the Black freedom movement has consistently been at the forefront of not only American but also global political change. It has often been forced to do its work from the margins while the rest of society catches up to its principled positions on human liberty. This was true of BLM before the eventful summer of 2020, and it was never truer than in the case of the antislavery campaign of the twentieth century, which is as forgotten today as its nineteenth-century forebearer is celebrated. What makes the neglect of this history even more remarkable is that it focuses on some of the very issues, including the carceral state, that lurk in the background of events now unfolding before our eyes. At a moment when the past is being reexamined with renewed urgency to carry on its unfinished work, it is all the more important to recover this forgotten legacy.

It is unthinkable to study the nineteenth-century international antislavery movement without considering the central contributions of Black abolitionists.[1] The same should hold true for the twentieth century. Yet when scholars have written about that subsequent period, they have almost always failed to mention Black people in their capacity of activists and theorists rather than victims.[2] This omission is enormously consequential not only to the understanding of history but also to how the twenty-first-century abolitionist movement traces its lineage and defines the states of unfreedom that persist today.

Black abolitionism did not end with the final rounds of emancipation in the Americas because slavery and its derivatives did not disappear. In the subsequent century the long shadow of slavery kept millions of Black people confined to coercive labor practices that exposed them to some of the same conditions as antebellum slavery, leaving them well short of the freedom they had been promised. The effects were felt across the African diaspora, including in the American South, where sharecropping and debt peonage entrapped a substantial proportion of African Americans as the constant threat of enforced prison labor loomed large. At the same time, this "new slavery"—as Black abolitionists called it and as I refer to it in the chapters that follow—recrossed the Atlantic so that forms of unfree labor menaced the liberty of an even larger number of Africans. This terrible transformation forced leaders of the Black freedom movement to carry the abolitionist struggle into the twentieth century, developing new Black abolitionist principles to combat the new slavery.[3]

The illustrious history of the antebellum antislavery cause does not predispose us to critically examine its successors for evidence of systemic racism. And yet a careful tracing of the twisting and turning of twentieth-century abolitionism is vital to understanding the full impact of the Black freedom movement on the world today. Its leaders bequeathed their own abolitionist legacy rooted in the idea that, for Black people around the world, the continuation of racial slavery anywhere jeopardized their freedom everywhere. The pages that follow offer the first historical account of this important chapter in the history of the antislavery and Black freedom struggle, filling in some of the less visible historical background.

This book reflects the influence and teachings of my mentors, colleagues, and friends Stephanie Shaw and Patricia Hill Collins in ways that even they will not be able to discern. It benefits as well from the impact of many people—more than I can name here—over a period of many years. A short list includes Richard Blackett, David Blight, John Bracket, Spencer Crew, Peter Ekeh, Cecil Foster, Graham Hodges, Jim Horton, Angelene Jamison-Hall, Robin Kelley, David Levering Lewis, Y. G.-M. Lulat, Alamin Mazrui, Nell Painter, Joseph Takougang, Rinaldo Walcott, and Lillian Williams. I also owe a debt of gratitude to the thousands of students in African and African American studies at both the University of Cincinnati and the University at Buffalo and the MA and PhD students at the latter that I have had the privilege to teach for two decades.

The research for this book was supported by a Charles Phelps Taft fellowship from the University of Cincinnati; by funding from the Weatherhead Initiative on Global History, Harvard University; by the Baldy Center for Law and Policy; and by funding and research leave from the College of Arts and Sciences at the University at Buffalo. While I served as chair of Africana and American Studies, Dean Bruce McCombe and his successor Bruce Pitman also provided me with a research assistant, PhD student Marta Cieslak, who carried out her duties with the excellence and extraordinary diligence that characterize everything she undertakes. A very special thank you to the great editorial team under Ashely Runyon at the University Press of Kentucky, especially acquisitions editor Natalie O'Neal, for their unstinting support and wise counsel. As always, my greatest debt is to Janina Brutt-Griffler for her patience in listening and reading, for the incisive critical feedback she always offers, and for accompanying me on many a trip to the archives, particularly in London, where her research interests take her as well.

Introduction

In 2018 activists in the Florida state prisons leveraged the symbolism of a protest held on Martin Luther King Day fifty years after his assassination. The disproportionately Black victims of America's carceral state were signaling their unwillingness to continue to be exploited by the prison-industrial complex. It was bad enough that most states paid inmates only a few cents per hour for their labor. Florida refused to compensate them at all. The protesters sought an end to this "modern-day slavery" consisting of unpaid labor in brutal conditions.[1]

When the war on drugs began in the 1980s, Black men, most of them younger than thirty, flooded Florida's penitentiaries, as they did in the rest of the nation. A 2019 *Florida Times-Union* exposé detailed the results of that history, beginning with the influx of young Black males into the state's prisons by the 1990s. First, they were forced to build the "work camps" where they would be housed and that subsequently became the basis for "forced labor that could power rural communities." One mayor went so far as to voice the same justification that had fueled the slave trade, bluntly declaring, "We need bodies." Race was once again at the root of the ability and readiness to supply those bodies, resulting in treatment that current and former prisoners describe as "subhuman." The secretary of the Department of Corrections lauded the system, which "provides . . . a valuable service to Florida's communities [by] reduc[ing] expenditures to taxpayers." A county commissioner cited the irreplaceable "value that the inmate labor contributes," which the *Times-Union* estimated at hundreds of millions of dollars. Calculations of the actual amounts involved in "Florida's shadow economy," reaped by the state, local municipalities, and even universities, are considerably greater. Another Florida official, alarmed at "the troubling optics of seeing mostly black incarcerated men working on the side of the road," described the stark reality: "We're still buying bodies." The prison-industrial complex also enmeshes white people, including in Florida, where they now make up a plurality of both prisoners and unpaid laborers. But these current multiracial demographics cannot disguise a history based unambiguously on the social acceptability of oppressing Black people.[2]

Despite identifying themselves as the victims of slavery, the Florida prisoners who engaged in the 2018 protest did not turn to the present-day antislavery movement for support. Instead, they timed their action for the day commemorating the nation's most revered civil rights leader and named it Operation Push in honor of King's disciple Jesse Jackson because theirs was a cause King would have understood and embraced. These present-day activists understood the inseparable connection between their fight and the history of the Black freedom movement that preceded it. The continuities across time are almost startling. In his iconic address on the centennial of the Emancipation Proclamation, speaking to the hundreds of thousands gathered for the March on Washington, King called for Lincoln's expansive purpose in that historic act to be fully implemented in America. It remained an unrealized dream a hundred years later because the issues of Black freedom and racial slavery were inextricably intertwined. King viewed the "task of emancipation" not as situated in the distant past but as an immediate and pressing problem that he must direct his activism toward solving.[3]

King shined a light on the inseparability of systemic racism, economic exploitation, and colonialism and neocolonialism, which formed the essential context for issues of freedom and slavery of Black and brown people. He recognized that ending segregation did not cost society anything, whereas the exploitation of Black labor involved deep-seated economic interests. King did not shy away from taking up controversial causes like that of the Florida prisoners, such as his Poor People's Campaign. By the last year of his life, he forthrightly declared that civil rights had not gone nearly far enough. In his 1967 exhortation to the convention of the Southern Christian Leadership Conference (SCLC) titled "Where Do We Go from Here?" King explained, "A nation that will keep people in slavery for 244 years will 'thingify' them. . . . They will exploit them and poor people generally economically." History showed that the Black freedom movement would have to set the standard of what constituted real liberty. King told his audience of civil rights activists that "racism, the problem of economic exploitation, and the problem of war" were all connected to the issue of slavery. He insisted, "America, you must be born again!" in part because slavery was not just a stain on its past but a taint on its present, so distorting American society that it needed to be fundamentally transformed. He prophesied the outcome if the "three evils" of "racism, economic exploitation and militarism" were not rooted out. Although the carceral state as we know it dates in part from the decades after King's death, he saw the seeds all around him. In time, the imprisoned population of African American men would expand tenfold, even as the nation staked claim to the civil rights revolution he had led.[4]

King also saw the link between the battle he was in the midst of and the previous history of the Black freedom movement. Just as the Florida prison activists traced their actions to the height of the civil rights movement six decades earlier, King went back some sixty years to the inception of the movement, drawing on a line of previous African American leaders, none more so than W. E. B. Du Bois. King knew he would be forever linked with that particular predecessor. As he stood on the dais erected at the Lincoln Memorial on August 28, 1963, King was handed a note passing along the news of Du Bois's death in Accra, Ghana, at age ninety-five. Moments later, as he gave his "I Have a Dream" speech, King must have felt the almost palpable presence of everything Du Bois had said and done looming over the immense gathering. Neither King nor anyone else realized that the occasion marked a symbolic passing of the torch from the most illustrious civil rights leader of the first half of the twentieth century to his even more revered successor.[5]

A few years later—months before his own tragic demise—King gave a lesser known oration, "Honoring Dr. Du Bois," in which he paid tribute to the man who had been an "intellectual giant" and "a radical all of his life." Counting himself among the followers of Du Bois, who was two generations older, King emphasized, "He would have wanted his life to teach us something about our tasks of emancipation." King avowed that he had assimilated the lessons of Du Bois, who was "in the first place a teacher." The young minister summed up that intellectual heritage: Black people were locked in a life-and-death struggle over the political, legal, and moral bounds of what could be done to them in the interests of economic exploitation. He declared that America's systemic racism "has justified the low living standards of the Negro, sanctioned his separation from the majority culture, and enslaved him physically and psychologically." His lecture concluded tersely, "We were partially liberated and then re-enslaved."[6]

A student of the Black freedom movement as well as a leader of it, King recognized that Du Bois had been among the first to articulate that proposition at the turn of the twentieth century. Here, the inter-connected threads of the freedom struggle's history become even more obvious. Du Bois's critique of what he would call the "new slavery" com-menced with his early exposé of the unremunerated labor of imprisoned Black men, women, and children. Together with sharecropping, Du Bois characterized such prison labor as one of the "direct children of slavery," which "to all intents and purposes are slavery itself." He traced its origins to the post–Civil War South, when former slaveholders "sought to evade the consequences of emancipation" and "restore slavery in everything but in name." Du Bois declared that nothing less than "a new slavery and slave-trade was established," and he began to rewrite the postemancipation history of African American bondage by empha-sizing that the coercive labor practices taking shape replicated some of the worst features of antebellum slavery.[7]

Du Bois realized that this state-sponsored new slavery in the South had far-reaching effects that extended beyond the tens of thousands caught up in it. First, it displaced Black workers from the skilled trades and other industries they would otherwise be paid to occupy, reducing the incentive to compensate African Americans to perform jobs they could be coerced into doing for nothing. More perniciously, it perpetu-ated a cornerstone of the ideology of slavery, which asserted that Black people would not work without the "discipline" of enslavement—or, in this case, the bondage of their incarceration. The resort to prison labor became part of the racist argument that Black people would rather be impoverished than to work. As Du Bois warned, all African Americans suffered from this gross injustice, as what he called the "legalized slavery" of even a few thousand became a material constraint on the freedom of many millions. He predicted the conversion of the American criminal justice system into a pillar of systemic racism.[8]

Those were precisely the consequences that gave rise to the carceral state in which the Florida prisoners found themselves enmeshed in 2018. It was the legacy of Du Bois's analysis, amplified by King's powerful historical presence, that the incarcerated Floridians invoked in their antislavery crusade. To understand why their struggle was such a lonely one and why they did not appeal to the current antislavery movement requires an examination of the historical inheritance of the previous century that forms an important, if little known, background to events playing out today. It is the integral connection of present-day events to little-known episodes of a century ago that motivates this book.

In the face of the most difficult circumstances it could have confronted, Black abolitionism, rather than its more celebrated antislavery rival, bequeathed an indispensable legacy in terms of understanding and combating the present-day derivatives of twentieth-century slavery. Even after the imprint of Black abolitionism was erased within the mainstream movement, it made its way into the Pan-Africanism that would help revolutionize thinking about the racialized modern world. It was this antislavery tradition that the Florida prison activists drew on to protest the conditions of their unpaid labor, which in their minds, could only be classed as slavery.

Antislavery today traces itself to the wrong lineage. Important Black freedom movement leaders from Du Bois to King maintained the urgency of a principled alliance between antiracism and antislavery. As Manisha Sinha argues, "at a programmatic as well as intellectual level," antebellum African Americans made that alliance "an essential part of the abolitionist project." The success of Black abolitionists in converting at least the most advanced antislavery advocates to an antiracism commitment was a potent force in bringing about the legal abolition of slavery in the Atlantic world. It was instrumental in producing not only the Thirteenth Amendment to the US Constitution, outlawing slavery, but also the Fourteenth, bestowing citizenship, and the Fifteenth, enfranchising African American men. The contemporary mainstream abolitionist movement undid much of that hard-won progress. To understand why the Florida activists and others like them found themselves on their own requires an analysis of the history of the "new antislavery" to emphasize its fundamental break with the past.

It began in the 1910s when an important segment of white abolitionism, centered around the British Anti-Slavery Society, abruptly turned its back on its abolitionist principles and jettisoned an earlier association with Black abolitionists in favor of an alliance with colonial officials to provide ideological cover for the new slavery. For the next few decades, the self-described abolitionists at the head of the venerable Anti-Slavery Society, which dated to the height of the antebellum crusade, actively worked against the interests of Black and brown people around the world, with devastating consequences. In addition to depriving the Black freedom movement of a vital source of support for its cause, the new antislavery sanctioned most of the extant forms of Black enslavement as it forged a closer relationship with Britain's Colonial Office, charged with overseeing the world's largest empire. Their joint work gave priority to imperial interests as the activists and colonial officials—sometimes the same people—arrived at a fundamentally colonialist division between freedom and slavery that reflected imperial Britain's dependence on the exploitation of Black and brown people. The Anti-Slavery Society acceded to the goals of British colonialism to such an extent that it finally ceased to resemble an antislavery movement at all. Meanwhile, the British Empire's cooperation with the self-professed vanguard of twentieth-century abolitionism helped exonerate it from charges that it participated in new forms of slavery in its vast African territories, with ramifications for Black people everywhere.[9]

The new antislavery therefore played a previously unrecognized role in the racialization of the international law that defines slavery today. Once it abandoned its antiracism principles, it was not a huge leap to advocate treaties that, far from abolishing the racial basis of the old slavery, actually built on it. In the 1920s the colonial powers adopted a global legal regime that created one set of laws applicable to the white workers of Europe and North America and quite another for Black and brown people everywhere else. In purporting to inaugurate an end to slavery once and for all, international law instead enshrined a dubious and racialized distinction between free labor and slavery that left people of color subject to conditions that would have been called slavery if white workers had been subjected to them. It seems almost incomprehensible today that a movement professing antislavery principles would sign off on any of this. Based on the more renowned period of nineteenth-century abolitionism, we have come to associate antislavery with combating rather than abetting such racialized institutions.

In the battle against their own conditions of slavery, the Florida prison activists invoked the tradition of the Black freedom movement rather than any present-day antislavery campaign because the latter excludes so many victims of the new slavery from the definition of slavery contained in international law. If it did not, the conditions they contested would not have been legal in the first place. Unpaid prison labor is permissible only because the new antislavery helped usher in a new classification system for human bondage that divided the unitary category of slavery into three allegedly separate variants based on the race of the enslaved and the enslaver. These three classifications—slavery, trafficking (originally known as white slavery), and forced labor—are indispensable to the history of the freedom movement examined in this book, especially how the term *new slavery* was used in the twentieth century.

By the time the European powers finished their "scramble for Africa," they had, by general consent, limited the term *slavery*, minus any adjective modifying it, to only one class: people of color subject to oppression at the hands of other people of color. Such usage was consistent with the European colonial nations' justification of their presence in Africa on the grounds of stamping out the slave trade, even though slavery still thrived there. It was true that European suzerainty marked the end of an epoch of slavery on the African continent. The vast extension of European colonialism beginning in the 1880s stifled the export slave trade, especially from East Africa. By the middle of the nineteenth century, that region's millennia-old external trade, largely in Arab hands, had replaced the west coast as the center of commerce in human beings, including to the Americas but mostly to the Indian Ocean world and the remaining slave plantations. More gradually, but no less surely, colonialism suppressed Africa's domestic slavery. To delimit the definition of slavery to what existed in Africa before Europe's conquest denied any continuation of the old racial slavery Europeans had brought to the Americas. To be sure, these officially recognized forms of slavery were themselves racial—but only in the sense that white people were ostensibly not involved.[10]

Beyond the conspicuous absence of Europeans as organizers and principal beneficiaries, there was not much to link the various systems of slavery found in Africa or to differentiate them from what the Europeans were involved with. Paul Lovejoy (Africa) and Gwynn Campbell (Indian Ocean) have revealed such slavery to be a widespread, varied, and ever-evolving institution. Campbell describes Indian Ocean slavery as based on protection and reciprocal relations and thus very different from the racial slavery of the Atlantic world. Joseph Inikori identifies three characteristics that differentiated slavery in the Americas: it entailed not simply forced *labor* but forced *migration*; it was based on the quest for a cheap workforce, largely for raw materials production; and it involved crass economic exploitation to produce goods for the world market. All these purposes remained, but not in what the colonial powers defined as slavery in international law. They were found instead in the crass forms of exploitation they employed themselves.[11]

As Adelle Blackett and Alice Duquesnoy write, "Neither the legal definition of slavery nor the international legal definition of forced labor shows any rootedness in the legacies of the racialized unfreedom of transatlantic slavery." Identifying the ownership relation as the essence of slavery was especially convenient for ideologists of the European empires. It denied the continuation of racial slavery by claiming that the only slavery that still existed involved the ownership of Black and brown people by other Black and brown people.[12]

A second category, *trafficking*, soon came to refer exclusively to the sexual exploitation of white women, principally at the hands of other white people. The European and North American activists behind the emergence of this classification and its introduction into the public consciousness at the turn of the twentieth century referred to the transportation of European women across national borders for purposes of sexual exploitation as *white slavery*. One of the first antitrafficking organizations founded in 1899 was called the International Bureau for the Suppression of the White Slave Traffic. As early as 1904, an International Agreement for the Suppression of the White Slave Traffic was adopted. It became an international convention in 1910 and was renewed under the aegis of the League of Nations in 1921, which sponsored an International

Conference on White Slave Traffic. What is important here is not the specific content of these instruments but that, in the late nineteenth and early twentieth centuries, the world's major powers did not give a second thought to signing treaties and sponsoring conferences that clearly limited their scope to white women.[13]

The term *white slavery* was intended to shock its white audience, evoking a sense of outrage and compassion for the victim, who was more or less in the position historically reserved for Black people in the Atlantic world. The phrase had deep historical roots, including its occasional use by white American abolitionists who found the racism of their fellow white citizens too ingrained to resist entirely. A case in point was the Underground Railroad's self-proclaimed "president," Levi Coffin. Though generous in crediting the African Americans he worked alongside as the backbone of the movement to which he devoted so much of his life, he recounted the story of "Rose, the white slave," as one of his best marketing campaigns among his white compatriots. Rose, he writes, was unlike any of the other runaways who passed through his Cincinnati home, "tall and graceful, her face beautiful, and her expression one of intelligence," with "long, straight black hair" and "hands . . . as delicate as those of any lady." "When her vail was removed it was difficult for us to realize that the handsome, well-dressed lady who sat before us was a fugitive slave. The tinge of African blood in her face was so slight that it was hardly noticeable." The issue of white slavery embedded not only the central question of race but also, and just as foundationally, that of gender. For Coffin, what proved Rose to be a white slave was not only her phenotype but also her ability to give birth to a son who was "as white as any child."[14]

Coffin acknowledges that Rose made such a distinct impact on him partly because he saw her as a rare opportunity. "We were deeply interested in her at once, and felt that we wanted to exhibit these white slaves to some of our acquaintances, whose sympathies had never been so strongly enlisted for the slave as ours had been." The ploy worked. "The gentlemen were greatly surprised, and said, 'Can it be possible that they are slaves, liable to be bought and sold? It is a shame.'" Coffin's experience told him that most white people could muster only limited sympathy for the racial other. He and activists like him believed they could elicit much stronger feelings when people identified with their own kind in a thoroughly racialized Western society.[15]

The twentieth-century antitrafficking movement was dependent on this same reaction to the unexpected discovery of white people in a condition reminiscent of slavery. For Coffin's generation, it was a moment of racialized opportunism that played a minor role in their antislavery agitation—always tempered by their ongoing collaboration with their Black coworkers. As it had in Coffin's time, the term *white slavery* employed by antitrafficking activists was meant to evoke the sympathies of the white public—albeit without any intended benefit to Black people. The notion of the *white slave* still resonated through the middle of the twentieth century, revealing that the connection between slavery and race had not yet been severed in the Western public consciousness. The enslavement of Black people remained the unmarked case—the implicit subject whenever the word *slave* was employed. *White slave* was the marked case, the deviant variety involving the unforeseen victim.

In the minds of both abolitionists and antitrafficking activists, *trafficking* was not to be confused with *slavery*, which continued to be defined by its application to Black and brown people. Nor did either movement conceive any essential connection between trafficked white women and the threat menacing African Americans and, increasingly, Africans, which would be given a different name. The respective activist groups maintained a rigid organizational separation. The antitrafficking movement did not concern itself with women of color, while antislavery activists who traced their descent from the abolitionists behind emancipation did not address the exploitation of white people. This division did not stop antitrafficking activists from borrowing the discourse of abolitionism to advance their cause in a familiar act of racial opportunism.

The distinction between *trafficking* and *slavery* was racialized in ways that we are prone to feel uncomfortable with today. That was no accident. The two were entirely different because of the historically developed edifice of race. Although these forms of human oppression might converge in some of their results, the virtually impenetrable barrier of race kept them apart. Both sides, but particularly abolitionists, recognized that the exploitation of Black and brown people was on an entirely different scale in terms of scope, extent, and consequences for the enslaved, as it had been for the past four centuries. The dichotomy that developed between trafficking and slavery in international law was racialized in acknowledgment of the historical condition that the definition of slavery inherently involves race in the modern world.[16]

The evolution of the international instruments on slavery attests to an abiding notion of modern slavery as *essentially* racial. Only in 1948, during its ratification by the United Nations, were the words "white slave traffic" stripped from the international convention's title and its provisions at least theoretically extended to women of color. Until that time, the antitrafficking movement had consciously excluded women of color from its purview and the legal instruments that arose from its activism. It was not that nonwhite women were not subject to this type of exploitation; on the contrary, as a result of colonialism, more women of color than white women were caught up in trafficking. The truth was, antitrafficking activists had no interest in protecting nonwhite women.[17]

Whatever their motives, in appealing to the racist sentiment that justified colonizing virtually all of Africa and much of Asia, antitrafficking activists contributed to the racialization of antislavery law and its impressment to the colonial cause. Their success planted seeds within mainstream abolitionism that exploited racial consciousness beyond the need to uphold antiracist principles. The colonial powers readily embraced the division between trafficking and slavery because it fit into the justification for their recent conquest of Africa. Europeans may have trafficked women but, more importantly in their own eyes, they did not enslave men. Because it involved women, trafficking was deemed a lesser civilizational offense.

The advent of the notion of trafficking or white slavery, which is taken up again in chapter 6, is important to this history mainly because it developed at around the same time and for the same reasons as the term describing its opposite: *forced labor*, or the labor practices to which the European powers subjected Black and brown men in their African and Asian territories. This racially demarcated usage ensured that, paradoxically, the term *slavery* no longer covered the coercion of Black people's labor by white people. Neither slavery in its colonial definition nor trafficking applied to the purely racial slavery of the old Atlantic world that Du Bois observed being resurrected in the American South and that he was about to discover had recrossed the Atlantic and been established across Africa on an unprecedented scale. This form of coercion fell under the third designation, *forced labor*, the category European colonizers used to describe the ostensibly more innocuous—but in reality brutally abusive—forms of subjugation they practiced on the peoples of Africa, Asia, and the Caribbean.

The claim that the European powers had colonized Africa to stamp out the slave trade there was rich in historical ironies and masked a stark reality: every colonial regime engaged in something that was very often worse than slavery. They boasted about it, denied it, justified it, and rationalized it, sometimes all at once. They were "teaching the natives to work," carrying out a "sacred trust," and making the colonial enterprise pay. What they could not do was credibly or convincingly refute the parallel to the earlier racial slavery in the Americas. Imperial authorities were better at discerning the iniquity of the bondage of workers of color when those workers labored under the flag of a rival. Britain's Lord Cromer called the "contract labour" in Portuguese Africa indistinguishable from slavery. Another English commentator decried the "servitude reposing too often upon fraudulent and oppressive practices" observed in the colonies belonging to Germany and Portugal, where "labourers [were] compelled to work on land which had previously been their own." A Brazilian minister included Britain among the "powerful grouping of European capital" that employed "black populations" in "semi-slavery," noting that these workers were "ill paid and bound to the soil," "absolutely destitute of any protection from modern society['s] laws," and "whose low standard of life makes greater expenses unnecessary." The Board of Foreign Missions of the US-based Methodist Episcopal Church, writing about conditions in the British Caribbean, concluded that the "slave trade forbidden by law exists on plantations under the name of contract labor." An expert witness before the US War Department's Philippine Commission said of contract labor there under the Spanish, "The coolie system is worse than human slavery, though it does not sound so badly. . . . It simply uses the man as long as he has got physical vigor—that is, has got any mark of value—and then throws him into beggary."[18]

As both gendered and racialized, the treaties enacted to protect white women would find their opposite in the 1920s in international covenants that encoded what had long been accepted colonial doctrine: coerced labor would be considered "free" so long as it was performed by Black and brown men. Forced labor was subdivided into the permissible and the impermissible under international law. Consistent with the racial taxonomy behind it, that distinction would be decided unilaterally by the European colonizers—backed up by the self-described abolitionists allied with them in the new antislavery movement—so as to justify the use of coercion in those situations of greatest importance to them. No matter where they elected to draw the line, it meant the de facto sanctioning of racial slavery where it was deemed allowable. This widely varied set of exploitative labor practices given the purportedly sanitizing name forced labor, together with the parallel forms in the American South, came to constitute the new slavery identified by Black abolitionists. The chapters that follow detail the complicated and often circuitous process of how and why this understanding took shape and how colonial officials and exponents of the new antislavery came to fashion the classification system described here into a seemingly coherent if specious abolitionist doctrine.

This volume traces the contested and evolving definition of slavery in the twentieth century, which was largely dependent on who was doing the defining. One point seems clear: tens of millions of Black people faced crassly exploitative conditions of labor that differed markedly from those of their white counterparts in Europe and North America. Their freedom was on the line—that is, it was literally dependent on where abolitionists drew the line between morally and politically proscribed slavery and free labor. Throughout the existence of Black abolitionism, it wrestled with the fundamental task of identifying the manifold permutations of racial slavery in the context of a self-described antislavery movement attempting to hide and justify slavery as states of freedom.

By the 1930s, inspired by the views of those directly impacted, Du Bois decisively threw down the gauntlet on behalf of Black abolitionism with what might be the simplest, perhaps canonical, definition of slavery: enslavement involved any leveraging of racism to extend the socially acceptable bounds of labor exploitation. As long as it was possible to subject a person of color to exploitative conditions of labor that would be categorically unacceptable for a white worker, Du Bois considered it slavery, no matter the particular circumstances. To draw the line anywhere else only justified the abuses, as in the case of the new antislavery turning a blind eye to those abuses found in British Africa especially. Black feminist abolitionists subsequently added the methodology we now call *intersectionality*, which was as necessary to the understanding of enslavement as any other analysis of oppression. The fight to complete the unfinished emancipation of 1865 would necessarily continue until the full dismantling of the global structural racism that made it acceptable to subject Black people to the very worst forms of exploitation.

In telling the history of twentieth-century Black abolitionism for the first time, *The Freedom Movement's Lost Legacy* centers on the thought and actions of the cadre of African American leaders who spearheaded the movement. They include, in chronological order, Frederick Douglass, Ida B. Wells, Alice Kinloch, W. E. B. Du Bois, Marcus Garvey, Cyril Briggs, George Padmore, Ella Baker, Kwame Nkrumah, Frantz Fanon, and Martin Luther King Jr. The book documents how and why they came to take up the question of the new slavery and the reasons why their understanding of it differed so fundamentally from that of the mainstream antislavery movement.

Du Bois occupies a central place in the narrative of this work, reflecting his role in history. This position is partly a matter of his almost unparalleled political career, which stretched from his physical attendance at the Pan-African Conference of 1900 to his symbolic presence at the 1963 March on Washington. But it is also true that at definite moments and in particular ways, Du Bois drove the development of twentieth-century Black abolitionism like no one else. He learned of the existence of the new slavery in Africa while attending a central and defining event for Black abolitionism—the Pan-African Conference of 1900 in London—and immediately connected it to the conditions experienced by African Americans in the South, which he had been studying since his relocation there a few years earlier. As he watched the new slavery spread in Africa, Du Bois became convinced that the global dimensions of racial slavery were greater than ever and that African Americans were caught up in the same system that imperiled the freedom of Black people everywhere. He therefore determined to bring the antislavery movement he had first encountered in London back home to America.

Du Bois was keenly aware of the transnational dimensions of antebellum slavery and abolitionism, having written his doctoral dissertation on the topic and subsequently studied nineteenth-century Black abolitionism. Manisha Sinha demonstrates that abolitionism had always been transnational in scope and understanding, just as racial slavery had been since its inception in the sixteenth century. Antebellum Black abolition-

14

ism in the United States drew inspiration from the Haitian revolution and the Jamaican Christmas rebellion. Denmark Vesey conceived his plan for an antislavery revolt in hemispheric terms. David Walker, in his great abolitionist tract, appealed to the "Colored people of the world" to liberate themselves from the uniquely oppressive modern institution. The Underground Railroad had its most important terminus in Canada, where African American exiles like Martin Delany devoted their efforts to ending bondage in America even as they conceived ventures to immigrate to Africa or Haiti. Prominent activists such as Frederick Douglass and William Wells Brown aligned themselves with abolitionism across the Atlantic, traveling to England in search of allies and safe haven. Beginning in the late 1890s, Black freedom movement leaders responded with a transnational resistance movement as they once again found themselves caught up in a transnational system of slavery. Like Douglass and Brown, their successors Wells, Du Bois, and King all journeyed abroad at key junctures in their political careers. Throughout most of the twentieth century, a close link was maintained between Black abolitionism and Pan-Africanism, one that foreshadowed and fed into the international dimension of the civil rights movement of the 1950s and 1960s, as meticulously documented by Carol Anderson, Penny Von Eschen, and others.[19]

In reviving Pan-Africanism after World War I, Du Bois helped ensure that the Black abolitionist movement of his time would be as transnational as its progenitor, because in his understanding, the new slavery was just as global as its forebearer. Du Bois's use of the term *Black world* to describe a conjoined geography of oppression and resistance spanning the Black Atlantic would be part of his theory and praxis from 1900 on, making that international scope vital to this historical account.

Du Bois's abolitionism nevertheless took root alongside that of a much larger group of Black intellectuals whose immense contributions are indispensable to the retelling of this history. Douglass, the preeminent Black abolitionist of the antebellum period, passed the torch to Wells, the famed antilynching and civil rights crusader, and to South African journalist and Pan-Africanist Kinloch. Du Bois absorbed the antislavery of all three. Twentieth-century Black abolitionism was effectively launched at the Pan-African Conference of 1900, in large part through the efforts of Kinloch. She, Wells, and civil rights icon Baker laid the important groundwork for the development of Black abolitionism beyond the Du Boisian brand and into its more fully realized intersectional form. Du Bois was also profoundly influenced by a number of Afro-Caribbeans who became his fellow Harlem-based political activists—especially Garvey, Briggs, and Padmore—all of whom made the connections between the predicaments of African-descended peoples across Africa and those of its diaspora. Their work, in turn, helped shape the thinking of later figures, such as Ghana's first postindependence leader, Nkrumah, and the enormously influential intellectual and revolutionary Fanon, both contemporaries of King.

The roles of three white Englishmen also require inclusion—Henry Fox Bourne as an early ally, and John Harris and Frederick Lugard as later determined foes. Fox Bourne worked closely with Kinloch in creating a short-lived, forgotten, but nonetheless important turn-of-the-century alliance of Pan-Africanism and British abolitionism discussed in chapter 2. Harris, who replaced Fox Bourne at the forefront of British antislavery, was the central architect of the new antislavery. Lugard was Britain's principal imperial expert on slavery; he, along with Harris, helped develop the empire's pseudo-antislavery doctrines that shaped international antislavery law. Chapter 3 recounts their central roles, providing indispensable background to an understanding of the development of Black abolitionism. Only in this full historical context can we adequately appreciate the role African Americans reprised a century after their essential contributions to the successful abolitionist movement that produced emancipation.

In attempting to be faithful to the history as Black abolitionists lived and interpreted it, I am mindful of the need to consider the particular circumstances of the new slavery to which Black abolitionists were responding. The history of twentieth-century slavery and antislavery has almost always been written jointly, for the very good reason that twentieth-century slavery has not achieved anything approaching the same notoriety as the slavery of earlier times. An exception is the "slavery by another name" that has attained a certain place in our collective consciousness through the valiant efforts of Douglas Blackmon and others. Here, I attempt to fill in the requisite historical context of the new slavery without diverting too much attention from the main narrative or shifting the focus from antislavery onto slavery itself. I therefore touch on the American side of the question only in passing, and then entirely in and through the writings of Black abolitionists. Beginning in chapter 1, the book provides more background on the new slavery in Africa, which is likely to be unfamiliar to all but specialists, to illustrate the principles the abolitionists put forward and, in some cases, to illuminate the labor practices they denounced. It is a difficult balance to strike when writing about the history of twentieth-century antislavery, but it is worth the effort if it makes this account accessible to all those who might be interested. The focus nevertheless remains squarely on Black abolitionists. The action unfolds through their eyes, and their analysis of what qualified as slavery is at issue throughout.[20]

Finally, it might be useful to describe the organization of the book. The first three chapters are arranged in historical sequence to make it clear that Black abolitionism gave rise to the alliance between Pan-Africanism and early-twentieth-century British antislavery and that the new antislavery broke that alliance. To credit the contributions of Black abolitionism fully, Kinloch's separate influences on Black abolitionists and their white counterparts in the late 1890s are divided between chapters 1 and 2 to ensure that the narrative does not convey the false impression that Black abolitionism was a response to that of its British ally. Chapter 1 chronicles Kinloch's foundational role in Pan-Africanism and her intellectual influence on Du Bois. Chapter 2 makes it clear that, in striking up an antislavery partnership with Fox Bourne, Kinloch also catalyzed a restoration of abolitionism's long-dormant militant spirit in the early 1900s. Chapter 3 recounts the entirely separate and spurious antislavery doctrine of British colonial officials that dates in part to the 1890s and forms the background for the new antislavery that developed in the 1910s and reached full fruition in the 1920s. The chapter on the new antislavery must follow chapters 1 and 2 to preserve the chronology, since it postdates both Black abolitionism and the British abolitionist movement it sparked. This presentation also emphasizes that the new antislavery was a reaction to Black abolitionism, not the other way around.

More specifically, chapter 1 examines in turn the roles of Douglass, Wells, Du Bois, and Kinloch in founding the movement, following these separate strands to their eventual convergence at the Pan-African Conference of 1900. The chapter culminates with a consideration of the effects that seminal gathering had on Du Bois, who took the leading intellectual and political role in the movement going forward. In tracing Black abolitionists' efforts to turn principle into action by reconstituting the interracial form of the antebellum movement, chapter 2 begins by examining a second side of Kinloch's work in the late 1890s. Once this necessary historical context has been established, the action shifts back to the United States, where, with the founding of the NAACP in 1909, Du Bois again channeled Kinloch in helping to launch a parallel movement across the Atlantic and eventually his transnational Pan-Africanist strategy.

Chapter 3 centers on the unraveling of that approach as Du Bois confronted the principals of the new antislavery in London in 1921. To make it clear why this occurred, I chronicle the profound alteration of the mainstream abolitionist movement over the first quarter of the twentieth century entirely outside Du Bois's cognizance, which left his grand plan in tatters. That previous history includes the advent of the specious abolitionism of Harris, Lugard, and other British imperial officials. The chapter ends with Du Bois forced to watch helplessly as the new antislavery becomes the basis for treaties adopted over the next decade, writing race into international labor law.

Chapter 4 picks up the story of the subsequent development of Black abolitionism, chronicling the response of Du Bois and other Black abolitionists to the ascendancy of the new antislavery. It begins by focusing on the growth of Pan-Africanism throughout the 1920s, which led to heightened scrutiny of the exploitation of Black workers globally. Forced to go it alone, Black abolitionism developed a far-reaching conception of antiracist human rights, with Du Bois again taking the lead. The chapter concludes by briefly considering how those ideas animated a line of activists extending all the way to the 1960s, when King took up the mantle.

A parallel line consists of women from Wells and Kinloch to Baker to later African activists, whose stories are recounted in chapter 5. In developing an intersectional version, they gave Black abolitionism a form that better fit later trends in the Black freedom movement. To bring the story up to the present, chapter 6 examines how antislavery in the twenty-first century continues to be shaped in important ways by the history chronicled in this volume. It also considers some of today's movements that have carried on the tradition of Black abolitionism, including the one that opens this introduction.

1

The Origins and Launch of Twentieth-Century Black Abolitionism

What did true freedom mean to African Americans deprived of their liberty since the inception of the American republic? The origins of twentieth-century Black abolitionism can be traced to the conclusion of the antebellum movement, when Frederick Douglass pondered that question. While his fellow African Americans recognized the need to pursue the struggle against the nation's entrenched racism, it was easy to assume that the abolition of slavery in the South would mark its end on American soil. Only in 1865 did Douglass first sound a warning that the aftermath of emancipation could take a very different course based on the events he saw unfolding.

Three decades later, the question of freedom and slavery was not merely a theoretical one for Douglass's successors at the forefront of the Black freedom struggle in the United States. Ida B. Wells discerned a connection between racial violence in the form of lynching and the effective enslavement of Black southerners, and like Douglass, she took the freedom struggle across the Atlantic to England in search of allies. Around the same time, W. E. B. Du Bois began to study sharecropping and its attendant debt peonage, supplemented by racial violence, that developed after emancipation, replicating in many particulars the legal slavery it replaced. As a result, he rediscovered Douglass's analysis of the problem of emancipation and used it to develop a more far-reaching understanding of freedom and slavery in the age of imperialism.

The twentieth-century Black abolitionism developed by those two civil rights pioneers found its launching pad at the Pan-African Conference of 1900, an indirect offshoot of Wells taking her antilynching activism to England. Although that seminal assembly would be associated primarily with the African independence movement, it was just as concerned with the new slavery taking hold globally. This dual focus was a result of the merger of Du Bois's analysis of conditions in the American South and Black South African journalist Alice Kinloch's exposé of the labor system taking root in the mines of that vital outpost of British colonialism.

In no small measure because of what he learned from his political associates at the conclave in London, Du Bois began to use the term *new slavery* for the conditions African Americans faced in the South. At the same time, he warily took note of developments in Africa, becoming more and more convinced that racial slavery not only retained its hold on the South but had also recrossed the Atlantic a century after the transatlantic slave trade had ceased. For Du Bois, these disturbing developments became a matter of practical urgency on which the outcome of the Black freedom movement depended.

Frederick Douglass and the Problem of Emancipation

Despite President Abraham Lincoln's issuance of the Emancipation Proclamation in 1862, Frederick Douglass experienced a strong and increasing undercurrent of anxiety as the Civil War progressed toward the hoped-for Union victory. As early as 1863, signs of trouble were already appearing. One was the sudden and marked increase in the maroon community in Louisiana's Great Cypress Swamp. On the surface, nothing seemed amiss in this enclave of runaways, who were following a three-centuries-long tradition in the Americas of escaping enslavement. By that time, the dislocation of war had greatly enhanced the chance of escape throughout the Confederacy, and more African Americans were running away than ever before—hundreds of thousands in all. They were running to Union lines to free themselves and, as

W. E. B. Du Bois later realized, the nation. In the Louisiana bayou, however, African Americans were fleeing Union-occupied territory. They wanted nothing more than to escape the sites of their historical bondage, the plantations and farms run so ruthlessly by the people who claimed ownership over both the land and the African Americans who worked it.[1]

The Emancipation Proclamation should have left them free to go where they pleased. Instead, Union troops under the command of General Nathaniel Banks served as an enforcement mechanism to keep them on the plantations, even as armed Black soldiers staged what amounted to guerrilla raids against Banks's forces in an attempt to free their families. The result was a war for freedom within a war for freedom, with some Black Union soldiers fighting against their own side to liberate their relatives from this new form of bondage.[2]

Banks, a Republican and an abolitionist, was in large part responsible for this situation. As the de facto military commander of occupied Louisiana, he issued an executive order that confined African Americans to the plantations on which they had been enslaved. Banks insisted that the newly freed people must be "preserved from vagrancy and idle, vicious habits." His decree forced them to sign what purported to be "labor contracts"—a misnomer, given the lack of choice involved. Although African Americans were paid for their work, they were forbidden to leave the plantations without permission. Banks's plan spread across the federally administered South in the immediate aftermath of the war. The rallying cry of preventing vagrancy became a pretext to deprive African Americans of what the Emancipation Proclamation promised when it stated that "all persons held as slaves" would be "forever free."[3]

Union officers opted for the alternative policy—giving African Americans land to work for their own benefit on their own initiative—only with great reluctance. Lincoln tried to entice Confederate planters to his side by promising the return of their abandoned land. General Tecumseh Sherman had gone so far as to destroy a bridge to rid himself of the "contraband" caravan of escaped enslaved children, women, and men dogging his steps. Finally, Union leaders gave in and permitted some twenty thousand newly freed African Americans to take over land on the Atlantic coast. To make this policy easier to enact and justify, the area chosen was largely devoid of its former white planter population.

What perhaps doomed the project was African Americans' reluctance to grow cotton rather than foodstuffs. Northern abolitionists found it difficult to convince them to do otherwise.[4]

In justifying his actions, Banks could point to the precedent set by slave insurrectionist Toussaint-Louverture some seven decades earlier. During the Haitian revolution, Toussaint encountered the problem of how to get newly freed people not only to work in the fields but also to produce the staple crops the economy depended on rather than crops to feed themselves. As the leader of an enslaved populace in open rebellion, he was forced to take increasingly draconian measures against his followers in the name of the revolution. Toussaint finally resorted to a series of orders confining a large portion of the Black population to plantation agriculture under the oppressive control of the planter class. His forced labor decree went so far as to proclaim that "field-negroes are forbidden to quit their respective plantations without lawful permission." His government enacted vagrancy laws and mandated child labor. As a result, the Haitian revolution was interrupted by what amounted to a rebellion within a rebellion, foreshadowing later events during the American Civil War. Plantation workers turned on Toussaint's state because, in their view, it was imposing the same conditions they had taken up arms to oppose. He responded by ruthlessly crushing the resistance and executing the leader of the rebellion—a man he thought of as his nephew—in the name of preserving the revolution, a decision that may have helped precipitate his downfall. It was a portent of the strange spectacle during the American Civil War of former slaves running *away from* Union lines to avoid the compulsory cultivation of cotton, even as hundreds of thousands of African Americans fled *to* Union lines to escape slavery.[5]

Douglass discerned something sinister at work here: despite being legally free, African Americans were attempting to escape Union-controlled territory to avoid being locked on plantations against their will. Before the war ended, Douglass posed the crux of the problem of emancipation: America might end one form of racial slavery only to permit another if it did not guarantee Black people a few essential human rights. As the conflict drew to a close in January 1865, Douglass gave an impassioned address on the meaning of freedom to a group of abolitionists attending the annual meeting of the Massachusetts Anti-Slavery Society in Boston. Despite the rapid approach of a triumphant conclusion of the antislavery war, Douglass was in no mood for celebration, even as his soul yearned to cheer the great vistas opening up before a long-suffering people whose ordeal was about to come to an end. He would later, as historian Stephen G. Hall notes, "use the postbellum period to outline and sketch the 'historical mind of emancipation.'" But Douglass knew that this time had not yet arrived. In his view, as an abolitionist, he had no choice but to sound the alarm among those devoted to the cause of Black freedom.[6]

As he contemplated Banks's confinement of African Americans to the plantations of Union-occupied Louisiana, Douglass drew a deeper lesson. When Wendell Phillips questioned whether Banks was right to say that African Americans needed to be prepared to exercise their liberty, Douglass got to the heart of the question. "What is freedom?" he asked his fellow abolitionists. For it to have any meaning, it must confer "the right to choose one's own employment." "When any individual or combination of individuals undertakes to decide for any man when he shall work, where he shall work, at what he shall work, and for what he shall work, he or they practically reduce him to slavery." According to Douglass, Banks's policy deprived African Americans of these four essential freedoms, continuing Black people's bondage. If occupied Louisiana's African Americans were no longer enslaved, they should be free to go where they wished and to do as they liked, whereas Banks's decree "makes the Proclamation of 1863 a mockery and delusion." Douglass remained dissatisfied with an emancipation limited to banning the legal ownership of African Americans while leaving other essential features of slavery in place.[7]

A few years later, Thaddeus Stevens, leader of the Radical Republicans in Congress during Reconstruction, came to the same conclusion. He acknowledged that land policy was where the battle of freedom versus slavery would largely be fought in the postemancipation South. The land question neatly bundled all the great issues, serving as a measure of when "forever free" would commence. Stevens realized that African Americans would seek ownership of the land they had previously worked for free, while their former enslavers would resist such a profound change. "Make [the formerly enslaved] independent of their old masters," he insisted, "so that they may not be compelled to work for them upon unfair terms." That "can only be done by giving [freed persons] a small tract of land to cultivate for themselves." Stevens warned, "Withhold from them all their rights, and leave them destitute of the means of earning a livelihood," and they would remain "the servants and victims of others." The veteran abolitionist predicted that without land redistribution in compensation for the work of so many generations of enslaved African Americans, their descendants would remain in a condition far removed from freedom.[8]

Stevens knew that landownership was only a proxy for the deeper issue of the republic's attitude toward African American bondage. The choice was to either break the power of the old planter class or watch its hold on African Americans reemerge. Stevens foresaw that the withdrawal of federal "protection" would leave African Americans "prey to the legislation and treatment of their old masters." He even worried—presciently, as it turned out—that "hundreds of thousands would annually be deposited in secret, unknown graves." Lynching was not quite that widespread, and it was as much public spectacle as clandestine terrorism, yet Stevens captured much of the essential spirit of the freedom struggle to come.[9]

The cogency of Stevens's point is attested by the circumstance that, although African Americans were not exactly "driven to defend themselves by civil war," they were forced to fight for their fundamental human rights for a full century after Stevens's untimely death in 1868. Martin Luther King Jr. was fully aware of the connection between the civil rights revolution he sought and what Stevens had been unable to achieve in Congress. Invoking the heritage of Black abolitionism, King would look back at this signal failure as historically decisive in sealing African Americans' fate. "In 1863 the Negro was granted freedom from physical slavery through the Emancipation Proclamation. But he was not given land to make that freedom meaningful. . . . And this is why Frederick Douglass would say that emancipation for the Negro was freedom to hunger, freedom to the winds and the rains of heaven, freedom without roofs over their heads. It was freedom without bread to eat, without land to cultivate. It was freedom and famine at the same time." King had much earlier concluded that what he called "the proclamation of inferiority" had "contended with the proclamation of emancipation, negating its liberating force." African Americans were still dealing with the consequences in King's time.[10]

Douglass recognized all this and more when he spoke to abolitionists in the closing months of the Civil War. He discerned that even in the absence of the master-slave relationship, the freed African American would discover that "if he is not the slave of the individual master, he is the slave of society." African Americans were not legally free if they could be compelled to work on behalf of others solely because they were Black. Douglass perceived that the pretext of a war emergency ultimately rested on racist premises so habitual as to be second nature to many white Americans and therefore too readily made permanent.[11]

On what grounds, then, did Banks issue his order confining African Americans to their plantations in Union-occupied territory? The question apparently never came up, as the right to legislatively control African Americans was simply taken for granted. The Constitution contained no provisions by which the federal government could single out African Americans for differential treatment other than their status as enslaved—which, following the Emancipation Proclamation, they no longer were. Douglass's indignation at how readily Banks and other Union officials ignored the lack of a constitutional basis for implementing such draconian measures aimed at African Americans—and the relative lack of protest it occasioned among white abolitionists—was justified.[12]

Given his own lived experience, Douglass understood that racial slavery was too deeply rooted to be reduced to a simple legal relation between individuals. Behind the enforcement of property rights, sanctioning of the slave trade, provisions for the return of runaways, suppression of rebellions, and myriad other means of enslaving African Americans rested the overwhelming force of the government—in whose name Banks promulgated his military orders to deny African Americans their freedom. The limits of emancipation ran deep, encompassing the ultimate expression of systemic racism that characterized the world in which Douglass lived.

Douglass's lived experience as a Black man born into slavery and stalked by racism even after his escape loomed large in his mind as he discerned the significance of Banks's policy. Douglass was an incisive critic of American society; he knew he lived in a society where African Americans were defined by race legally, politically, and socially. Years earlier, in 1852, Douglass had been asked to speak at an Independence Day celebration in his adopted hometown of Rochester, New York, and he could not help but ask his audience of white Americans, "Fellow-Citizens—pardon me, and permit me to ask, why am I called upon to speak here to-day? What have I, or those I represent, to do with your national independence? Are the great principles of political freedom and of natural justice, embodied in that Declaration of Independence, extended to us? . . . What to the American slave is your Fourth of July? I answer, a day that reveals to him, more than all other days in the year, the gross injustice and cruelty to which he is the constant victim."[13]

Douglass's fellow abolitionist Charles Langston expressed that idea even more candidly during his trial in Ohio for his Underground Railroad activities: "The courts, the laws, the governmental machinery of this country are so constituted as to oppress and outrage the colored men. I cannot, then, of course, expect, judging from past history, any mercy from the laws, the Constitution, or the courts." Langston created what the newspapers called a "sensation" in the courtroom when he characterized himself "as a citizen of Ohio" and then quickly corrected himself. "Excuse me for saying that, sir," he told the presiding judge. He meant to say he was *an outlaw of the United States.*" The Supreme Court agreed with him.[14]

A few years before his address on emancipation, Douglass would feel the full impact of the status to which Langston referred. Following the Harpers Ferry antislavery rebellion, Douglass was compelled to flee the country just ahead of the federal marshals pursuing him for his connection to John Brown. But his real crime was his active opposition to slavery and his role in the Underground Railroad, by which he had escaped and in which both he and Langston played active roles.[15]

The name of the Underground Railroad—the assistance rendered to African Americans' largely spontaneous flight from slavery—unintentionally points to a crucial quality of the movement. In an ostensibly democratic nation allegedly committed to the principle that "All men are created equal," it was left to an *underground* movement to champion African Americans' cause. When these activities attain quasi-mythic status, such as the French and Polish underground during Nazi occupation, they are generally organized against foreign occupiers. Here, the movement arose to secure the liberties that white Americans had systematically denied their fellow countrymen for centuries, solely on the basis of race. The Underground Railroad constituted an illegal movement in a land of political liberty as, essentially, a band of guerrillas fighting against the Constitution, with its fugitive slave clause; the laws that protected the human property of the slaveholding class; and the federal government that united white Americans while dividing them from Black.[16]

Movement stalwart John Brown referred to his planned raid on Harpers Ferry as "the Rail Road business on a somewhat extended scale." Like every other antislavery rebellion, it was an insurrection against an oppressive state. Brown had even drafted a constitution for what amounted to a revolutionary regime. He was convicted of treason, even though he was charged with subversion against Virginia rather than the federal government, whose armory he had attacked. But as Douglass put it with his characteristic lucidity, Virginia was acting for the federal government: "Slavery seemed to be at the very top of its power; the national government, with all its powers and appliances, was in its hands, and it bade fair to wield them for many years to come."[17]

Even a moderate abolitionist like William Lloyd Garrison denounced the world's great liberal democratic constitution as a "devil's pact," and African Americans did so with considerably more urgency. What other choice did they and their white allies have but to fight an essentially revolutionary war against a constitution that enshrined slavery? What alternative did they have but to act against the democratically elected government that had turned Brown over to Virginia to be hung for treason and had passed the Fugitive Slave Law, which decreed that freedom seekers be surrendered to the South? That African Americans in the North had few options in their quest for liberty represents a signal failure of American institutions.[18]

Douglass, like all African Americans both enslaved and free who resisted tyranny, knew that the enemy came not directly from the institution of slavery but from the power behind it in the form of the American state. The determination of race meant that this ostensibly liberal democratic regime, like the one from which it had successfully rebelled and separated itself, applied a policy of systemic racism to the enslaved that extended to all African Americans—to all Black people in the Americas. Atlantic slavery, Robin Blackburn writes, manifested a "radically new character compared to prior forms of slavery," displaying an internal consistency in the form of "a system of social identification and surveillance which marked [slaves] as black, and closely regulated their every action." The slave trade—both transatlantic and domestic—was essential to racial slavery. *Racial* here conveys all the specific historical conditions that *slavery* by itself does not. The slave trade was a principal source of global capitalism involving one of the most important articles of commerce: human cargo.[19]

Douglass perceived that the antebellum enslavement of Africans and their descendants in the Americas had determined *where* and *at what* millions upon millions of them would labor. The *where* encompassed the long history of what Joseph Inikori highlights as the forced migration of the Atlantic slave trade, which entailed the transportation of Africans to the West Indies and from those islands to North and South America. Later, for their descendants, it meant forced relocation from the upper to the lower South at the height of cotton plantation slavery. These conditions imposed on millions of Black workers contrasted with the liberty of their white counterparts. The latter could come and go as they pleased and were permitted not to work at all if they could find an alternative. White workers were free to rise into a higher sphere or descend into a lower one. Not so Black workers, who were sent to the sources of the earth's natural resources, whether agricultural land or mineral deposits, through complex mechanisms of forced migration. Whatever the specific type of force, its primary aim was to restrict their freedom of movement. The *where* served the purposes of the *at what*, locking Black workers on plantations and farms spread across two continents. As Inikori concludes, "raw materials were produced by Africans where the cost for British manufacturers was lowest." For centuries, Africans and their descendants had labored where it was most profitable for others. All that lived history—his own and the collective experience of Black people in the Americas—would have been on Douglass's mind when he realized that African Americans would not be able to determine *at what* they worked until they had the free choice of *where* they worked. Banks's policy struck at the heart of the most important of Douglass's four essential freedoms.[20]

If the US government could continue to protect and even promulgate slavery during an avowedly antislavery war, the same danger lurked everywhere. Though the danger receded during Reconstruction, even the legal revolution that accompanied it could not uproot the systemic racism that continued to give rise to racial slavery. In his address to fellow abolitionists in 1865, Douglass warned that the very term *emancipation* could effectively disguise a quite different process. He exposed the reasons why it would be so difficult in practice to abolish racial slavery in its manifold forms, despite the taint that periodically sparked abolitionist movements among Black people's white allies. According to Douglass, even with the old slavery dead, a new slavery remained possible. Twentieth-century Black abolitionism would name it, describe it, and pick up the fight against it.[21]

Ida B. Wells, W. E. B. Du Bois, and the Postemancipation South

Ida B. Wells and W. E. B. Du Bois were still children as the promise of triumphant abolitionism faded. The powerful alliance of antislavery and antiracism had revolutionized America—producing not only the Thirteenth Amendment to the Constitution, banning slavery, but also the Fourteenth and Fifteenth Amendments, granting African Americans citizenship and voting rights for males. By the time Wells and Du Bois reached adolescence, however, Reconstruction would be over—and with it, virtually all vestiges of African American liberties in the South and increasingly in the North as well.[22]

As segregation engulfed both regions, either de jure or de facto, the Supreme Court put its imprimatur on the wanton violation of the now antiracist Constitution. In its landmark 1896 *Plessy v. Ferguson* decision, which dominated the American legal landscape for half a century, the court declared, "Legislation is powerless to eradicate racial instincts or to abolish distinctions based upon physical differences, and the attempt to do so can only result in accentuating the difficulties of the present situation. If one race be inferior to the other socially, the Constitution of the United States cannot put them upon the same plane." The Supreme Court had stated in the 1857 *Dred Scott* case that "a Black man has no rights that a white man is bound to respect." It now claimed that relations between Black and white had nothing to do with rights in the first place. The Constitution could not guarantee African Americans anything. All that counted was race. Here, the Supreme Court was not interpreting the Constitution; it was attempting to nullify it almost entirely as it applied to Black people. Voting rights in the South were simultaneously revoked by a resurgent and unrepentant proslavery regime that confined most African Americans living there—still a large majority—to sharecropping and debt peonage. Even northern politicians like Theodore Roosevelt could be heard lamenting the end of slavery and obliquely calling for its reinstitution.[23]

Freedom was at best a tenuous condition for African Americans living in the South, as Wells experienced firsthand. Born into slavery in Mississippi in 1862, she had been freed as a result of the Emancipation Proclamation. She remained in the South, relocating to Memphis in 1883. An educator and activist, she waged a tireless battle against segregation, turning to journalism and launching a one-woman crusade against the scourge of lynching sweeping the South. Wells identified that form of racial violence as rooted in the "civil and industrial slavery" that endured decades after emancipation. She also sought to expose the "prisons and convict farms" where Black southerners were collected in large numbers to serve long sentences on false charges. When she found white American audiences too hostile to her message, she opted to rekindle the antebellum Black abolitionist tradition of traveling to England in the cause of freedom.[24]

At some of their most challenging moments, Black activists had crossed the Atlantic to find encouragement, allies, and financial supporters in Great Britain. Douglass had done so for the first time in 1846, spending two years there to escape the fallout from the publication of his tell-all slave narrative. A highlight of his speaking tour was his introduction to the venerable Thomas Clarkson, then eighty-six years old, "feeble," and "at the edge of the grave." Douglass recalled their poignant encounter decades later: "He took one of my hands in both of his, and, in a tremulous voice, said, 'God bless you, Frederick Douglass!'" Douglass returned to England in the aftermath of Harpers Ferry, a wanted man for his association with John Brown. To his surprise, "On reaching Liverpool, I learned that England was nearly as much alive to what had happened at Harper's Ferry as the United States, and I was immediately called upon in different parts of the country to speak on the subject of slavery." For six months he found more than a safe haven, noting that he was "chiefly occupied in speaking on slavery, and other subjects, in different parts of England and Scotland, meeting and enjoying the while the society of many of the kind friends whose acquaintance I had made during my visit to those countries fourteen years earlier."[25]

Another freedom seeker, William Wells Brown, was accorded the same reception during a five-year sojourn in the late 1840s and early 1850s. That warm embrace of both himself and his cause contrasted strongly with the attitude of his native land. The Fugitive Slave Law was passed soon after his departure, making it clear that he would not be welcome back. Brown too found himself in demand as a lecturer, delivering more than a thousand public addresses while crisscrossing Britain. Venturing to the Continent, Brown shared a stage with Victor Hugo, Alexis de Tocqueville, and Richard Cobden at the Paris Peace Conference of 1849, where he was "received with marked attention." The American refugee chaired a mass meeting in August 1851 in London, where a "committee of fugitives" from slavery sat on the dais next to "some of the most noted English Abolitionists" and members of Parliament.[26]

From the lectern, Brown denounced his nation's hypocrisy in purporting to love freedom while perpetuating slavery and enacting the Fugitive Slave Law. He declared, "posterity will blush at the discrepancy between American profession and American practice." In recalling the experience much later, Brown took considerable satisfaction in being able to reproduce his words from decades-old press clippings, gratified that Britain, at least, had accorded him the respect he deserved as both an abolitionist and a human being. He, in turn, had helped rouse public opinion there against the institution he abhorred, using what historian Stephen Hall calls a method of "present[ing] freedom as a teleological process and as a moment of unfettered possibility." Britain presented a stark contrast to the United States, where, as Brown told his British audience, he and Douglass were treated as "fugitives from their native land," though they were decidedly not "fugitives from justice."[27]

In reviving the tradition of crossing the Atlantic, Wells laid important groundwork for a resurgence of the antislavery movement on both sides of the ocean. Douglass admitted, "I have spoken, but my word is feeble in comparison" to hers. In 1893 Wells cofounded an antilynching and antiracist organization, the Society for the Recognition of the Brotherhood of Man. Following Douglass and Brown to Britain, Wells became a bridge between the nineteenth- and twentieth-century antislavery movements. Calling out the blatant hypocrisy of the nation of her birth, she appealed to the many who recognized the inconsistency between the proclamation of principles of freedom and the tyranny of government-sanctioned control over the lives and labors of others. Wells knew this palpable contradiction had played a role in the abolition of Haitian slavery during the French Revolution, as well as the movement to abolish the slave trade in Britain and the fledgling United States at the end of the eighteenth century. But Wells was also keenly aware of the indispensable historical role of Black abolitionists such as Brown, Douglass, and Harriet Tubman, among many others, which she aimed to replicate.[28]

The America that Wells lived in seemed even more hostile to her antilynching cause than it had been to Black abolitionists such as Douglass and Brown decades earlier. She conveyed her disgust to English audiences, noting that "the pulpit and the press of our own country remains silent on these continued outrages and the voice of my race thus tortured and outraged is stifled or ignored whenever it is lifted in America in a demand for justice." Douglass admitted, "It sometimes seems we are deserted by earth and heaven," given the conspicuous silence among the descendants of white American abolitionists on the plight of African Americans. He supported Wells's quest for allies with testimonials addressed to his network of overseas contacts, many of whom rallied to her assistance. The holdover *Anti-Slavery Reporter* introduced her to its readership as Douglass's follower, describing her speaking tour as a sequel to his. Wells worked from the same script. Her biographer Mia Bey writes, "Like her abolitionist predecessors, Wells aimed to mobilize the British press and pulpit to address their American counterparts." Her efforts exceeded her own expectations, Bey notes, because she "offered British reformers the chance to reclaim the glory days of their antislavery campaign."[29]

African Americans were conscious of, yet sometimes ambivalent toward, British antislavery credentials at the time. Lawrence Little demonstrates that the Disciples of Liberty, who formed the leadership of the African Methodist Episcopal Church, appreciated Britain's role in suppressing the slave trade and slavery in Africa. However, although they saw Britain as "an already liberal and enlightened" colonial power, that did not blind them to "the complex realities of self-determination and racism in Africa." Wells too felt these countervailing forces, but she focused on the opportunity offered by Britain's more active antislavery heritage as she forged ahead with her antilynching work. Back in the United States, Du Bois, born six years after Wells in the abolitionist stronghold of Massachusetts, took note of her success as he headed south in 1897 with a Harvard doctorate in hand to take up a faculty position at Atlanta University.[30]

As he journeyed around the South, Du Bois chronicled much of what he encountered, later including his travel log in his *Souls of Black Folk*. Amidst "the remnants of the vast plantations," he wrote, "the whole land seems forlorn and forsaken." Here and there he could discern signs that "the Negro is rising" as the twentieth century approached. But the unmistakable imprint of slavery showed through too. New methods of compelling African American labor had emerged. After the Civil War, former slaveholders imitated General Banks by passing vagrancy laws that allowed African Americans to be arrested and confined to plantations if they attempted to claim their newly decreed freedom by deserting their former masters.[31]

When Reconstruction-era legislation put a stop to that practice a few years later, Du Bois observed, "the courts sought to do by judicial decisions what the legislatures had formerly sought to do by specific law—namely, reduce the freedmen to serfdom." Black people were tried, convicted, and legally bound to work for employers who had no obligation to pay them. "Gangs of Negro convicts" substituted for the formerly enslaved workforce for decades as "a way of making Negroes work." Du Bois heard "hard tales of cruelty and mistreatment of the chained freemen." Commenting on a county prison, he wrote, "The white folks say it is ever full of black criminals,—the black folks say that only colored boys are sent to jail, and they not because they are guilty, but because the State needs criminals to eke out its income by their forced labor."[32]

Du Bois appreciated that such a shocking indictment of the persistence of purely racial slavery required extraordinary evidence. Ever the pioneering social scientist, Du Bois led a contingent of students into the field to study the conditions of African Americans in the rural South. He involved them because "these young persons, born and bred [here], have unusual facilities for first-hand knowledge of a difficult and intricate subject." He was tacitly admitting that, as a northerner, he had the status of an outsider. His willingness to employ students because they were better able to understand Black southerners indicated his determination to confront a problem he saw all around him as he ventured into the heart of the Black Belt. For him, this study helped unlock the meaning of postemancipation racial slavery, which was assuming greater importance in his thinking about the long freedom struggle ahead.[33]

In a series of writings, Du Bois cataloged the results. He cited the case of a "young girl" in Georgia who in 1895 "was repeatedly outraged by several of her guards, and finally died in childbirth while in camp." He detailed the practice of whipping and "torture," the woefully inadequate diet, the twelve-hour or longer workdays, the unsanitary pens the prisoners were kept in, the absence of medical care, and the exceedingly high mortality rates. With a nod toward Wells, Du Bois called this regime the legal version of lynching—two sides of the same oppressive coin for African Americans across the South. He presciently forecast that this system would evolve into newer and more outrageous forms. That prediction quickly came true in the infamous "chain gang." In the era of the automobile, chain gangs built the highway systems of southern states like Florida, making them accessible to tourists from the rest of a nation, the entirety of which tangibly benefited from and silently sanctioned the continued enslavement of Black people.[34]

African Americans now worked the land on which they had been enslaved a generation ago. Yet they were subjected to other means of accomplishing the same ends, as landlords extracted extortionate rents from tenant farmers. Planters had figured out that they "could squeeze more blood from debt-cursed tenants. . . . The shadow-hand of the master's grand-nephew or cousin or creditor stretches out of the gray distance to collect the rack-rent remorselessly." Du Bois described one tenant, aged twenty-two and "just married," who was doing well until the price of cotton fell. Suddenly he lost his rented land as local law enforcement "seized and sold all he had." The young farmer was forced onto a much worse parcel that actually cost him more. A disgusted Du Bois remarked, "Only black tenants can stand such a system, and they only because they must." Their "hard battle with debt" was the inevitable result. "Poor lad!" Du Bois lamented, "a slave at twenty-two." Du Bois cautioned that this unfortunate man was not alone; millions like him were "in danger of being reduced to semi-slavery" in the rural South. In entrapping close to a majority of African Americans located there, sharecropping, which Du Bois identified as "slavery in everything but in name," conditioned the poverty and segregation that facilitated the rise of mass incarceration not only in the South but also elsewhere in the nation. African Americans were forced to flee their bondage under the worst circumstances, leaving them disproportionately impoverished and segregated in inner cities, where the carceral state would exert its repressive force.[35]

Du Bois could only conclude, "Here lies the Negro problem in its naked dirt and penury." His fertile mind continued to range far and wide, and much of African American life came under his scrutiny at one point or another. Still, what he famously called "the problem of the twentieth century" never left him. Motivated by the dire situation of Black people, he was in the midst of a decades-long formulation of a political program for the continuation of the Black freedom struggle, which he now realized included a battle against the persistence of slavery. The more he studied the conditions under which African Americans lived and labored in the turn-of-the-century South, the more clearly he discerned the unresolved problem of emancipation. But only when he too, like Wells, went on a pilgrimage to England did he fully realize what African Americans were up against. And this insight was the result of his exposure to another founder of twentieth-century Black abolitionism: Alice Kinloch.[36]

Alice Kinloch and the Pan-African Conference of 1900

Three years after Ida B. Wells cofounded the Society for the Recognition of the Brotherhood of Man, the society's journal published two essays by South African journalist Alice Victoria Kinloch. These articles brought to public attention a related campaign single-handedly launched by Kinloch. Within the span of a few years, these two solitary, pioneering Black female activists and journalists would travel to England to expose ongoing racial oppression. This produced a marked change in tone on the part of the British antislavery movement and briefly restored it as an antiracist ally—a position it had not occupied for decades. Neither woman received the credit she deserved at the time, overshadowed by their male co-organizers and white allies, although Wells, at least, has subsequently been acclaimed.[37]

Little is known about Kinloch's life. She was born in the early 1860s in South Africa's Cape region. By the 1870s, her parents, both domestic servants, had relocated to Kimberley, site of a diamond rush. There she eventually took up journalism, steadfastly chronicling the

conditions to which African workers in the diamond industry were subjected as the migrant labor system emerged out of a combination of
employers' needs, African workers' skills, and the racist ideology underpinning colonialism.[38]

In her writings and speeches, Kinloch gave riveting descriptions of
the "compound system" that was "imposed on" Africans "enticed" to work
in the diamond mines of Kimberley, the gold mines on the Rand, and
other industries across the region. She decried the "herding [of] a thousand or more" workers "in enclosures each measuring about 150 yards
square," where they were forced to live and work in "degrading captivity."
In stark language rarely heard in Britain for more than half a century,
Kinloch characterized that nation's expanding empire and the plight of
African workers as "conditions of slavery in an aggravated form."[39]

Kinloch was relaying the sentiments of African workers caught up
in the new slavery, and her activism channeled theirs. According to
Charles van Onselen, for "black mine workers" in southern Africa, the
legal regime of British colonialism "relegated them to what they considered to be slave status." Van Onselen notes that their term for this labor
system, *chibaro*, and its equivalents were "synonymous with contract
labour, forced labour and slavery." Kinloch's brother Geoffrey provided
her reports from Zimbabwe, and she discussed that nation's compound
system in her lectures. The sense among African workers that their conditions of labor amounted to slavery would continue for as long as colonialism lasted. For instance, when the British ruthlessly suppressed a
strike of mine workers in Zambia's resource-rich copper belt shortly
after the outbreak of World War II, Katwishi Chowa posted a notice
addressed to "my fellow workers": "This fact embitters my mind—the
Europeans left their work without any trouble falling upon them. Cannot a slave, too, speak to his master?"[40]

"The issue of what was free labor and what was coerced," writes
Frederick Cooper, "and how narrowly to limit the legitimate use of the
latter, would be the focus of international discussions in the 1920s and
1930s." He adds, "These discussions had little to do with the lives of
African workers or even the daily decisions that colonial officials and
African chiefs had to make except to make clear what could not be said,
what could not be seen, and what could not be asked." It was equally a
question of *who* could not be asked. Africans caught up in the new slav-

ery, like enslaved African Americans before them, were the first to point to their bondage, as Kinloch well knew. Twentieth-century Black abolitionism would be rooted in the antislavery activity of the enslaved, just as it had been in the antebellum period.[41]

Kinloch presented reform-minded Britons with a somewhat different challenge than Wells did. Whereas Wells asked them to take a stand against atrocities in America, Kinloch illuminated practices for which their own government was responsible. Her criticism hit home, leaving British colonial officials on the defensive. Earl Grey, who objected to the term *slave cages* for the compounds where African mine workers were housed, was ridiculed by his fellow parliamentarians for characterizing them instead as *garden cities*. With no provision for families or personal autonomy, these compounds might easily be judged inferior to the slave quarters of the antebellum American South. In some respects, the worst of them were reminiscent of slave ships or the holding pens where the captives waited to board: enormous brick barracks stuffed with up to thousands of men, with cement bunks for beds, no furniture, and no electricity or lighting. In this updated version of slave quarters, no women were permitted. According to Liberal critic John Atkinson Hobson, the "'compound' slavery system," as a turn-of-the-century pamphleteer called it, "converted a labour contract into a period of imprisonment with hard labour." The barbed wire fences and a local population authorized to shoot on sight anyone attempting to escape gave force to the analogy.[42]

The parallels to slavery cataloged by Kinloch were documented in reports compiled by the British authorities themselves throughout their African territories. The compound system persisted essentially unchanged for nearly half a century. A 1943 report about British mines in Zambia called the compounds "labour camps," with echoes of other contemporaneous places that were condemned when Europeans were the victims. Like those infamous labor camps, the ones in British Africa reduced internees' lives to shifts of eight to ten hours or more of intensive labor, often underground, for stints of six to twelve months. Tanzania's British administration insisted that the camps be organized "on semi-military lines" for purposes of domination. According to a South African mining official, the pass systems enforced against Africans "enable us to get complete control over our labourers," a sentiment echoed by authorities in other British colonies and with which American slaveholders would have heartily concurred.[43]

Examining the practice across decades, historian William Beinart points out that migrant workers would never be "totally controlled." "Despite pass laws, compounds and police, many Mpondo workers found it possible to desert," he notes. Of course, the same was true for enslaved African Americans whose escapes had powered the Underground Railroad. The response of the authorities was similar. Throughout the compound system's decades-long history, van Onselen explains, it was aimed at preventing migrant workers from "running away." He adds, "the bulk of the extra-economic coercion was applied by the state, through the agency of the 'native police,' who roamed town and countryside enforcing the Pass Laws."[44]

Kinloch argued that compound inmates had no enforceable rights, and extensive documentary evidence from subsequent years corroborates her charge. When allegations emerged that workers were subjected to beatings on the slightest pretext, a turn-of-the-century government inquiry revealed "habitual assaults" against them. Transvaal's governor remarked, with considerable understatement, the compounds "cannot be said to have been constructed with a full appreciation of hygiene or of the number of cubic feet of air supposed to be required by a human being." "The general state" of the worst compounds Kinloch had visited, a South African journalist reported, "baffled description." He noted that "almost all of the natives in the compound at Springs Colliery were found in a state of starvation," the result of thirteen hours a day in the mines and inadequate rations.[45]

Van Onselen opines that the compound system, with its "quasi-military appearance," was "unique in capitalist development." He adds, "everywhere in southern Africa, the compounds served to isolate, regiment and exploit" workers. "It was the compound, with its state-sanctioned system of industrial violence, which converted reluctant and forced labour into forced production." In the 1920s the South African minister of mines acknowledged that African workers were still preferred over whites "owing to the compound system, pass laws, apprenticeship, right of prosecution for desertion, and so on." He added, "In fact we cannot deny that the natives of the Witwatersrand—nearly 190,000—are there really in a semi-servile condition." It was a tacit admission that Kinloch's critique three decades earlier had been squarely on the mark.[46]

Kinloch was describing the same problem of emancipation that Douglass had warned about in America. The migrant labor system of British colonialism, if not openly announcing itself to be slavery, at least tacitly admitted that it was, couching its coercive measures in the kind of language once used by Union general Nathaniel Banks. Even when Britain embarked on its war to save freedom and democracy in 1939, the British administration in Malawi, a principal supplier of labor for its larger neighbors, insisted that, in British Africa, "indentured labour is better than free labour" and added, in the spirit of Banks, is "in the interests of the natives." The number of migrant workers who were apparently voluntary did not change the nature of the system, given that the very notion of work freely entered into imagines very different circumstances from those in British colonial Africa. As historians of slavery in the Americas have made clear, the enslaved there also negotiated the terms of their enslavement without altering its nature.[47]

Kinloch harnessed the legacy of the earlier abolitionist struggle to promote that of the African workers of her day. Twentieth-century Black abolitionism owed an enormous debt to her, though she would become the least known of its progenitors. Here, in embryonic form, was everything Du Bois and others would subsequently forge into a powerful anti-slavery doctrine. Due in no small part to Kinloch's influence, the term *new slavery*, used to describe these colonial labor systems, would gain considerable currency in the first few decades of the twentieth century.[48]

Posterity would commit a grave injustice to this African woman who was so instrumental in launching the Pan-Africanist movement, which helped usher in the postcolonial world. The official report of the Pan-African Conference of 1900 declared, "The public's attention for the first time in England was called to the existence of the aforementioned condition in South Africa principally by Mrs. A. V. Kinnlock [*sic*], a native lady." Among those she reached was Trinidadian law student Henry Sylvester Williams, who heard her speak not long after she arrived in Britain in 1895 or 1896. Her talk exposed him to the realities of British rule in Africa just as his own anticolonial ideas were taking shape. Pan-Africanism would be launched in no small part because of their fateful meeting. Williams later told an associate that the formation of the African Association in September 1897 was "the result of Mrs. Kinloch's work in England." His admission, in effect, acknowledged Kinloch as the guiding spirit behind the antislavery impetus that formed a significant part of the mission of nascent Pan-Africanism. Ironically, her return to South Africa in the late 1890s to take up farming meant that Kinloch missed her opportunity for lasting renown, as she was unable to attend the inaugural Pan-African Conference.[49]

One of the organizers' goals was to convene a meeting of the minds among leaders of the Black freedom movement from across the Atlantic world. As David Levering Lewis notes, Booker T. Washington's sponsorship secured African American participation among the delegates in London, who included Du Bois and Anna Julia Cooper. Contrary to how history—and even Du Bois himself—would remember it, Du Bois had no part in organizing the event that would leave such a lasting imprint on him and perhaps change the trajectory of his entire life, leading to his last Africa-based political project. The agenda was one that Washington could readily endorse. As Lewis writes, if "the congress itself was an unmistakable harbinger of distant restiveness," it was nevertheless modest enough in its "moderate, trusting appeal for an imperialism that lived up to its highest pieties." Even "a clairvoyant Du Bois" did not yet foresee independence as the goal of the movement and probably did not imagine that he would live to see it, let alone end his days in an Africa that was newly liberated from external rule.[50]

If this nascent Pan-Africanism did not yet demand an end to European rule, it did call on Europeans to stop enslaving Africans. Antislavery was in certain respects more central to the new organization's expressed purpose than anticolonialism. Resolutions pointed out the existence of outright slavery in Africa promoted by European colonization, but equally they decried the "acute ill-treatment of the natives in South Africa." The conference condemned "the degrading and illegal compound system of native labour in vogue in Kimberley and Rhodesia"; the system of "indenture, i.e., legalised bondage of native men and women and children to white colonists"; "compulsory labour on public works"; the pass system; and legal segregation. Kinloch was quickly forgotten as Williams's collaborator in launching the 1900 conference, but both its existence and its unmistakably abolitionist tenor bore her distinctive imprint. Kinloch was largely responsible for Du Bois's change in thinking after his sojourn to London, even though he never met her and knew almost nothing about her. He would hear only faint echoes of the words and deeds of the person who would so deeply impact his own role in the movement.[51]

W. E. B. Du Bois and the New Slavery

Both the Pan-African scope and the abolitionist content of the Pan-African Conference worked its way into Du Bois's consciousness as he carried the torch for Black abolitionism into the new century. He immediately connected the new slavery in Africa he learned about in London to what he had been studying in the American South. His subsequent writings evince the meeting's significant influence in cementing two related trends in his thinking. The first involved the link among African-descended people that provided the scope and purpose of the Pan-African Conference. Though in every other way Du Bois played only a supporting role in those proceedings, his fellow delegates appointed him to deliver the closing address titled "To the Nations of the World," which was duly adopted as a call to action. Du Bois more than rose to the occasion. He put his immense literary gifts to use by stating, "The problem of the twentieth century is the problem of the colour line." As he explained it, the question was "how far differences of race . . . are going to be made, hereafter, the basis of denying to over half the world the right of sharing to their utmost ability the opportunities and privileges of modern civilisation."[52]

Du Bois also probed the theoretical basis of what drew him and his fellow attendees together, advancing an idea that would become an influential intellectual movement in the second half of the twentieth century. In calling Pan-Africanism an outgrowth and expression of the "black world," he pioneered the construct of transnational worlds linking peoples and geographies across national borders. That idea later became most closely associated with Fernand Braudel. Du Bois, however, holds the earlier claim, describing Africa and its principally American diaspora as one connected historical, political, intellectual, and cultural realm. Across three continents and varying economic conditions, race constituted the social determinant of not an *Atlantic* but a *Black* world. Du Bois was less interested in what linked Europe, North and South America, and Africa than in the historically constructed notion of transnational Blackness through which the modern world economy forged the common bonds of Black workers and inexorably divided them from white.[53]

The second idea that crystallized in Du Bois's mind was the persistence of racial slavery. He linked it to the very notion of global blackness, asking whether "the black world is to be exploited and ravished and degraded." In his address in London, his references to the resurrection of slavery across the Black world, including in the United States, were still rather indirect. He invoked the "spirit" of Frederick Douglass alongside fellow abolitionists William Lloyd Garrison and Wendell Phillips to tweak "the conscience of a great nation" and avert its present course of "unrighteous oppression toward the American Negro." He asked the same of Britain in its African and Caribbean dominions. Du Bois was nevertheless part of a convention animated by an abolitionist spirit that, in its resolutions, denounced the persistence of racial slavery more directly. That nascent twentieth-century abolitionist discourse would immediately make it into his writings about the plight of African Americans in the Black Belt.[54]

Within a year, Du Bois produced two essays that forthrightly described the labor system of the South as de facto slavery. When he revised one of them for inclusion in *Souls of Black Folk*, he sharpened his language even further. His attendance at the Pan-African Conference played a key role in his decades-long quest to understand the connection between the Black world and the problem of emancipation first raised by Douglass. The more Du Bois studied the conditions under which African Americans lived and labored in the turn-of-the-century South, the more he discerned exactly what Douglass had prophesied.[55]

This new clarity was especially evident in Du Bois's 1901 essay "The Spawn of Slavery: The Convict Lease System in the South." He noted that both the prison labor system and what he called the "crop-lien system" were about "controlling human labor," which made them both "the direct children of slavery" and thus "a new slavery." For Du Bois, as for Douglass, none of this happened in a vacuum. It was not possible to end the enslavement of Black people without getting rid of the *racial* content underlying racial slavery. The historical context for this evolution of racial slavery was racism, and its continued existence would continually produce, as Du Bois put it, "children." Du Bois reduced it to this ideology: "The black workman existed for the comfort and profit of white people, and the interests of white people were the only ones to be seriously considered." Given the realities of racism, racial slavery would mutate, "spawn[ing]" new forms. Here was the incisive critique that Du Bois's work of only two years earlier had lacked.[56]

Du Bois had previously witnessed firsthand how oppressive systems such as sharecropping and prison labor would continue to stalk African Americans in the United States, but the Pan-African Conference alerted him that racial slavery extended much farther. In *Souls*, Du Bois again states, "The problem of the twentieth century is the problem of the color line"—now defining it as "the relation of the darker to the lighter races of men in Asia and Africa, in America and the islands of the sea." The next sentence reveals exactly what is on his mind: "It was a phase of this problem that caused the Civil War." The influence of Pan-Africanism is clearly in evidence as Du Bois extracts that conflict from its usual purely American framing and views it from a Black world perspective.[57]

Du Bois was already keenly aware of the transnational dimensions of both slavery and abolitionism in the nineteenth century. His doctoral dissertation, *The Suppression of the African Slave-Trade to the United States of America*, had been published just before he headed south. At the outset, his concern was clearly centered on the United States itself. But he could not ignore that "the slave-trade [was] an international problem." He writes, "The question of the suppression of the slave-trade is . . . intimately connected with the questions as to its rise, the system of American slavery, and the whole colonial policy of the eighteenth century." The African slave trade, after all, supplied two continents, and where any individual African ended up was largely a matter of chance. He notes that what happened in the Caribbean shaped the slavery of states like South Carolina and Georgia, resulting in a "police system" to ward off the kind of rebellions that would later occur there and encourage "check[s on] the further importation of slaves."[58]

Du Bois also documented the power of an international antislavery movement that spanned the Atlantic world. He devoted an entire chapter to "Toussaint L'Ouverture and Anti-Slavery Effort," noting that "the role which the great Negro . . . played in the history of the United States has seldom been fully appreciated. Representing the age of revolution in America, he rose to leadership through a bloody terror, which contrived a Negro 'problem' for the Western Hemisphere, intensified and defined the anti-slavery movement, became one of the causes, and probably the prime one, which led Napoleon to sell Louisiana for a song, and finally, through the interworking of all these effects, rendered more certain the final prohibition of the slave-trade by the United States in 1807." He cited the impact of English abolitionism in particular in convincing one European nation after another to ban its participation in the slave trade. Though his focus was primarily elsewhere at the time, the seeds of his later understanding were already planted.[59]

As he immersed himself in the study of the problem of emancipation, Du Bois found that not only modes of analyzing it but also means of combating it were very much on his mind. In 1903, soon after the appearance of his critically acclaimed and lastingly influential *Souls of Black Folk*, a major publishing house asked Du Bois to contribute to a series of biographies of prominent Civil War–era figures. He eagerly chose Frederick Douglass as his subject. Soon Du Bois would feverishly be securing his own place in history by launching the Niagara movement and the National Association for the Advancement of Colored People, and he welcomed the opportunity to assimilate the thinking of the preceding generation, especially that of the man he viewed as its preeminent representative. Some months later, after being informed that Douglass's biography would instead be assigned to Booker T. Washington, Du Bois fixed on Nat Turner. As Lewis writes, he envisioned a project that would "trace slave insurrections from Toussaint L'Ouverture to John Brown." But the editor of the press rejected the suggestion, alleging that Turner was too obscure to be featured in the series, and he assigned Du Bois John Brown instead.[60]

Du Bois accepted the commission, but with his characteristic iconoclasm, he chose an unorthodox approach that effectively salvaged his plan to study Black abolitionism. He characterized Brown as significant because he, rather than Abraham Lincoln or William Lloyd Garrison, was "the [white] man who of all Americans has perhaps come nearest to touching the real souls of black folk." Du Bois's biography would explore "the little known but vastly important inner development of the Negro American." In Du Bois's hands, the Harpers Ferry movement was much larger than the man who led the antislavery rebellion. It was important for what it revealed about Black abolitionism. Though ostensibly a biography of Brown, the work was really an opportunity for Du Bois to understand the political legacy of nineteenth-century Black abolitionism.[61]

To restore Douglass to the full context of African American history from which he emerged, Du Bois radically reinterpreted the abolitionist movement, anticipating the recent argument advanced by Edward Baptist. Denied the opportunity to write a biography of Douglass, the undisputed great man of his time, Du Bois opted instead for an early version of bottom-up history, diving deeply into the African American experience. His focus was what he called the "black phalanx." Typical of the cosmopolitan author of *Souls*, which traced the African roots of American cultural forms, he chose as a central metaphor a Greek military form taken from the Egyptians. In battle formation, the phalanx marched in unison to engage the enemy; it was so powerful that it helped write the history of conquest in the ancient world for nearly a millennium. Du Bois seemingly borrowed the term, without acknowledgment, from the title of a volume about Black US soldiers by Joseph Wilson, an otherwise obscure Black soldier who had fought in the Civil War. Du Bois also adopted Wilson's description of the ethos of the "black phalanx" as a fighting force that could claim "no reserve—no reinforcements behind to support them when they went to battle; their alternative was *life or death*. It was the consciousness of this fact that made the black phalanx a wall of adamant to the enemy."[62]

Du Bois applied Wilson's evocative name and the animating spirit of the troops he wrote about to a metaphorical antislavery army, its ranks formed by "a widening, hurrying stream of fugitives [that] swept the havens of refuge, taking the restless, the criminal and the unconquered—the natural leaders of the more timid mass." Du Bois again quoted without attribution a nineteenth-century African American intellectual, historian George Washington Williams. Two decades earlier, Williams had argued that runaways constituted the "safety-valve" of slavery by emptying the South of "the leaders . . . among the slaves," who otherwise would have "enacted . . . the direful scenes of St. Domingo," and "the hot, vengeful breath of massacre would have swept the South as a tornado." Du Bois repeated Williams's argument, clarifying that because of the absence of Haiti's "disproportion of races," such a "desperate and bloody" struggle was doomed to failure. Du Bois queried the afterlife of those revolutionaries who disappeared neither from sight nor from history following their escape from slavery. His corollary to the "safety-valve" theorem was that while the act of flight drained the South of its "natural leaders," it simultaneously filled the ranks of the antislavery resistance located in the North and especially in Canada. Having evaded the reach of slavery, freedom seekers banded together with free African Americans, "organizing themselves into a great black phalanx that worked and schemed and paid and finally fought for the freedom of black men in America."[63]

The genius of the phalanx was that it allowed an army to dispense with the usual officer corps to direct it in the fog of war. Du Bois used the term to aggregate the mainly obscure figures who led in egalitarian unison. In doing so, he unearthed the memory of the unknown martyrs one generation older than himself who had not survived the Civil War era but provided the shock troops behind Douglass's leadership. They thus prefigured not only the Civil War's Black soldiery but also—and perhaps even more so—the runaways who turned the tide of that conflict.[64]

Du Bois effectively divided the black phalanx into two groups animated by different impulses. First, he depicted the mass of freedom seekers who expressed the irrepressible desire to be free and would stop at nothing to achieve their liberty. He illustrated the soul of this mass component of the movement through the story of one of the five African American participants at Harpers Ferry, Shields Green. That young freedom seeker, in his twenties, manifested the "attitude of the slave" in choosing to follow Brown not long after his arrival in Canada via the Underground Railroad. The man who embodied the second group—the intellectual leadership of the black phalanx—was Green's friend Douglass, who introduced him to Brown and who made a very different choice.[65]

The analysis of the "real souls of black folk" in *John Brown* pivots around the question of why one opted to participate in the antislavery rebellion and the other did not. As a freedom seeker on the cusp of realizing his lifelong dream but who chose instead to "go down to John Brown and to death," Green stood in for other freedom seekers prepared to risk everything. Du Bois recognized in them Brown's inspiration for his life's work and for his Harpers Ferry venture, which had started out as "a plan of increasing and systematizing the work of the Underground Railroad by running off larger bodies of slaves." Du Bois wrote, "some Negroes of the right type were needed and to John Brown's mind the Underground Railroad was bringing North the very material he required." For Brown, nothing was more convincing of his chances for success than the prevalence of the self-determining act of escaping to freedom that yielded the Harriet Tubmans, Frederick Douglasses, and Shields Greens. Du Bois discerned in them the hidden basis of Harpers Ferry that others had missed.[66]

The phenomenon of freedom seekers reached a vast scale and impressed Du Bois immeasurably, as he divined how many more Shields Greens had still been enslaved in the South and how much heroism they had been capable of. Here was the germ of the idea Du Bois later developed in *Black Reconstruction*: that the single greatest political victory in the history of the African American freedom struggle stemmed from a spontaneous movement that welled up from the souls of Black folk and changed the course of American history. Here was one of the most important lessons Du Bois drew from the antebellum history of Black abolitionism. Coming when it did, *John Brown* was almost a prophecy of the civil rights movement, whose mass phase was still half a century away.[67]

Just one generation younger than the Harpers Ferry martyr Green, Du Bois believed the legacy of freedom seekers was more than a question of history and memory. Du Bois saw Green's life story as just one chapter of the larger Black freedom movement of which he was now a part. As he wrote about this history, he was conscious of doing so during what would have been Green's natural life span. Green would have been in his sixties had he not forfeited his life to the antislavery crusade, and this circumstance invited Du Bois to look at his own times through the freedom seeker's eyes. An Underground Railroad that had already assumed its place in American lore masked the realities of American society for those who had survived the ordeal of slavery. Du Bois wistfully recorded some of their stories in *Souls*, including "one big red-eyed black" man who for "forty-five years had labored" on the same farm, "beginning with nothing, and still having nothing . . . hopelessly in debt, disappointed, and embittered." What would Green, this man's contemporary from a neighboring state, have made of his predicament? Would he have seen in postemancipation America the fulfillment of the goals he set out to accomplish by joining John Brown?[68]

Du Bois rigorously applied a freedom seeker's standard in insisting that emancipation had left African Americans far short of freedom. His acute historical vision encompassed all of what occurred in the South even as he came of age in the North: the rise of sharecropping, segregation, disfranchisement, and lynching. How could the emancipation that promised African Americans so much deliver so little to so many? It was the answer to that question that prompted Du Bois to turn to the study of Black abolitionism.

And yet, as much as he admired and credited Shields Green, Du Bois made it clear in *John Brown* that he saw himself more in the role of black phalanx leader Douglass than his rank-and-file comrade. In going to Harpers Ferry as a combatant, Green was, in Du Bois's judgment, emblematic of the courage, the love of freedom, and the capacity for action of the mass of the black phalanx. Green's self-sacrifice was noble and brave; Douglass's refusal to join the suicide mission demonstrated that discretion was the better part of valor. Whereas the newly escaped young man represented the "attitude of the slave," his older comrade personified the accumulated wisdom and acuity of judgment of Black abolitionist leadership. Green would leave a lasting imprint on Du Bois's consciousness, and he would come back to Green's story as he attempted to understand how to end the slavery of his own times. But first he needed to understand the problem of emancipation: why had slavery managed to persist beyond its ostensible abolition? Here, Du Bois could not help but realize that Douglass's assessment of the anti-slavery rebellion's bleak chances for success had proved right and Brown's optimism had proved wrong. As a result, the doyen of Black abolitionism survived to establish the theoretical foundations of its reemergence in Du Bois's time. It is not difficult to read in Du Bois's portrayal of the black phalanx as the central core of nineteenth-century abolitionism an insistence that their political successors—the African American leaders of the Black freedom movement, which included himself—must play a similar role in the twentieth century.[69]

Douglass, the theoretically acute Black abolitionist, remained on Du Bois's mind as he revived his predecessor's analysis of the problem of emancipation to explain the rise of sharecropping, debt peonage, and racial violence that replicated in many particulars the legal slavery they replaced. Du Bois's fieldwork in the rural Black Belt convinced him that

Lincoln's 1863 Emancipation Proclamation and the Thirteenth Amendment that followed had not permanently eliminated the evil they addressed. The impetus behind the Civil War—racial slavery—continued to pose an existential threat to African Americans' freedom aspirations. Du Bois realized the significance of Douglass's conclusion, decades earlier, that racial slavery was capable of giving birth to other forms—taking on new guises that masked the same content.

Du Bois's understanding of racial slavery as inherently transnational would only be reinforced by his investigation of Black abolitionism for *John Brown*. He discovered that Brown shared his appraisal of the Haitian revolution and had studied it thoroughly as a model of what he hoped to replicate in the South. Brown's continentwide viewpoint went even deeper, as he found equal inspiration from the Jamaican Christmas rebellion, which provided the impetus for the 1834 abolition of slavery in the British dominions. Du Bois could not help but draw a direct connection to the black phalanx, since Canada, which became a key center of antebellum Black abolitionism, was a free territory only because of that earlier emancipation. Only a few years before the rebellion in Jamaica, David Walker had issued his "Appeal to the Colored Citizens of the World" to band together to overthrow the slavery that deprived them of freedom. He was representative of Black abolitionists whose outlook was always transnational. So was their praxis, as exemplified by the large and growing component of the black phalanx that waged the freedom struggle from Canadian exile. Even Douglass fled the United States for England in the aftermath of Harpers Ferry. Britain had always been an important center of international abolitionism and a resource for Black abolitionists.[70]

Du Bois found Shields Green so captivating because he embodied the Black world that had assumed a prominent place in the aspiring freedom movement leader's mind. Green had been born and raised in Charleston, South Carolina. The history of that state epitomized the conditions of racial bondage Green had been born into and so willingly sacrificed his life to change. Planters from the British Caribbean had first brought plantation slavery, with its Black majority, to the North American mainland, creating the British colony that would eventually become the American state. The introduction of rice production by these plantation owners established the conditions of slavery in

South Carolina, which included reliance on the skills and knowledge of Africans and their descendants and a surprising degree of autonomy.[71]

South Carolina's landscape was marked by both Black resistance and racial slavery. It was the site of the eighteenth-century Stono rebellion, in which Jemy and the leaders of that revolt set off for freedom in a foreign territory—in this case, Spanish Florida—only to forsake their own freedom in a valiant attempt to raise an antislavery rebellion. A century later, a decade or so before Green's birth, Charleston would be the site of Denmark Vesey's conspiracy with the same objective, one of many in the Black Atlantic tradition of the Haitian revolution. A few years after Green's escape, South Carolina was also the locale of the assault on a federal military installation that started the Civil War—the culmination of a historical process that the runaway slave–turned–antislavery rebel had, in small measure, helped set in motion. Charleston's Fort Sumter looked out on the body of water that has fittingly been described (along with the four continents it joins) as the Black Atlantic for the four hundred or so years of history that created the bondage and the freedom struggle that shaped Green's life and death.[72]

Green's epic journey out of slavery took him from the Atlantic seaport of Charleston to Canada via the Underground Railroad. The ocean that carried Green to freedom on a cotton vessel bound northward was the same one his ancestors—including his own father, according to one tradition—had been transported across as part of the centuries-long slave trade. When Green stowed away on that ship out of Charleston, he symbolically crossed the Black Atlantic—the world of racial slavery, racial colonialism, and Black resistance—on his way to freedom. The links between enslaved South Carolinians Shields Green and Jemy and the larger phenomena of runaway slaves, maroon communities, the Underground Railroad, and slave rebellions were found across a much wider geography than that of the United States. Green was not just incidentally joined in the same cause as Haitians and Jamaicans; he did not accidentally share the same martyrdom as Toussaint-Louverture and Denmark Vesey.

All this history of slavery and antislavery that Du Bois studied firmly implanted the conviction that nothing could be more natural than for twentieth-century slavery and the Black abolitionism that resisted it to be every bit as transnational as that of the nineteenth century. This understanding was represented in Du Bois's use of the term *Black world*, and it was consistently present in his theory and praxis from 1900 on.

Du Bois considered the possibility that the ship carrying Shields Green might have been bound for a destination other than New York. If so, the young freedom seeker might have escaped the fate that awaited him at Harpers Ferry, and he would have found slavery abolished across most of the Americas. And yet, Du Bois seems to say, wherever Green might have gone in the Atlantic world, he would have found that he was defined out of whiteness and into blackness, with everything that came with it. Racial colonialism was far from losing its defining role in the Atlantic world. Since the problem of the twentieth century—systemic racism—was global, so was the resultant racial slavery.

It is with this larger picture that Du Bois chose to conclude his analysis of nineteenth-century Black abolitionism. In *John Brown* he writes, African Americans "see the world-wide effort to build an aristocracy of races and nations on a foundation of darker half-enslaved and tributary peoples." Therefore, the "debate" between pro- and antislavery forces "was not closed by the Civil War. Men still maintain that East Indians and Africans and others ought to be under the restraint and benevolent tutelage of stronger and wiser nations for their own benefit." In exposing the inadequacy of what would become the canonical definition of slavery under international law to cover slaveries rooted in race, Douglass had anticipated not only slavery in the United States being resurrected in new guises but also racial slavery recrossing the Atlantic. The understanding that it extended the length and breadth of the Black world would become a defining feature of the twentieth-century Black abolitionism that Wells, Kinloch, and Du Bois brought into being. The distribution of the new slavery also suggested that England, which had played host to its Pan-African Conference launching pad, would be especially important to its growth and influence.[73]

2

Reactivating the Antislavery-Antiracism Alliance for a New Century

The political activities of Ida B. Wells and Alice Kinloch established a model that would go a long way toward shaping the trajectory of twentieth-century Black abolitionism. Seeking the white liberal allies she could not secure in America, Wells's speaking tour in Britain in the mid-1890s laid important groundwork for the revival of the antislavery-antiracism alliance. The antislavery press covered her extensively and sympathetically, renewing British interest in the oppression of African Americans. In addition to providing the impetus for the formation of Pan-Africanism, Kinloch drew the attention of British abolitionists to a question they might have thought had been solved long ago: slavery in the British Empire. The new slavery's close resemblance to the old, which they had publicly pledged to stamp out, proved very troubling to a few influential Britons, reigniting British abolitionism and catalyzing the reactivated alliance.[1]

Their encounter with Kinloch and the African Association encouraged some British abolitionists to see the problem of the new slavery as empire-wide as the twentieth century dawned. A few came to understand that British imperialism itself was the problem. Upon entering into an alliance with a nascent turn-of-the-century Pan-Africanism, these liberals—for all their shortcomings on questions of race—suddenly and lucidly penetrated to the core of the problem. They recognized that, by using the overwhelming force of the colonial state to coerce labor from a racially demarcated class, the labor systems taking shape in British Africa preserved the spirit and essence of the African slave trade and racial slavery.

A witness to and a direct personal beneficiary of these developments, W. E. B. Du Bois determined to bring the antislavery movement in England to the United States. In 1909 he got his chance as a principal mover in the founding of the National Association for the Advancement of Colored People (NAACP). The association's other leading figure, Oswald Garrison Villard, was the grandson of distinguished abolitionist William Lloyd Garrison and was not shy about leveraging his ancestry to buttress the NAACP's claim to the august heritage of antislavery as an interracial movement concerned with African American rights. That lineage was more than enough for Du Bois to ensure that antislavery constituted a crucial component of the new civil rights organization's agenda. In the end, the victories would prove meager. After a decade of tireless work, by the end of World War I, Du Bois was convinced that the NAACP's antislavery campaign had reached the limits of what could be accomplished in the current American political context.[2]

Finding himself stymied at home, Du Bois developed a transnational strategy that attempted to replicate the tactics of Wells and Kinloch. The revived antislavery-antiracism alliance would need to be reconstructed on the same international stage it had occupied in the antebellum period. To fulfill that bold ambition, Du Bois used the occasion of the 1919 Paris peace talks to relaunch the Pan-Africanist movement that had been the springboard for Black abolitionism's revival. In doing so, he counted on the British antislavery movement to provide the trustworthy and politically powerful allies he lacked at home. He expected that the international institutions of governance taking shape to cement freedom and democracy worldwide would have to take up the case of African Americans and people of the Black world as a whole.

Alice Kinloch, Henry Fox Bourne, and the Alliance in Britain

In the last years of the nineteenth century, Kinloch joined Wells in the grand tradition of Black abolitionists who traveled to Great Britain and left their mark there, electrifying listeners with accounts of slavery and oppression in places closely associated with British society and history. Making use of the institutions Wells had established and the memories she had awakened, Kinloch and her collaborators in the African Association similarly inspired an antislavery movement to confront a looming problem in which Britain's government was complicit.

Du Bois was not the only activist to come under the sway of Kinloch's abolitionism centered on the new slavery emerging in Africa. In its brief three-year existence, the African Association had attracted the support of some of the biggest names in British politics. Among its honorary members were the noted reformer, mathematician, and educator Henry Gurney. More prominent was George W. E. Russell, a Liberal member of Parliament (MP) who, only a few years earlier, had been a cabinet secretary. Best known was Philip Stanhope, MP, whose ancestor had been granted an earldom in the sixteenth century. Although this Philip Stanhope was a younger son elevated to the peerage fairly late in life, his family name was among the most illustrious in England. Coming into contact with the Black Britons, Africans, and Afro-Caribbeans in the African Association seemingly exerted a significant influence. Stanhope, for instance, came out against Britain's notorious Boer War in South Africa, an unpopular position in the ruling Liberal Party. Joining this group of converts was an officer of the British and Foreign Anti-Slavery Society (BFASS), Francis William Fox.[3]

The African Association's most important ally was one whose conversion was directly attributable to Kinloch: Henry Fox Bourne, secretary of the Aborigines Protection Society (APS). Then half a century old, the APS had emerged from a parliamentary select committee established in 1835 "to consider what measures ought to be adopted with regard to the native inhabitants of countries where British settlements are made, and to neighboring tribes, in order to secure to them justice and the protection of their rights." Under the energetic leadership of Fox Bourne, the APS would become the foremost antislavery organization in Britain and would eventually merge with the BFASS, which traced its lineage to the heyday of the fight against slavery in the British Empire. What Kinloch had to say affected Fox Bourne so powerfully that he set up the speaking tour that introduced her to Britain, reaching large audiences across the country. Taking turns at the lectern, the two created an antislavery stir in Britain that would reinvigorate the long-dormant abolitionist movement there.[4]

In a letter published in a liberal British paper, Kinloch listed the important purposes of the African Association, one of which was to "help the Aborigines' Protection Society" in its antislavery work. Fox Bourne spoke at the official launch of the African Association, pledging cooperation on their "common aims." Together with a few of his APS colleagues, he became an honorary member of the association and duly noted its formation in his journal the *Aborigines' Friend.* He called it a "very interesting and promising society" dedicated to "protecting the interests of all British subjects," a goal squarely within the purview of the APS's mission. The BFASS also pronounced itself "pleased to give our hearty good wishes to this newly-formed body." Both organizations invited Henry Sylvester Williams to their annual meetings as an official delegate representing the African Association and the prospective Pan-African Conference. Williams addressed each body and joined in its political deliberations. At the 1899 convention of the APS, which Booker T. Washington attended, Williams engaged in a disagreement with another delegate, Earl Grey, that was detailed in the *Aborigines' Friend.* In response to Grey's positive characterization of Africans' position in British colonial Zimbabwe, Williams quoted a letter he had received (perhaps through Kinloch) from a Zimbabwean denouncing colonialism's racist rule. It was, perhaps, a measure of how secure Williams felt that he boldly challenged such a prominent figure, yet it simultaneously revealed how alien an environment it remained for a Pan-Africanist. In the short term, nevertheless, Williams's position seemed to be in the ascendancy.[5]

Even in Kinloch's absence, the resolutions of the Pan-African Conference radiate the sense of expectation about the new movement's ability to count on an old ally. The first resolution passed, titled "The British and Foreign Anti-Slavery Society," thanked the BFASS "for the great and noble work" it had undertaken in the past and for its prospective "achievement of like, if not greater, heroism for Christ and humanity," a tribute the BFASS quoted in full in its encouraging account of the proceedings. Similarly, the third resolution, "The Aborigines Protection Society," "gratefully acknowledged" the APS's past support and "pray[ed] that the Society may be greatly encouraged in carrying on its work." The conference specified a list of particulars that antislavery activism should focus on, including abolishing the compound system, indentured labor, the pass system, and discriminatory legislation in British colonial Africa. The founders of Pan-Africanism not only believed in the importance of such partners but also interpreted the sentiments emerging from the antislavery movement as portending the extension of the old alliance in the new century.[6]

What happened in Britain mattered to the Black freedom movement for three reasons. First, there was the important historical connection to Black abolitionism. Second, Britain's colonial policy made that nation central to the new slavery's spread beyond the Americas; hence the British antislavery movement was crucial to its suppression. Finally, the long-standing influence of British antislavery assured that it would play a principal role in twentieth-century abolitionism and the international conventions it would sponsor.

In establishing fraternal relations between British antislavery and Pan-Africanism, Fox Bourne and his colleagues rededicated themselves to the antiracism that had been a distant afterthought for decades. Working cooperatively with Black abolitionists, as had his forerunners during abolitionism's heyday, Fox Bourne gave important backing to Pan-Africanism, shared the stage with its founders, promoted their cause, showed respect for their ideas, and gave serious weight to their position on the new slavery in Africa. British abolitionists acknowledged the presence of slavery in the United States as well, attentively reading Du Bois's writings and enthusiastically receiving the American civil rights leader when he returned to London a decade later. They greeted the Pan-African Conference with the same support they had shown the African Association.[7]

Though she worked closely with several other English reformers, especially a number of prominent women, it is not difficult to see why Kinloch put so much stock in Fox Bourne. A lawyer by training and a journalist and man of letters by profession, he had virtually been born to the role of serving as her ally. Fox Bourne had come into the world in 1837, during his father's mission to Jamaica in support of abolitionism. Following two decades in the War Office, during which he spent much of his time on various scholarly endeavors, Fox Bourne took up the political journalism that was nearer to his heart. He first edited the *Examiner*, a moribund penny paper that he sought to revive. He described the editorial line as "deprecating all foreign complications [and] oppression of subject races, as in India," but also championing women's rights. Contributors included such luminaries as John Stuart Mill, Herbert Spencer, John Elliott Cairnes, Frederic Harrison, and Henry Fawcett. Upon the failure of that venture, which he later attributed to his being "a too sanguine Radical," Fox Bourne pitched these views to a working-class audience through yet another publication, the *Weekly Dispatch*. This time he succeeded, and it helped propel him to the forefront of radical politics. During what he called his "ten years' heresy," Fox Bourne critiqued the Liberal regime of William Gladstone as persistently as he did the Tories. "Venturing to claim for Radicals the right of thinking and acting for themselves" finally doomed Fox Bourne's career as a journalist when he too vociferously condemned Gladstone's 1886 Irish home rule bill as a half measure inconsistent with the principle of "complete justice, political and social."[8]

Fox Bourne shared many of the pervasive racial attitudes of his class and his European nationality, but his views were distinct from those of his antislavery peers even before he came under Kinloch's influence. Although he professed to agree with Europe's self-described mission of lifting the "weaker races" out of their age-old "backwardness," he had peculiar ideas about how colonialism should work. He believed the European powers should limit themselves to establishing "ports and trading stations, with roadways between them," but otherwise leave economic development almost entirely to African initiative, since "we have no warrant for breaking down [Africans'] independence." He termed European territorial claims "preposterous" because they professed "to deal with the human beings in [Africa] as though they were no less 'chattel' or 'game' than its elephants or lions." He added sententiously, "So long as such claims are put forward our vaunted condemnation of slavery and the slave trade is little short of a mockery."[9]

On the death of its longtime secretary in 1889, and with no successor in place, the APS leadership approached the BFASS about a merger. The latter declined, citing its unwillingness to increase its existing responsibilities. Spurned by its traditional partner and faced with the formidable task of filling a burdensome position that offered little compensation, the APS turned to Fox Bourne, whose personal finances allowed him to indulge his love of politics and vindicate his father's views. After taking the helm of the organization, Fox Bourne served as the movement's sole full-time activist and resident expert on a wide range of interests, its guiding spirit, and by far its most influential theorist, even though he is virtually forgotten today.[10]

Before Fox Bourne became a Kinloch disciple, the APS seemed oblivious to the realities of British rule in South Africa, the empire's focus on that continent. The APS did not quite join the Anti-Slavery Society in extolling the now notorious Cecil Rhodes as the one "man in South Africa who deserves the title of the black man's friend." However, Earl Grey, member of the House of Lords, Rhodes's close friend, and director of the British South Africa Company's mining empire, was an APS supporter with whom Fox Bourne engaged in a collegial exchange of letters. Fox Bourne approvingly printed Grey's admonition that "to abolish [slavery] at once . . . would . . . destroy what might be made a useful instrument for gradually bringing a barbarous population under the discipline of civilized life," calling it an "extremely valuable and suggestive letter."[11]

Still, in the 1890s the APS was a more propitious ally for Kinloch and the African Association than its sister organization the BFASS. A key partner of antebellum American abolitionists, by the late nineteenth century the group used its august tradition to wield considerable moral authority. In practice, however, the APS's attitude toward slavery had already manifested signs of becoming increasingly equivocal. In any case, it showed little interest in the practices in Africa with which Kinloch was concerned. For its part, the APS had shifted its attention to Africa from its earlier concern with British policy in Canada toward indigenous people. Increasingly prominent on the APS's list of concerns were the methods by which every colonizer, including Britain, created a labor supply for the extractive and agricultural enterprise that made colonies pay.[12]

In the face of a public exposé in Parliament, the APS criticized the British government for its hypocritical version of emancipation in Africa, which in its view embraced slavery in the name of abolitionism. As early as 1894, an APS-affiliated MP rebuked his fellow governing Liberals, noting that "only half-a-dozen or a dozen opposed" the resurrection of slavery by the British in Africa. Fox Bourne declared the "labor tax" instituted in South Africa by the British regime a "modified form of slavery," locating the immediate origins of this "class legislation" in the racial slavery used decades earlier in the Cape. He traced it even further back, pointing out that "the European 'scramble for Africa'" began not in 1885 but with the advent of the transatlantic slave trade. "The pass laws and labour laws, the political and social disabilities, and other arbitrary and unjust restrictions, to which natives are still subjected in Cape Colony" were the progeny of that age-old injustice. If Fox Bourne were not already convinced that the British were reneging on their pledge to permanently abolish slavery in their overseas territories, Kinloch's descriptions and analysis persuaded him. But only when she introduced him to what she was already calling the new slavery taking hold in the mining industry did Fox Bourne believe that nothing less than racial slavery was being resurrected under the British flag, underpinning the entire colonial enterprise.[13]

Despite Kinloch's mentorship, Fox Bourne did not entirely reprise the radical views on race held by the most advanced nineteenth-century white abolitionists such as John Brown, John Rankin, and Wendell Phillips. For instance, he shared the nearly ubiquitous antipathy to the Chinese. The post-Kinloch Fox Bourne did, however, steadfastly oppose the numerous taken-for-granted colonial proscriptions against Africans. He also bore the traces of Du Bois's intellectual influence, as he accepted the American's critique of industrial education as a component of the "plans for inducing natives to work for whites by an educational system designed solely for the training and organising of a servile class." Fox Bourne insisted that Africans living in towns should have all the "privileges" of whites. Echoing positions he had spent hours listening to Kinloch champion, he objected to the pass laws and other discriminatory legislation, called for political and voting rights, and advocated that Africans be allowed "to rise . . . to any success their enterprise and talents render possible to them." Above all, they should not be "induced" to labor in any way. Fox Bourne's criticism of European missionaries became as unstinting as Kinloch's, and he remarked, "the way in which these ministers of the Gospel pass from the assertion of excellent doctrine to advocacy of unblushing tyranny is certainly remarkable." Kinloch must have been under the distinct impression that she had found someone who listened to her.[14]

Kinloch provided Fox Bourne with a crash course on the new slavery in Africa. Though he trailed behind a group of dissident liberals who had denounced it earlier, after his close association with Kinloch, Fox Bourne emerged as the leading voice of militant abolitionism until his death in 1909. Even as the woman who had educated him so thoroughly in the realities of British rule in Africa slipped into obscurity, Fox Bourne used her pioneering abolitionist analysis in his crusade to "prevent the setting up of a new slave trade and a new slavery under new and specious names." The necessary pillars for the resurrection of the antislavery-antiracist alliance of yesteryear were now firmly in place.[15]

There were, to be sure, deeper forces at work in producing this convergence of British antislavery and Pan-Africanism. Many factors account for the stirring of antislavery sentiment among those who are not enslaved themselves. One of the most potent across time has been the activism of the enslaved. The emergence of abolitionism among a small minority of white people in the northern United States was inextricably tied to the steady stream of freedom seekers from the South. The movement that came to be known as the Underground Railroad roused sympathy for the enslaved and moral indignation at the institution that held them in its yoke—even forming the central plot element in Harriet Beecher Stowe's enormously influential antislavery novel *Uncle Tom's Cabin*. No matter how small their numbers compared to those who remained behind, the freedom seekers who fueled the Underground Railroad raised the profile of abolitionism internationally.[16]

Turn-of-the-century British abolitionists also heard the clarion call of what David Walker describes as the "one continual cry" of the enslaved. As African Americans had before them, Africans found ways to make their presence felt and their voices heard. Like runaways during the Civil War, runaways in British Africa would get the attention of many principals in the debate over the nature of slavery that raged for the next half century. Albeit lacking the celebrity of their predecessors, with whom they shared many commonalities, the women (in particular) who transformed themselves from victims to rebels by escaping slavery played a similar role in the twentieth-century antislavery movement. Among northern white people in the United States, assisting runaways had been their most tangible antislavery activity. Similarly, a few missionaries in Africa found themselves moved by the desperate plight of the refugees seeking their aid. It would once again be the voices of white abolitionists relaying the message of Black people all but silenced by bondage that raised the public cry against slavery.[17]

The antislavery activity of Africans caught up in the new slavery dated back to the British conquest of East Africa in the early 1890s. The British defended their African conquest on the grounds that they were suppressing the slave trade and slavery (echoing the justification of the Union army). Some enslaved Africans responded precisely as enslaved African Americans had: by seeking refuge among the liberating troops. The leader of the British expedition reported coming face-to-face with a woman who had "escaped" from her captors and sought shelter with his troops. This freedom seeker's situation seemed to personify the very institution the British were allegedly in Africa to stamp out. She had been captured during a raid by British-aligned forces, whose ranking officer then handed her over to a nearby French mission. The Catholic station, in turn, put her and her fellow captives—all women—to "menial work" before distributing them among "various influential chiefs of the R[oman] Catholic region," evidently in an effort to curry favor with the missionaries. Fleeing her bondage, the newly enslaved woman took refuge with the British forces, but, upon learning of her whereabouts, her erstwhile master demanded her return. The British commanding officer would decide her fate, as well as that of a second woman who presented an even more heartbreaking sight: she wore "irons . . . welded on her ankles," so that "it was necessary to file these through to release her." The British had not only the power to free these two women but also the obligation to do so under both British and international law.[18]

In posing this dilemma for British authorities, African freedom seekers were reenacting the antislavery activism of African Americans during the Civil War. Historical memory credits Lincoln with being the Great Emancipator, but it generally forgets the African American fugitives from slavery who precipitated the chain of events leading to his order authorizing them to free themselves via flight. Against Lincoln's will, they had in no small part made their freedom central to the war effort. When the Civil War first broke out, Lincoln prioritized preserving the union, to the point of, in Frederick Douglass's words, "fighting to keep [slavery] in the Union," even as "the South was fighting to take slavery out of the Union." Lincoln initially ordered that African American refugees who sought the sanctuary of Union lines be returned to slavery. The endless stream of fugitives, however, eventually forced the president's hand. Some of his officers refused to comply with his policy, and events soon overtook the leader we remember as the Great Emancipator, because on this issue, at least, he did not get his way. African freedom seekers attempted to foist the same results onto the colonial powers that ruled them. By whatever means Africans resisted their enslavement, their activism played a significant role in inspiring the antislavery movement that hailed the advent of Pan-Africanism.[19]

The resulting antislavery-antiracism alliance got off to an auspicious start as Fox Bourne took the torch from his abolitionist forebearers by making good use of the momentum Kinloch had kindled. For some time, the BFASS had limited its activities to urging the imperial powers in Africa to stamp out African slavery. With the Fox Bourne–led APS teaming up with Kinloch to prick its collective conscience, the BFASS would finally be prodded into expanding its attention to the new slavery introduced by the colonizing nations. The British antislavery movement briefly converged around the program of nascent Black abolitionism. The BFASS leaders who were most critical of the new slavery were APS stalwarts who cited Fox Bourne as the resident authority in British reform circles, symbolically transferring to this relative newcomer the mantle of leading abolitionist and acknowledged movement theorist.

To announce its expanded charge, the BFASS used the occasion of the bloody Boer War in South Africa, by which the British Empire reasserted its control over a breakaway republic of mainly Dutch-descended colonists. The BFASS declared in 1901 that "although South Africa has for many years been understood to be the special sphere of the Aborigines' Protection Society," the BFASS now demanded assurances that there would be no "recognition of any form of Native slavery." The *Anti-Slavery Reporter*, its official organ, decried the "exceedingly sinister appearance" of the maneuvering of the Transvaal gold mining industry in the attempt to secure "cheap labour at all costs." It noted that the mining interests were resorting to, in the words of their leading critics, "unconscious repetitions of the oldest arguments for slavery."[20]

Kinloch's partners in British abolitionism absorbed the lesson that the adoption of an explicitly racial basis indelibly imprinted the developing labor systems in colonial Africa with the stamp of *racial* slavery.

A Liberal MP summed up their emerging position to a large antislavery meeting in London, stating that British abolitionists once again needed a "clear enunciation" of principles. The "frightful development of negro slavery" in the Americas to serve the labor needs of empire could not be allowed to repeat itself in Africa, especially in British territory. "What I consider the most urgent danger," he declared, "is to the natives who are, or may be brought into the Transvaal [gold mines] from other parts of Africa." Evidence would convince these abolitionists, as it had Pan-Africanists, that this migration was anything but voluntary. "This shifting of coloured people from one portion of the world to another," the antislavery MP declared, "is one of the most serious dangers in the possible development of slavery." This was, he had come to understand, the forced transport of individuals.[21]

Decades later the League of Nations admitted what Kinloch had reported: "In its crudest and most primitive form, recruitment was undoubtedly analogous to slave-trading." That body described the methods used to round up workers as "taking men by force and transporting them far from their homes to places where they were obliged to work sometimes for several years," after which they were forcibly returned. Similarly, a British Malawi government inquiry characterized the ordeal its nationals endured on the two-month journey to the mines as one of privation, exhaustion, sickness, and death. Migrants, it said, "are obliged to travel continually and at a high rate of speed. Many become exhausted and die by the roadside. Many get ill in uninhabited places, and are left to the mercy of wild beasts."[22]

As Kinloch had first exposed, the grueling migratory labor trail, the labor camps where the men were housed, and their poor diet made for a lethal combination—both then and, as she forewarned, for decades to come. Even if the workers spent six months of the year back in the reserves to "clear their lungs" of "crushed quartz" and the "fumes of dynamite explosions," a British government official noted that the expected working life span of a miner "was not more than seven years." This figure is a particularly haunting echo of what historian Herbert Klein calls "the mythical seven years," describing the foreshortened life spans of the enslaved in parts of the Caribbean at the height of plantation slavery. The death rate in the African mines was even more appalling because the workers were adults younger than forty-five years and had been screened for health problems prior to arrival. An even larger percentage of mine workers were "repatriated" as "permanently incapacitated for work by physical infirmity or disease."[23]

Making matters worse, sending the sick back to their rural homes, like the one to which Kinloch retired, meant that they were forced to march back to their villages. Once there, the survivors tried to recover their strength, only to start the whole process over again. Medical authorities in Kenya described the inevitable results:

A somewhat dilapidated African appears at the dispensary complaining of an ulcer of the leg of long duration. Quite clearly he has an ulcer. But is it all that is the matter with him? If we examine him even superficially we will probably find, firstly that he is ill-nourished, secondly that he is anemic, thirdly that he has pyorrhea, fourthly, that he has an enlarged spleen, and fifthly that he has "the itch." A more careful examination would probably show that he was infected with malaria, and infested with intestinal worms. Still further investigation might reveal that his Wassermann re-action is positive and that he is still suffering either from yaws or syphilis. If he were to die, and if a post-mortem were to be performed we would probably find that he had a fine cirrhosis of the liver, and not improbably some changes in the vascular system of the covering of his brain.

Citing the case of a thirteen-year-old boy who weighed thirty pounds when he died of malnutrition, the *East Rand Express* observed, "It seems to be the practice for a certain class of persons to allow their sick and dying boys to go adrift on the veld, by which means they escape the trouble of providing medical treatment for the natives, and also the inconvenience of burying them when they succumb." As bad as conditions were on the Rand, they were by all accounts worse in the mines of neighboring colonies such as Zimbabwe and Zambia. Kinloch's British abolitionist followers recognized it as a system of purely racial slavery revived to fill the same age-old purposes.[24]

For British antislavery activists under Kinloch's Pan-Africanist guidance, what constituted slavery in the aftermath of its centuries-long racial form required explicit consideration of the role of race. The *racial* means of organizing labor linked *racial* colonialism to *racial* slavery. The

Atlantic slave trade found its basis in what Joseph Inikori calls "the forced migration of Africans to the Americas" to produce raw materials for industry cheaply. Slavery in the Americas was a system built on conveying bonded workers to remotely located colonial processes of production, with people from one continent enslaving those of a second continent in the territory of a third. These turn-of-the-century British abolitionists warned that the same principle could be applied within Africa. Workers could be forcibly moved around to meet the labor needs of colonialism, whatever the consequences to them. As the Liberal MP who doubled as an antislavery activist put it, there was an inherently close connection between slavery and the "shifting of coloured people from one portion of the world to another."[25]

British abolitionists now warned that, as Europe's imperial powers had once seized on the internal slave trade and slavery of Africa to build a transatlantic racial system of giant proportions, they were again exploiting race to transform the preexisting domestic slavery into a new racial slavery. It was a potent and dangerous combination. The new system appropriated the justification of the old one, replete with its racial demarcation of a class subject to the coercive laws of colonialism. At the very heart of the British abolitionists' point about the determination of slavery lay *race*, as Douglass had divined much earlier.

Unlike those who reserved the designation *slavery* for labor practices of the Belgian Congo or Portugal, Fox Bourne and turn-of-the-century British antislavery advocates followed Kinloch in applying it to the British Empire itself. She had observed its oppressive policies firsthand. Fox Bourne echoed Kinloch in taking aim at the compound system, warning that "the authorities have established a rule of forced labour which threatens to develop into, if it is not already, slavery under another name." He proclaimed, "If slavery has been abandoned in theory," British labor policy in South Africa "imposes on those subject to it a degrading bondage scarcely distinguishable from slavery."[26]

Having borrowed so much of Kinloch's understanding, Fox Bourne could confidently and effectively dismiss colonial officials' characterization of their African workforce as free based on the existence of labor contracts and the payment of wages. The allegedly voluntary agreement, Fox Bourne explained, amounted to a "pretence." Its limited duration meant little, since "slavery for five years may be, while it lasts, more oppressive than slavery for a life time." He shrewdly noted that it gave the employer incentive to "get as much as possible out of his slave while the mastery lasts," foreshadowing Kevin Bales's notion of "disposable people." Nor did the "promise of wages" convert it from slavery to free labor. "The cruelest slave-driver," Fox Bourne averred, "where slavery exists without subterfuge, will tell you that the food and shelter he provides for his slave are equivalent to wages, and that the promises he extorts from his slave under fear of the lash satisfy the conditions of a contract."[27]

Kinloch had witnessed and reported that African workers under colonialism may have fared worse than their enslaved predecessors in the Americas with respect to their diets, if historians' fragmentary conclusions about slave nutrition are at all accurate. Similar to the practice on large plantations in the Americas, migrant workers in Africa would be issued "rations" that were calorically and nutritionally deficient, especially in protein. Authorities in Uganda acknowledged that "health cannot be maintained on [the] diet" prescribed in its ordinances and admitted, "When a similar ration was used for the contract labour employed by Government, the death rate amongst the Banyaruanda reached the appalling figure of 105 per thousand per annum." Colonial authorities later professed to be astounded at the results of augmenting rations to achieve a life-supporting standard. That discovery did not compel most British territories to follow suit. Instead, one colonial official described workers "looking for, earning, buying or otherwise procuring the food extras (including, probably, animal products) . . . to make the basic ration appetizing." It was a fitting commentary on the inadequacy of the diets of so many colonial African workers. Their experience would have been familiar to the enslaved in the Americas, who spent much of their spare time gardening, hunting, and fishing to satisfy their need for food. The Sunday practice of engaging in extra work to procure food instead of getting much-needed rest was a page out of the playbook of enslaved African Americans.[28]

The results were also much the same. When a worker became too "sick or too fatigued," he had to forgo the opportunity to supplement his diet, and "as his official ration [was] not enough for adequate nutrition, [a] vicious circle [was] established, and he [went] further down hill in health." At the compounds like the ones Kinloch encountered at the Kimberley diamond mines, colonial employers, like American slaveholders, provided rations not to ensure the well-being of their workforce but to take advantage of economies of scale that saved them money—the same ruthless and reckless calculation with the same potentially disastrous results. The food rations provided to migrant workers in Africa, as one colonial official put it, constituted "the minimum required for the maintenance of the labourer as a working animal."[29]

Fox Bourne got to the heart of the hypocrisy. He wrote, "Not a few of those who condemn the enslavement of blacks by blacks have no compunction in adopting tyrannical methods differing only in degree from those they deprecate. Compulsory service is not the less servile because there is pretence of paying for it." Pretexts aside, the labor regime in African colonies amounted to "a revival of such forced labour as, when practised in other days and by other nations, English people had no hesitation in denouncing as slavery." An APS "charter" showed the distinct trace of Kinloch's teachings and demanded that African workers' "freedom of action shall be as complete as that recognised by law in the case of white and other citizens," absent which racial colonialism "condemned them to a bondage that, however much it may object to call it so, is in fact slavery." After Kinloch's retirement from politics, Fox Bourne and other British abolitionists took up her work of documenting the horrors the new slavery inflicted on Africans. Having paid careful attention from afar, Du Bois determined to replicate Kinloch's success in galvanizing an interracial movement that similarly exposed the impact of America's racist practices on African Americans.[30]

The NAACP and the Alliance in the United States

A decade after he attended the Pan-African Conference, Du Bois declared a "crisis" in American race relations. When "a friend" wrote to suggest that Black Americans should "depend on their own resources to advance themselves," Du Bois replied that they could not afford to do so as "farm laborers [working] under conditions of semi-slavery." In an era of entrenched racism, lynching, and segregation, he deemed the support of prominent white liberals and reformers essential. Many white abolitionists had closed up shop after emancipation, forcing African Americans to fend for themselves in the absence of an organized interracial antiracism movement on the scale of antebellum abolitionism. That seemed to change for the better with the founding of the NAACP.

Topping the new group's priorities were basic civil and voting rights, which were proving to be elusive even half a century after emancipation. But as the association's most prominent Black officer and editor of its official journal, which he pointedly named *The Crisis*, Du Bois ensured that opposition to the new slavery in the South was part of the organization's broad mission.[31]

Du Bois extensively chronicled the existence of and resistance to debt peonage, laying bare its inner workings for all to see. He published a letter that described how the states and the courts participated in this practice—withholding the author's name, at his request, because otherwise he "would be dead in a short time." A Black person would be prosecuted for some alleged crime, perhaps something as simple as purportedly breaking the contract tenant farmers were forced to sign with landowners. "I am brought in a prisoner," the correspondent explained, and "go through the farce of being tried." Absent all pretense of due process or any legal protections, the African American victims of these proceedings found themselves legally indebted to any propertied white person who paid the fines imposed by the court. From there, the debt perpetually increased, with no legal relief possible. Although Du Bois understood the new slavery in broader terms, his focus on debt peonage was strategic, since a sizable proportion of politically prominent Americans considered debt peonage to be a form of slavery. In 1911 the US Supreme Court issued key rulings acknowledging that the practice violated the Thirteenth Amendment. The first case it heard was backed not by the NAACP but secretly by Du Bois's old political nemesis Booker T. Washington. In *Bailey v. Alabama*, the Supreme Court began chipping away at the legality of practices like those described by Du Bois's anonymous informant, starting with statutes aimed at empowering states to enforce labor contracts. This and future rulings, however, did little to stop the practice. The results were widely lamented in the press, as Du Bois painstakingly chronicled in *The Crisis*, but nothing came of the grumbling.[32]

Kinloch's imprint on Du Bois as the leading force in the NAACP was also strongly evident in its journal. In the years since the 1900 Pan-African Conference, Du Bois had not forgotten about the dangerous existence of the new slavery in Africa. Even as he focused his efforts on the predicament of African Americans in the South, Du Bois called attention to developments in Africa. He pointedly linked the new slavery in Africa "to race and color prejudice" for his American audience. He explained, "One has only to remember the forced labor in South Africa, the outrages in Congo, the cocoa-slavery in Portuguese Africa, the land monopoly and peonage of Mexico, the exploitation of Chinese coolies and the rubber horror of the Amazon to realize what white imperialism is doing to-day in well-known cases, not to mention thousands of less-known instances." After the outbreak of war in Europe in 1914, abolition of the new slavery in Africa took on greater urgency as a central pillar on which the outcome of the Black freedom movement depended.[33]

Directly addressing his core constituency, Du Bois advised Black voters to insist that four demands be met in exchange for their support: ending segregation, "enforcement of the Thirteenth Amendment by the suppression of peonage," education, and enfranchisement in the South. Before every election, the NAACP lobbied American politicians to take on racism, but with little success. The Republicans, the party of Lincoln and the authors of the Fourteenth and Fifteenth Amendments, had long since lost interest in championing the cause of Black people. In the 1912 presidential election, Du Bois opted to support Democrat Woodrow Wilson. His white "progressive" associates had encouraged him to seek entry into Theodore Roosevelt's Bull Moose Party, despite the former Republican president's well-known racism. Progressivism was the movement of the day among white reformers, including a number of NAACP stalwarts. But Roosevelt had firmly rebuffed the olive branch, telling one of Du Bois's progressive associates to be "careful" of the "dangerous" Du Bois.[34]

Embracing a Democrat was a bold move for an African American leader, given the party's proslavery history and status as the mainstay of the one-party white supremacist South. Wilson claimed he would be the candidate of a reformed Democratic organization that would henceforth champion Black rights. Du Bois was skeptical, even after his NAACP colleague Oswald Garrison Villard personally assured him that Wilson had pledged to be "president of all the people." Believing he lacked a better alternative, Du Bois publicly endorsed Wilson's candidacy, only to see him introduce segregation into the federal government and famously endorse the white supremacist film *Birth of a Nation*.[35]

The start of conflict in Europe in 1914, followed by America's inevitable entry into World War I in late 1917, pushed domestic reform off the agenda. Even as African Americans continued to fight for freedom, Du Bois counseled them to support the war effort and postpone the battle for civil rights until after the war's conclusion. But contrary to his expectations, the postwar period saw the crisis in American race relations worsen considerably. The end of World War I was celebrated in America by the lynchings of Black soldiers—some in uniform—and a series of race riots that became known as "Red Summer" for all the African American blood shed at home. It did not end until two years later with the infamous Tulsa massacre of more than two hundred African Americans by a racist mob targeting the "Black Wall Street" located there. Lynchings were nothing new. Du Bois's NAACP colleague Walter White rose to prominence as a journalist by documenting dozens of these brutal murders across the country.[36]

As the preeminent scholar of the Black experience set out to document the illustrious history of African American soldiers in the late war, racial violence engulfed them on what should have been their triumphant repatriation. Du Bois zeroed in on some of the same "real causes" Wells had discerned behind lynching: failure to enforce the Thirteenth Amendment, "vestiges of the slave trade in the convict lease system and the arrangements for trading tenants," and, above all, the "slavery" of debt peonage. The ferocity of the racist hate directed at Black people after their contributions to the war effort belied any notion that freedom was at hand, that America was making progress, or that politicians like President Wilson could be trusted to keep their promises to African Americans.[37]

A decade after Du Bois had first proclaimed the crisis in American race relations, he found that little had changed. There was no mass antiracist political party nor significant progress through the courts. It was even more discouraging to him that the NAACP had failed to replicate anything close to the scale of the antebellum abolitionist movement, despite the widespread acknowledgment of the continuation of slavery in the South. Booker T. Washington had stepped in to bankroll the *Bailey* case because Villard had demurred. NAACP national president Moorfield Storey took to pleading with his fellow white liberals: "We appeal to every warm-hearted, high-minded man or woman in this country, and urge them to organize a new anti-slavery movement." But they did little to take up the call. Du Bois had vainly hoped that the civil rights association would catalyze an interracial movement focused on antiracism and antislavery that had been absent for so long in America. As he directed his gaze across the Atlantic to London, where the Pan-African Conference had revolutionized his thinking, he could not help but notice signs of the very alliance that was proving impossible to reconstruct in the United States.[38]

As his American-based movement seemed to falter, Du Bois watched with growing interest as the transnational strategy pursued by Wells and Kinloch seemingly produced very different results. Increasingly frustrated with American liberalism, Du Bois judged that such an approach could be of decisive importance for African Americans. Some of the lure Du Bois felt was British abolitionism's embrace of him personally. He had achieved standing in those circles over the years, a development that probably surprised and certainly pleased him. His renown would only grow after the favorable review of his *Souls of Black Folk* in the British abolitionist press three years after his attendance at the Pan-African Conference. In 1910 the *Anti-Slavery Reporter* featured a collection of essays by Du Bois and Booker T. Washington, noticeably siding with the NAACP leader in detailing his charges of the resurrection of slavery in the United States.[39]

A year later, unable to convince others in the NAACP leadership to back *Bailey*, Du Bois would embark on a highly publicized speaking tour in Europe centered on the antiracist Universal Races Congress in London. That gathering, held in July 1911, attracted more than two thousand participants, including some of the leading lights of British and European intellectual society, as well as the official representatives of some twenty nations. Years later, Du Bois still believed the congress "would have marked an epoch in the cultural history of the world, if it had not been followed so quickly by the World War." In addition to his two addresses there, Du Bois gave another at the behest of the Anti-Slavery Society. The *Anti-Slavery Reporter* enthusiastically endorsed Du Bois's European tour, and its coverage of the congress centered on his contributions, portraying him as perhaps the most distinguished intellectual among that globally renowned group of statesmen and thinkers. Du Bois came away satisfied that he had been listened to. For the next decade, as the movement languished in America, British antislavery gave Du Bois the platform he craved.[40]

Du Bois was experiencing firsthand the profound changes Alice Kinloch had wrought in Great Britain's antislavery movement, as she almost single-handedly redirected it toward a renewed commitment to antiracism. Whether he fully understood her role in bringing about these welcome developments, Du Bois found himself a direct beneficiary. The British movement that had captured his attention—as he had its—would feature in his future plans for the freedom movement.

Du Bois's Transnational Pan-African Strategy

As the victorious Allies gathered at Versailles in 1919, Du Bois thought he discerned an opportunity to emulate the success of Wells and Kinloch. The timing seemed perfect. Calling it "the Revolution of 1914–1918," he thought World War I marked "the Beginning of a mighty End," including the end of "the world slavery in Africa." He was certain that what was true for Africans would pertain to their descendants in the Americas. His success at the Universal Races Congress, which he called "the greatest event of the twentieth century so far," loomed ever larger in his mind. Both the British prime minister and the leader of the opposition had attended the international antiracism conference in London. Liberal leader John Morley, an antislavery activist, anti-imperialist, and close collaborator of Fox Bourne, had been particularly outspoken in his opposition to the new slavery. The contrast between Britain and the United States in this respect could not have been greater. Du Bois therefore undertook to revive Pan-Africanism as part of his transnational strategy to pursue the struggle for equality at home. His idea was to build on the antiracism-antislavery alliance that Wells and Kinloch had reestablished in Britain and use it as a lever to apply pressure on the US government using the postwar institutions of international governance under construction at President Wilson's behest.[41]

Du Bois believed he held a trump card. Upon US entry into World War I in 1917, he had issued a call to African Americans to "close ranks" and put aside the struggle for equality to win the war, confident that President Wilson and white America would reward them upon its successful conclusion. With African Americans' crucial role in the Allied victory, Du Bois boasted, "we are in a position to come before the world saying: 'Behold us. Here we are clean-handed and with pure hearts. You must listen to us. We black people, in addition to our rights of ordinary consideration, have proven ourselves worthy of extra consideration.'" Du Bois set out to write the history of the African American soldier in the Great War with a political purpose in mind. He believed the victorious European Allies would be grateful to African Americans and would work with the Pan-African Congress (led by Du Bois) to reform colonialism in Africa and transition the continent to self-government. Combined with the African American freedom movement at home, which had been turbocharged by the war and its aftermath, this would put irresistible pressure on the US government to enact the civil rights legislation seemingly promised by Wilson as part of his war aims known as the Fourteen Points.[42]

In developing his plans to overcome the hostile American climate, Du Bois was clearly channeling Wells, but he was also responding to grassroots movements at work in post–World War I politics. The Black abolitionist movement was being shaped by what had historically been its ultimate basis: the antislavery activity of the enslaved themselves. It is no coincidence that Du Bois's abolitionism commenced when he immersed himself in ethnographic research among African Americans caught up in the new slavery of the turn-of-the-century South— listening not only to their lived experiences but also to their reasoned judgment that twentieth-century labor systems preserved the spirit if not the legal form of the old slavery into which many of them had been born. Perhaps partly because of this early exposure, Du Bois would be the first to discern the essential role of what he called, in *Black Reconstruction*, the "general strike" of African Americans during the Civil War in bringing about emancipation. According to his pioneering analysis, African Americans liberated themselves from slavery through the simple act of escaping to the forbidden territory of Union lines.[43]

As Du Bois realized, voluntary migrations have constituted the root of epic freedom struggles of workers of the Black world, from maroon communities to the Underground Railroad to the exodus from slavery during the Civil War. Stephanie Camp writes, "Though freedom had no specific location within or outside the postwar South and resided at no certain destination, it nevertheless had a spatial nature grounded in one of the same principles that had guided slaves' antebellum rival geography: motion." Similarly, Isabel Wilkerson calls the Great Migration "the first mass act of independence by a people who were in bondage in this country for far longer than they have been free." It was a material factor in creating the postwar New Negro movement that would help convince Du Bois to relaunch Pan-Africanism with a focus on the new slavery found across the Black world.[44]

Many attempted to capture the essence of the "New Negro," but perhaps no one did it better than Howard University professor Alain Locke, a former Rhodes scholar with a PhD from Harvard and the leading contemporary commentator on the Harlem Renaissance. He located the basis of the New Negro in the Great Migration, the movement of millions of African Americans from the South to cities in the North at an ever-accelerating rate from 1910 to 1920. Locke perceived that the New Negro found its basis in the Black tenant farmers, sharecroppers, and agricultural and other workers from the South who packed up their belongings and moved north, often having to overcome physical intimidation and violence by southern authorities determined that African Americans should remain the region's primary labor force. Locke considered these Black workers the moving force behind the migration. In contrast, the relocation north of African American professionals—doctors, lawyers, teachers, and others—represented a response to this mass exodus of agricultural workers. Locke observed, "It is the rank and file who are leading and the leaders who are following."[45]

The Great Migration, according to Locke, was the expression of a mass movement in its most fundamental sense: an upsurge from below, in which working people were determining their own destiny, exchanging the intolerable conditions of the South for the promise of the North, and transforming both themselves and the African American community. A profound alteration in social consciousness underlay this grassroots process, which Locke called "a transformed and transforming psychology." That the African American psychology had been transformed was evidenced by the scale of the migration. It forced an adjustment by the Black middle class and the society at large, indicating the degree to which it was transforming. The mass exodus from the South was the expression of a new worldview. Originating in the South as a revolt against conditions there, it would impact race relations in the North as African Americans moved there, seeking a new life.[46]

Harlem, where Du Bois had moved to edit *The Crisis*, was in no small measure a part of this resistance to the new slavery. This Black enclave in New York was one of the many products of the New Negro, the very embodiment of the spirit of seizing opportunity, as African Americans improved their living conditions in New York by buying up the upper-middle-class and previously all-white Harlem block by block. Its dramatic appearance led Locke to refer to this hard-won space as "the sign and center of a renaissance of a people." James Weldon Johnson proclaimed it "the greatest Negro city in the world." Harlem would also be the center of the political expression of the New Negro.[47]

As Locke discerned, the new spirit among African Americans sprang from deep within the people and was not attributable to any political leaders or organizations. In politics as well, the rank and file led and the leaders followed. Locke noted that one of the most salient characteristics of the transformed and transforming consciousness of the New Negro was that African Americans had switched their allegiance from the "officially recognized and orthodox spokesmen" of the NAACP and similar groups to those "of the independent, popular, and often radical type." Southern migrants helped determine that new voices would give coherent political expression to the social movement under way, and Du Bois concluded that he needed a strategy to win their political allegiance.[48]

Du Bois and the NAACP faced a new political rival with the emergence of Marcus Garvey and his Universal Negro Improvement Association (UNIA). Its increasingly popular slogan, "Africa for the Africans," called for the liberation of Africa from European colonialism and "the entire Negro race . . . from industrial bondage, peonage and serfdom." Garvey promulgated an appealing vision of a unified Africa and called for African Americans to immigrate to the continent, where they would make liberation possible by providing leadership and an army. Painting a picture of African glory unsurpassed in the ancient world, Garvey proclaimed that the continent would once again attain those same heights.[49]

Garvey's many critics among African American political leaders, including Du Bois, were perpetually suspicious of the "Back to Africa" message, but the Garvey movement was much more than this outer shell. Underneath was a conception of transnational Black identity—a consciousness of the inherent interconnection of all people of African descent throughout the world. Du Bois had long been attracted to that notion, but he was skeptical that African Americans would widely embrace it. Garvey proved him wrong. His movement linked Africans, Afro-Caribbeans, and other Black Latin Americans with African Americans. Garveyism proclaimed the African peoples one unified whole and encouraged them to embrace a common identity, despite different nationalities and languages. Du Bois called Garveyism "one of the most interesting spiritual movements of the modern world."[50]

Garvey promoted knowledge of and interest in African culture among African Americans. He organized one of the first exhibits of the works of African artists in Harlem. His reach was extensive, and Arna Bontemps later credited a speech by Garvey as helping to awaken his poetic voice. Garvey was, to a large extent, the political spokesman for what came to be known as the New Negro and the more assertive brand of Black politics that, in some crucial respects, foreshadowed the Black Power movement of the 1960s. As Bontemps later recalled, Garvey "gave voice to dreams that literally blew the minds of a large segment of his impoverished generation of black humanity in the New World." Claude McKay, one of Garvey's rivals, acknowledged, "If Marcus Garvey did not originate the phrase, New Negro, he at least made it popular." James Weldon Johnson, as much of a Garvey critic as McKay was, added that his political foe had "stirred the imagination of the Negro masses as no Negro ever had."[51]

Garvey's notion of transnational Blackness was nothing new. "The Negro has always regarded his social problem as a world problem," declared Black radical Lovett Fort-Whiteman. Despite its evident exaggeration, his assertion reflected a meaningful reality. In his famous 1829 abolitionist tract, David Walker had addressed the "Colored Citizens of the World." African Americans would claim the heritage of the Haitian revolution as their own as soon as news of it reached them, and they continued to do so throughout the nineteenth century. The Black nationalism of Martin Delany was tied to movements to leave the United States, which were essentially rooted in transnational realities of Blackness—a point embraced by the Black Power activists Martin Luther King Jr. appealed to in the late 1960s. Du Bois's generation was heir to that earlier tradition. As colonial powers spread racial labor systems across Africa, the Pan-African Conference of 1900 issued an updated version of Walker's appeal written by Du Bois, denouncing the renewed enslavement of Black people in the name of "we, the men and women of Africa in world congress assembled." A decade and a half later, Garveyism, with its international outlook, took firm hold across the United States and beyond, insisting that this new slavery had to end.[52]

Du Bois did not need Garvey to remind him that racism was global. Still, it might not be an exaggeration to say that Garvey spurred his older rival into action, given that Du Bois later admitted that the African American response to Garvey was "astonishing." He would experience Garvey's long shadow as far away as Britain, ensuring that Du Bois would be mindful of just how much New Negroism and Garvey had changed the African American political context at home.[53]

Facing the perplexing dilemma of where to turn for support in the fight against the continued enslavement of Black people, Du Bois's postwar frustration with white America prompted him to leave the United States in search of antiracist allies. Knowing that nineteenth-century Black abolitionists had found supporters in Britain—as had Wells and Kinloch more recently—he set off for London in 1919, where the Pan-African Conference had met in 1900. He next decamped for the Paris peace talks. As part of this transnational Pan-African strategy, Du Bois decided to redirect the reconstituted movement almost entirely to the postwar Africa question, which involved, in part, the disposition of defeated Germany's former colonies. Tying African Americans' circumstances to Africans' was the best means, in Du Bois's judgment, to get on the agenda of the negotiations that would secure not only peace but also the postwar world order. He proposed that former German territory fall under international jurisdiction as an interim measure toward African self-rule. But this was merely an entry point.[54]

Du Bois had something much greater in mind, including the creation of an independent African state that would span much of the continent. But just as centrally, he was concerned about the fate of African Americans across the Black Atlantic. Du Bois reasoned that, when viewed from an international perspective, antiracism spanned the Black world, as it had at the Universal Races Congress, which considered "the problem of the Negro in Africa and America." For the reconstituted Pan-African movement "to agitate the Negro problem in any particular country"—including the United States—it needed to be "plausibly shown to be part of the future of Africa."[55]

When Du Bois returned to Europe in 1919, he did not only set out to reconstitute the Pan-Africanist movement. He specifically modeled it after the antislavery version to which Kinloch had given direction. The Kinloch-generated antislavery movement in Britain served as the basis of a strategy to focus Black abolitionism on the new slavery in Africa and fight for its elimination everywhere. Du Bois had himself dispatched to Paris on behalf of the NAACP to reconvene Pan-Africanism, which had lain dormant for nearly two decades in the absence of a sponsor. The new body would represent the Black world with all the moral authority it had earned for its role in winning the war. The international alliance of antislavery and antiracism, previously revived, seemed to Du Bois to be as strong as ever. Responding to the same currents as Garvey and other activists who shared his Harlem home, Du Bois concluded that the only solution consisted in "larger and larger unity of thought among Negroes and through this, concerted action." He considered the NAACP inadequate for this transnational goal; the Pan-African Congress was his answer to Garvey's UNIA.[56]

It was not unreasonable to conclude that what Du Bois had been unable to accomplish in America he might achieve on the international stage. It was there that African Americans could spend the political capital they had built up by helping the Allies win the war to save democracy. When Du Bois sojourned to the Versailles peace talks, he still harbored faith that colonialism could be reformed and that the European powers would voluntarily give up their African possessions. The 1900 Pan-African Conference, for which Du Bois had written the appeals to the governments of Britain and France, had advocated that course. Kinloch herself had focused her colleagues' attention on what imperial regimes allowed the private entrepreneur to get away with, rather than what they did on their own behalf. That emphasis remained true when Du Bois revived Pan-Africanism. He thus invited representatives from both the French and Portuguese colonial administrations to his gathering.[57]

Du Bois sought to plant his flag in Paris, where a visitor could observe every other "nation," "group," or "race" assembled with "not a single great serious movement or idea" missing. He conspicuously reprinted in *The Crisis* the call of the Anti-Slavery Society's new leader, John Harris: "Another European and American International Congress should be held to amend the existing agreements for maintaining the rights, liberties and welfare of native races." That was exactly the opportunity Du Bois was looking for. Like Wells—who was planning to attend what would become known as the First Pan-African Congress—he reasoned, "What we cannot accomplish before the choked conscience of America, we have an infinitely better chance to accomplish before the organized Public Opinion of the World."[58]

"I went to Paris because today the destinies of mankind center there," Du Bois explained to readers of *The Crisis* upon his return to the United States in mid-1919. He was certain that the peace talks would determine the future "for a hundred years to come"—including that of African Americans. He had hastened to Europe before acknowledging the purpose of his trip, claiming that he "knew perfectly well that any movement to bring the attention of the world to the Negro problem at this crisis would be stopped the moment the Great Powers heard of it." That turned out to be true, as the US government subsequently denied passports to Wells, Madame C. J. Walker, and William Monroe Trotter, who had intended to travel to Europe for the congress. It was a fatal blow because, to Du Bois's mind, a sufficiently large presence of representatives from across the Black world "could have settled the future of Africa." Even he could not argue that his "mission" had been a success, but Du Bois consoled himself that the hastily called and sparsely attended meeting had at least got "the ear of the civilized world." What it heard, he asserted, was that the issue of global racism fell squarely within the mandate of the Leagues of Nations, the new instrument of international governance created at Versailles. Du Bois called the league "absolutely necessary to the salvation of the Negro race" and characterized it as a "supernational power [able] to curb the anti-Negro policy of the United States and South Africa."[59]

Undeterred, Du Bois recalibrated his transnational Pan-African strategy to take account of the success of Wells and Kinloch two decades earlier. With their example in mind, he was convinced that a second Pan-African Congress in Europe could succeed where the first had failed. It would do so by leveraging the movement Kinloch had cofounded with Fox Bourne, one aimed specifically at British responsibility for the new slavery in Africa rather than its manifestation in the United States. What impressed Du Bois most from the vantage point of the post–World War

I crisis in American race relations was that the Kinloch–Fox Bourne association had drawn their respective organizations together. Du Bois felt certain he could replicate that accomplishment with his revived Pan-African movement. Unlike his ascending rival Garvey, Du Bois remained committed to securing the support of politically well-connected white allies. He decided to return to Europe in 1921 to gain an audience with the powers determining the fate of the world for the next century. Surveying the landscape, he targeted the British Anti-Slavery Society and the Labour Party.[60]

Du Bois's relationship with longtime collaborators in British abolitionism seemed closer than ever. He might have been in the background when Kinloch and Fox Bourne reestablished the antislavery-antiracism alliance, but the Universal Races Congress of 1911 had cemented his reputation among British antislavery activists. Du Bois reciprocated by regularly highlighting their work in *The Crisis*, contrasting what he saw as the flourishing British abolitionist cause and the largely dormant American one. According to him, British campaigners were "working for justice . . . [for Africans] in all matters." He hailed them for objecting to the British release of the racist film *Birth of a Nation* and for showing as much interest in the "future of African colonies" and international mechanisms for governing them as Du Bois himself did. Relations seemed to be at a high point by the end of World War I, when the Anti-Slavery Society solicited Du Bois to set up a library of suitable works on the Black world in London, presumably featuring his own. This evidence of the abiding alliance between antislavery and antiracism encouraged him to think that the Black freedom movement could rely on its old abolitionist friends when it was otherwise so isolated. Nothing was more natural than Du Bois approaching that association to help organize the Second Pan-African Congress that would put it firmly on the political map.[61]

Du Bois also counted on the suddenly politically ascendant British Labour Party. In his newest book, *Darkwater*, published on the eve of the Second Pan-African Congress, he highlighted this new force in British electoral politics, which "disclaim[ed] all sympathy with the imperialist idea" and advocated "the transfer of the present [African] colonies of the European Powers" to the supervision of the "League of Nations." This British political party, on the eve of its accession to power, endorsed Du Bois's plan for African self-rule—a stark contrast to the attitude of American politicians. Moreover, Du Bois was familiar with Sidney Webb, Labour's most influential intellectual, having been introduced to his work at Harvard during the 1890s.[62]

Webb was the very embodiment of the progressivism that had once attracted Du Bois. The moving force behind the founding of the London School of Economics, where he was appointed to a professorship in public policy, Webb had for decades produced a steady stream of work exposing the flaws of industrial society and charting comprehensive plans to improve it. Arguably, no one in England was a more dedicated, ambitious, and insightful reformer. Webb had always preached patience in preference to the violent extremism of the more Jacobin elements of socialism, holding that capitalism's critics could achieve nothing until the majority of society had been convinced to regulate its worst excesses and modify its productive powers toward humane ends. The Great War had accomplished that goal. Webb's long-awaited moment had arrived, and he became the prototypical ally Du Bois sought.[63]

The war suggested that Western civilization needed the guidance of its leading intellectuals more than ever, and Webb's Fabian Society included George Bernard Shaw, H. G. Wells, Virginia Woolf, and Bertrand Russell. The Fabians collectively occupied a prominent position in the socialist wing of the Labour Party, founded in 1900 and in the midst of a swift rise to power by the 1920s. Webb used the crisis of faith in capitalism ushered in by the war and the resultant economic turmoil to entrench Labour's socialist principles.[64]

Webb drafted and successfully campaigned for the landmark clause 4 of the party's program. This best known and most controversial provision called for Labour "to secure for the workers . . . the full fruits of their industry and the most equitable distribution thereof" through "the common ownership of the means of production." Webb also advocated universal human rights, along with "the improvement of the social and economic standards and conditions of work of the people of the world." This goal would be accomplished through state regulation, to which Webb attributed "the permanent elevation of the standard of life" in the English working class since the grim days of early industrialism. Livable wages and humane working conditions required "that there should be an inflexible inferior limit below which the conditions of employment must not be permitted to fall." The existence of less privileged workers, Webb affirmed, "appears to me to aggravate our responsibility in the matter."[65]

Webb's principles seemingly suited him and his party to the role of antiracist ally. His address as chairman to the party's convention just before it formed its first British government pledged that a Labour administration would "be outspoken in our denunciation of every form of governmental tyranny, whether 'white,' 'red,' black or any other colour, at home or abroad, in Asia and Africa as well as in Europe and America." Future prime minister Ramsay MacDonald added, "The Labour Party would insist, that the whole of the Empire cannot help being made responsible for the acts of its States." He asked to be judged by a high standard when in office: "If the Home Premier condones the conduct of Imperial officers who played a leading part in [the British Empire's own] disgraceful episodes, it is sheer hypocrisy on the part of our Foreign Secretary to threaten the Congo Government for allowing the murder of natives in the rubber forests." The choice was to reform the evil perpetrated by both the British and the notorious Belgian rule or admit culpability for it. Mindful of the model of Wells's antilynching campaign, his own increased stature in England, and the encouraging words he heard from British abolitionists and Labourites, Du Bois crossed the Atlantic triply confident. He arranged a meeting with Webb and the Labour Party's executive committee, as well as with John Harris and the Anti-Slavery Society. To Du Bois, it all appeared promising.[66]

Dark clouds, however, had long since appeared on this seemingly bright horizon. Even at the height of British antislavery activists' sense of embarrassment, shame, and outrage real or feigned, there were clear indications that twentieth-century abolitionism differed from its predecessor. Wells found an audience for her antilynching campaign but at times was nevertheless forced to take a backseat to her English collaborators. One of them brazenly appropriated her work, publishing it under his own name without crediting her. Historian Mia Bey observes that some journalists manifested more interest in Wells's "exotic appearance" than her intellectual arguments. Wells's cofounder of the Society for the Recognition of the Brotherhood of Man, Catherine Impey, resigned from the organization after only two years because it opened its doors to segregationists on the pretext that African Americans "prefer to have their own institutions, and to keep to their own race." The society professed opposition to "customs, laws, observances and regulations" that promoted racial segregation but would not ask its members to put their avowed principles into practice.[67]

Kinloch may have shared a stage with Fox Bourne, but neither she nor any other Black person was invited to chair or address a mass antislavery meeting, as William Wells Brown and Frederick Douglass had been in their time. And although Kinloch's pamphlet was published by a trade union group, it was never widely circulated and generated no income, compelling her to return to South Africa to earn a living. The antislavery movement she helped launch never offered to pay her fare to London for the Pan-African Conference when she could not afford passage. It was not just these two Black women, Wells and Kinloch, who were abandoned. British abolitionists soon ceased to provide any forum for Black activists to set out their ideas or recount their experiences, opting instead to be an all-white movement.[68]

In a 1910 review of Du Bois's work, the *Anti-Slavery Reporter* acknowledged his point that the new slavery continued to thrive in America but concluded, "It is not for us to judge censoriously those who have this terrible heritage of slavery confronting them within their own borders." This apparent concern for American sovereignty—in stark contrast to nineteenth-century British abolitionists, who threw their weight behind African Americans and against American slavery—masked a different motivation. "The colour question to-day is not one for America alone, but it is one which all colonizing nations have to meet, and which it is not too much to say, is severely testing the meaning and worth of modern civilization." British abolitionists did not want to be held up to the standard implied if they criticized racism in America.[69]

The apparent success of Wells, Kinloch, and others notwithstanding, something essential had changed since the time of Douglass and Brown. The 1899 meeting of the Aborigines Protection Society, where Williams rose to challenge Earl Grey, had already revealed the ambiguities of British abolitionism's relation to the imperial project at the heart of the nation's politics. Though Du Bois would later attribute the retreat to the impact of World War I, it dated from an earlier and deeper conflict that he failed to notice. Despite his high hopes, the stage was set for the failure of Du Bois's transnational Pan-African strategy.[70]

3

The Rise of a New Antislavery

So great was Du Bois's faith that World War I marked a decisive break with the past that he became convinced that European colonialism was ready to change its ways. As a centerpiece of the First Pan-African Congress's program in 1919 he included an appeal to Britain, France, and other colonizing nations "to establish a Code of Laws for the international protection of the Natives of Africa similar to the proposed international Code for Labor." He counted on his presumed allies in the British Anti-Slavery Society and the Labour Party not only to fight for that principle but also to ensure a place at the table for himself and his fellow Pan-African leaders.[1]

But much had changed in the decade since Du Bois's 1911 trip to London, when he had been warmly received by the Anti-Slavery Society. Behind the scenes a more complicated political drama was unfolding: British colonial officials and the nation's celebrated antislavery movement were converging around a new antislavery that sanctioned the new slavery. British officials influential in the abolitionist movement had long abandoned its nineteenth-century principles as they established labor policy in Africa. It became their central mission to redefine slavery to permit them to exploit African workers more profitably.

At the forefront were two figures. Frederick Lugard, despite his reputation as an abolitionist, developed the policy of "permissive freedom"—a euphemism for resurrecting slavery and dangerously transforming it from a domestic institution into a full-blown system of racial slavery. John Harris, an avowed segregationist, lent the indispensable moral cover of abolitionism when he assumed the helm of the Anti-Slavery Society in the 1910s, following the death of Henry Fox Bourne. So decisive was its break with the past that mainstream abolitionism fully embraced colonialism's racist worldview under Harris and executed an about-face on the new slavery. His organization was drawn into an alliance with Lugard and Britain's Colonial Office—the arm of the government charged with overseeing the empire. A leading imperial figure, Lord Cromer, proclaimed a paradoxical doctrine holding that forced labor constituted slavery only when employed by private enterprise and not by the state charged with stamping out its use.

Du Bois was unaware of these developments until his 1921 visit, when all his hopes and expectations would be rebuffed. His miscalculation was most evident in his unrealistic vision that Europe's principal imperial nations would accept a coequal role for his Pan-African Congress in the midst of a desperate struggle to keep their African empires in their clutches. On the contrary, Du Bois would find that the international antislavery-antiracism alliance had been irreparably severed, and the mainstream abolitionist movement had entered into a close relationship with racial colonialism.

When the legal instruments Du Bois called for were passed over the next decade, instead of accomplishing his objectives, they would show the depth of the betrayal of Black workers by the new antislavery. With the plight of African Americans in the South ever in mind, Du Bois needed two measures in particular enacted into international law: provisions to prevent the kind of debt peonage that menaced southern tenant farmers, and an outright ban on prison labor and its derivatives. But quite to the contrary, these treaties would inscribe race into international labor law, leaving the new slavery firmly entrenched.

Frederick Lugard's Racial Colonialist Antislavery

Squarely in the middle of the rise of the new antislavery was no less distinguished a figure than Sir Frederick (after 1928, Lord) Lugard, whom the Anti-Slavery Society counted as perhaps its most influential supporter. Lugard played a role that Du Bois never would have suspected of such a celebrated abolitionist and one that would somehow escape the censure of history. Black abolitionists could have been forgiven for concluding that Lugard represented something of a twentieth-century successor to Abraham Lincoln in the cause of ending slavery. Europe's claim that it was stamping out slavery in Africa derived in part from Lugard. Like Lincoln, his name is closely associated with a historically significant antislavery instrument, in his case, the draft of the 1926 Slavery Convention that he authored. Lugard's status in the pantheon of antislavery heroes is more complicated, however, beginning with his record in the last two decades of the nineteenth century as military administrator for the Imperial British East Africa Company. He helped bring much of that region under British control as his forces advanced into the continent's interior during the "scramble for Africa." The nation that had pioneered the abolition of slavery in 1834 attempted to portray its territorial conquest as the work of an army of liberation that would serve as a beacon to the enslaved population it had come to free. Lugard's declared antislavery objectives obtained the ardent support and active lobbying of the Anti-Slavery Society for what might otherwise appear to be a naked land grab.[2]

It was Lugard who determined the fate of the two women freedom seekers whose stories are recounted in chapter 2. Ominously, despite his legal obligation not to do so, Britain's designated expert on slavery ultimately opted to return the two women to their captors. His decision, together with his audacity in openly bragging about it in his widely read chronicle of the campaign, should have sounded alarm bells among abolitionists everywhere. Lugard's callous treatment of these two African women demonstrated that he would not follow the nineteenth-century abolitionist practice of granting agency to the formerly enslaved. A principal means of doing so was fighting for the freedom of those who embarked on the powerful and self-determining act of escape.[3]

For colonial powers like Britain, proclaiming antislavery objectives was easy. The British especially could afford to suppress the preexisting institution of slavery without harming their own interests, which, over the course of the nineteenth century, had altered almost completely. The real test would be how their professed abolitionism fared as they sought to meet their own labor needs. Lugard's retreat from established antislavery principles helped justify the British colonial policy that set the stage for racial slavery to recross the Atlantic.[4]

Lugard showed little interest in even the most basic antislavery principles from the beginning of his career. He freely admitted that "all [European] nationalities alike" used slaves as carriers or porters who hauled supplies into Africa's interior and then hauled the products of African labor back to the coast for export. He acknowledged that this involved "a paltry subterfuge, [in which] slaves would be enlisted as free and voluntary labour, though the real state of the case was fully known alike to the British authorities and to the employers." In endorsing the practice as "a distinct good" to the slaves so employed, Lugard revealed nothing not already in the public domain, as reports of these practices had already reached London. What might have been dismissed as a pragmatic defense of the exigencies of war in the interests of a greater crusade, as in the case of Union troops in the American Civil War and during the Haitian revolution, quickly morphed into something far greater. Lugard soon sanctioned the deployment of enslaved labor for the purpose of creating a supply of workers for the labor-intensive construction of the infrastructure of colonial rule.[5]

There were, Lugard declared, two competing emancipation policies from which Britain could choose. The first, which he labeled "abolition," entailed the principle that "neither can an owner retain a slave, nor can slaves remain in slavery whether they desire their freedom or not." This standard, Lugard explained, was the one adopted in the 1834 emancipation enacted in British possessions. In his view, that policy, championed by the antebellum abolitionist movement, was not appropriate for British East Africa, since it would disrupt "existing social conditions," especially the labor supply on which European enterprise depended. He called his rival plan "permissive freedom": abolishing the "legal status" of slavery while forcing enslaved Africans to buy their freedom by working as contract laborers for the British. He simply chose to ignore that, as opponents charged in Parliament, it violated the spirit and quite probably the letter of British law and doctrine since 1834. More than a temporary postponement of abolition, permissive freedom set the stage for the new slavery that Black abolitionism had organized to combat.[6]

Lugard's permissive freedom was anything but the principled antislavery the British professed, and colonial officials rushed to exploit the ambiguities it introduced. Colonial secretary Joseph Chamberlain, among the most ardent imperialists of his time, joined one of the top administrators in southern Africa, Earl Grey, in resurrecting the thoroughly racist pretext for the use of force to which General Nathaniel Banks had resorted in the United States. They claimed that the threat of "vagrancy" necessitated a system of coerced labor centered on men only. Rhetorically inventing a problem, Chamberlain asked during a 1901 Parliamentary debate, "What will happen if [African men] do not work? . . . There is nothing left in that case but the extinction of the native or his return to the servitude from which he has emerged." He pronounced, "In the interests of the natives all over Africa we have to teach them to work."[7]

The method Chamberlain favored for disguising the policy of forcing African men to work in the mines and construct the infrastructure of European colonialism was a "labor tax" to be paid in the money they obtained working for the colonialists. Labor taxation was invented by the now notorious imperialist Cecil Rhodes during his tenure as premier of the Cape Colony in 1895. Rhodes's friend and codirector of the British South African Company, Earl Grey, imported it into other parts of the British Empire, beginning in Southern Rhodesia. As the South African system of labor taxation, migrant labor, and white supremacy took hold across the region, workers from as far away as Malawi became enmeshed in it.[8]

According to officials like Grey, the British were in fact developing a system of free labor, albeit one whose definition differed considerably from its common meaning. Four illuminating decades after Karl Marx's *Capital* first elaborated a political economy of free labor, Grey claimed that "the principle of freedom of labour" must be judged by whether it left the mining corporations "free to obtain the unskilled labour we require from the most economical source." Lugard's notion of permissive freedom was only the first embodiment of the new slavery that Grey preferred to view as free trade in African workers. As Britain imported the Atlantic world's racial slavery to Africa, this reprise of one of the greatest injustices in world history was even more galling because it was undertaken in the name of abolitionism itself.[9]

Justifying Twentieth-Century Racial Slavery in the Name of European Colonial Rule

As British imperial officials sought to meet the ever-expanding labor needs of colonial rule, they attempted to redirect attention from their own government's practices to those of Britain's rivals. Imperial champions seized on Belgian Congo as the perfect foil. By the early twentieth century, its labor practices had become notorious and synonymous with slavery. As humanitarians exposed the appalling conditions there to a scandalized Europe, it allowed the British to deflect criticism of their own colonial practices. Earl Grey's brother Sir Edward Grey, an important leader of the Liberal Party, emerged as a vocal critic of the slavery on Belgian territory. Upon becoming foreign secretary in 1905, Edward Grey charged that requiring Congolese men to discharge their tax obligations in labor amounted "to a system of forced labour, differing in name only from slavery."[10]

Grey soon followed Lugard's lead in formulating a new antislavery doctrine to cover up the similarities between Belgian and British practices. He declared in 1908 that the problem was not the principle of labor taxation, which Grey acknowledged the British also deployed, but the ends to which the workers labored. If the "proceeds . . . are used for the purposes of private profit, instead of being employed solely for the benefit of the State, then this labour is not a tax, but slavery," he pronounced. When employed for "the furtherance of private interests," he reiterated in Parliament, "in the opinion of His Majesty's Government," the practice could "only be expressed in unqualified terms as slavery pure and simple." At the same time, he insisted, when the same measures were undertaken by the state, as in the British case, it was an ethically sound policy. A decade and a half earlier, Earl Grey had formulated essentially the same principle, writing to Fox Bourne, "abolish[ing slavery] at once . . . would . . . destroy what might be a useful instrument for gradually bringing a barbarous population under the discipline of civilized life." The objection, instead, should be to those "seeking to make money by industrial enterprises carried on by forced labour."[11]

In early 1914, as world war loomed, Lord Cromer adopted the formulation of the two Greys and declared that it demarcated the bright line between slavery and free labor that seemed so difficult to draw in the era of the new slavery. Here, allegedly, was the distinction between the labor practices of the British and the Belgians, Germans, and Portuguese. Cromer, a preeminent figure in Britain's colonial service, took to the pages of the influential Conservative publication *Spectator* to prosecute his case. He asked, "When and under what conditions is forced labour justified?" and "At what point is it synonymous with slavery?" Cromer ignored abolitionists' classification of all forced labor as slavery and Britain's long-standing denial of employing it. No one seemed to notice or care that Cromer had entirely reframed a long-standing debate. Claiming to speak for the British Empire directly and for abolitionism indirectly, Cromer explained, "The answer to [the] question [of] what we mean by slavery is that we reluctantly admit the necessity of compulsory labour in certain cases, and that we do not stigmatize as slavery such labour when, under all possible safeguards against the occurrence of abuses, it is employed for recognized and indispensable purposes of public utility. On the other hand, we regard the system, when employed for private profit, as wholly unjustifiable and as synonymous with slavery." Though Cromer cited Grey, the impact of Anti-Slavery Society leader John Harris's work should not be overlooked. Cromer took careful note of Harris's version of this new antislavery doctrine a year before giving it canonical expression. The Anti-Slavery Society itself would consistently credit Cromer, but Harris might hold the earlier claim.[12]

Critics noted the inconsistencies that riddled this allegedly antislavery principle. Former Portuguese foreign minister Freire d'Andrade cogently noted that, if the aim was the elimination of forced labor, it would have been more rational for the government to "begin by setting the example." He was not alone in discerning a double standard. The chairman of the Tanganyika Sisal Growers Association, under fire for his members' dedication to the "restrictions on the liberty of movement of natives," countered: "Regarding this question purely from its economic and industrial aspects it should be remembered that the only instances of forced labour in this territory known to planters, instances continually under their notice, are the actions of Government in compelling tax-defaulters to work on road maintenance and other Government work until their taxes are paid." As this exponent of British capitalist enterprise in Africa perceived, the greatest demand for forced labor came from a colonial administration that was by far its biggest beneficiary, relied on it immensely, and was loath to part with it.[13]

With their dependence on forced labor to maintain their colonial governments in Africa, the British found themselves in a precarious position. British abolitionists, following Alice Kinloch, had denounced such forced labor as the foundation of the new slavery—just as Du Bois had identified prison labor in the American South. A 1907 parliamentary inquiry showed the pervasiveness of the practice, especially in East Africa, where the British commandeered the labor of African men for up to one month per annum for the construction of infrastructure. A Ugandan Anglican bishop exposed the widespread presence of "forced labourers" on road construction crews. The result, according to the cleric, was disruption of the agriculture on which Ugandans depended, the outbreak of famine, and depopulation of the region. Forced labor extended to West Africa as well, where Gambia, Gold Coast, and Southern Nigeria required it of "all able-bodied men" and Northern Nigeria made it compulsory for "all Natives." In British Natal, Africans were expressly required to form "native labour gangs," with public works defined to include not only "road work" but also "telegraph construction" and "postal runners." Although the colonial state primarily requisitioned men, women were not exempt. An Anglican archdeacon in Kenya witnessed "gangs of girls from the ages of 10 to 16 years [who] were called out for collection of thatching material in the North Gem area of Central Kavirondo, involving some of them in a daily journey of 30 miles."[14]

Absent other ways to get products to market from remote areas, British colonialism did so on the heads of forced laborers from the time the British took possession of African territories. Porters transported mining machinery in one direction and bags of metals weighing sixty-five pounds in the other direction, for hundreds of miles. In 1926, when the British still employed seventy-eight thousand porters in Tanganyika, they admitted, "the economic development of the country still largely depends upon head porterage." This ancient mode of transportation lasted into the second half of the twentieth century, as the world entered the age of the jet airplane and was in the process of conquering space. It was backbreaking, exhausting, dangerous work that no African would do voluntarily. A Labour MP claimed, "When I was in East Africa I saw 90,000 of these wretched devils die carrying loads for us."[15]

Road and railway construction and maintenance generated a greater demand for coerced labor. A British colonial undersecretary admitted in the late 1920s that those sectors involved "by far the most important use" of compulsory labor for the state, which was "practically universal in Uganda . . . and in British West Africa." Ghana's colonial governor boasted that forced labor had produced and maintained nearly seven thousand miles of roads. A representative of the International Labor Organization (ILO) noted that forced labor was employed almost exclusively for this purpose—men in construction and women to provide them with food. Britain's African empire became so reliant on this forced labor that the governor of Uganda declared in 1929 that it was "essential" to exclude it from the international treaty enacted a year later to ban forced labor, which it was.[16]

The ILO representative admitted that, "juridically speaking," the League of Nations commission was permitting a violation of the terms of the mandate by not requiring monetary compensation for work requisitioned under the guise of taxation paid in labor rather than money. He reported Nigerian "men being employed for seven months [consecutively] without payment." But this representative of the interests of the working class nevertheless approved of the violation, explaining that "he preferred to look to the practical effects upon the native population" than to uphold the recognized international policy that discouraged such practices. He could not help, however, blushing at the "altogether excessive" death rate of eighty per thousand among the Nigerian workers from a combination of overwork and "ill-treatment" under this colonial fiscal tax system.[17]

There was no better rescue for an embarrassed British colonial administration than a new antislavery, which gave its stamp of approval to its exploitative practices. Speaking on behalf of his fellow abolitionists, Lugard insisted that international law uphold the Cromer doctrine. "There was no dispute as to the right of a Government to use compulsion . . . for works of public utility or emergency," he claimed before a postwar international regulatory body. Lugard meant for that principle to apply only in Africa. The British adopted a different position for the Soviet bloc, denouncing the practice as slavery when it was employed there. Even the British could see the parallels between what they perpetrated in Africa and denounced behind the Iron Curtain. An experienced British administrator noted that, "in the sphere of production and marketing . . . in many [British colonies in Africa] a standard of organized State Socialism has been reached which might be the envy of the Russian Government." Nowhere was this truer than in the extensive use of forced labor. The doctrine of the permissibility of forced labor for "public utility" became as indispensable to colonialism in Africa as the notion of the exigencies of "socialism in one country" was to Stalin's industrialization campaign.[18]

As southern planters disguised their exploitation of African Americans behind bogus criminal convictions and fraudulent debt relations, Africa's British overlords attempted to justify themselves on the basis of precolonial African communal service obligations. Confidentially, they admitted it was not the simple "continuance of old indigenous services, due to the chief or tribe, but . . . really new services due to the introduction of European rule." A British colonial authority suggested, "It is better to be honest and say that recourse to compulsory labour for these constructive services can only be justified on the basis that [they] are essential to the economic advance of the native communities." The British did their best to maintain the legal fiction. What British colonial authorities referred to as "minor village services" by "men, women and children" entailed "an obligation incapable of exact definition or measurement by hours of labour." The lack of specificity was convenient, since the characterization of services as "minor" was far from matching the job description. The Colonial Office privately acknowledged that "the object of dealing with this labour under" the category of "minor communal service" was "clearly" intended to ensure "that it may continue to be unpaid." That it was, as one official admitted, "universally unpaid" removed any pretense that it was anything but forced labor.[19]

Du Bois documented that the South's economy depended on its ability to coerce African American tenants to sign on to a desperate bargain, and the same held true for their counterparts in colonial Africa as well. Ghana's colonial governor admitted that the purpose of forced labor "has been to secure" labor at "an economical cost," saving his administration hundreds of thousands of pounds annually. A British official responded to criticism by an American investigative committee of the use of forced labor in West Africa: "Were the Government to rely solely on such labour as can be recruited individually at [the] current labour rate, it would be impossible to build railways or to undertake any other public work of magnitude." No employer paid less than colonial African governments, and none had the power to circumvent the payment of wages altogether. Imperial powers needed forced labor, despite their public pledges to end it. Du Bois first went wrong in believing those assurances while ignoring the underlying dependence on and ideological justification of forced labor by British colonialism. He was equally oblivious to British officials' influence on the nation's antislavery movement.[20]

John Harris's Segregationist Antislavery

The choice of John Harris to replace Henry Fox Bourne as full-time organizer behind British abolitionism cemented the movement's embrace of a new antislavery. While Fox Bourne maintained his hold on the Aborigines Protection Society, there remained a formidable counterweight to these colonialist machinations. After his death in 1909, the APS once again (as it had twenty years earlier) approached the BFASS about a merger. This time, the offer was accepted. In 1889 they had been allied organizations with separate missions and concerns. In the intervening decades, Fox Bourne had turned the APS into the antiracist wing of abolitionism formally allied to Pan-Africanism. The amalgamation, renamed the Anti-Slavery and Aborigines Protection Society, blotted out virtually all traces of his influence. Harris owed his appointment as the organization's front man in no small part to the colonial administrators in and around the British antislavery movement. He, in turn, obliged by removing the movement's gaze from British colonial policy.[21]

From Du Bois's vantage point in New York, there would have been little reason to suspect what would follow Harris's ascension to the forefront of British antislavery. Of relatively modest means but well educated, Harris had started his career as a clerk in a commercial house engaged in African trade. Following his ordination as a Congregationalist minister, he turned to missionary work on that continent. His resultant understanding of African colonialism retained both a commercial and a missionary bent, supplemented by an extensive apprenticeship under the tutelage of leading imperial administrators. Du Bois would not have comprehended its significance, but it was not a good sign that, when cataloging his principal abolitionist influences, Harris listed some of the most prominent figures of the British Empire—especially Edward Grey and Lord Cromer. Harris asked Cromer to write the preface to his 1912 statement of his antislavery agenda, signifying his aspirations to be the intellectual leader of the British movement. In laying out his vision for colonial Africa, Harris could not have been more fulsome in his praise of Britain's imperial officials, whose "hearts and consciences pulsate with lofty principle and humanitarian sentiment." He proclaimed Cromer "Africa's greatest constructive Administrator."[22]

As Britain's leading abolitionist from 1909 until his death in 1940, Harris perfectly embodied the spirit of the new antislavery, just as Fox Bourne had the old. Given his rise to prominence in agitating against the new slavery in Belgian Congo, Harris's modus operandi was arousing British public opinion against a foreign wrongdoer. Even if he had the appetite to oppose his many sponsors within the imperial apparatus, he lacked the requisite gravitas. But that quandary never arose. The Anti-Slavery Society's leaders immediately stopped criticizing their own government, executing an about-face on the indentured, contract, and migrant labor they had so recently classed as slavery. The society now reserved that term for the labor practices in Belgian, Portuguese, French, and German possessions, as the new antislavery ignored the new slavery in British-controlled areas of Africa. The Kinloch-influenced period was now firmly in the Anti-Slavery Society's rearview mirror.[23]

Whereas Fox Bourne had been a prototypical twentieth-century integrationist, Harris was a confirmed segregationist. As subsequent events would show, Harris would have objected as much to Fox Bourne's association with Black abolitionists as to his embrace of their doctrine. Harris sanctioned the "inter-mixing of the races" solely for "industrial purposes," and then only if Africans worked for Europeans and produced for the "white consumer." Politically and socially, Harris deemed what he called the "child race" of "primitive" Africans unfit for a greater role. He thus viewed Black intellectuals and abolitionists like Du Bois not as potential partners but as nuisances to be managed. Fox Bourne denounced incipient apartheid in South Africa as scandalously unjust; Harris embraced it as a "model policy" that Britain should adopt across the continent. He hailed the advent of apartheid's first pillars: the forced removal of Africans from most of their remaining land, the strict industrial racial bar, and the more stringent enforcement of pass laws. In justifying white supremacy, Harris deceitfully claimed, "General Botha's policy is not segregation of peoples, but a separation of land ownership."[24]

Though a minister of the gospel, Harris was prepared to sacrifice religious principle at the altar of what he regarded as a more sacred cause. "The full brotherhood of man does not mean miscegenation," he pronounced, sounding a favorite theme of American segregationists and the slaveholders before them. Harris too professed special anxiety about white womanhood. The possibility of interracial "sexual relationships" disturbed him, but he pronounced the "question of the relationship of Black men towards white women" "far graver" than the less threatening liaisons of white men with Black women. He was perfectly willing to subordinate African girls and women to white men, but rather than expose their white counterparts to the unattended and tempting presence of young Black males working in their homes as domestics, he advocated that girls replace men and boys as the domestic servants of colonial Africa. The exposure of African females to sexual violence at the hands of white men did not move the former missionary, who considered their welfare secondary to that of Europeans and to the needs of colonial governance.[25]

On behalf of the British Empire, Lord Cromer pronounced his gratitude that the antislavery movement was no longer headed by an "enthusiast" like Fox Bourne, who had allowed his "emotions to dominate [his] reason." Cromer much preferred Harris, who possessed "a solid appreciation of the difference between the ideal and the practical," which was "consonant with the . . . material interests of the Empire at large." Alluding to Fox Bourne, Cromer gloated, "the excellence of British rule has not been always fully recognized in those circles in which Mr. Harris principally moves," as it would be by Harris himself. Cromer's praise for Harris spoke volumes about the ever-tighter embrace of British abolitionism and the Colonial Office. Where Fox Bourne had partnered with Pan-Africanism against British colonialism, Harris would do the reverse.[26]

Under Harris's leadership, the Anti-Slavery Society made progressively less effort to hide the racism that had previously lurked beneath the surface. Rather than opposing indentured labor as slavery, it now advocated the use of Indians over Chinese workers on the grounds that South Asians were "easily controlled" and eliminated the "serious moral question" of sexual liaisons between Chinese men and African women. Having once denounced debt peonage in the American South as slavery, British abolitionists took to praising Theodore Roosevelt's overt racism in handling what they cynically called "The Native Problem in the United States" so as to solicit understanding of the British share of the "white man's burden."[27]

While British abolitionists had once sympathized with African Americans' predicament as portrayed by Ida B. Wells, they now professed pity for their white counterparts in America, who strove for progress against the retarding force of "less advanced races." The *Anti-Slavery Reporter* quoted Harvard philosopher Josiah Royce, who asserted that, in contrast to Jamaica, where "the negroes are orderly, law-abiding, and contented, and the English white men, few in number, control the country with extraordinarily little friction," in the US South "it is found necessary constantly to remind the negro of his proper place, and to keep him in it, and this causes acute irritation on both sides." The situation in the South was entirely comparable to "the native questions which confront us and other European nations to-day, in different forms, in all parts of Africa." Since the principal liberal democracies on either side of the Atlantic shared a dominant racist ideology justifying oppression, it could be employed to remind them of their common racial interests. With its turn away from antiracist abolitionism, this exploitation of racism for pragmatic economic ends implicated the leaders of Britain's premier antislavery organization. The British *African Times and Oriental Review* charged Harris and the organization he led with being "patronizing," being "out of touch," and "consider[ing] themselves capable of dealing with" the concerns of Black people without consulting them. Du Bois reprinted that critique in *The Crisis* but somehow failed to heed the perceptive warning and soon found himself confronted by the truth it contained.[28]

Du Bois's Transnational Pan-African Strategy Unravels

Upon Du Bois's arrival in London in 1921, two years after he believed he had laid the groundwork for his transnational Pan-African strategy, he encountered the first of several disagreeable surprises that woke him up to the reality of the new antislavery. The very man he was most counting on for support, John Harris, greeted his ostensible American ally with a dismissive review of Du Bois's newly published exposé of global racism, *Darkwater*. Du Bois was completely blindsided by this personal slight. Only months earlier, Harris had requested that *The Crisis* editor publicize his own latest volume. In response to Du Bois's highly complimentary notice, Harris reciprocated by damning with faint praise Du Bois's book. Harris's characterization of *Darkwater* as "impassioned, [and] glowing with a sense of wrong and injustice" was

97

not meant to be a recommendation of either Du Bois or one of his greatest works, which is as celebrated today as Harris's is forgotten. Harris deemed *Darkwater* overly emotional and too focused on what he considered the incidental historical force of racism. Du Bois's alleged fixation with race, Harris insisted, "leads the author into some exaggerations, and not infrequently, into somewhat confused generalisations and vague denunciations." The Englishman chastised his American counterpart for being too critical of Europeans and too laudatory of people of color. To Du Bois's assertion that Europeans were not a superior race, Harris sniffed, "Not many will be found to accept this dictum." Harris described Du Bois's work as "not so much an argument on the colour question as a cry from one who is keenly and bitterly conscious of the wrongs and sufferings of the race to which he belongs." Most disheartening, perhaps, Harris summarily dismissed Du Bois's call for an end to colonial rule.[29]

Even that uncollegial treatment did not prepare Du Bois for the shock to come. The review foreshadowed Harris's supercilious conduct toward his fellow abolitionist when they met. Harris made it quite clear that there would be no reconstitution of the alliance between Pan-Africanism and British abolitionism that Alice Kinloch and Henry Fox Bourne had spearheaded two decades earlier. Shortly after their meeting, Harris took the highly unusual step of publishing an account of it, as well as detailing their communications "for some months past," including his suggestion that they "confer privately" about "subjects of interest before the Congress." Harris conditioned his support for the Pan-African Congress on Du Bois's agreement that the conference's resolutions would be worked out in advance and would meet with Harris's personal approval. He admitted ambushing Du Bois with "certain resolutions on subjects to which the Society attached great importance." His pro-British imperialist stance and what historian Kenneth Janken deems Harris's "paternalist bearing [that] eventually placed him at odds with British Blacks" led to a "heated conference" between the organizers of the Pan-African Congress and officials of the Anti-Slavery Society. In Harris's retelling of his arrogant attempt to dictate what positions Du Bois's conclave should adopt, the English antislavery leader led his audience to conclude that the Pan-Africanist was unreasonable in demanding that his congress decide its own program. The insulting public airing of the ostensibly confidential meeting was a slap in the face. Making matters worse, at Du Bois's subsequent hourlong gathering with Labour leaders, he had to endure being mistaken for an emissary of Marcus Garvey and his congress for an offshoot of the Universal Negro Improvement Association, which, as his NAACP colleague Walter White recalled, noticeably "frightened Downing Street." "Dr. Du Bois tried to obtain some definite statement from Ramsay MacDonald as to what the Labour Party proposed to do to correct glaring evils in the colonies, but we received only vague evasions." The brush-off was hardly what Du Bois had anticipated.[30]

Though caught off guard, Du Bois quickly assimilated the political lesson. White confided to his NAACP colleague James Weldon Johnson, "Dr. Du Bois most scathingly denounced so-called philanthropic organizations which believe in working for the natives in Africa and refuse, meanwhile, to work with Africans." Du Bois explained to White that "the Anti-Slavery Society occupies the same position in England that the Tuskegee–Urban League group of whites [does] in America—believing that the Negro should be developed up to a certain point as laborers and no farther."[31]

Du Bois was almost certainly comparing Harris to Oswald Garrison Villard, his colleague in the NAACP generally remembered for his civil rights work. Villard had cofounded the National Urban League and was an enthusiastic supporter of Booker T. Washington's Tuskegee Institute model of "industrial training" for African Americans. White might have missed the oblique reference, but he did not agree with Du Bois—at least not publicly. He would write that Villard was one of "only a handful of supercourageous white Americans [who] dared speak out boldly for unqualified freedom for Negro Americans."[32]

Du Bois was less convinced. He still remembered Villard's review of his biography of John Brown. With undisguised condescension, William Lloyd Garrison's grandson had written, "That so gifted a writer as the author of 'Souls of Black Folk' should be tempted to write a new life of John Brown from the point of view of the negro is easily understood." Since "the negroes themselves [have] as yet done [so little] to honor the memory of John Brown," a "volume of appreciation" was long overdue. To Du Bois, this dismissal of his landmark biography—still celebrated today, even as Villard's own treatise on Brown written a year later has been forgotten—spoke volumes. He later commented, "To a white phi-lanthropist like Villard, a Negro was quite naturally expected to be humble and thankful or certainly not assertive and aggressive." To Du Bois, this expectation of Black gratitude meant that white antislavery activists should be left to define Black freedom and Black slavery, and decades of experience convinced Du Bois that they could not be trusted to do so. What irritated Villard about *John Brown* in the first place had been Du Bois's insistence on the centrality of Black abolitionism to the advent of emancipation.[33]

When Du Bois consigned Harris to the British equivalent of "the Tuskegee–Urban League group of whites in America," he meant that the Anti-Slavery Society's leader had no interest in even discussing any question of principle with a Black person. If he had bothered to learn about it, Harris no doubt would have been as dismissive as Villard of Du Bois's trenchant analysis of the shape of slavery in the twentieth century. Harris took it for granted that it was his natural place to speak on behalf of Black people as European authorities worked out the acceptable limits of the exploitation of Black labor. As if to give force to Du Bois's characterization of him, Harris never again mentioned the Pan-Africanist leader in public and dissociated himself from the con-gress's advocacy of "social equality."[34]

Du Bois had sought refuge in Britain, where African Americans' appeals had long enjoyed an audience, but he found, to his dismay, that both its abolitionists and its Labour Party leaders were thoroughly immersed in the racist ideology of colonialism. The old antislavery had both recognized and denounced the racial character of slavery. The new antislavery proved to be willing to countenance racism. In the age of imperialism, a shared Anglo-American racism spanned the Atlantic, one that proved socially acceptable to an important group of reformers in Britain. Being deprived of dependable allies marked a serious setback to the Black freedom movement. It was not that African Americans had no supporters, either at home or abroad. A small Geneva-based organization not only took part in the Pan-African Congress but also gave what Walter White called a "scathing and meticulously docu-mented" indictment of France's treatment of Africans. But what had previously been and still purported to be a powerful collaborator, the British antislavery movement, had abandoned antiracism. It was not such a great leap from there to aiding and abetting the cover-up of the enslavement of Black and brown people. Du Bois had entirely missed the British antislavery movement's shift in direction a decade earlier, when its leadership had transferred from Fox Bourne to Harris. The sponsor of Pan-Africanism's revival would now come face-to-face with the realities of interwar imperial politics that belied his idealistic expectations. Having met this unexpected check in London, Du Bois would be forced to watch his transnational program stood on its head amid the measures taken by the colonial powers in the aftermath of World War I. With their outsized influence in the interwar period, Harris's Anti-Slavery Society and Webb's Labour Party would soon profoundly impact international labor law.[35]

If any outcome of the postwar treaty negotiations indicated Du Bois's chances of success on the international stage, it was the League of Nations Permanent Mandates Commission, formed to oversee the administration of Germany's former colonies distributed among the victorious Allies. At the core of its mission was the obligation to ensure the immediate cessation of the forced labor extensively employed there. The delegation of two particular members of the commission by their home nations would have seemed quite propitious from Du Bois's point of view. Representing Great Britain was the celebrated British abolitionist Frederick Lugard. Portugal sent no less powerful a statesman than former foreign minister Freire de Andrade, whom Du Bois had managed to attract to his First Pan-African Congress as a delegate. Du Bois had sought prominent and well-placed allies in Europe, and the attitude of these men would indicate whether he had succeeded in making any. The extent of Du Bois's naïveté in believing that he could work with colonial authorities to reform the new slavery in Africa was brought home by d'Andrade's contributions to a remarkable discussion at a meeting of the commission.[36]

At the apex of their imperial might in the 1920s, the European colonial powers represented on the Permanent Mandates Commission registered alarm at a potent new specter haunting their rule in Africa. It was not the communist menace threatening to encircle the globe, not Pan-Africanism, and not even the danger of Western public opinion suddenly deciding to apply Wilsonian self-determination to Africans. The Belgian delegate warned his colleagues, "at the rate at which this process was going forward, it would not be possible to continue [the colonial project] for very much longer." For once, consensus reigned among the officials from the various states. In the view of the French member, the threat was grave indeed: "the native population was diminishing" and possibly "dying out," which was "not the case before the arrival of the white population." Lugard did not dispute the ominous conclusion: "there seems to be little doubt that since the partition of Tropical Africa between the European Powers the native populations in most territories have not increased and have probably decreased." D'Andrade added, "the high death-rate . . . is all the more alarming as affecting men who are young and in the prime of their powers."[37]

Just six years after Du Bois believed he had lined d'Andrade up behind his program to liberate the people of the Black world, the high-ranking Portuguese official revealed just how meaningless his participation at the Pan-African Congress had been. He blithely attributed the catastrophic death rate to what he called the "predestined" "disappearance" of "the African races," assuring his fellow imperial custodians of Africa that all the inhabitants of that continent, and presumably their descendants in the diaspora, were fated to vanish from the face of the earth. His British colleague brushed aside such a patently absurd explanation and, more in keeping with antislavery sentiments, acknowledged that the depopulation was due to European colonialism's labor regime, as attested by the decimation of the young male population. Commission members had been presented with enough data in the body's marathon sessions to comprehend the underlying reasons. An analysis by the ILO showed that the "remarkably heavy" mortality in British Cameroon could be traced to forced labor in locales far from Africans' homes. The world's new regulating body dedicated to the welfare of the working class also informed the commission that forced labor in French Equatorial Africa was producing mortality rates of up to 25 percent, according to data furnished by the French government. The Belgian official, representing perhaps the most notoriously brutal colonial regime, observed that a careful examination of the testimony presented to the colonial body showed an average annual death rate of between 7 and 10 percent. He remarked that even this enormous figure "passed over in silence the number of individuals sent back to their villages permanently incapacitated, or with organic diseases which were incurable."[38]

The inescapable conclusion put the leading European democracies in an embarrassing position. They had to confront the contradiction of employing forced labor while attempting to distinguish themselves as enlightened colonialists in contrast to the Germans, whose African subjects they had appropriated. "It has *long* been a *guiding* principle among the liberal and democratic peoples of the world," Britain's Colonial Office would declare in a 1951 memo, "that an individual *should not be required* to perform labour which is not of his own free choosing: the boundary between such forced labour and slavery is a tenuous one." Any violation of such an ingrained democratic principle posed delicate questions of public perception in a world newly challenged by the Soviet regime, which openly denounced imperialism and publicized the secret treaties for the division of colonized peoples. It looked bad for the "liberal and democratic peoples of the world" to engage in the renewed ravaging of Africa's population after barely a century's hiatus since the cessation of the slave trade. It appeared worse that these nations were again systematically depopulating whole regions of Africa of men. That the cause was coerced labor for its own enrichment seemed more than even Western civilization might be expected to tolerate.[39]

However damaging it was from a public relations standpoint, representatives of all the colonial powers, including Britain, admitted they could not do without forced labor. The Dutch member of the Permanent Mandates Commission reminded his colleagues that "literal compliance" with any prospective ban on the practice, even if it exempted "essential public works and services," was "impracticable." "Anyone with experience of colonial life," he cautioned, "knew that there was always need of such labour." In a signal of the realities Du Bois and his Pan-African Congress were up against, d'Andrade agreed, remarking that the use of forced labor in the colonies "is inevitable, and we are all sufficiently experienced to recognise the fact." The French and Belgian representatives backed them, in a revealing show of imperial unity on the "labor question." It was, however, the concurrence of Lugard on behalf of Britain that really told the tale.[40]

As Du Bois later admitted, his usual political acumen deserted him in the postwar period. He thought he "knew my Europe pretty well," having studied there while working toward his doctorate. He subsequently acknowledged he had failed to recognize the storm brewing, which fatally undermined his plan to secure the allies he sought. A disappointed Du Bois later concluded he had not "realize[d] that the intertwining threads of culture bound colored folk in slavery to, and not in mutual co-operation with, the whites." The short-lived twentieth-century antislavery-antiracism alliance was all but dead. And worse times lay ahead when the colonial powers finally got around to enacting the ban on unfree labor Du Bois had called for at the First Pan-African Congress.[41]

The Forced Labour Convention of 1930 and the Racialization of International Labor Law

In 1926 the League of Nations adopted the Slavery Convention that gave direction to subsequent treaties. Drafted by Frederick Lugard and embodying the novel antislavery doctrine for which the Anti-Slavery Society now stood, the covenant among the colonial powers tacitly acknowledged that all unfree labor qualified as slavery at some level. The treaty included a plea to its "High Contracting Parties" to "endeavour progressively and as soon as possible to put an end to the practice" of "compulsory or forced labour" and "to prevent forced labour from developing into conditions analogous to slavery."[42]

British authorities were keenly aware that their numerous critics, both influential and ignored, perceived the analogy between the forced labor in British colonies and the older forms of slavery in Africa the British professed an intention to suppress. Officials were exceedingly anxious to draw attention away from that similarity. As pressure mounted from a world still horrified by the barbarity of the Great War, a select committee of the British Parliament declared: "While not denying that [forced] labor is almost invariably in the interests of the Natives themselves, the Committee concluded that the practice is no longer in accordance with the ideas of modern civilization and should be discontinued." Imperial officials were anything but clear on where they could make a plausible case in drawing a line between permissible and impermissible, so the issue of which analogies would count was left open until settled by enactment of the Forced Labour Convention in 1930.[43]

A comprehensive treaty years in the making and filling hundreds of pages with detailed regulations with the force of international law behind it, an ostensibly prolabor body in the ILO charged with monitoring its implementation, and the weight of global public opinion to ensure enforcement, this second addition to international law was touted by its framers as a permanent solution to the problem of unfree labor. It was all the more fitting that it was signed and sealed on behalf of Britain by its newly elected Labour government. Nothing contributed more to the appearance of the abolition of slavery than this outright ban that antislavery activists had long demanded. The convention seemed to herald the dawning of a new era. There seemed every reason to believe that, in a time marked by such progress and promise, a reform movement enacting enlightened principles for European workers would curb the excesses of rampant free-market capitalism in the colonies too.[44]

The fingerprints of the new antislavery principals were all over this convention. As the voice of British abolitionism, John Harris was a frequent visitor to Geneva, where he served as an adviser to the international governance structures there and actively participated in the shaping of the treaty. The ILO commended the working relationship of the British antislavery movement and the British Colonial Office so that the world's largest colonizing power "came out [looking] better" than its rivals. The Anti-Slavery Society boasted, "It is admitted on every hand that it was largely due to the efforts of the Society that the League of Nations is committed to the 'total abolition of slavery in all its forms,' the ultimate abolition of all forms of forced labour, excepting that required for emergency purposes, and the reform of contract labour as it obtains in certain territories."[45]

There were testimonies all around to the unprecedented prestige and influence of British abolitionism. The *Manchester Guardian* informed its liberal readership, "Yesterday the Anti-Slavery Society did the cause of civilisation a real service by re-stating in a series of formal resolutions the elementary principles of colonial government. Today those principles are nominally accepted by almost every one; they are the explicit basis of Liberal and Labour and of enlightened Conservative Colonial Policy." The *Guardian* noted that this abolitionist blueprint for enlightened colonialism was "embodied in the whole mandatory system" under which the League of Nations oversaw the World War I victors' rule over the former territories of their defeated rivals. As proof of the antislavery movement's sway over Britain's imperial policy, one of its most active steering committee members, Sir Robert Hamilton, took up the position of undersecretary for the colonies in 1931. From the other side, Lord Robert Cecil, a Foreign Office insider, accepted appointment as Anti-Slavery Society vice president, joining numerous other imperial luminaries in such roles. There was less distance than ever between abolitionists and the empire they allegedly watched over to ensure that it adhered to antislavery principles.[46]

Du Bois got the treaties he wanted, but without the impact he sought. The League of Nations' slavery committee publicly declared, "In Africa, the age-long home of most of the slaves of the world, there is no reason for any disquietude concerning any of the colonies of the European Powers." Privately, the British acknowledged that this optimistic public assessment was far from warranted. Although the ostensible purpose of the treaty was to limit the acceptable bounds of labor exploitation in African colonies, no one believed that outcome was possible. Two key members of the British delegation to the conference that passed the convention acknowledged upon their return: "While we may congratulate ourselves that we have obtained what is upon the whole a satisfactory Convention it must be realised that the prospects of its having any great practical results for the benefit of native races are none too good." Their colleagues understood that what made it a "satisfactory Convention" was the room it left for powers like Britain to evade it. A Colonial Office staffer complacently observed, "The Convention is so confusing that it is extremely difficult to say whether its provisions were contravened." This was not an accidental result. The British had joined the French, Belgians, Dutch, and Portuguese in secret diplomacy to ensure that the Forced Labour Convention they signed left colonial production unaltered. They emphatically succeeded in this goal, as the subsequent history testifies.[47]

British colonialists confessed that forced labor persisted long after its purported abolition, mirroring the postemancipation South. In 1952, five years before yet another Forced Labour Convention would be adopted professing to end the practice for all time, a Colonial Office expert admitted, upon reading documents submitted by Tanzania's British administration, "We have never been quite sure just how Forced Labour still works and this correspondence throws some light on it, particularly the District Officer's view that he can interpret the law to suit circumstances." The authorities in Tanzania readily conceded, "It is not, of course, claimed that forced labour has been abolished, or that the end of it is in sight." Two decades, a world war, and a growing anticolonial movement later, British officials confirmed what their colleagues at the time had so accurately predicted about the ease of evading the provisions of international law when they involved Africans under European rule. How could this not be the case, so long as colonial authorities were permitted to judge what was forced labor and what was not?[48]

In the United States, the Supreme Court had ruled that the kind of forced labor common in colonial Africa was a violation of the Thirteenth Amendment banning slavery, declaring in its 1911 *Bailey v. Alabama* decision that "slavery or involuntary servitude [is] established or maintained through the operation of the criminal law by making it a crime to refuse to" labor. "The State," it explained, "may not compel one man to labor for another in payment of a debt, by punishing him as a criminal if he does not perform the service or pay the debt." In that case, "the compulsion to such service by the fear of punishment under a criminal statute is more powerful than any guard which the employer could station" as the overseer of any enslaved person. "The essence of involuntary servitude" is, the court ruled, "control by which the personal service of one man is disposed of or coerced for another's benefit"—and it did not matter whose. Though the US Supreme Court had no jurisdiction in Britain's African colonies, it drew on the same common law that made such contract labor impossible in Britain itself. How could it then be justified in British colonies? And yet the Forced Labour Convention did nothing to stamp out the tenancy arrangements in agriculture that were among the "spawn of slavery" identified by Du Bois in the American South.[49]

British officials recognized the problem, particularly with respect to contract labor. Hungary's accession to the Slavery Convention raised this question, as the central European nation signed the treaty only on the condition that doing so did not entail any obligation to limit its right to enforce labor contracts via the legal coercion of workers. Britain was faced with a dilemma. Defending its fellow newly independent neighbor, the Czechoslovakian government suggested that such contracts fell entirely outside the scope of the convention, and the Foreign Office eagerly sought to accede to the Czech position, already embraced by the French. A Colonial Office undersecretary discerned a problem with this approach. "If we associate ourselves with Czecho-Slovakia," he minuted to his colleagues, "we acquiesce in the view that the application by public authorities of coercive measures to enforce voluntary contracts is not contrary to the Convention." This objection touched off a spirited debate within his department, as one of his colleagues amplified the concern: "Accepting the Czecho-Slovak idea—sensible as it is—will open the door to all sorts of abuses because the Portuguese or others will say that the [forced] labour [they employ] is quite voluntary." Another official countered, "If 'coercive measures' means no more than a fine for breach of contract, with the possibility of imprisonment in default of distress for non-payment, do not we apply 'coercive measures' to contract labour? If so, it would seem more in our interest to agree that a voluntary contract to labour (if such a tautology is permissible) is altogether outside the convention." His colleague agreed: "We do not want to become involved now in any discussion of 'contract labour.'"[50]

Even British imperial officials could not help but admit that contract labor in their colonies was associated with indefensibly oppressive practices. The contract in question, as these officials well knew, was not an agreement *with* the African worker as much as an obligation to labor imposed *on* him and enforced by the state for the benefit of the employer. This compulsion was clearly and unambiguously reserved for British colonial subjects, just as debt peonage in the United States was limited to Black people. Within a few years, Colonial Office staff would unanimously concur that a draconian ordinance regulating agricultural workers in Kenya was such an egregious case of debt peonage that it amounted to a de facto form of "serfdom." Yet undersecretary of state Lord Dufferin blithely determined that "only two trifling amendments to the Bill are required to bring it into conformity with" Britain's treaty obligations. The decision to let the legislation stand struck one of Dufferin's subordinates as so inconsistent with Britain's public pronouncements that he was moved to record a highly unusual dissent: "from the labour standpoint its provisions seem to me indefensible and I am sorry for anyone who has to attempt it."[51]

The convention was also silent on the state's employment of prison labor, which menaced Black people on both sides of the Atlantic and had first attracted Du Bois's attention to the persistence of racial slavery. In 1936 the *Times* ran a story under the headline "Tax Resistance by

Kenyan Natives," which sounded the alarm about an imminent "break-down of the tribal system." "Half-educated youths," the paper charged, "now prefer to spend money made in the towns and on the farms on themselves and on their women friends," a violation of the established social order "under which young men accepted responsibility for the taxation of their parents and elderly relatives." The *East African Standard* quoted a member of Kenya's settler colonial legislature, who insisted "it was neither good for the Natives themselves nor Nairobi and it was bad for the country as a whole to allow thousands of young men to become demoralized in the town." The journalist added, "on what they lived he did not know"—and the authorities did not care. They wanted Africans out of urban areas if they were not serving the purposes of the colonial project. The response by Kenya's administration could only be called draconian: locking up boys as young as fourteen in detention facilities—more accurately called labor camps or, in Russia, the gulag.[52]

As the seeds of the prison-industrial complex were planted in the United States, the British enthusiastically employed unpaid prison labor in Africa. Kenya, according to the Colonial Office, "freely used" internment in detention camps to get around the legal obstacles to labor taxes imposed by international conventions. A commission set up ostensibly to investigate rather than instigate abuses recommended that defaulters serve three months at "hard labour" to deter the "many able-bodied and well-dressed young men who prefer detention to the trouble of working." An Anglican archdeacon described it differently: males aged fifteen to eighteen had been "driven out of the reserves and when they cannot get work they are arrested and put into detention camps," in a chilling echo of the vagrancy laws of the post–Civil War South. The Colonial Office reported that the number of detention camps was increasing rather than decreasing, providing an important source of labor for roadwork. The Forced Labour Convention had changed nothing in this regard. The earlier evolution of British antislavery doctrine had foretold that the British would refuse to endorse any ban on prison labor or penal sanctions.[53]

Even absent such loopholes, representatives of the colonial powers were nothing if not skilled in circumventing the intent of the ban on forced labor. One favored method was to label the requisitioning of forced labor a form of taxation. The French delegate to the Permanent Mandates Commission, backed by his Portuguese and Belgian counterparts, insisted that a colonial regime was not guilty of employing forced labor so long as it did not pay the worker for the labor he was forced to perform. While remunerating the worker would acknowledge the existence of coercion, not doing so discursively converted his would-be enslavement into part of the "fiscal system." In colonial logic, the proof that forced labor constituted a "tax applied in almost all countries without giving rise to objections of principle" was that it was *not* paid. "If the work were remunerated, it would no longer be a fiscal tax." This French official simply took for granted that enslaving Africans could be justified based on the same principle that allowed Europeans to be taxed. True, European governments levied taxes on Europeans at home in money and on Africans in Africa in labor, but that, he claimed, was owing to the innate difference between Europeans and Africans. Nor did it matter that this practice violated the treaty provision stipulating that all compulsory—legally speaking, forced—labor was to be paid. This mouthpiece for French colonialism claimed that labeling forced labor a tax "avoid[ed]" a "difficulty" "by means of an interpretation." Even Lugard, by no means squeamish on the subject of forced labor, disavowed this tortured logic, observing that the practice "introduced . . . 'corvée' . . . under a new label"—referencing a system long acknowledged to be slavery.[54]

Lugard, however, could not make too much of his objection without admitting that the British profited from slavery, as his empire resorted to precisely the same argument as this French official. During the drafting of the convention, the Zambian colonial governor had rationalized that the labor taxation to which his colony resorted was "no more 'forced' than similar labour is 'forced' in civilised communities where householders are 'forced' to pay rates for the maintenance of essential services." He continued, "The term 'forced labour' . . . is a misnomer. There are many things which require to be done in a native village connected with its good order, sanitation, etc., where it is by far the simplest and least expensive way for the able-bodied male villagers to do them themselves. In a more highly organized community they would be done by paid labour, paid out of the proceeds of a local rate." European powers would not hold themselves to the standards they applied at home vis-à-vis Africans, precisely as Du Bois had predicted decades earlier. On discovering that the forced labor used for the construction and maintenance of roads in his colony did not qualify for the "minor communal service" exemption in the convention, Nigeria's colonial governor proposed substituting a labor tax. His colleague in Ghana simply chose to interpret the international treaty differently, and the same staff meeting in the Colonial Office that accepted the Nigerian governor's view "agreed that there was no need to question" that of his counterpart in Ghana either.[55]

The League of Nations scolded the British as late as 1936 for their continued violation of the convention by levying taxes to be paid in labor. It was revealed that many workers in Tanzania paid their "tax liabilities by labour" for up to forty days a year, which included a period of work to defray the cost of the food they were provided. As one commissioner commented, "It was . . . a strange system that men should be compelled to work in lieu of paying taxes, and to work an extra period in lieu of food. If they had no food, they would obviously be unable to pay such high taxes." This was precisely the point. It constituted the very purpose of the taxation advocated by Earl Grey and Cecil Rhodes in South Africa, the discovery of which had helped activate the British antislavery movement in the late 1800s.[56]

Elsewhere in the empire, spurious subterfuges served to evade the ban on labor taxation. Failure to pay the monetary tax in Malawi meant a prison term of six months at hard labor. This was "not an uncommon sentence," according to a Colonial Office staff member who could "not help feeling that a maximum sentence of three months, as elsewhere in East Africa, is really adequate." His colleague noted, "It is contrary to Conventions to say 'if you don't pay your tax you must work,'" and then he detailed the artifices employed by British colonial administrations to get around that stipulation. The Colonial Office admitted that its own representatives on the ground were violating "the spirit if not the letter" of the ban on taxes paid in labor. In the late 1930s tens of thousands of Tanzanians remained subject to the practice. A commission in Kenya uncovered evidence of authorities "arresting" women to hold as "hostages," as well as accusations that they engaged in torture and, it was alluded, rape to induce payment. Tanganyika's administration actually introduced a new labor tax in 1935, which prompted a Colonial Office staffer to admit, "This, I suppose, is forced labour under Article 10 of the

[Forced Labour] Convention." In 1957, on the eve of the end of British rule, a colonial official in Kenya still claimed, "No payment is made for work of this nature [communal services] because it ranks as a normal civic obligation of direct interest to the community concerned." Africans, it seemed, were being enslaved in their own interests, and that was justification enough for the European colonial officials charged with enforcing the international antislavery law they themselves had written.[57]

One of these officials was the Labour Party's secretary of state for the colonies, Lord Passfield—which was how Sidney Webb signed official documents since being raised to a baronetcy. On assuming a position of power, Webb—in whom Du Bois had once expressed such trust—never sought to enact the kind of state regulation on behalf of Africans that, based on his own research into English working-class history, would have profoundly improved their living standards and working conditions. He would not even publicly advocate on African workers' behalf to raise the consciousness of his fellow voters in the British democracy.

Webb's hostility to workers of color in the colonies, so contrary to his position with respect to English workers, did not go unnoticed. His subordinates in the Colonial Office chided him for not "signify[ing] the intention of Government to deal with" the use of force against African workers. Under his direction, the Colonial Office only reluctantly acquiesced in the creation of the Forced Labour Convention, which it had sought to delay—and then mostly to offset censure. Six months before the treaty was adopted, the British representative noted: "It must be realised that the British Government is under some suspicion at Geneva, and is regarded as not having made a very good show with regard to the ratification and application of International Conventions relating to labour."[58]

It was now clear that one of the twentieth century's most celebrated reformers, who had sounded such unpopular themes in the past for the benefit of British workers, would not do so on behalf of Africans. By this time, Webb was even less concerned with Du Bois than he had been a decade earlier when the leading Black intellectual of his time had paid a visit. Webb was simply not interested in Pan-Africanists' appeals that he live up to his views about the rights of workers when it involved Africans. It was a far cry from the alliance of antislavery and antiracism at the turn of the century.

The Labour Research Department, established by Webb's Fabian Society in 1912, had noted the consequences of this neglect of Africans three years before Webb became secretary of state for the colonies in 1929. It wrote, "The whole organization and administration of Government is directed towards compelling the African inhabitants to work for European masters, and is based on the absolute subjection of the native population. Labour is recruited and controlled by the Government, and every possible device, including actual conscription, is used to force the natives into the labour market." A Colonial Office staffer confided to a colleague: "What we are really establishing is a system of black conscripted labour in order to make money for the white farmer and business man." He meant *we* not merely in the sense of Western society as a whole but specifically himself and his fellow imperial functionaries. It was a natural statement to let slip for an official who spent much of his career shaping the living conditions of millions of human beings he would never meet and whose existence was something of a theoretical proposition from his office in London.[59]

Given that colonialism was racial, here was the international labor law to match. The essential flaws in the Forced Labour Convention ran much deeper than its many loopholes, deliberate ambiguities, and unenforceable provisions. Its very spirit was racist and proslavery, backing up Du Bois's characterization of the politics of the British antislavery movement, which played such a pivotal role in its adoption. Together with the Slavery Convention—and the related antitrafficking instruments—the Forced Labour Convention wrote that racial reality into international antislavery law. The forced labor for "public utility" that was legal in no European country; the penal sanctions for the violation of labor contracts, struck down by the US Supreme Court; the taxes to be paid in labor: none of this was intended to apply to white workers anywhere. This hypocrisy was made clear by Britain's strenuous objections when the same measures tolerated in Africa were employed in Russia or Hungary. Du Bois had hoped that international law would serve as a check on American racism. Instead, international labor law now mirrored overtly racialized American law, especially as applied in the South. There was already differential enforcement of labor laws in the United States in the case of African Americans, such as nonenforcement of the Supreme Court's *Bailey* decision, which had sent Du

Bois seeking solutions in international political institutions. Now the provisions of these conventions ensured the racialization of international labor law in conformity with the racially determined construction of the global working class—as alive in the twentieth century as it had been during the height of slavery in the Americas. There would be one set of legal principles applicable to the industrial workers of Europe and North America and quite another for workers of color in the rest of the world.

The European imperialist nations—justifying their presence in Africa on the grounds of eliminating the slave trade and the slavery that still thrived there—sought to shift the focus away from the racial nature of their labor practices. They did so by wielding the power of what critical race theorists term *colorblind racism*. Leslie Carr points out that the US Constitution sanctioned racial slavery without overtly referring to race. International treaties adopted at the behest of the colonial powers followed that precedent—and with seeming consistency once "white slavery" was removed from antitrafficking legislation in the coming decades. Like the US Constitution, international law did not need to invoke race overtly to enforce racism. The colonizing nations used the simple expedient of entrenching a purportedly colorblind definition of slavery on a racialized institution to disguise the centrality of race, permitting them to draw a perfectly racial division in international law.[60]

Like the US Constitution, the Forced Labour Convention did not overtly allude to race. It was universally understood to cover only colonial, or native, labor, although both terms were omitted from the final version. As the Colonial Office acknowledged, the international labor conventions "deal with matters arising mainly out of social and industrial conditions prevailing in highly-developed Western countries, and for this reason the question of the extent to which they have been applied in Colonies etc., has not received very much attention on the part of the International Labour Office." Six months before ratification of the Forced Labour Convention, the British representative at the Fourteenth International Labor Conference wrote "of the difficulty of applying to Colonies and Dependencies Conventions which are originally drafted mainly with reference to highly organized industrial communities." The Committee on Forced Labor at the Twelfth International Labor Conference in 1929 admitted, "The question of native labor is an entirely new sphere of activities." The new treaty would mark the first international "convention [to] be applied primarily, though not exclusively, to Colonies and Protectorates [and which] has been discussed with their conditions in mind." Of course, "colonial conditions" were those of systemic racism. A treaty that purported to be the culmination of the century-long effort to inscribe antislavery principles in international law represented their signal betrayal.[61]

The positions taken by the Anti-Slavery Society after the Forced Labour Convention came into force made this betrayal clearer. It not only endorsed Britain's continued use of forced labor but also approved Lugard's opposition to any immediate abolition of domestic slavery where it remained in Africa. "In the interests of the slaves themselves," Lugard declared to the approbation of the society's 1932 annual meeting, "until they have been taught methods of responsibility and self-control, and have opportunities for employment, it would be cruel to emancipate them forcibly." American slaveholders had argued the same point a century earlier—without, however, the support of abolitionists. This was the same principle Du Bois had discerned at work in justifying the enslavement of African Americans decades after emancipation; it stemmed from the same racist ideology that menaced Black people wherever they lived under white supremacist rule. To argue that slavery protected the enslaved, echoing the rhetoric of slaveholders of yesteryear, might have seemed a peculiar stance for an abolitionist organization to take. Even more incongruous was that Lugard was recapitulating the same policy the Anti-Slavery Society had excoriated four decades earlier, when it drew on the principles of nineteenth-century abolitionism to decry the rebirth of slavery in Africa under British rule.[62]

The new antislavery also accepted Lugard's contention that domestic slavery offered better "protection" of the enslaved than their emancipation did, a particularly contradictory position for an organization that claimed to advocate the "total suppression of slavery in all its forms throughout the world." Yet Lugard's view was entirely consonant with the society's proclamation on the centennial of the abolition of slavery in the British dominions: "the general acceptance of the doctrine that the child races of the world constitute for the stronger races a Sacred Trusteeship." This hierarchy—straight out of the racist ideology of imperialism—had caused Du Bois to give up on the idea that British abolitionism was willing to fight racism. But even he probably never imagined that Harris and the Anti-Slavery Society would succeed in enshrining racist principles into international antislavery law.[63]

It was clear that the European democracies—or even their anti-slavery and reform movements—would not be pressuring the United States to modify the oppression of Black people. Prior to the Second Pan-African Congress, Du Bois had warned, "Slavery still exists in the United States . . . and it will go on until one day its red upheaval will shake the civilized world." That day was seemingly a long way off. The Forced Labour Convention did not even directly impact African Americans, who were not covered by its provisions. And that was the problem, from the standpoint of Du Bois's now failed transnational Pan-African strategy. International governance manifested no concern for African Americans' plight.[64]

A deflated Du Bois would hold two more Pan-African Congresses in 1923 and 1927, with noticeably less enthusiasm and ever-diminishing returns—although the third meeting did attract socialist literary luminary H. G. Wells. After the fourth, Du Bois abandoned the effort, citing African Americans' lack of interest. That was only partially true, as evidenced by Marcus Garvey's flourishing movement. Du Bois nevertheless concluded that for the foreseeable future, the Pan-African Congress had run its course without achieving his ambitions. His decision signaled his abandonment of the transnational Pan-African strategy to advance the US freedom movement.[65]

In some respects, the situation was now worse than when Du Bois had first embarked on his postwar project. In abandoning antiracism, the new antislavery, as codified in international law, tied the fate of African Americans and Africans more closely than ever. The Forced Labour Convention constituted a threat to Black and brown people everywhere, including in the United States. The exemption of forced labor "for public purposes" helped open the door for states like Florida to extract unpaid labor from prisoners today. Du Bois imbibed what he thought to be the lesson of his folly. When duly elected, Britain's Labour government proved to be as faithful a guardian of the nation's vast empire of colonial workers as any Liberal or Conservative predecessor. A disgusted Du Bois would remark bitingly: "The . . . color caste founded and retained by capitalism was adopted, forwarded and approved by white labor, and resulted in subordination of colored labor to white profits the world over. The majority of the world's laborers, by the insistence of white labor, became the basis of a system of industry which ruined democracy and showed its perfect fruit in World War and Depression." Du Bois and a new generation of Black abolitionists assimilated these political lessons and believed they had no choice but to develop their own understanding of the new slavery and their own program to abolish it.[66]

4

"The Emancipation of Man"

Faced with the permanent severance of the antislavery-antiracism alliance as a result of the advent of the new antislavery, Black abolitionists would be forced to change tactics. From the commencement of their rebirthed movement in the 1890s, they attempted to replicate the united front that had become a powerful interracial movement in the antebellum period. Some turned to more left-wing sections of the working-class movement, especially Marxists. In the wake of a second failure to secure allies, Black abolitionism would be forced to cement its existence as an independent branch of the antislavery movement.

Led by Cyril Briggs, founder of the African Blood Brotherhood, a group of radicals tried to get communists to acknowledge and combat the existence of the new slavery practiced on Black and brown people. In 1931, a year after the adoption of the Forced Labour Convention by the League of Nations, one of them, George Padmore, published *The Life and Struggles of Negro Toilers*, cataloging in minute detail the racial slavery the treaty left untouched. Padmore's subsequent expulsion from the communist movement indexed the failure of this working-class internationalist strategy. It had been undone not only by the dominant colorblind, orthodox Marxism but also by the young Black Marxists who signed onto it and dismissed the need for either Black abolitionism or Pan-Africanism.

If Du Bois could not lead a transnational movement, he could at least develop a comprehensive elaboration of Black abolitionism.

Unconvinced by the younger Black Marxists who vocally rejected his Pan-Africanist abolitionism, Du Bois set out a comprehensive under-standing of postemancipation racial slavery in his magnum opus *Black Reconstruction*, which built on Frederick Douglass's notion of the four freedoms. Du Bois reconceptualized slavery as part of the historical development of capitalism's racialized labor system, inseparable from the economic functioning of racial colonialism. In his Black abolitionist definition, slavery consisted in using racism to exploit Black workers in ways that were impossible in the case of whites. As the "ultimate exploited," their enslavement was the product of the concrete conditions of global racism, which he called "color caste" to emphasize that it was hereditary, historically entrenched, society-wide, and often independent of the law. It was therefore a moral imperative to emancipate them. That simple proposition, true to the spirit of antebellum abolitionism but radically different from the ostensibly colorblind new antislavery, proved to be influential on some Black theorists and activists as they pursued civil rights and decolonization in the decades to come.

Competing Perspectives in the Interwar Black Freedom Movement

Du Bois was not the only Black abolitionist searching for allies in post–World War I America in the midst of Red Summer. At such a desperate juncture, with African Americans facing racial violence and the NAACP ill-equipped to deal with it, Cyril Briggs believed there was only one alternative to Du Bois's futile attempt to work with British abolitionists and the Labour Party. Born in the British Caribbean territory of Nevis and based in Harlem, Briggs founded the all-Black African Blood Brotherhood in 1919 as an underground organization advocating self-defense against postwar racial violence. The group gained a measure of national attention in 1921 for its role in organizing the protection of African Americans during the Tulsa riot. Jamaican Claude McKay was its best-known member.[1]

Like Garvey's UNIA, the African Blood Brotherhood was an expression of the New Negro movement aimed at working people in the industrial North, the agricultural South, the Caribbean, Latin America, and Africa. Briggs too considered all persons of African descent one political entity, and followed Garvey in calling on the "Negro people of the world" to unite in a political movement. Garvey's influence no doubt

119

played a role in encouraging Briggs to focus on the enslavement of Black people. Garvey told his mass following, "We declare to the world that Africa must be free, that the entire Negro race must be emancipated from industrial bondage, peonage and serfdom; we make no compromise, we make no apology in this our declaration." Briggs reprinted in his *Crusader* Garvey's global reworking of Lincoln's famous principle: "Half the world can't be free and the other half slave." Briggs was equally persuaded by Du Bois's campaign against debt peonage under the auspices of the NAACP. Like Du Bois, Briggs denounced the "'New Slavery' in the South, where Negro men and women are to-day being sold as openly and irretrievably into slavery as in the worst days of the 'Old Slavery.'" While professing to be mystified at the lack of an interracial successor to the antebellum antislavery-antiracism alliance, Briggs had no faith that the NAACP could become a twentieth-century abolitionist movement in the United States.[2]

Briggs was nevertheless not ready to conclude, as Garvey preached, that people of African descent throughout the world must unite to win freedom completely on their own. Like Du Bois, Briggs initially felt the appeal of Woodrow Wilson's vision of postwar self-determination for all nations. For Briggs, the litmus test for Wilsonianism was whether it extended to Africa and the Caribbean. He was as bitterly disappointed as Du Bois when both regions were excluded from the national independence given to the Poles, Irish, Hungarians, and Czechs. Briggs next looked to socialism, a tradition dating to the late 1840s, when Peter H. Clark was first attracted to the radical doctrine. Inspired by the Russian Revolution, Briggs eventually steered his African Blood Brotherhood into the nascent US communist movement. Unlike Clark and other Black socialists such as A. Philip Randolph, Briggs did not temper his Garvey-like dedication to achieving Black liberation. He told his readership, "No race would be more greatly benefited by the triumph of Labor and the destruction of parasitic Capital Civilization with its Imperialism incubus that is squeezing the life-blood out of millions of our race in Africa and the islands of the sea, than the Negro race." He taunted white liberals and conservatives for having "the gumption to express 'surprise' at the Negro for fighting against new slavery in the company, as in the old abolitionist days, of radicals."[3]

Above all, Briggs insisted there was a connection between the new slavery in the United States and that in Africa and the Caribbean. He agitated on this issue within the communist movement for the next decade, as colonialism shaped international antislavery law to its liking. He could not have been more delighted when Padmore's *The Life and Struggles of Negro Toilers* was published, chronicling the existence of the new slavery that had allegedly been banned by international treaties. Briggs judged that this comprehensive survey "brilliantly analyzed world conditions in their relation particularly to the Negro people." Padmore had risen to a high position as head of the International Trade Union Committee for Negro Workers, a division of the Communist International's union wing. His political work on behalf of the African working class had already marked him as a danger in the minds of Britain's imperial administration.[4]

Padmore was the first to realize the full implications for Black people of the hypocritical façade of international antislavery law. In the United States, the new slavery Du Bois had identified three decades earlier remained entrenched as a result of "lynching, peonage, Jim-Crowism, political disfranchisement and social ostracism." Echoing Douglass's four freedoms, Padmore noted that "it has always been the prerogative of the ruling class of the South to decide when the Negro workers should leave their service, or under what conditions they are bound." The "labour recruitment" of Black workers, including the "chain gang," was used "to oppress and enslave." African Americans in the South remained subject to "a sort of feudal contractual relationship which bound them to the land like serfs."[5]

On Latin American banana plantations and in the building of the Panama Canal, Black workers were "transported in the same way as chattel slaves of former days" and "prohibited from having anything to do with the native working-class population." According to the Trinidadian-born Padmore, Afro-Caribbeans were enmeshed in an economy of forced migration and coerced work centered on plantations and peasant agriculture. In South Africa, "czarist methods of police terrorism" meant that "millions of Negro toilers are enslaved within their own country." On the continent as a whole, "Blacks, who form the majority of the entire population, have been robbed of their lands and are segregated on Reserves, enslaved in Compounds, and subjected to the vilest forms of anti-labour and racial laws (Poll, Hut, Pass taxes) and the colour bar system in industry." European colonialism in Africa relied on "black colonial slaves." With the "different forms of forced labour, peonage, expropriation of their lands, extraordinary laws and unbearably heavy taxes, lynchings, [and] segregation," millions of Black workers around the world could not be considered free in any meaningful sense of the word.[6]

Briggs and Padmore were both surprised and dismayed when *Life and Struggles* ran afoul of the leaders of the movement with which they had aligned. When Padmore called for the building of "a steel bridge of international solidarity between the toilers in the metropolis and those of the colonies and oppressed nations," he was expelled from the Communist International on grounds of "petty bourgeois" nationalism. Shunned from mainstream Marxist politics, Padmore turned to a race-based variety. History would remember him for his postwar leadership of the Pan-African movement, not for his efforts to interest the international working-class movement in the plight of Black people. Padmore's fate mirrored that of other Black communists in the 1930s—among them Briggs, McKay, and Richard B. Moore—but it was no quixotic episode in the history of a cynical and corrupted Stalinist Left. Sidney Webb's tenure in a Labour administration testified that socialists and social democrats, together with the trade unions they controlled, were just as uninterested in the enslavement of the workers of the Black world. The ability of the international working-class movement to ignore the new slavery was made easier—and, to an extent, less obvious to history—given the rise of a new US strand of Black Marxism that repudiated the older variety.[7]

The economic cataclysm that commenced with the stock market crash of 1929 led a number of leading African American intellectuals to reassess the world around them, including the literary renaissance that had been one of the most visible products of the 1920s New Negro movement. Langston Hughes would say, "Ordinary [Black people] hadn't heard of the Harlem Renaissance. And if they had, it hadn't raised their wages any." Claude McKay would call it a "pseudo-renaissance." In the 1930s many other Harlem Renaissance intellectuals, including its principal contemporary interpreter Alain Locke, would see the literary movement as a manifestation of an elite that was out of touch with working people, especially sharecroppers and other rural southern workers, however their particular form of bondage was defined. Judged from the standpoint of people deprived of basic freedoms and struggling to get by, the artistic and cultural concerns of intellectuals like Hughes and Locke seemed less urgent.[8]

In the climate of crisis, a group of young African American intellectuals rushed headlong into the revolutionary vanguard of Marxism to do battle on behalf of all African Americans with what Marx called the weapon of criticism. Born of a circle of graduate and professional students at Harvard and centered at Howard University, where many of them served on the faculty, these young radicals felt a sense of urgency. Abram Harris, Ralph Bunche, John P. Davis, and their colleagues embraced working-class politics and became proponents of what Marx called the "class struggle." Racial oppression, according to this view, was merely a minor skirmish in the larger class warfare that would be won by taming capitalist production. The socialist revolution (or perhaps evolution) loomed on the horizon like the Second Coming—a tidal wave of working-class political self-determination poised to wash away oppression in its wake. The prophets of that regeneration were the socialists, and their shock troops were the industrial workers, the working-class vanguard organized in trade unions. Few were more zealous proponents of unionism than these Black Marxists. In their writings, at national conventions, and in the program of the political organization they founded, the National Negro Congress (NNC), these would-be leaders of the Black liberation struggle trumpeted industrial unionism. When "progressive" elements in the American Federation of Labor, frustrated with the narrow "craft" outlook of that largest American trade union, split off to form the Congress of Industrial Organizations (CIO), NNC leaders were right there with them. While CIO activists organized white industrial workers, the NNC organized their Black counterparts. The young radicals rode the whirlwind of American socialism's heyday.[9]

Steeped in the Marxist conventions of the day, these Black radicals took aim at Garveyism and Pan-Africanism, which touted transnational rivals to the working class as the means of liberating the oppressed. Repeating a theme white labor leaders had pushed for decades, Bunche warned in a 1936 pamphlet entitled *A World View of Race* of "the dark, blind alley of black chauvinism" found in the "not very consistent myth" of a Pan-Africanism that had no potential to effect real change. People of African descent certainly endured ruthless oppression throughout the world, but that stemmed from their status as part of the "peasant and proletarian groups" in the United States and the "subject peoples of the world" in the colonies. "The 'racial' nature of the Negro problem in the United States has been greatly exaggerated," just as it had been globally. The "all too simple racial interpretation," Bunche wrote, expressed "a widespread misconception [of] the true position of the Negro in society" and had "no scientific basis." "With the intensified development of monopoly capitalism in the modern world," there was nothing Black people could do on their own. They, like everyone else, could be liberated only by the pending revolution, the battle lines of which had been drawn in the powers of "the dominant populations of the world." Black workers wasted their time dreaming of Pan-African utopias when their only real path was to throw their weight behind the "white working class." Bunche blamed not white workers and their political representatives but Black intellectuals like Garvey and Du Bois for the lack of unity between white and Black workers. African American leaders, he insisted, laid too much "stress on the element of race in the Negro problem." The young radicals rejected a politics based on race for one constructed on class—specifically, the class analysis of Marxism, with its socialist millenarianism predicated on a hierarchy of workers with the white industrial proletariat at the pinnacle.[10]

Alone among these young Marxists, Abram Harris remained in close touch with Du Bois throughout this tumultuous period. They even joined forces briefly in the early 1930s in an attempt to radicalize the NAACP. The much younger political economist, Howard professor, and activist even assured his older associate that if "a fight brings into existence a new movement there is no one to lead it but yourself." Du Bois took the challenge from his colleague seriously, and it apparently played a role in his intellectual trajectory. The venerable elder statesman, now back at Atlanta University, surprised and greatly pleased his Howard colleague by announcing that he too was making a thorough study of Marxism. Du Bois had surveyed Marxism to varying degrees since studying it in Germany some four decades earlier, but he now asked Harris which works besides *Capital* "the perfect Marxian must know." Harris obliged and offered some unsolicited advice about adhering to the orthodox interpretation then in vogue. Du Bois thought Marx uninformed about the real conditions of African American workers in the South, where Du Bois had done fieldwork decades earlier. Harris disagreed: "I doubt that [Marx] would have said anything very different than what he did say had he been more closely in touch with the problem." Harris seemed to imply that however ill-informed about Black people Marx had been, he provided the last word on class analysis. Du Bois apparently paid little heed to Harris's criticisms of his unorthodox understanding of Marxism.[11]

The maverick intellectual, as eclectic as ever, evidently read Padmore's work with great interest and was much more deeply impacted by it than by Marx or Harris. He corresponded with his future collaborator in Pan-Africanism on the eve of the anticolonial revolution while completing the draft of *Black Reconstruction*, where he would set out his fully matured views on slavery and antislavery. That seven hundred–page treatise gives the broad outlines of a profoundly new interpretation of modern world history that supports Padmore. The central argument of *Black Reconstruction* demonstrates that although his transnational Pan-African strategy built on the antiracist-antislavery alliance may have been dead, Du Bois was not done with either Pan-Africanism or his transnational understanding of twentieth-century racial slavery. *Black Reconstruction* is, at least in part, a product of Du Bois's political dispute with the young Marxists. The illustrious longtime activist was deeply engaged in a battle against the Marxist orthodoxy of the day— especially that of its Black exponents.[12]

For all their mutual respect, and despite their close association, Harris and Du Bois represented rival camps within the leadership of the Black freedom movement in the 1930s United States. They were divided over the role of race in the determination of class. On the one side, Du Bois and like-minded activists loosely grouped themselves around Pan-Africanism, while on the other side, self-described Marxists hewed to the orthodoxy of the day by aligning themselves with the progressive labor movement. At stake was the very notion of a Black freedom movement—or at least the degree to which the interests of not only African Americans but also Africans were distinct from those of white workers, necessitating a separate struggle. Harris and the Marxists believed that Du Bois put too much emphasis on the role of race, both theoretically and politically. Du Bois thought his protégé and his followers credulous and naïve about the realpolitik of international left-wing politics. In his mind, there was something more fundamental about the historical role of race than Marxian class analysis postulated, and nowhere was it more obvious than in the twentieth-century new slavery of Black workers.[13]

Harris readily granted that his friend and mentor had been the most important and influential African American intellectual of his era, but he was convinced that Du Bois's time had passed. In a 1935 review of *Black Reconstruction*, Harris wrote that Du Bois "has been for more than a quarter of a century the militant theorist of the Negro's struggle for equal rights." But since the start of the Great Depression, Harris continued, "Dr. Du Bois' leadership has been on the wane" because his approach to the Black freedom movement "did not touch the basic realities of Negro life" in the current economic emergency. Younger rivals, more in tune with the moment, "saw the race problem as part and parcel of the proletarian class struggles and felt that its solution lay in the alignment of black and white workers." Du Bois remained to Harris and the new generation of Black radicals a "racialist" who could not grasp the principles of Marxism that provided the roadmap to liberation. Du Bois's *Black Reconstruction* proved as much, and Harris had little good to say about the newly published work, despite his professed admiration for its author. It was, however, Du Bois's understanding that would prevail—and it would not take long for everyone involved to realize it.[14]

Though scholars have uncovered much that the young Black Marxists and their allies achieved in the 1930s, they quickly became disillusioned with the Left and with the labor politics of the Depression. However significant their victories, Harris and his comrades felt the defeats even more keenly, driving them to believe, like Garvey and Du Bois, that the white working class and its leaders had not done nearly enough to justify the Black Marxists' faith in them. A case in point was the CIO's failure to organize Black workers, the majority of whom were either agricultural or female domestic laborers. The CIO declared share-croppers impossible to organize, despite evidence to the contrary in the form of the Southern Tenant Farmers Union, which the labor federation refused to assist. The NNC would receive no CIO aid in its efforts to unionize Black women in domestic service. In both cases the purported reason was that "progressive" union leaders did not want to antagonize white southern workers. If the earlier "industrial revolution" had produced cotton plantation slavery, the more recent one consisting of mass trade unionism had ushered in the "underclass"—remnants of the destitute Black working poor left virtually as a class unto itself by the merger of the white industrial working class and the larger white middle class. The American institution of Jim Crow, together with colonialism in the global South, emerged from the epic struggles of the Great Depression virtually intact and largely unfazed.[15]

In contrast, the race-based movement Bunche had once dismissed as "black chauvinism" proved a more viable long-term vehicle for change. The worldwide struggle Bunche forecast did materialize, but not in the form he assumed it would take. Colonialism's demise was attributable not to the class struggle in Europe and North America conceived by Marx—the revolution by what Bunche termed the "dominant populations of the world." Instead, the "subject peoples" with whom Pan-Africanism had sought alliance succeeded in freeing themselves within decades of Bunche's pronouncement that they were too weak to play any meaningful role in world history. In turn, the US-based civil rights movement of the 1950s and 1960s would be stimulated by the rural, largely agricultural African American population of the South rather than the urban, industrial workers of the North. There seemed to be some truth to "the not very consistent myth" of Pan-Africanism after all, as the next wave of Black radicalism emanated from that source.[16]

Half a century after Marx declared, "Labour cannot emancipate itself in the white skin where in the black it is branded," his followers put an end to such illusions on the eve of mass unionism in the United States, marking a watershed for white industrial workers. The radicalism of this generation of Black freedom movement leaders would lift with the Depression, as they severed their ties with working-class politics and buried the memory of their socialism. Bunche moved on to a career in diplomacy, becoming the first Black US ambassador to the United Nations. Davis turned his attention to writing an African American reference book. Harris took a position at the University of Chicago. In the end, even his erstwhile rivals agreed that Du Bois had been right: Black abolitionism needed to forge ahead without these ostensible class allies. His understanding of the foundational role of race in the determination of class could not be so easily dismissed, nor could its implications for the new slavery. It would be Du Bois's ideas outlined in *Black Reconstruction* that stood the test of time, while Harris would later repudiate the views he had once expressed so dogmatically.[17]

The Enslaved as the "Ultimate Exploited"

Black Reconstruction begins with an unexpected question: "What did it mean to be a slave?" Du Bois explains that it was neither a question of cruel treatment nor "the absolute negation of human rights." It was not a matter of the length of the workday nor the malnutrition from which the enslaved suffered. It was not "merely a matter of name" either. Slavery for African Americans was in part "the enforced personal feeling of inferiority." It was, first of all, about racial subordination, "the calling of another Master," "the submergence below the arbitrary will of any sort of individual." The position of enslaved workers could not in any sense be compared with that of white industrial workers in Europe or America, however bad their conditions. Enslavement was surely about standards of living and the act of being bought and sold, but it was also much more than that. "Above all, we must remember the black worker was the ultimate exploited; that he formed that mass of labor which had neither wish nor power to escape from the labor status, in order to directly exploit other laborers, or indirectly, by alliance with capital, to share in their exploitation."[18]

Du Bois signals that he is taking the view of the enslaved themselves. He is not concerned with how slavery is defined from the standpoint of the law or the abstract theoretical realm of political economy, including Marxian. He asks instead what it feels like to the enslaved. Black abolitionism must have its own political economy, its own ethics, and its own perspective on the inadequacies of the law. To an extent, Du Bois anticipates later bodies of thought such as critical race theory. He is calling out any uncritical acceptance of the ideology of colonialism in all its ramifications. He wants the doctrine of Black abolitionists to be rooted in the experience of the oppressed.

By implication, Du Bois is also asking whether their conditions feel like enslavement to the Black workers of his day. Du Bois concludes that they must and that slavery's "analogue today is the yellow, brown and black laborer in China and India, in Africa, in the forests of the Amazon." He continues:

That dark and vast sea of human labor in China and India, the South Seas and all Africa; in the West Indies and Central America and in the United States—that great majority of mankind, on whose bent and broken backs rest today the founding stones of modern industry—shares a common destiny; it is despised and rejected by race and color; paid a wage below the level of decent living; driven, beaten, prisoned and enslaved in all but name; spawning the world's raw material and luxury—cotton, wool, coffee, tea, cocoa, palm oil, fibers, spices, rubber, silks, lumber, copper, gold, diamonds, leather—how shall we end the list and where? All these are gathered up at prices lowest of the low, manufactured, transformed and transported at fabulous gains; and the resultant wealth is distributed and displayed and made the basis of world power and universal dominion and armed arrogance in London and Paris, Berlin and Rome, New York and Rio de Janeiro.[19]

Du Bois alerts us that we have seen this process before: the ruthless exploitation of a virtually or actually enslaved workforce to supply the conveniences and extravagances of industrial societies. The brutal oppression began, after all, in the early modern period for the sake of precious metals, three hot beverages, a sweetener, a clothing dye, the leaves of a plant that could be smoked, a material for inexpensive clothing, and another for a luxury cloth. Over time, this merciless and relentless coercion of labor encompassed more commodities in perpetually growing amounts—perhaps none more important than the rubber needed to launch the *tour de monde* of the automobile. The plethora of raw materials included vegetable oils and important supplements to domestic metal and mineral production, the rare and the precious alongside the common and widely dispersed. In each case, there was an individual, even idiosyncratic reason that industrial society wanted the particular product of a labor-intensive process delegated to an expanding class of human beings sacrificed to that purpose. That justification was enough to seek the commodity at any cost—always at someone else's expense, the product of someone else's pain, suffering, deprivation, and, ultimately, slave labor. It did not matter to what uses the products were put or how indispensable they were to those who oversaw their production and distribution. If the consumers of industrial societies wanted them, the market would stop at nothing to obtain these objects of desire. There was a class of people to do the necessary work, and moral scruples did not sufficiently trouble these evolving civil societies, based on individual liberty, to preclude the methods used to extract labor.[20]

Du Bois discerns the common purpose: the wealthy industrial societies of the colonial powers wish to acquire the goods and services they cannot produce for themselves and do not want to pay fair value for. It began, of course, with the raw materials that fed the factories of Europe and North America, including the cotton that enslaved African Americans provided to the nascent textile mills that launched the Industrial Revolution. As Du Bois details, the underlying basis of both the old slavery and the new had grown exponentially in the century since then. From the start, European colonial powers had not felt morally compelled to safeguard the same conditions for nonwhite workers in their colonies as for white workers at home. The colonialists themselves affirmed as much. Surveying centuries of colonialism, one of Britain's most experienced imperial administrators, Sir Hugh Clifford, concluded in a memorandum for Britain's Colonial Office, "Agricultural enterprises conducted upon any really large scale under European management and supervision have found that, in order to maintain a regular labour force of sufficient strength and reliability to meet their requirements, recourse must be had to some organized system of immigration from without the areas in which the agricultural operations in question are being carried on, or, failing that, to some form of more or less open compulsion." By 1920, the centuries-long history of colonialism clearly demonstrated that "the very existence of these European agricultural enterprises undertaken on a large scale in the Tropics, is shown to be dependent upon a regular and adequate supply of *immigrant* labour—that is to say, upon highly artificial conditions." By "immigrant labor," Clifford meant the most overt forced labor of Africans and Asians—slaves, coolies, and indentured and contract workers brought from a distance.[21]

The earliest modern roots of the system lay in the sugar plantations of Italy's Mediterranean colonies. Termed the "sugar-slave complex" by historians, this form of agriculture—which involved backbreaking labor and large capital investments—made use of a workforce comprising mainly Europeans alongside a small number of Africans. Initially, it remained a regional economy. It spread first to the islands off the coast of Africa claimed by Portugal and, later, other European powers; eventually, it reached the colonial possessions in the Caribbean dominated by Britain and France. As this expansion occurred, an epochal transformation took place: the local labor supply in the east Atlantic paved the way for a transatlantic slave trade exclusively in Africans. This fundamental alteration in the workforce gave modernity's vast empire of commercial plantation slavery its characteristic racial form.[22]

Du Bois is also concerned with what came after the demise of this Atlantic world slavery. In his judgment, agrarian servitude remained a fixture in the Caribbean and North and South America, taking the form of sharecropping, tenancy, and indentured servitude. He is equally alarmed by what Clifford was alluding to: Europe's global empire was guided by a policy sanctioning the use of forced labor on an even larger scale. Plantations were established with enslaved labor in the Americas and with indentured and contract labor in Indonesia, Malaysia, Sri Lanka, India, and large parts of Africa. Indentured Indians and Chinese peasants were transported to the Americas, to Africa, and across Asia to work the plantations and the extractive industries established there. To the long-standing practice of exploiting peoples and their land, European colonialism added the innovation of transporting millions of people to other territories to exploit them on a scale that would never be matched.[23]

Clifford did not include extractive industries in his consideration, but Du Bois realized that precisely the same circumstances applied. He observes that it was not simply agricultural undertakings that hewed to the pattern; colonial enterprises of all descriptions meant slave labor or its close "analogue." He was enough of a student of history to know that this bondage was not new. From ancient times, human society relied on unfree workers to accomplish its most labor-intensive feats— anticipating the solution adopted by the British across much of their territory in Africa. Even confining the inquiry to the modern era amply confirms industry's dependence on the unfree status of a large segment of the workforce. Two of the quintessentially modern systems of bondage were spread across vast geographic expanses—slavery in the Americas and eastern European serfdom—and a significant component of each was devoted to industrial purposes. Although American slavery is largely identified with plantation or agrarian production, in its earliest stages, it was at least as much about mining. Before the enslaved became almost exclusively Africans and their descendants, indigenous peoples were caught up in the industrial extraction of precious metals and minerals. In Brazil, more than half of all Africans imported in the first half of the eighteenth century and a third in the second half were destined for mining operations. What Herbert Klein calls this "entirely new type of slave economy" spread to Spanish colonies as well.[24]

Slavery also permeated the larger economy, as the enslaved dominated the skilled crafts and were, according to Klein, "spread widely through the cities and rural areas of the nation engaged in every possible type of economic activity." Enslaved men and women were prominent in the workshops of towns and were strongly represented on the docks that facilitated global trade. Joan Casanovas notes that they worked alongside free workers in "all branches of the urban economy, often doing the same tasks." North American slaves in the colonial period exhibited a range of occupations, "from printing to mill work," according to Ira Berlin; they formed a significant component of urban "skilled workers" and were often owned by their fellow artisans. Early iron factories constituted an important center of the colonial American slave economy, as their forges and furnaces were fed by highly skilled enslaved people. In the antebellum period, historian Jacqueline Jones writes, the largest plantations featured their own workshops where men labored, while women "formed the bulk of the agricultural labor force." When factory production was introduced to the South, it too featured slave labor, including the famed Tredegar ironworks in Richmond, Virginia— that bulwark of the Confederacy central to Du Bois's purpose in *Black Reconstruction*.[25]

Du Bois keeps all this history in mind as he contemplates the problem of emancipation in the Americas resulting from four centuries of racial colonialism. He concludes that what changed was the name. Ashamed of their own behavior, enslavers no longer called it *slavery*, attempting to disguise it from the world and possibly from themselves. They refused to listen to what either the workers themselves or Black abolitionists had to say. Du Bois is aware of the manifold reasons he cannot trust the canonical definition of slavery as newly enshrined in international law enacted by European colonialism pursuing racist ends.

When the US Supreme Court judged debt peonage to be tantamount to slavery in *Bailey v. Alabama*, famed liberal jurist Oliver Wendell Holmes wrote a dissenting opinion defending the institution of debt peonage as "a perfectly fair and proper contract," pronouncing that he could "see no reason why the State should not throw its weight" behind it. Otherwise, "contracts for labor" would be invalid, which would be "as great a misfortune for the laborer as for the man that employed him," and it would do material harm to workers in the North. Holmes's dissent embodied the ostensibly colorblind new antislavery taking hold. It was disingenuous to deny African Americans the protection of the law on the pretext that it might hurt white workers—and subsequent history confirmed that no such harm would result. Holmes completely ignored that the labor contract for white workers in the North protected them, while the corresponding legal agreement for Black workers in the South enslaved them. Nor did he acknowledge that African Americans were the main victims of debt peonage and other manifestations of the new slavery. The failure to protect them only exposed others to risk as well. This refusal to recognize the impact of racism, a harbinger of the new antislavery, sanctioned the new slavery for African Americans as effectively as the Forced Labour Convention would for Africans.[26]

Du Bois, however, does not particularly care what slaveholders considered to be slavery; what matters to him is what it meant from the standpoint of the enslaved past and present. Though he traces the origins of the new slavery to its roots in the system abolished by the Civil War, Du Bois does not derive his understanding from antebellum American law. The meaning of slavery is not a question of what the law specifies, as he well knows from Douglass. For Du Bois, slavery is not fundamentally a question of legal status. He comprehends quite well from experience that law and social practice can be very different, and he is more concerned with the real circumstances of Black workers. To him, identifying the essence of slavery requires a deeper level of analysis than the law; it consists in the conditions experienced by the enslaved, which include the lowest levels of material remuneration for labor in the world. And that impoverishment is the result of the maximum allowable coercion directed against the worker. Du Bois is not concerned with the criteria to judge which worker qualifies as being subjected to enslavement, forced labor, or just very bad conditions of standard wage labor. The real problem lies much deeper than the name for this contemporary iteration of age-old servitude.

It comes down to one consideration before any other: the condition of being the "ultimate exploited." That was true under the system of antebellum racial slavery, and it was still true when he wrote *Black Reconstruction.* For Du Bois, the enslaved in antebellum America were not the only or the last people to occupy the position of the "ultimate exploited." His definition of slavery in those terms means that anyone subjected to that status is, for all practical, moral, and political purposes, enslaved because they fall at the far end of the spectrum of labor exploitation. This "ultimate" exploitation is enforced by society on behalf of the employer, whatever it is called and however it might be legally disguised. Slavery, then, is not a legal status as understood for millennia. In a world dominated by racism, it becomes a state inseparable from the racial structuring of class because it is built on top of it. It is a condition that must be understood through the lens of how racism has impacted the world and Black workers. When Du Bois writes that the analogue of antebellum slavery "today is the yellow, brown and black laborer in China and India, in Africa, in the forests of the Amazon," he directly invokes the Slavery Convention of 1926, which called on its signatories to abolish "conditions analogous to slavery." He makes it clear that all forms of forced labor employed by the colonial powers are analogous to slavery and, by the admission of the treaty's framers, they have an obligation to abolish them.[27]

In Du Bois's estimation, Douglass was proved right: even if the legal form of ownership is abolished, a Black worker can still be converted from the property of an individual to the "slave of society." It only requires that the worker still be subject to the conditions of the "ultimate exploited." Wherever Du Bois looks in the Black world, that is precisely what he observes, consonant with the colonial powers' purposes in employing Black and brown people to furnish them with the goods and services they want at a price they determine. To Du Bois, that represents a continuation of the spirit, if not the name, of slavery. It does not matter what white authorities call it. To the Black people forced into this labor, it is a continuation of their bondage. And any theoretical understanding that defines it otherwise is justifying the exploitation of Black people—denying them the allyship of the antislavery movement, which was, at the time, the only major historical interracial movement for Black freedom.

For Du Bois, the essential context of the new slavery is not about any form, either legal or economic. Rather, it is about conditions and the results of those conditions for both the worker and the employer. It comes down to one simple test: can employers do to white workers what they can to Black? If not, what Black workers endure is racial slavery. In Du Bois's analysis, the question of the boundaries of slavery disappears into the realities of racism. The new slavery is a form of racial slavery because it involves the use of *socially enforced difference* (in this case, race) as an instrument for the exploitation of labor that would be impossible in its absence. Slavery in the age of imperialism is necessarily racial because racism is the dominant form of socially enforced difference.

Du Bois's definition of the new slavery involves employers of any kind taking advantage of racism to treat their workers of color in a way that is impermissible for their white counterparts. Slavery is determined any time racism is used to exploit Black workers beyond what is categorically acceptable for their white counterparts. To Du Bois, it is that last part—exploitation above and beyond what is normally inflicted on white workers—that marks the conditions as slavery. There was no getting around the fact that the worst treatment, the greatest use of force, and the least remuneration were all reserved for Black workers. European colonial powers were using race to exploit workers of color. From the Manchester factory hands that Friedrich Engels so poignantly described to the white sharecroppers of the post-Reconstruction American South, European workers and their descendants in North America faced conditions that approached and at times matched in sheer brutality those found among their non-European counterparts. But Du Bois still discerns an all-important difference that determines the circumstances of Black workers as slavery.[28]

The "Color Caste" behind the New Slavery

Du Bois generalizes the understanding of Padmore and other Black abolitionists in conceiving a second essential condition of racial slavery. The individual Black enslaved worker's experience is personal and tangible. But the new slavery, like the old, is transnational and not local; it is built on the edifice of colonialism as the systemic racism endemic to the world economy. It is no accident that the slavery that ushered in capitalism was racial, nor that it remained so even after the era of emancipation. A categorical understanding of race as social difference requires not an ad hoc explanation based on historical contingencies. It does not matter what happens in any particular colony—or in the states of the US South—because the enslavement of Black workers occurs in the context of *global* white supremacy.

Historians have highlighted the significant differences across racial slavery's transnational reach, including the peculiarities that made slavery in the southern United States, as David Brion Davis puts it, "the ultimate form of inhuman bondage" and a "shining anomaly." And yet, again in Davis's words, it "was an institution common to virtually all New World colonies," being "the joint creation of the maritime powers of Europe." Colonialism extended the racial demarcation within the Atlantic world across the African continent as it partly merged with the Indian Ocean world, transforming the Black Atlantic into the Black world. That essential context, as Du Bois's Black abolitionist definition of slavery emphasizes, gave meaning to the new slavery of the twentieth century whether in the Americas or in Africa.[29]

If enslavement, for its victims, involved material deprivation and overwork, what permitted some people to enforce that condition on others? What allowed the codification of differential standards of freedom for white as opposed to Black and brown workers? What gave colonial powers the license to enslave Black workers for the production of raw materials in the twentieth century, just as it had done in previous ones? Or, as Douglass put it, what lay behind the privilege of determining *where, at what, when,* and *for what* Black workers would be forced to labor? Du Bois is interested in what enabled the League of Nations, supported by the British Anti-Slavery Society, to sanction forced labor for workers of color in the name of banning it. He knows it comes down to the same causes that allowed the United States to write racial slavery into its founding constitution and maintain the institution for nearly a century. Du Bois solves this conundrum by looking not at individual cases but at the totality of the different conditions of Black workers and their white counterparts, the same approach taken by Cyril Briggs and George Padmore.

The first essential condition is what we now call systemic racism, or, as Du Bois puts it, human beings "despised and rejected by race and color." The enslaved have no role in the laws and social practices that enforce their slavery, but it is not accurate to say that the enslavers alone are responsible. Those who actively aid the slave owners or simply give their tacit consent through silence are indispensable to the functioning of all forms of slavery, so long as they contribute to the systemic conditions in which it takes root. The new slavery was, in Du Bois's estimation, above all the new *racial* slavery, meaning that it was not truly new. Du Bois traces it back to the process of emancipation and what followed:

> The slave went free; stood a brief moment in the sun; then moved back again toward slavery. The whole weight of America was thrown to color caste. The colored world went down before England, France, Germany, Russia, Italy and America. A new slavery arose. The upward moving of white labor was betrayed into wars for profit based on color caste. Democracy died save in the hearts of black folk.
>
> Indeed, the plight of the white working class throughout the world today is directly traceable to Negro slavery in America, on which modern commerce and industry was founded, and which persisted to threaten free labor until it was partially overthrown in 1863.[30]

For Du Bois, the essential context manifests itself in the concrete conditions of global racism. Du Bois replaces the standard notion of class with the term *caste*—borrowed from an entirely different and seemingly culture-bound context—and attaches the adjective *color* to emphasize its racial character (thereby leaving room to extend his analysis to forms of caste that are not racial). He does so to emphasize that the notion of class obscures the condition that the circumstances that bind workers of color in the global context of colonialism are hereditary, historically entrenched, society-wide, and independent of the law. As has always been true of racial slavery, to be enslaved constitutes a heritable, societally determined status—one the victim is born into. The taken-for-granted nature of racism makes it easy to ignore the slavery of

Black people, including on the part of both purported abolitionists and alleged class allies.

Du Bois, by this stage, is no longer so impressed by "white labor." He concedes that some of the worst off among white workers have sporadically—and at their finest, heroically—made common cause with those whose degradation helped secure their ascent. But he does not perceive that either the shared suffering or the exceptional principled politics has bridged the chasm between the two components of the world's disunited workers, a divide at once material and political. Sharecropping, for instance, constituted a local, temporary, and exceptional condition for whites that, like contemporaneous eastern European serfdom, had no categorical implications for all white people or for the existence of race globally. Because it was not a racially based status for its white victims, both individuals and the class of workers collectively had a means of escape that did not exist for their Black counterparts. Refugees from eastern European serfdom could take their place in the American industrial proletariat as it was merging into the middle class, not as "in between peoples" but as beneficiaries of the privileges of whiteness. It was this process that also allowed former white sharecroppers to lose themselves in the westward migration, however long it took. Du Bois perceives a *categorical* movement toward free labor for white workers that is not true for Black. Under the economic, political, legal, and social conditions of the South, the Black sharecropping that so quickly degenerates into debt peonage represents a problem of a fundamentally different order.[31]

Du Bois judges the dominance of race over class to be of the same essential nature under European colonialism in Africa. His conclusion would be perfectly illustrated a few years later as the British ruthlessly suppressed the 1940 strike of Katwishi Chowa—the very man who called himself a "slave"—and his fellow mine workers in Zambia's resource-rich copper belt. The African workers demanded wages of more than ten times their actual rate of pay. That is, they asked to be remunerated on the same scale as the European workers who had just concluded a successful strike of their own. So unthinkable was this demand that it was not even acknowledged by the commission formed to investigate the labor action. Above all, mining corporations sought to avoid paying Africans the same wages as Europeans, even at the cost of depriving Europeans of a lucrative source of employment in an avowedly white supremacist society.[32]

Colonial workers continually pressed up against the "colour bar" in industry, and imperial authorities, joined by privileged white workers, beat them down. Zambia's secretary for native affairs reported that during a meeting of strikers, the African workers agreed that "the Europeans were lazy and did not know the work." The miners believed the European "presence in the mine was entirely unnecessary." Another Black abolitionist then based in the United States attempted to make that conviction clear to the guardians of British imperial interests. The earnest twenty-six-year-old son of a prominent Kikuyu traditional leader, Mbiyu Koinange had earned a bachelor's degree from Ohio Wesleyan University and was later a student at Cambridge. He appalled staffers at the Colonial Office by warning them that Africans "have a general ambition to rise and become something other and higher than merely unskilled laborers." But non-Europeans were not allowed to do so, or if they were, only on the condition that their wages did not permit a "European standard of living." The phenomenon Koinange pointed out was familiar to officials. A confidential British colonial report warned ominously:

The African workers often find themselves performing skilled jobs under the perfunctory supervision of Europeans who know less of the work than those they supervise and who draw several times the amount of pay received by themselves. Frequently in the case of piece work the size of the cheque received by the European miner depends on the degree of efficiency and industry of the African workers under him. It is true the African workers receive a proportion of the extra pay by way of bonus or unofficial tips but they feel that the European is being paid not for what he does himself but for what the African workers themselves do. Again they are aware that if they were given the necessary training they could efficiently perform some of the more skilled work from which they are at present debarred. . . . They know in fact that they are artificially being held in a subservient position by the white man. They have been accustomed to acquiesce in the principle of might being right and to being "hewers of wood and drawers of water" for their European masters but are now beginning to realise how much some Europeans, especially the inefficient ones, are dependent on them and to realize their power. This feeling is not at present very articulate but it is growing and it is dangerous.[33]

In Du Bois's distinctly non-Marxist political economy, "unskilled labor" is a euphemism for racialized labor. African workers came cheaply only *because* they were so skilled. This counterintuitive principle held true even in the most capitalized production sectors, such as the gold mines of South Africa's Rand. African workers replaced drills to break up rock on the narrower reefs, making it possible to engage in operations where it otherwise would have been unprofitable. African labor in the mines provided material advantages, as the workers recovered more gold than the most advanced technology of the day. At various times and places, African workers constructed their own on-site housing, secured and prepared their food, fashioned and maintained their tools, and taught one another the required skills to do the work. The same broadly skilled African labor played a key role not only on the plantations of the Americas but also in the metallurgy industry. Subsequent scholarship corroborated the understanding of twentieth-century Black abolitionism on this point. Joseph Miller writes, "Knowledge of livestock handling, agricultural techniques, metallurgical and other artisan skills, and hunting were the attributes by which masters recognized the human property they had purchased by their commercial value." Frederick Knight emphasizes that "craft" skills were as much a part of the African knowledge system "mobilized" by the "Anglo-American colonial project" as agricultural expertise.[34]

Nonagricultural know-how was equally crucial to Anglo-African colonialism. African laborers in the mines required a panoply of skills and knowledge. Mining capitalists in colonial Africa complained that employing European workers in place of African would result not only in higher wages but also in a loss of skill in the workforce. Zimbabwean mines could easily replace skilled white workers with Black, but the reverse was never the case. African workers were a more economical option than the technology employed in contemporary mining operations, and their skilled labor recovered more gold than such machinery, as attested by South African mining magnate Sir George Farrar. The need for substantial capital investments in machinery and other fixed costs did not obviate the demand for skilled labor in this labor-intensive production process, as evident from the earliest days of sugar production.[35]

As Africans brought the requisite knowledge for rice cultivation to the Americas, their productive knowledge also made coffee, tea, and even rubber production possible in Africa. A British official remarked that "experienced tappers and primers come almost within the category of skilled labour"—a concession of no small import in East Africa, where "skilled labour" served as a euphemism for white labor. African knowledge was also clearly responsible for independent African food and cash crop production, as it was a prerequisite for plantation production in Africa and in the Americas.[36]

While historians and economists have remarked on the agricultural knowledge of Africans, Du Boisian political economy lays the groundwork for even more far-reaching conclusions. The full extent of their role goes much further, and their contributions did not begin and end with agriculture. Crucial to the question of migrant labor that occupied Du Bois and Padmore, the role of African productive knowledge did not end on arrival at industrial sites. African male migrant workers brought much of the requisite productive knowledge of European capitalist enterprise with them, including the incredible adaptability and resourcefulness of the small cultivator. So dependent on this African knowledge economy did colonialism become that its overseers could complacently lament the alleged inefficiency of the production regime while doing little to alter it and continuing to export the vital raw materials on which industry relied, particularly those judged "strategically important," as Joseph Inikori notes.[37]

The skills and knowledge of African workers proved indispensable before they employed them in the myriad on-the-job tasks they undertook at industrial sites. The migrant labor system was itself a testament to the dependence of European colonialism on African knowledge systems. Much as slavery in the Americas rested in part on the ability of the enslaved to produce their own subsistence needs, male migrant labor depended on the productive and reproductive labor of women in rural areas. The system presupposed men's ability to migrate on their own, largely outside the purview of the colonial state or European employers. Africans' migration was possible because of their ability to live off the

141

land, including obtaining support from other African communities, and to traverse long distances to places of employment on their own, before the establishment of infrastructure offered other options.[38]

The authorities watched in wonder, tempered by their characteristic callousness. A Ugandan official marveled, "These 100,000 annual migrants [from Burundi and Rwanda] constitute perhaps the most intractable feature of the present problem. Purposeful, silent, not readily to be deflected, they may be seen in groups on almost any day in the year on the south-western roads pressing relentlessly towards Buganda, reminiscent of nothing so much as a stream of ants." Officials confessed that they knew few details of these journeys, which often lasted for weeks and covered hundreds of miles over treacherous terrain. A committee of inquiry into the "labour situation" of British Uganda was so impressed by the tens of thousands of workers trekking from Belgian Rwanda and Burundi that it likened their epic journey across vast "expanses of empty and largely waterless country" to the Irish crossing the Atlantic in the nineteenth century. While the Irish migration was a one-time trip, African migrants traveled annually in two directions, leaving them exhausted, weak, and susceptible to disease.[39]

Du Bois considers this multilayered reality in making the case that African miners, African American sharecroppers, and Black workers across the world are enmeshed in a quintessentially modern form of racial slavery. Like Douglass, Du Bois concludes that this bondage cannot be defined by the master-slave relationship; it is about the exploitation of labor in the context of systemic racism. If the labor of Black and brown workers is not defined by its allegedly unskilled character, what explains the conditions they are forced to endure? European colonialism's dependence on race took root in the creation of divisions within the working class along racial lines. "Racial slavery in the Americas," Davis concludes, clearly echoing Du Bois, "widened the gap between slaves and descendants of slaves, in one castelike group, and a nonslave population that, despite their internal hierarchies, now appeared to be forever 'free.'" The enslaved were racially marked property, Robin Blackburn observes. That entailed the hereditary status that Orlando Patterson finds common to systems of slavery across time and space. As Douglass foretold, the Emancipation Proclamation settled almost nothing because it left race intact, so Du Bois must conclude that the bonds of race that once held people of African descent in slavery in the Americas remain intact.[40]

In his redefinition of slavery from a Black abolitionist standpoint, Du Bois also realizes that the racial slavery of the Americas is rooted in settler colonialism. Inikori explains why European capitalists preferred to generate their colonial produce with African labor in the Americas rather than in Africa: "By far the most important of these factors was the colonization of the Americas, the destruction of the indigenous populations and polities, and appropriation of the vast natural resources by the economic and political entrepreneurs of Western Europe." The land was the key natural resource, and controlling it was paramount to any plantation-based economy. The basis of settler colonialism, the impetus and consequences of European colonization of the Americas, consisted in the displacement of indigenous peoples. But that appropriated land was inseparable from the slave labor that would work it.[41]

A key principle of twentieth-century Black abolitionism, particularly as expounded by Du Bois, consists in the contention that the racial division of the land was also at the heart of European colonialism in parts of Africa. Du Bois was far from alone in this realization. None put the question more forcefully than Koinange in his impassioned appeal to British prime minister Ramsay MacDonald in 1933 "on behalf of the African youth, whom I love so dearly." Koinange might have expected a sympathetic hearing, like Du Bois, counting on the liberal reputation of the Labour Party. He was perhaps familiar with the renowned reformer's words from three decades earlier, when MacDonald wrote, "our Imperial history . . . we read with but little pleasure now," as it makes "a sorry comment on the white man's civilisation." MacDonald insisted that "the expression 'British' . . . implies something more than a mere description of racial or national origin . . . carry[ing] to our minds certain qualities of justice, honour, and administration." "The task of the democratic parties of the Empire," declared the man who would lead Britain in the crucial years 1929–1935, changing the shape of Western society through ushering in the welfare state, "is to establish guarantees that this moral quality will be preserved untainted." Western democracies like Britain must safeguard "certain axioms regarding human liberty and the administration of justice," none more important than the proposition that "no man can be a slave under the British flag."[42]

Koinange sought to alert this self-professed champion of human liberty to several cases of "the removal" of Africans "from their land." He explained the significance of the matter: "Among the natives of Kenya it is the common belief that the land is the mother of all the inhabitants of the earth and that without the land no living creature can exist." The "dreadful problems that exist in Africa today"—among them gross inequality, starvation, depopulation, and slavery—began when the "land was seized for the private possession of the white man." The future Kenyan minister and author of the influential 1955 book *The People of Kenya Speak for Themselves* lamented, "the settler took all the land"—or at least a large portion of it—to the point that "the natives at the present time very naturally look upon the coming of the whites to their country as the cause of their misfortunes." From the beginning, historian Jonathan Crush details, Swazi rulers understood that the establishment of reserves meant "to place us in the position of kaffirs to the whites." Koinange asked MacDonald to end this iniquitous policy afflicting a large portion of the African continent. The Colonial Office staffers with whom the letter was unceremoniously deposited indignantly dismissed it as "'Negro Worker' stuff," referencing Padmore's proscribed publication and the challenge it posed to British rule.[43]

Here again, Black abolitionists could point to British colonial officials' own words as backup. Two years later, Frederick Lugard denounced the land policy in Kenya in even more strident terms. In a confidential note to the Colonial Office, he surveyed the aftermath of British rule in East Africa, which he had done so much to advance, striking at the very cornerstone of its settler colonialism. He bluntly characterized British policy there: "land in private or communal ownership" was "compulsorily expropriated by the State . . . in order that ownership may be transferred to a third party on racial grounds." Lugard was not the only architect of empire to become uncomfortable with colonialism's racial organization as its demise loomed on the horizon. Donald Cameron, governor of British Tanzania in the late 1920s, reported that his counterpart in Kenya aimed to turn East Africa into "a great White State," "a country with dominant Whites," in pursuance of which "we must put our natives into Reserves." He used the British colonial name—reserves—for the rural "African locations" established principally in South Africa, Zimbabwe, Zambia, and Kenya. By the end of World

War II, a decade after MacDonald's death, his former party no longer believed it could continue to ignore the wrongs cited by Koinange. Its Advisory Committee on Imperial Questions admonished in a confidential memorandum in 1946, "It is a perpetual reproach to this country that our friends and enemies, and above all our subject peoples, the Africans themselves should be able to accuse us of having reserved the lands for white settlement only, while there is acute hunger among Africans. This country cannot go to any discussion of colonial policy, whether with our allies, or with colonial peoples, with clean hands, so long as this policy of reservation continues."[44]

British policy sought to ensure that the division between Europeans and Africans permeated most of colonial society, but it began with the land, and this usurpation had profound consequences for African workers. Buttressing the connection Du Bois and Koinange drew to settler colonialism, a land commission in British Zambia pronounced, "The Territory in which [African] tribes live, is a country where Europeans rule and to which Europeans have come intending to live and settle." Given European colonial rule, "it is a country in which white and black will have to live side by side, separated socially and politically." An undersecretary of state in the British Colonial Office declared that "any system of native peasant tenure in the Highlands [the part of Kenya where British settlers preferred to live] would be inconsistent with [the] policy" of "reserving the Highlands for European occupation." "It follows," he explained, "that the only permissible relation between European and native in the Highlands is that of master and servant." Land policy was not meant to simply reserve productive tracts of land for European ownership; it was also intended to provide servile labor to work there. "Reserving" Kenya's Highlands "for European occupation" did not mean emptying the region of Africans. For every European in the Highlands there were ten Africans, but they had no landownership rights and were rendered tenants ("squatters" in colonial parlance), subject to a minimum of 180 days and a theoretical maximum of 270 days per year of unpaid labor for the landowner. It was difficult to separate the issue of land from the creation of unfree workers. This was true not only for the Africans converted into squatters and tenants but also for those who were removed, as Koinange so bitterly complained, to facilitate the expansion of the new slavery.[45]

From the standpoint of Black abolitionism, the rise of the new slavery in Africa depended on land policy that deprived Africans of the ability to support themselves through subsistence production, reestablishing the battleground of the ambiguous US emancipation to which Thaddeus Stevens objected. As Padmore documented, the demand for forced labor would be heaviest in the colonies with the largest European settler populations—especially South Africa, Zimbabwe, Zambia, and Kenya. Their British administrations divided these territories into the parts open to European development and the "reserves," where such enterprise was off-limits. The former often included the most fertile areas, and their populations might have to be moved. These alienated territories could be parceled up and sold to corporations or individuals, or they could be set aside for later allocation. The reserves, critics charged, were often located in the least fertile or most remote territories—land the Europeans were least desirous of. The Zambian Native Reserves Commission observed, "The great majority of [the reserves'] native inhabitants live along the banks of rivers in country of low altitude where there is little temptation for Europeans to settle. Nor is there likelihood, as far as we can discover, of it being a locality of mining development." The British colonial regime made it illegal or otherwise untenable for Africans to reside anywhere other than the reserves, outside of which they could be considered temporary residents subject to eviction unless they were under contract to a European employer or landowner. The reserve policy reached its peak in South Africa after 1948, but its history extended back a century earlier. Black abolitionists like Padmore had exposed this system, which created a working class dependent on perpetual enforced migration and constituted the heart of what came to be known as *apartheid*.[46]

Just as important from the standpoint of Black abolitionism, the effects spilled over colonial borders into neighboring countries, both indexing and determining the new slavery as transnational. Lesotho, Swaziland, and Botswana were all absorbed into the South African orbit as sources of migrant labor, joining Mozambique and Namibia. Malawians made their way in smaller numbers to the Rand mines and more frequently to Zimbabwe and Zambia. Land policy played a role in these colonies as well. British Swaziland established its own reserves, against the spirited resistance of the population. When British rule extended to Malawi in the last decade of the nineteenth century, part of its populace was compelled "to enter into agreements . . . by which in return for the right to remain upon the land the tenant agreed to work for a certain period during the planting season of the year." As a memorandum by the colony's governor put it, although the "tenants" had been "on the land at the time of its purchase by the European proprietor," the British presumed their right to seize Africans' land and turn them into a bound labor force. Colonial authorities reported, "What the landlords wanted was not rent but work." The period of such labor was fixed at "one or two months during the planting season" but could be as long as six months. The work did not necessarily have to take place where the laborers lived, at times entailing "travel [of] many miles daily to and from their tasks" or even to distant locales for the whole of the corvée period. Jonathan Crush notes that "Swazi chiefs and people . . . rejected the whole principle of tenancy," which nevertheless gained a significant hold in Swaziland as it did in Malawi.[47]

Black abolitionists recognized that such control over the movement of Black workers, a holdover from the Atlantic world slavery of an earlier epoch, required measures in evidence in both periods. Padmore zeroed in on the existence in some colonies, including pre-apartheid British South Africa, of pass laws enslaved African Americans would have readily recognized. These measures enforcing the reserve system sought to create a regime in which every non-European had to carry an identity document, amounting to an internal passport, at all times. Historian Martin Chanock notes that the master and servant acts, along with "the pass system for African workers and the policy of influx control for urban areas," created "an ecology of coercive laws designed to limit the numbers of permanent African residents in towns and cities."[48]

Pass systems were a prime example of the coercive instruments of labor and racial control that linked the old slavery in the Americas to the new slavery in Africa. A Kenyan colonial administrator claimed in 1927 that "registration is not a labour measure" but one aimed "to develop a conception of individuality and stability." The problem it addressed, he insisted, was that "under the Pax Britannica [the African worker] can wander anywhere, changing his name and his identity with each contract lest he dislike it and wish to break it, and with each offence against the law, lest more than one be proved. To establish identity, and stabilize individuality is the real administrative problem which after various experiments has in Kenya found its solution in a registration system which claimed to be far less harassing to the native than the South African pass system based on the same necessity."The British Empire's leading labor expert in the 1930s echoed those sentiments, remarking that without a pass system of some kind, "control or supervision naturally remains impossible. . . . It further greatly prejudices any effort to encourage repatriation"—that is, the requirement that Africans return to the reserves or rural areas following stints in European employment.[49]

Du Bois agrees with Padmore that colonialism established oppressive conditions for migrant African workers that demarcated them from their European counterparts. Rather than being allowed to concentrate in urban areas like the free European proletariat, Black workers were moved around as it suited racial colonialism, starting with the Atlantic slave trade. In the new slavery of the twentieth century, the imperial consensus was that the best solution to the potential problem of African workers' concentration in cities was "repatriation to rural areas—the reserves—of all but the minimum required in towns." "In the reserves," according to the British governor of Kenya, "the children have a very definite place in the tribal organization. The various ceremonies of their lives are largely based on discipline and self-control." When justifying the use of child labor, such as on the tea estates of Malawi, British imperial officials became more candid: "Were they not so employed they would doubtless be less wholesomely occupied in their insanitary villages." Authorities seemed convinced that Africans raised on the reserves made for a more exploitable workforce.[50]

Padmore observed that, despite the special notoriety of its postindependence South African form, British colonial policy throughout a significant portion of its east, central, and southern African empire was constructed on somewhat the same basis. This foundational British strategy long predated apartheid, which merely formalized the reserve policy, decreeing that Black South Africans could only be residents or citizens of the so-called Bantustans and eventually appending the legal fiction that these African "homelands" constituted self-governing, independent nations.[51]

As Black abolitionists emphasized, the use of political rhetoric to mask racial oppression was hardly new. The US Constitution had transformed the declaration that "All men are created equal" into the institutionalization of slavery, the traces of which can never be removed from the original text. The Supreme Court's 1857 *Dred Scott* decision extended that exclusion by ruling that African Americans are not citizens and therefore not entitled to the rights conferred by that status. The South African regime joined the American in refusing citizenship to its Black inhabitants, a form of the social death—at least vis-à-vis the state—that Orlando Patterson discerns at the root of slavery. Though their legal, social, and political expressions could be and generally were quite different, the effects on African Americans and Black South Africans tended to be analogous.[52]

Padmore perceived that the racial and the transnational went hand in hand in colonial Africa. A principal manifestation of the new slavery in Africa, forced migration, took root in reserving urban areas as European racialized space. Land policy denied Africans the right to reside in cities and places of concentrated production—or anywhere outside the limits of the territories designated for them—unless they were there to work for an authorized employer. Given the colonial project's dependence on African workers, they would be needed wherever Europeans were found in Africa. Much of this labor that Africans were forced to do was, by its nature, transitory. Some of the first Africans to pass regularly through European population centers were porters, who "had to be housed near the townships while waiting during the period between the discharge and the receipt of loads." The Zambian administration believed such locations should be "within a reasonable distance of European settlements" but not so close as to be uncontrollable. Colonial authorities viewed Africans' unconstrained urban presence as a recipe for revolt, just as slaveholders in North America had been suspicious of clandestine gatherings of the enslaved. When their jobs were finished, workers were deported back to their "home district," since there would necessarily be "intervals of idleness."[53]

A decade after Padmore's scathing indictment, a colonial official in Zambia confessed that the "policy of encouraging the workers to return to their villages . . . is, in effect, a policy of segregation." Since seasonal migration remained necessary in the colonial economy, migratory labor patterns were still seen as indispensable—or at least convenient. Rates of migration were so high that in colonies such as Malawi, which served as virtual labor reserves for other territories hundreds of miles away, the male absentee rate was 50 percent. An anthropologist found some areas in Zambia where the proportion of males away at labor centers reached 80 percent.[54]

In the early 1930s the British Colonial Office succumbed to external pressure to investigate the "effect on labour" of its own version of apartheid in East Africa. For appearances' sake, it asked territorial administrations to "limit racial discrimination in the townships to the minimum." But it would not consider eliminating the racial basis of townships: "There can be no doubt that segregation must continue." In 1951 the Colonial Office still declared that it was "obvious [that] racially discriminatory legislation of this nature cannot be continued indefinitely without serious challenge," yet it acquiesced in the maintenance of pass laws, claiming that they would "be abolished as soon as practicable." Nor did British officials contemplate removing what an in-house Colonial Office minute baldly referred to as "Restriction on Movement of Natives." As a leading South African mining capitalist explained, while "the whole country is open to the white man who wants to make this country his home," the same would never be true for the nonwhite person. "Properly indentured," such non-European workers would be "solely under Government control," and the state would "repatriate them to the country whence they came, not letting a single man remain behind." The transnational scope of the system expressed itself in racial terms.[55]

In Du Bois's comprehensive analysis, the racial basis of the bonds shared by workers across the Black world condemned African workers to, in Douglass's terms, the status of the "slave of society"—*society* in this case being colonial. Du Bois can now fully account for how British colonialism, which began by channeling victims of East Africa's slave trade into the construction of railways and other purposes, fashioned a new slavery of far greater proportions. From Du Bois's point of view, nothing is more significant than a policy that deprives Africans of the right to own or occupy land in what colonialism deemed the European zones of Africa. Racism is the only basis on which African subjects of the British Empire can be banished to reserves or forced to work for Europeans on land they traditionally occupied. The only legal principle that can exclude Africans from urban areas is the assumed right to use race to legislate injustice.

The forms of legal and extralegal racial control erected by British colonialism in Africa kept Africans, like their enslaved predecessors in the Americas, outside the realm of political freedom to which white workers were increasingly admitted. If slavery is social death, so too is colonial land policy and the laws that buttress it. As Lugard acknowledged, the grounds on which these policies were imposed were explicitly racial. Within the historical context of race and the transnational economy built on top of it lies the key to understanding the new slavery in colonial Africa as much as in the American South.[56]

Fighting for the "Emancipation of Man"

For Du Bois, the systemic, racialized basis of the new slavery, wherever it is found, leads inexorably to an overarching conclusion about antislavery. If the ostensibly "free labor" systems of racial colonialism are necessarily forms of slavery, and if the new slavery is inherently racial, then antislavery has to take the form of antiracism. Du Bois puts it this way: "Here is the real modern labor problem. . . . The emancipation of man is the emancipation of labor and the emancipation of labor is the freeing of that basic majority of workers who are brown and black." Black liberation does not depend on working-class freedom. On the contrary, human freedom depends on Black freedom. In this proclamation, Du Bois refines his better-known principle of some three decades earlier that the color line is the problem of the twentieth century. He declares it the global problem for all time. The emancipation of workers of color is the emancipation of man. Du Bois agrees with Marx that the goal is to eliminate exploitation, but he recognizes the indirect exploitation of Black workers by white.[57]

Du Bois is directly challenging not only Marx but also the young Black radicals who followed him. Liberation will have to be accomplished by the world's people of color, who, in contrast to white workers, lack not only the "power" to exploit others but also the "wish." European society and the movements it spawned cannot be trusted to emancipate all members of society, having become too accepting of racism and the exploitation of workers of color, for which Du Bois lays partial blame at the door of the white working class. Emancipation did not solve the problem of the "ultimate exploited"; in fact, the problem got much worse. And neither abolitionism nor the working-class movement seems to care. Taking aim at John Harris and British antislavery, Du Bois enunciates the principle that if abolitionism does not acknowledge the racial nature of the new slavery, it is itself racist. To Abram Harris and his fellow radicals, Du Bois directs the conclusion that a working-class movement that does not recognize that liberation necessarily means liberation of the "ultimate exploited" is not itself working class. Du Bois thus foreshadows not European socialism but the African and Asian anticolonial movement as the great hope of humanity.

Du Bois replaces Marx's essentially European-based working class as the revolutionary vanguard with its historical other side—the working class of color. He discerns that it was no accident that Pan-Africanism took shape as racial slavery recrossed the Atlantic. That development meant the Black world encompassed not only a shared ancestry but also a shared form of oppression. In the broad terms of Pan-Africanism, there was a common instrument of oppression and thus the need for joint modalities of liberation. For Du Bois, this historical reality of the Black world—including the oppression of Black people based on the systemic racism built into the structure of the world economy—necessitates liberation as a Black world. But the emancipation of Black people entails freeing all people of color, which in turn will liberate not just all workers but humanity as a whole. Stripped of its veneer of class struggle, the antiracist struggle is not only inherently abolitionist but, more profoundly, the sole path to universal human rights. In a racist world, the notion that Black lives matter implies that all lives matter, even though the reverse would never be true.

Du Bois understands race not as a *social construct* but as what would better be termed a *historical construct*. Race as a social construct implies that exposing the social origins of race might be enough to get rid of racism. But Du Bois believes that neither a colorblind class struggle nor any struggle that is not explicitly antiracist can undo the historical effects of race. Du Bois does not condition the liberation of workers of color on working-class freedom or on class struggle. He envisions human freedom as dependent on the freedom of workers of color. Du Bois has done more than turn Marxian class analysis on its head. He has charted a new abolitionism for the twentieth century and beyond and added an important dimension to any postcolonial notion of human rights. Du Bois foreshadows the need for a post–civil rights Black Lives

Matter movement as a natural and necessary next step in the freedom struggle. Despite the triumph over some of the worst manifestations of racism, the antiracist form of the movement cannot be dispensed with. Five hundred years of history determines otherwise, as do the extant links between the Black world and the broader racism impacting all persons of color. The implications are with us today, expressed every time activists insist on the cogency of the principle that Black lives matter and reject the colorblind nonequivalent that all lives matter.[58]

The main lines of the distinctive Black abolitionism developed by Du Bois and Padmore made their way into the thinking of some of the key figures in the African anticolonial movement. Antislavery requires antiracism, and in the absence of abolitionist allies, it would be up to the Black freedom movement in the United States and Pan-Africanism in Africa to end the new slavery. In important ways, subsequent developments upheld their hopes in this respect. Richard Wright highlighted Padmore's importance to the post–World War II Pan-Africanist movement, exerting a direct influence over a generation of leaders including Kwame Nkrumah and Jomo Kenyatta. Du Bois declared him "the organizing spirit of [the Fifth Pan-African] congress." To Du Bois, that year, 1945, was "decisive . . . in determining the freedom of Africa." To Nkrumah, that meeting gave "concrete expression" to the movement, and he could take satisfaction in thinking so, since he joined Padmore as the congress's co-organizer.[59]

Nkrumah characterized the fifth incarnation of the congress as unlike the first four, which "had been supported mainly by middle-class intellectuals and bourgeois reformists." This one, he boasted, "was attended by workers, trade unionists, farmers and students, most of whom came from Africa," where the center of gravity had by then shifted. Nkrumah argued that anticolonialism needed to serve their interests above all. "The great millions of Africa, and of Asia," he declared, "have grown impatient of being hewers of wood and drawers of water, and are rebelling against the false belief that providence created some to be the menials of others." Having imbibed the thinking of his mentor Du Bois, Nkrumah adopted his position that "European capitalism" exploited "enslaved" African workers.[60]

Though locating himself largely outside Pan-Africanism, the widely influential Frantz Fanon adopts essentially the same position. Europe,

Fanon writes, kept the global South "in slavery for centuries." Economically, "Europe is literally the creation of the Third World." Its riches "are those plundered from the underdeveloped peoples." Indeed, "Europe's well-being and progress were built with the sweat and corpses of blacks, Arabs, Indians and Asians." Fanon calls particular attention, as did Du Bois, to the direct correlation between "Europe's tower of opulence" and "the geography of hunger" in the global South. "In concrete terms Europe has been bloated out of all proportions by the gold and raw materials from such colonial countries as Latin America, China, and Africa." "Deportation, massacres, forced labor, and slavery," argues Fanon, "were the primary methods used by capitalism to increase its gold and diamond reserves, and establish its wealth and power." He cogently notes, "For centuries the capitalists have behaved like real war criminals in the underdeveloped world." Europe enriched itself to the extent that it impoverished the peoples of the colonial world, "drain[ed] their heads and bellies of all their substance to feed it." In a strong echo of Du Bois, Fanon concludes, "The colonized peoples" constitute the "slaves of modern times."[61]

According to Fanon, underlying this whole system is the historical category of race:

> Looking at the immediacies of the colonial context, it is clear that what divides this world is first and foremost what species, what race one belongs to. In the colonies the economic infrastructure is also a superstructure. The cause is effect: You are rich because you are white, you are white because you are rich. . . . This European opulence is literally a scandal for it was built on the backs of slaves, it fed on the blood of slaves, and it owes its very existence to the soil and subsoil of the underdeveloped world. . . . And it is only guaranteed by the slaves of this world, toiling in the oil wells of the Middle East, the mines of Peru and the Congo, and the United Fruit or Firestone plantations.

Fanon's analysis highlights the transnational bonds of a new slavery built on global structures with far deeper roots than those recognized by the contemporary mainstream antislavery movement or international conventions.[62]

The influence of the Black abolitionist tradition extended to Martin Luther King Jr., and key aspects were also adopted by Black Power.

It formed part of the background for the term *institutional racism*, coined by veteran activist Stokely Carmichael, of the Student Nonviolent Coordinating Committee, and Charles V. Hamilton in their 1967 book *Black Power: The Politics of Liberation*. In distinguishing institutional racism from the more common notion of individual racism, they write, "Black people in this country form a colony, and it is not in the interest of the colonial power to liberate them. Black people are legal citizens of the United States with, for the most part, the same *legal* rights as other citizens. Yet they stand as colonial subjects in relation to the white society. Thus institutional racism has another name: colonialism." Although "the black communities of the United States" might not produce raw materials, they do "export . . . human labor." The "colonial relationship" is "essentially" the same.[63]

Carmichael and Hamilton conceive the larger connection across the Black world that Du Bois made the centerpiece of his understanding. As "colonial subjects," African Americans "have their political decisions made for them by the colonial masters." Black people are "faced with a 'white power structure' as monolithic as Europe's colonial offices have been to African and Asian colonies." Economically, Carmichael and Hamilton focus on "dependency" rather than the new slavery in Africa. They emphasize that Africans' role in the extraction of raw materials was as cheap laborers, and in that context, they reference the still visible spectacle of the African Americans "cultivating cotton" ten hours a day for ten cents an hour. They argue, conveying the spirit if not the letter of twentieth-century Black abolitionist analysis, "The colonial power structure clamped a boot of oppression on the neck of the black people and then, ironically, said 'they are not ready for freedom.' Left solely to the good will of the oppressor, the oppressed would never be ready."[64]

As of the early 1970s, by which time the principal figures of twentieth-century Black abolitionism were dead, it seemed that the problem of emancipation, at least to outward appearances, had been permanently solved. The civil rights movement combined with mass migration out of the South had largely destroyed the remnants of peonage in the United States. In Africa, decolonization was well on its way to completion. Pan-Africanism had receded, and what remained had taken on a different political content. That appearance constituted a false dawn. In the United States, the menace of prison labor soon became apparent. In

Africa, as colonialism gave way to neocolonialism, the new slavery lingered and morphed, still serving Western interests even as the West derived benefit but incurred no blame. Subsequent history would show that people across the Black world had not been freed from the new slavery after all. The analysis of Black abolitionism would be as necessary to understanding the problem as ever, especially as modified by an intersectional abolitionist doctrine developed principally by Black women theorists.[65]

5

The Emancipation of Women

In 1935 *The Crisis*, which W. E. B. Du Bois had been editing for two decades, published an article that signaled the beginning of a transition to a post–Du Boisian Black abolitionism. He had valiantly carried the torch for Black abolitionism, albeit far from single-handedly, from the conclusion of the 1900 Pan-African Conference to the publication of his landmark *Black Reconstruction* in 1935. That same year a young Ella Baker—future civil rights legend and a recent transplant from the South—went undercover with a colleague to learn how the "slave market" operated in the Bronx. What she discovered shocked and disgusted her, stripping bare the face of the new slavery for northern Black women. Large groups of them assembled on the street corners of New York and other cities every morning at 8:00 a.m. during the Great Depression to attend a public auction—of themselves. In better times, these Black women had worked in a variety of jobs, but when times got hard, they were replaced by white women, who, taking advantage of their desperation and humiliation, hired Black women as domestics to lighten their own household burdens. Able to exercise power over Black women, these white women made far from sympathetic employers. They offered as little as fifteen cents an hour for an exhausting day's labor scrubbing filthy windows and floors and laundering coarse bedding, linen, and clothing. The Black women who accepted this harsh bargain did so only because it was the better of two grim alternatives, even though, at the end of the day, they knew they might simply be dismissed without pay.[1]

Baker understood perfectly how this exploitation leveraged systemic racism. The director of an employment agency that refused to list African Americans once white women became available told Baker, "The women who sell their labor thus cheaply have but themselves to blame," given their willingness to engage in such "slavish performances." "Unlike the original slaves who recoiled from meeting their masters," the unfeeling businesswoman continued, these women "rush to meet their mistresses." Baker, however, knew that "actual starvation" was the "slave driver" here. But she also emphasized an aspect of the new slavery that Du Bois had barely touched on, one that drew on and anticipated the analysis of other Black women abolitionists. "The lower-middle class housewife, having dreamed of the luxury of a maid, found opportunity staring her in the face in the form of Negro women pressed to the wall by poverty, starvation and discrimination." Baker's acute analysis mirrored Du Bois's in one respect, as she charged that "the exploiters . . . are the wives and mothers of [white] artisans and tradesmen who militantly battle against being exploited themselves, but who apparently have no scruples against exploiting others." But she also advanced beyond Du Bois's understanding in recognizing that these women were able to take advantage of white privilege to escape their gendered labor only because Black women confronted the double burden of race and gender.[2]

The intersection of race and gender had far-reaching implications for the Black abolitionist cause. Though he meant to encompass all of humanity under "the emancipation of man," gender analysis remained an area of weakness for Du Bois and for Pan-Africanism in general. Still, as Patricia McFadden writes, "The anticolonial struggles provided a unique opportunity for women to become political and to embark on the path toward citizenship—to becoming autonomous subjects, with a consciousness of rights and entitlements that enables one to demand protections and obligations from the state." That they were forced to do so had everything to do with Du Bois's reasons for conceptualizing "the emancipation of man" as "the freeing of that basic majority of workers who are brown and black." The racial colonialism that spanned the Black world in both space and time, as McFadden remarks, meant "the systematic exclusion" of Black people "from even the most limited meanings of citizenship as an imagined and performed status," including "the use of extra legal mechanisms to ensure that black women in particular" were the victims "of these exclusionary state policies."[3]

In response, a group of women activists that included Baker pioneered an intersectional Black abolitionism. It expanded and refined Du Bois's definition of the new slavery to include any use of social difference as a basis for denying the rights and protections afforded other workers for purposes of exploitation beyond what is otherwise societally acceptable. They also conceived the need for definite measures to end forms of the new slavery reserved for women. The deprivation of civil rights made all Black people vulnerable to what Ida B. Wells called "civil slavery," drawing on Douglass's notion of the "slave of society." The issues involved were more salient to Black women theorists in no small part because their impact often fell disproportionately on women, as McFadden argues. Kimberlé Crenshaw's extremely influential work has taught us that, when considering the oppression of Black women, we must examine it from the standpoint of intersectionality, or the "hierarchies" that govern "multiple systems of subordination." Intersectional analysis proved vital to understanding and combating the new slavery of the twentieth century.[4]

Abolitionism and Gender

Du Bois's inattention to gender was something he took from Frederick Douglass and nineteenth-century Black abolitionism. Abolitionists tacitly assumed that emancipation would solve the special forms of oppression women faced under slavery. That is not to say that Douglass was unaware of the impact of gender on the institution of slavery. He showed himself attentive to the particular problems of enslaved women when, in his earliest narrative, he detailed the plight of a female neighbor who was being persecuted by her mistress because she feared the young girl, who was just undergoing puberty, would soon attract her husband's sexual interest. Douglass knew as well as other abolitionists that the domestic labor to which the girl was confined pervaded the institution of slavery in the Americas. From the colonial period in North America, Ira Berlin concludes, "the division between house and field remained open and ill-defined." With the rise of the cotton plantation South, Jacqueline Jones estimates that perhaps "5% of all antebellum adult slaves served in the elites corps of house servants trained for specific duties." They were mostly women, although "the lines between domestic service and fieldwork blurred during the day and during the lives of enslaved women." Enslaved children provided "an acceptable alternative source of labor" when women were needed elsewhere. Barry Higman finds that a significant proportion of the enslaved in the nineteenth-century British Caribbean performed domestic duties. Cuba's 1871 slave lists recorded similar proportions engaged in domestic labor. Laird Bergad attributes the preponderance of women among the urban enslaved in Cuba, Brazil, and the United States to the demand for domestic labor.[5]

Even as a child, Douglass was aware of the role gender played in assigning the differential functions of enslaved women, who were often designated "half-hands." The episode with Douglass's young female neighbor was meant to delicately allude to the reality that, as Jones writes, a "woman's childbearing capacity set her apart from boys and men, as revealed by the preoccupation of auctioneers and buyers with women's breasts and genitalia." Male enslavers' obsession with Black women's bodies also indexed the sexual subordination they perpetrated. In colonial times, Berlin writes, "sex stood high on the list of commodities for sale" in North American markets. In the antebellum period, too, the commodification of the Black female body went beyond the famed marketplace in New Orleans for unofficial wives (in addition to those who were legally recognized), effectively creating a polygynous system. In Brazil, "even women of respectable households commonly required their slave women to earn money for them by selling themselves." In the British Caribbean, owners of brothels, inns, and taverns employed their slaves as prostitutes.[6]

Du Bois too recognized the role of gender in antebellum slavery, at least in the legal principle that a child's status followed that of the mother. Reducing a woman to "an article of property" and permitting the sale of her children in infancy ensured reproduction of the enslaved population. At least a portion of slaveholders took full advantage of the law, to the detriment of enslaved women. In *Black Reconstruction* Du Bois claims that the practice amounted to "slave breeding," although that notion has been disputed by subsequent scholars. Higman's comprehensive review of practices in the British Caribbean finds that slaveholders merely took measures to increase the incidence of childbirth. Historians have broadly concluded that the typical enslaved woman in the antebellum period first gave birth at about age twenty and continued to do so every two and a half years for the next one and a half decades. Still, the fact remains that women's reproductive labor was unambiguously part of slavery in the Americas, and Du Bois took its importance into account.[7]

Du Bos did not, however, apply that gender analysis to the new slavery, even as Baker's investigations revealed it to be profoundly gendered. When Du Bois exposed the kinds of slave labor colonialism depended on for the production of raw materials, he omitted the agricultural and reproductive work of women on which male migrant labor depended. Perhaps he had not foreseen the worst feature of a separate international labor code for workers of color: its silence on the special forms of oppression reserved for women that gave the colonial powers an even freer hand with them. Baker demonstrated that gender lay at the root of the slave market for Black female domestic workers. It was also omnipresent in the prison labor system. At its inception, Du Bois noted that the prison labor system enmeshed men, women, and children almost indiscriminately, but as it evolved, men became its principal targets. This trend intensified as mass incarceration reached its zenith after 1970. More subtly, gender made its presence felt in the division of labor within sharecropping, including the supplementary cash earned by women in domestic service that helped sustain it. The same patterns emerged in the migration-based political economy of the Caribbean, where, in the aftermath of slavery, women engaged in much of the subsistence production and, as time went on, increasingly reproduced a labor force in the absence of the external slave trade.

Intersectional Black abolitionism sought to publicize the differential effects of the new slavery on men and women in the Americas, even as it menaced all Black people. In Africa, under a European colonialism that was both patriarchal and racial, the gendered nature of the new slavery was just as apparent. The Du Bois–led abolitionist movement tended to focus on the new slavery for men, but something even more sinister and enduring was taking shape for women, with US slave markets serving as a case in point. Alongside this gendered new slavery developed intersectional Black abolitionism, which exposed the conditions oppressing Black women as insightfully as Du Bois had those for men, even as it rectified the faults of gender-blind abolitionism.

Women and the New Slavery

Now in his tenth decade, Du Bois wanted to attend the Conference of the Women of Africa and African Descent in Accra, Ghana, in July 1960. He hoped to live out his final years on the African continent as the civil rights movement he had helped bring about was peaking at home. This determination was a tangible demonstration of his commitment to Africa that stretched back six decades, as well as his intense concern that Black abolitionism focus as much on Africa as on the United States, where he had first encountered the new slavery. Du Bois must have been particularly gratified to see that the symbiotic relationship between US civil rights and African decolonization had prompted others to cross the Atlantic to witness the interrelated struggle play out. He was aware that the fight was far from over in America, but he also realized how much remained to be done in Africa. As a founding member of Pan-Africanism, he saw an opportunity to participate one last time. Moreover, the Pan-Africanism that had long been home to Black abolitionism was finally turning its attention to women's issues, and Du Bois was interested. But because the US government had confiscated his passport a decade earlier, he arrived in Ghana too late.[8]

Du Bois's delayed departure caused him to miss Shirley Graham Du Bois's keynote, as well as Kwame Nkrumah's opening address. Nkrumah's message was supportive, in keeping with his sponsorship of the meeting. Yet one of his remarks was unintentionally revealing: "Who would have thought in this year 1960, it would be possible to even hold a conference of all Ghanaian women, much less of women of all Africa and African descent! But today that is a reality and an achievement which constitutes another landmark of progress in Africa's irresistible march to emancipation and victory."[9]

It might have been more apt to remark that without the indispensable contributions of women like Ida B. Wells, Anna Julia Cooper, Alice Kinloch, and the two Amy Garveys who helped launch the UNIA, Pan-Africanism might never have gotten off the ground. Without the Women's War in Nigeria in 1929 and the Women's March in South Africa that gave rise to the Women's Charter, Nkrumah might not have been in the position of power from which he spoke. The Conference of the Women of Africa and African Descent was followed by an explosion of

Black women's activism across the Black world in the 1960s and beyond, and the emancipation of women that consequently became a key component of Nkrumah's "irresistible march to emancipation and victory."[10]

Awareness of the gendered nature of the new slavery began long before Ella Baker's analysis of the slave market of the 1930s. Alice Kinloch laid the groundwork for an intersectional abolitionist analysis of the differential oppression of women that eluded Du Bois. Although we know little about her, there are important hints of what might have been her proto–Black feminist outlook, such as her gravitation to "an association of progressive minded women" while in England. It was likely Kinloch who influenced Henry Fox Bourne to consider the standpoint of African women under colonialism.[11]

Fox Bourne was thus armed when he confronted Earl Grey, Joseph Chamberlain, and the Rand magnates, who claimed to be championing African women allegedly enslaved by their male relations. One of the first expressions of the new antislavery dates to Chamberlain, a former member of the Liberal Party's radical wing who later became an ardent imperialist. Eager to justify Britain's racial labor policies, which Kinloch denounced as the new slavery, Chamberlain, who was colonial secretary at the turn of the century, came up with what he considered an ingenious angle, declaring that the African male migrant workers' "so-called wives are really slaves who work to keep him in idleness." Grey joined him in deploring the plight of these "slave wives."[12]

Fox Bourne exposed what he called this "hypocritical perversion of the facts." African marital "arrangements," he wrote, "may be at variance with English sentiment, but they are not slavery. Nor is the work that women have to do regarded by them, or to be regarded by any one else, as servile." Fox Bourne discerned that this entire campaign was an attempt to distract from the more sinister ambitions toward these women. He wrote:

It is true that, in the wine-producing districts of Cape Colony and other parts in which white men exploit the country and its inhabitants, native women are constrained to toil for their masters in uncongenial ways, but this is an innovation for which [European] civilisation is responsible. Much worse will surely happen if the mining capitalists are allowed to have their way and to compel [the] male population to work under them. The wives will then be reduced to a state of slavery indeed, compelled to do all the farming and pasturing while their husbands and fathers are earning money at a distance.[13]

Fox Bourne warned that the potential enslavement of the female relatives of male migrant workers in feminized agricultural and reproductive labor took root not in African marriage traditions but in the racialization of African colonial space by its imperial occupier. He applied Douglass's test of the four freedoms to the wives of migrant workers consigned to the reserves being established in South Africa. The absence of urban employment opportunities for women was neither a reflection of the age-old patriarchy of Europe (or Africa) nor a fortuitous circumstance; it was a policy choice by British authorities that legally tied male workers' female relatives to the fields of "African locations"—British colonial lingo for the rural areas designated for Africans. In the Douglass–Fox Bourne understanding, such racialized spatial confinement for labor purposes determined where and at what these women worked, an unambiguous condition of slavery, whether on North American plantations or on the farms of a British colonial "location."[14]

John Harris's new antislavery completely inverted that interpretation. Since "the most precious asset in Africa is [male] labor," women should play their proper role in providing it. He wrote, "To the forces of Christianity belongs the obligation of . . . preparing the girls—the future women of Africa—to do women's work and to take a woman's stand, and thus help to prevent one of the greatest and most rapidly-growing evils of Africa." Harris did not attempt to clarify the seemingly obscure connection between African women's domesticity and the suppression of interracial sexual relations. Evidently, it was important only that he link the two ideologically. He nevertheless made it clear that African women's rightful place was not only in the domestic sphere but specifically in the reserves, whose existence he enthusiastically lauded as the basis of a segregated society. His segregationist antislavery ensured his support for British labor policy. Segregation required reserves, which conveniently buttressed the exploitation of Africa's "most precious asset"—male labor. At the height of its authority, British abolitionism abandoned women when they most needed protection from colonialism.[15]

The retreat from turn-of-the-century antislavery therefore hurt women most of all. To be sure, the new antislavery endorsed depriving Africans—men and women alike—of political and human rights. The Anti-Slavery Society declared that Africans belonged to what it termed "the child races of the world." Sir Donald Cameron, a member invited to address the society's 1931 annual meeting as an expert on Africa, had starkly stated this view a few years earlier while serving as governor of British Tanzania. He described the African under colonialism as not "a member of the State" but "a member of a *servile community* without political duties or rights," employing the very term the Slavery Convention of 1956 would stigmatize as synonymous with slavery. But Cameron judged that even the paltry freedoms associated with this lowly status were too great for impoverished rural African women. In response to a 1930 inquiry on the "status of women" in the empire, he opined: "African women at the present day enjoy a degree of freedom which easily degenerates into license . . . their need is for more, and not fewer, restraints." The British obliged with innumerable curbs on the liberty of African women. As Fox Bourne had predicted, their fate seemed to be enslavement by the labor policy of racial colonialism.[16]

Once again, the new antislavery backed British colonialism's oppression of Africans. If Fox Bourne was right, and British officials' attempt to position African women as their husbands' slaves was a "hypocritical" diversion from the realities of the new slavery, then it was apparent that the colonialists could not be trusted to protect their female subjects any more than their male. The same was true of the apostles of the new antislavery. Their colorblind abolitionism was equally gender blind, despite Orlando Patterson's conclusion that "the great majority of persons ever enslaved were women"—as they are, in his estimation, today.[17]

Du Bois and George Padmore noted the gender dynamics of British policy in Africa, but they focused on the impact on men. In their minds, the new slavery in Africa was a system that, instead of concentrating workers around the centers of industry, forced them to be migrant laborers, deployed to perform mining, infrastructure construction, porterage, and other forms of labor central to the colonial mission. Because they needed to be mobile, they were removed from their land. They were meant to live temporarily in the areas set aside for European enterprise as the unavoidable prerequisite for working there. Toward that end, land policy first deprived Africans of the ability to support themselves through subsistence production. Aided by the imposition of stiff taxes that had to be paid in British currency, male workers were forced into "oscillating" or "circular" migration patterns from the reserves to urban production spaces in mining towns and similar locales. The resultant "migratory system," the British Central African Council acknowledged, was "unknown in more highly developed countries," with their more familiar urban working classes. As Du Bois and Padmore documented, British policy aimed to free men for migrant labor without making proletarians of them. The Northern Rhodesian Native Reserves Commission commented in 1926, the "distance of Reserves from labour centres would not affect the supply [of workers]. . . . With notable exceptions, the general view was that labour from a distance was more constant and dependable if only because it was from a distance."[18]

Du Bois and Padmore were less interested in the far-reaching results for women. Perhaps they reasoned that since the pass laws in colonial Zimbabwe and elsewhere did not apply to women, their movement was less circumscribed. They seemed to miss what Kinloch and Fox Bourne recognized: this migrant labor policy relied on banishing women *to* rural areas and banning them *from* urban areas. With their female relations bound to the land, men were forced to return to what colonial authorities called their "rural homes." Calling this system *migrant labor* to stress its mobile quality is inherently one-sided and gendered, since more than half the total working class is *immobile*. Teresa Barnes concludes that, because of the "more common . . . travel and urban residence restrictions for women, especially in central and southern Africa," the absence of pass laws was "fundamentally irrelevant." The urban-rural divide was very much gendered, Barnes writes, since women's "economic and spatial mobility were curtailed because the codification of the colonial 'invention of tradition' boxed them into a state of permanent legal minority."[19]

The constraints on women confined to the reserves were manifold. By colonial policy, the reserves were not open to urban development. Northern Rhodesia's Native Reserves Commission, for instance, specified that they be "homogeneous and not intermingled with areas of European settlement," "permanent and perpetual," and suitably remote from sites of European industry. Stuck on the rural side of the urban-rural divide, women were not free to do what they wanted, go where they desired, cohabit with their husbands, or benefit from the labor of their husbands and other adult male relations. They had none of the rights that defined the liberal democratic regimes at whose behest and in whose interests they toiled. The organization of labor in Africa meant that women would be tied to the land and isolated from the migrating men—the basis of what Kinloch and Fox Bourne characterized as an even more onerous new slavery for women.[20]

Du Boisian abolitionism was not adequate to the task of emancipating Black women from the new slavery and its feminized forms of labor—especially domestic work in the United States and agriculture in Africa. In failing to grasp the full implications of the new slavery's gendered structure, Du Bois did not adopt the Kinloch–Fox Bourne position that male migrant labor in Africa needed to be abolished, if for no other reason than its effects on women. He did not take account of the ways women were excluded from key aspects of civil society, including labor unions, state benefits, education, and—especially in Africa—urban citizenship. Here too, an intersectional Black abolitionism was needed to more effectively combat the new slavery.

Civil Slavery Absent Civil Rights

Ella Baker began the work of addressing the constellation of issues Du Bois left untouched. She concluded, "The real significance of the Bronx Slave Market lies not in a factual presentation of its activities, but in focusing attention upon its involved implications. The 'mart' is but a miniature of our economic battle front." The Black women caught up in it were victims of the racially exclusionary practices of both "relief administrators and investigators"—that is, the government—and "organized labor," which ostracized them. Black women resorted to the mart because American racism positioned them outside the state protection that afforded white workers the ability to organize into unions.[21]

Black women remained of little interest to America's principal union federations at the height of their power and influence. The problem, Baker judged, was "organized labor's limited concept of exploitation, which permits it to fight vigorously to secure itself against evil, yet passively or actively aids and abets the ruthless destruction of Negroes." In unionizing Black women domestics, she and her fellow Harlem labor activists, together with John P. Davis and the National Negro Congress, would have the field to themselves.[22]

In her penetrating analysis, Baker drew on the thinking of Ida B. Wells, who not only followed the Black abolitionist trail to England but also built on the analysis pioneered by its principals. Her notion of racial violence and terrorism as part and parcel of what she called "civil and industrial slavery" elaborated on Douglass's idea of the postemancipation new slavery, converting African Americans from the chattels of individual slave owners to the "slave of society." Wells recognized that the slavery in the postemancipation South remained racial. She was particularly interested in a related question: how did racial slavery operate? In her formulation that racial slavery is "civil slavery," she meant to highlight that it is rooted in the denial of the rights and protections afforded to those whose full citizenship is recognized in the governance of society.[23]

Wells zeroed in on the mechanism of the new slavery. Du Bois, influenced by Marxism, had focused on the overarching economic structure responsible for the new slavery, ignoring civil society altogether in both *Black Reconstruction* and the demands he put forward on behalf of the Pan-African Congress. Wells, in contrast, drew from Douglass's emphasis on the social character of the slavery he feared would persist after emancipation. The subsequent denial of civil rights made African Americans vulnerable to what Wells termed "civil slavery." She specified that the forms of such slavery already observable by the 1890s functioned through the exclusion of African Americans from those rights and protections government should offer citizens. By then, the US Constitution purported to recognize African American personhood and citizenship, as it had not in antebellum times. As Douglass already understood, however, racial slavery is not, by its nature, an individual condition. It is embedded, as Du Bois recognized, in a racial context, but it takes a civil form. Whether or not it includes what Patterson calls social death, it at least entails civil exclusion, which was enough to open the door to the new slavery.

Wells connected that civil status to the question of state-sanctioned violence both directly, in the form of lynching, and by extension to the kind of state-perpetrated violence that African Americans face today at the hands of the police that sparked the Black Lives Matter movement. Decades before Baker, Wells had already pointed to African Americans' exclusion from the protections of citizenship by describing lynching as America's "national crime," prefiguring the later notion of "crime against humanity." That lynching was not treated as lawbreaking in America demonstrated that African Americans were not entitled to the state protections due citizens of the nation. It was not only "civil" but also "industrial" slavery because Wells perceived that the same forces at work in the definition of lynching also served as the basis of the new slavery of debt peonage. Lynching could be the "national crime" only because African Americans were positioned outside the boundaries of US citizenship and thereby, like other noncitizen workers, were subject to exploitation that was not effectively limited by law.

Wells fleshed out Douglass's idea of "the slave of society" in what she called "civil and industrial slavery," distilling it down to the entirely separate racialized legal regime that underlay all forms of the new slavery. This insight was a notable and prescient contrast to Du Bois's attempt to use the vehicle of the revived Pan-African movement to seek legal redress through international institutions that Wells prophesied would not be forthcoming absent the end of systemic racism. It foreshadowed Du Bois's later conclusion that a much more far-reaching emancipation was needed.

Wells's understanding is also vital in recognizing racial slavery as simultaneously gendered. Following up on Wells's analysis, Baker discerned in the slave market for African American women domestic workers their exclusion from government benefits and labor unions, which enforced their slavery. Their African counterparts had the added burden of being denied fundamental human rights, such as basic urban citizenship—with profound consequences.

Baker's intersectional Black abolitionist analysis applied equally to a British colonialism that did more than simply segregate African cities. More fundamentally, it carved out entire racial zones that, much like the roots of the new slavery in the twentieth-century United States, determined where a large proportion of Black people could live and labor. In America, it involved confining African Americans to the Black Belt via the combination of economic, legal, social, and violent coercion. In colonial Africa, this racialized space centered on reserving urban areas for Europeans, with African men allowed to enter as temporary servile labor and unmarried African women permitted to enter, if at all, as sex workers. As slavery locked a large proportion of Africans and their descendants in the fields of the plantations and farms of the Americas, colonialism in Africa trapped a significant proportion of women in the fields of the rural locations to which they were bound. The situation of African women demonstrated the power of Baker's Black abolitionist understanding, which differed so markedly from the new antislavery. As Baker made clear, African women were not confined to sex and domestic work in urban areas and agrarian production and reproduction in rural areas by some unaccountable accident. This was a central intent of the racial labor system of British colonialism, a racial model that was, by its nature, also gendered.

Rendering African women vulnerable to slave market forces did not always require separate enforcement measures. As Baker made clear, because the racial organization of space, labor, and the production process was inherently gendered, enforcement of the racial was perforce enforcement of the gendered. As occurred in the urban American North, the colonial state converted *Black and female* into a de facto social category subject to state enforcement, and in so doing, it gendered the rural-urban divide. The consequences of this positioning of women outside of urban industrial capitalist society would be lasting. In forbidding their entry into cities, colonial authorities denied women the fundamental right to urban citizenship that underlies the status of the free in civil societies. Colonial policy was significant for how it positioned African women vis-à-vis urban industrial capitalist society—particularly the poorest and most vulnerable among them. The very attempt to establish African cities without women emphasizes that the existence of zones of exclusion within urban areas was less important than who could inhabit them in the first place. To examine the urban from the standpoint of race is to focus on segregation. The perspective of gender reveals that, alongside racial segregation, gender segregation—excluding women from cities—has received considerably less attention, although it is a more fundamental, if closely connected, form.[24]

The results of British policy were evident in the urban demographics of colonial Africa. In East Africa in the 1950s, on the eve of colonialism's demise, only in Dar es Salaam were there as many as seventy-two women for every hundred men. In the mining districts of Northern

Rhodesia, the number varied from fifty-eight women to every hundred men in Mufulira to forty-seven in Broken Hill to only forty-three in Chingola. Authorities in Nairobi reported in 1941 that "it is known that there are eight men to one woman" in the city. These raw figures tell only part of the story, since most of the women in question were married and resided temporarily with their husbands. Most of their children remained in the rural locations, as attested to by the presence, on average, of only one child for every woman in towns and cities, at a time when fertility rates were four or five times higher than that. Equally important, these married women greatly outnumbered unmarried women—in Broken Hill, for instance, by a ratio of six to one, while there were no fewer than seven single men to every unattached woman. The demography of the rural hinterland featured the mirror opposite. In a 1964 report devoted to improving the conditions of African women, the International Labour Office noted that "by far the majority of Africans—and this is even more true of females than males—are to be found in the rural areas." In sub-Saharan Africa today, there are 116 women for every 100 men between the ages of fifteen and forty-nine in rural areas. International agencies call this phenomenon the "feminization" of the rural global South—although its impact varies considerably from region to region.[25]

Taken together, an intersectional Black abolitionist standpoint revealed that African women were not merely *left* to engage in agrarian production by their migrating male relations; this predicament was *forced* on them by the coercive mechanisms of racial colonialism. It was partly a question of legal enactment, in the shape of banning Africans from urban areas. It was partly a matter of certain categories of employment being closed to women, as was also the case for African American female domestic workers in the North. From the intersectional Black abolitionist perspective, the agrarian production of African women was therefore just as compulsory as the migrant variety imposed on African men or the debt peonage of African Americans in the South. Wells and Du Bois probed the purely race-based legal means that undergirded debt peonage in the United States, while Kinloch and Fox Bourne did so for the rural captivity of African women. They were the first to note that British colonial policy gave African women's circumstances the distinctive appearance of the essentially premodern conditions of serfdom.

The racial organization of space, labor, and the production process in colonial Africa meant that African women would be tied to the land across the continent, even in the absence of migrating men, bearing a striking resemblance to a kind of gender-specific quasi-serfdom in some parts of British Africa.

Wells's notion of "civil slavery" applies especially well here. African women were as effectively bound to the land by a combination of the law and the structure of production as any European serf—even absent the familiar form of personal servitude to a landowner on which serfdom is generally understood to be based. Large numbers of African women experienced the essential conditions of serfdom, despite the absence of a class of feudal lords. Though disguised as an attempt to conform to and respect Africans' customs as part of the policy of indirect rule, British colonial authorities did not leave this outcome to African initiative. Its alleged "tribal" pedigree notwithstanding, women's serfdom rested on colonialist measures to control women's movement.[26]

Even British officials acknowledged the analogue. As Pan-Africanism began to penetrate Africa, thanks in no small part to Padmore's writings, one British assistant colonial undersecretary acknowledged privately that the terms of a 1938 ordinance in Kenya would leave Britain "open to attack on the ground that [it] reduce[d] the labourer's family to a condition approximating to serfdom." Another Colonial Office expert agreed with this assessment: "Serfdom may be serfdom even if the head of the family has, for lack of any other choice, accepted the conditions." Kenya's governor bristled at the criticism. "It has been accepted," he insisted to the colonial secretary, "that the resident labourers' position is that of a servant." The assistant colonial undersecretary observed, "any system of native peasant tenure in the [Kenya] Highlands would be inconsistent with [the] policy" of "reserving the Highlands for European occupation." "It follows," he explained, "that the only permissible relation between European and native in the Highlands is that of master and servant." Enshrined in the ubiquitous "masters and servants" ordinances, this legal status of African workers had a distinctly feudal ring to it. British officials came to acknowledge that it applied most of all to the female relatives of male migrant workers living in the reserves, affirming intersectional Black abolitionist doctrine.[27]

The reserve system as a means of organizing a working class ensured that women formed a hereditary class bound to the land and experienced all the essential conditions of serfdom—and of the "civil and industrial slavery" identified by Wells. "The moment a native woman is married, she has duties which tie her to a hut and its adjacent garden in a way that the man is not tied," claimed the Northern Rhodesian Native Reserves Commission in 1926, attempting to justify herding women onto the reserves and making it illegal for them to leave. In reality, however, it was the other way around. In both feudal Europe and colonial Africa, class stratification had to be enforced, as difference must always be reproduced. In each case it required the state's restriction of movement—an underlying determinant of all unfree labor. That control of movement is perhaps nowhere more obvious than under serfdom, a condition that ties the class of producers to the land as much as to servitude under the landowner. The agricultural serfs of Poland, for instance, could not permanently reside in towns, acquire legal title to land, or move freely about the countryside. The same was true for Africans subjected to the reserve system, although in this case, the restriction of movement took a different form for men than for women.[28]

African peasants might have seemed to be landowners under colonialism, but a Black abolitionist perspective shows otherwise. This peculiar gendered serfdom owed its existence to the need to produce raw materials for the world market under a system of settler colonialism that Du Bois and Padmore effectively laid bare. Reserves required and facilitated state enforcement not of African landownership but of labor and tax or rent obligations, along with the same lack of liberal democratic rights experienced by serfs—both markers of unfree status. African women in the reserves thus found themselves subject to administrative control analogous to that faced by European serfs. Imperial authorities refused to settle the issue of African landownership in the reserves or even in the colonies without significant European settler populations; nor would they allow Africans to "alienate" their land to non-Africans. Lacking anything resembling the unimpeachable legal title the British refused to grant, Africans could remain only so long as they furnished a reliable labor supply. Failing that, they were assured recurrent shifts in policy, endless relocation, and continuous diminution of the land area or augmentation of the population density of the reserves. African land tenure too often had to satisfy colonial ends, just as serfs, who could never claim landownership as the condition of their bondage, served the production needs of the feudal lord. The size of the peasant holdings in reserves was as carefully calculated as those of the serfs in nineteenth-century Poland—that last bastion of European serfdom—and for the same reason: to provide for bare existence while leaving the peasantry in a state of insufficiency that compelled labor for the ruling class. Allotments of land in each case were strictly limited, although a select few received more than others. Even in colonies like Tanzania and Malawi, where there was no need for a reserve system, given the absence of a significant number of settlers, the British abided by the principle that land should be restricted to "sufficient quantity to enable [cultivators] to provide for the sustenance of themselves, their families and their posterity."[29]

The most salient difference between the position of African women and that of serfs might seem to be the absence of a feudal landlord. And yet the reserves were precisely the expression of that hereditary class of overlords who owned the land and the means of production and who reaped the windfall of class exploitation and exercised political power. Africans were not oppressed by the vague, disembodied force of the world market. They were not simply, like so many wageworkers, laid low by the encroachment of the capitalist mode of production. They were, instead, directly confronted with and subjugated to a resident class of Europeans determined by an impenetrable wall of heredity, however imaginary. African women were confined to the land solely because of the existence of the settler colonial population and in the interests of a policy of complete subordination and effective control. They were menaced by the presence of the landlord in its most meaningful form—the hereditary side of serfdom that does not exist in the case of a free peasantry. These conditions, together with their ramifications, were exactly what Douglass and Wells had foretold.

As the heaviest user of male migrant labor, the British colonial state conceived an interest in keeping those workers' female relatives confined to rural locations. Even in West Africa and Uganda, where legislation was lacking, the Colonial Office demonstrated its dedication to the rural location of women by choosing to ignore what it called the inevitable trafficking of girls for prostitution rather than relax its prohibition of wives residing in mining areas. This priority manifested itself in the effective exclusion of women from most forms of legal urban employment, as well as in a lack of education for girls. In early twentieth-century South Africa, for instance, "any form of wage labour was considered to be a male occupation, domestic service included." A meeting of colonial officials in Zambia in 1938 concluded, "Any wholesale extension of female domestic labour to industrial areas is not desirable at present." In much of Africa, the transition of domestic service from a male- to female-dominated sector was largely a postindependence phenomenon, although women started to gain a foothold much earlier.[30]

The results were the same as those Baker uncovered. While conducting her field research in the "slave market," she witnessed firsthand the fate of those women who lacked "luck." If white women did not offer them domestic work, "maybe their husbands, under the subterfuge of work, [would] offer worldly-wise girls higher bids for their time." Baker explained, "Not only is human labor bartered and sold for [a] slave wage, but human love also." And it was not simply that "labor or love" was "sold" or that "economic necessity compelled the sale," it was the totality of the circumstances that differentiated the slave-market variety from other street-corner sex work. As was the case with domestic work, the opportunities presented to these Black women at this time and in this place determined their character as the new slavery: the use of social difference as a basis for denying the rights and protections afforded other workers for purposes of exploitation beyond what is otherwise societally acceptable.[31]

Although Baker did not know it at the time, her analysis of African American female domestic workers applied to unmarried African female urban dwellers, whose lack of civil protections subjected them to the same "slave market" forces. At its worst, it became a literal slave market. Within a few years of her exposé, across the Black Atlantic a "startling disclosure" by British colonial officials made it into the pages of the English-language magazine *West Africa*. At first glance, it might have seemed to be a scene straight out of the Atlantic slave trade. It involved a shipload of some eighty young persons being transported into bondage in a "country distant [and] unknown." These children would take their place beside the "several hundreds of these poor little wretches" already there. "African girls not yet in their 'teens" were being transported into what the paper called "sexual slavery," in this case to service the migrant male workers at mining centers. When *West Africa* accused the colonial authorities of "connivance" in the trafficking of these girls, it was a vast understatement. A British official acknowledged the "considerable traffic in young women" in West Africa but explained that any curtailment of it would be "full of difficulties and obvious costs."[32]

The sexual servitude of women in colonial African cities was the concomitant of their forced attachment to rural space. The passport for young, unmarried women to enter urban space harkened back to one of the most quintessential expressions of Atlantic world slavery for women, and it revealed an aspect of the new slavery entirely invisible in Du Bois's analysis, like so much that afflicted women. Authorities conceded that migrant male communities necessitated the presence of a certain proportion of women to men, and they lent official sanction to the trade in women's bodies. There was what Elizabeth Elbourne calls a "tight link between prostitution networks and the provision of migrant labor by men across the workfaces of empire."[33]

The lack of attention to the exploitation of Black women allowed the colonial powers as free a hand as the white American women who took advantage of the "slave markets." Although the British Colonial Office was worried about the verdict of the court of global public opinion in the case of ordinances in East Africa that prohibited Africans from walking on the sidewalks in cities and towns, it was not in the least concerned that anyone would notice that unmarried women could gain residence there by virtue of being figuratively but inexorably forced to walk the streets.[34]

Women's Resistance to the Gendered New Slavery

As Black freedom movement leaders called attention to their plight, African women waged their own abolitionist campaign hidden in plain sight. Du Bois's "emancipation of man" could not occur in the absence of the emancipation of women, and women were pioneering one of the most potent tools in bringing about both. They occupied the same position as freedom seekers in the antebellum abolitionist movement in materially advancing the objectives of twentieth-century Black abolitionism. As African Americans had during the Civil War, African women were engaging in an unexpected form of antislavery activism for their self-liberation. In these circumstances, African women's resistance, like that of African Americans before them, involved voluntary migration as a principal means of claiming a measure of freedom—or at least attaining a better position from which to wage a war of liberation. The numbers in Africa were parallel to those of the Underground Railroad— tens of thousands among a population of millions. That was enough to exert an economic impact, sound the alarm of coming changes, and scare those who upheld the existing order that they were losing control.[35]

What Camilla Cockerton concludes for colonial Botswana often held true in other colonies in British Africa: "much of female migration took the form of unauthorized escape." These "runaways," as she calls them, sought relief from "arranged marriages" or were "'runaway wives' [from] violent or unhappy marriages," and this "'running away' only intensified as the twentieth century progressed." More broadly, she writes, "female migration was an escape from patriarchy."[36]

This movement across the Black Atlantic was analogous to the early twentieth-century Great Migration or the antebellum Underground Railroad that Black abolitionists like Du Bois might have recognized. In the Great Migration, millions of African Americans released themselves from the grasp of white supremacy in the South and its system of tenancy and debt peonage. Like the Underground Railroad, which relied on African American front-line communities along the border between free and slave states, African women waged a valiant struggle to create an urban beachhead from which to leverage freedom from rural bondage. Du Bois was quite familiar with the Great Migration, which had built the Harlem community where he lived and worked. Du Bois appreciated the worldwide historical importance of freedom seekers from slavery, but what he so brilliantly deduced in history, he missed in the living present. Even as the ongoing migration from the South gradually broke the back of the new slavery, Du Bois believed for much of his activist life that abolitionism in the twentieth century, especially in Africa, required working with the colonial powers toward reform. He did not recognize the connection between the voluntary migration of African Americans and the movement of African women who fled rural areas and stole into cities.[37]

Similar to the Underground Railroad, African women's resistance provoked a draconian response that might be likened to the Fugitive

Slave Law. The discovery that even a small number of women from Malawi were migrating to Zimbabwe was enough to galvanize colonial authorities to "refus[e] to admit women" who were not "accompanying their husbands." In the Ndola province of Zambia, an ordinance specified, "No woman may leave her village except with her properly married husband and also with the permission of the headman." The legal code took particular aim at the unmarried: "No single woman is to leave the area for the towns without the written permission of the Chief. Parents or guardians allowing a woman to go to or remain at towns for immoral purposes will be prosecuted." Legislation in British Lesotho also required the permission of a woman's "guardian" before she could leave the territory unaccompanied. Even where legislation did not restrict unmarried women to rural localities, colonial administrations attempted to accomplish the same purpose by forbidding them to enter urban areas. The policy reached its zenith in the principal British territories of east, central, and southern Africa, every one of which, with the exception of Uganda, had legislation on the books to exert what an official called "the control of the influx into the city."[38]

The goal of colonial authorities was the "repatriation" of those who succeeded in escaping, just as the mission of slaveholders had been to recover their runaways. That held true even for insurrectionaries. The Colonial Office included under the "rehabilitation of Mau-Mau adherents" in Kenya the preliminary punishment of sending women "to the work camps to work on irrigation schemes." The goal remained, however, to restore women to their state-mandated rural existence. Though they admitted that "reabsorption into village life . . . was an even more difficult problem than rehabilitation," British authorities retained that objective. They remained steadfastly dedicated to the rural confinement of women, on which they sought to structure a significant part of the economy of empire.[39]

The urban areas to which women escaped were no promised land, any more than the antebellum North had been for African Americans. Even as African Americans left the racialized zone of the South only to enter another one in the North, African women left one gendered zone for another. Their flight to towns and cities removed women from the main site of their bondage and gave them the capacity to contest it. Depending on time and place, the fate of women migrants varied, with some finding employment in various forms of trade and small businesses, such as brewing. Yet there is abundant evidence that many of the women who took refuge in the towns and cities of British Africa ended up in sex work or its equivalent and, as time went on, domestic labor. There were simply too few alternatives for unmarried African women. Urban location too often resulted in dependence on men in one form or another—as clients or through temporary marriages that, according to authorities, "verg[ed] on prostitution." The large numbers of women locked into sex work and domestic labor ensured the lasting consequences that still gender the urban world of the poor.[40]

The intersectional feminism of Ella Baker is crucial to an understanding of the complex interplay of the forces at work. The sex work of those bartered at the Bronx "slave market" was no less slavery because it offered the false veneer of choice to those in a state of "desperation." In her view, to give it another name would be to deny the manifold circumstances that substituted for any individual "slave driver." It was no different for a significant proportion of African women. At its worst, the state restricted their movement within cities—whether that meant being confined to a brothel or to the streets of a certain district—and they were subjected to the will of those who controlled the sex trade: urban authorities, police, pimps, and male clients. Though women used prostitution as an instrument of urbanization, the constraints it imposed on them only extended the restrictions of their movement, constituting a tangible sign of their unfree status in the gendered urban domain where they remained subject persons. It was as much a component of the new slavery as the sexual servitude of slave women was of the old slavery, even when women acted, for all intents and purposes, on their own initiative. It was no different from enslaved people in the antebellum United States working their own land, marketing the product, and hiring themselves out. The purpose of restricting their movement in Africa was to maintain control over African women's bodies.[41]

Prostitution was a means of women's escape from rural bondage, but only because they still lacked the essential economic freedom that Douglass identified as the sine qua non of liberation from slavery: the ability and the right to choose one's occupation. Wherever the line between trafficking and sex work may have lain in other parts of the world, British policy in Africa ensured that prostitution bore little resemblance to work freely chosen. It was indelibly stamped with the taint of continued bondage, albeit transferred from the rural world to the urban.

The pass laws and the location policy they enforced across British east, central, and southern Africa rendered women presumptive fugitives in urban centers. Even those who engaged in sex work were not criminals because of their profession; rather, large numbers of women were forced into prostitution in significant part because of their tenuous legal status outside rural areas. The colonial state did not merely tolerate their existence but legally circumscribed it, with the intent of ensuring that unmarried women were fugitives in the urban areas where they sought refuge.

To be legally rendered a fugitive outside of rural locations has deep resonance across the Black world. It was, after all, represented in the very title of the 1850 Fugitive Slave Law enacted to prevent African Americans from escaping to the US North and Canada on the Underground Railroad. Females who were unattached to males in urban areas were positioned as the enemy by colonial authorities, who, as Carina Ray writes, "were predisposed to thinking that single, mobile, and entrepreneurial African women were prostitutes." Even as this perception conformed to what Ray calls "racist colonial ideologies about African female sexuality," it also conveniently constituted a pretext to disguise women's state-enforced subordination. In this sense, *prostitute* was merely another word for *rebel*, and the rebellion took the form of the illegal migration of women to urban areas.[42]

The municipal African affairs officer in Nairobi, Kenya, declared that that colony's pass laws—so reminiscent of those in the antebellum American South—needed to be strictly enforced if the British were to achieve their policy goals. He insisted, "we must confine Africans to locations," clarifying that he was referring primarily to women. He declared, "We want to keep prostitutes out as much as possible. The real object is to reduce the number of these persons." In language that resonates today, he called it a "war against prostitutes." We have come to recognize in such ballyhooed crusades the hidden agendas that often underlie them, and the British colonial war against prostitutes was no exception. It was a thinly disguised campaign against the freedom of women. The British Empire was blasé about prostitution in West Africa that resulted from the trafficking of young girls, yet it was positively incited to action in eastern and southern Africa, where engagement in sex work represented women's own initiative against coercive colonial rule. Prostitution was not the target. As Luise White concludes about colonial Nairobi, "prostitution was essential to the smooth running of a migrant labor economy."[43]

The objective of the war against prostitutes was to stem the tide of women migrating on their own. Strictly speaking, British colonial East Africa featured cities without unmarried women who were not positioned as fugitives and sex workers. Single women in colonial African cities were always under suspicion of being prostitutes. Even if colonial authorities could not successfully bar unmarried women from cities, Africans' exclusion from full citizenship rights, privileges, and state protections in urban industrial capitalist society impacted women more heavily. The fundamental gendering of the urban-rural divide in British colonial Africa via women's de facto rural serfdom meant that an indeterminate but not insignificant number were effectively at war with a colonial state intent on confining them to the reproductive captivity of rural marriage. This war on women indexed their ongoing rebellion as much as the numbers of freedom seekers who poured into the American North and across the border to Canada.

The victims of the forms of new slavery reserved for women, whether African American or African, were of little concern to the mainstream antislavery movement or anyone else, no matter the source of what Baker called their "slave wage." The International Abolitionist Federation, initially based in Britain but with an increasing presence across Europe, was organized in the 1870s to, as Stephanie Limoncelli writes, "combat the sexual exploitation of women." She notes that it "consciously" adopted "the abolitionist terminology used by the earlier international movement to combat slavery." By the twentieth century, "the abolitionists . . . helped to sway the League of Nations and the United Nations to incorporate universal, gender-based abolitionist language in their trafficking conventions and in their stance toward prostitution." Limoncelli chronicles how these activists' efforts included broadening the crime of trafficking from an initial focus on "'the white slave traffic' to the 'traffic in women,' so as to include women of color." In truth, however, the renaming did little or nothing to protect Black women caught up in the new slavery. Of all the extant varieties of anti-slavery or antitrafficking in the twentieth century, only intersectional Black abolitionism paid any attention to the sexual exploitation of Black women. But despite its efforts to highlight these conditions, combating them would be left largely to the tangible antislavery activism of the affected women themselves, especially in Africa.[44]

In not following up on Wells's analysis of the role of what she called civil slavery, Du Bois missed a crucial component of the new slavery that disproportionately impacted women. Baker, therefore, meaningfully advanced twentieth-century Black abolitionism in recognizing the need to end civil society's exclusion of women and to ensure equal state protections and benefits. These goals found particular expression in Africa, where women activists remained unsatisfied with how the triumph of the anticolonial movement affected their lives. Battling the poverty of the countryside, women's sporadic if determined resistance in the form of their escape to cities in the first half of the twentieth century took on the shape of a mass movement in the second half. In a racially bounded coercive labor system founded on the restriction of movement, voluntary migration became a means of claiming some measure of personal autonomy, as well as disrupting state-sponsored racial subordination. Urbanization was a battleground that pitted rural Africans against the colonial regime, just as the Great Migration put African Americans in conflict with southern authorities. British policy decisions were largely intended to maintain low wages, preserve the new slavery, and uphold imperial control of Africans. For both African men and women, urbanization was more than a temporary respite from a life of permanent migration—it represented an escape from the oppressive conditions of migrant labor and the collapsing subsistence that supported it.[45]

Intersectional Black abolitionism advances an understanding of urbanization in gender terms. Since cities in colonial Africa were gendered spaces, urbanization took African women out of the principal site of their bondage without taking them to a place of freedom. An intersectional Black abolitionist standpoint comprehends urbanization as a vastly underappreciated component of the twentieth-century women's liberation movement—one that involves rural women in large parts of the global South, but especially in Africa. It renders the women involved not as passive participants in urbanization but as active agents. Their insistence on being included in urban migration significantly disrupted the system of migrant labor. Women's defiance of colonial Africa's gendered space and property law via this urban foothold was, despite its limitations, of great importance in colonial times, and it remains so today to the cause of combating oppression. Intersectional Black abolitionism links the resistance of Africans, women in particular, to the history of those seeking to escape bondage in the Black world since the rise of modern racial slavery.[46]

However important—and however remarkable the feat for those who accomplished it—urbanization was only a partial solution. Not all could escape. As fertility rates rose and infant mortality declined, the population of Africa increased and, largely unnoticed, so did African women's burden of labor, both productive and reproductive. If, as the ILO found, "the uneducated woman living in the country working on the family land . . . works physically very hard practically all her waking hours" in "conditions of work [that] are particularly unsatisfactory," it was the result of colonial policy and not a legacy of precolonial African society. Colonialism produced precisely the same effects on women as those found under slavery: an increase in the amount of labor, both productive and reproductive, under significantly worse material conditions compared with precolonial times.[47]

The key role of African women activists in advancing the aims and the practice of Black abolitionism has continued into the twenty-first century. A 2012 conference in Dar es Salaam, Tanzania, launched the Women to Kilimanjaro movement, which organizers advertised as "aim[ing] to create space for us as rural women to be able to participate in decision making processes about land and natural resources." McFadden chronicles that in Zimbabwe, for instance, the "neocolonial state" that emerged after independence "fell short of the transformative changes needed to shift society from one embedded in exclusionary state and legal practices to one that provides all citizens access to the most fundamental resource in the society—arable land." She continues, "The collusion of white farmers with the neocolonial state in the exclusion of black farm workers from the protections and entitlements of citizenship" helped ensure continuation of "the practice of indentured black labor and child labor until recently (the late 1990s)." Women, in particular, were subject to "unpaid labor" that maintained the "luxurious lifestyle for the white settler family" amid the "hundreds of thousands of dispossessed people." Similar processes across eastern and southern Africa led to the Kilimanjaro Initiative, which its organizers described as "a rural women's mobilization across Africa towards an iconic moment at the foot" of Africa's highest mountain.[48]

African rural women demanded "access to use, control, own, inherit and dispose [of] their land and natural resources" as part of "an all-inclusive African women's charter"—reviving a decades-old South African goal. This political program filtered up through rural women's assemblies and "women farmers' forums" involving half of Africa's postindependence nations, and it called for "women empowerment." The activists sought a real voice in their own affairs, codification of their land rights, and an end to unregulated pollution of their land, themselves, and their children. They called for a "ban [on] harmful and oppressive cultural practices that undermine women's rights including those that prohibit women to inherit land and other resources." The transnational rural women's collective insisted that "government should enact laws to provide security and protection of women's rights defenders." These activists accomplished their historic Women to Kilimanjaro march outside the considerable spotlight of the resurgent twenty-first-century antislavery movement. No one would think to link the history of the one movement to that of the other. And yet the legacies of both the new slavery and the new antislavery live on today, including in the United States, which was the primary home of Black abolitionism. Because they do, twentieth-century Black abolitionism remains as relevant as ever.[49]

6

Black Abolitionism and the New Slavery in the Twenty-First Century

Several months after the 2018 Martin Luther King Day protest of incarcerated Floridians, a nationwide strike was launched, with work stoppages, sit-ins, and hunger strikes spanning nineteen days. Like its predecessor, it was a response to what the organizers, themselves prisoners, called "a systematic problem born out of slavery that this nation must come to grips with and address." Bennu Hannibal Ra-Sun, founder of the Free Alabama movement, launched the action to address the twin problems of "mass incarceration and prison slavery." Writing in the *San Francisco Bay View*, which advertises itself as the "National Black Newspaper," he insisted that because "our slave labor" is key to "helping to keep the empire running . . . as incarcerated and enslaved people the POWER to effect change, immediate change, lies exclusively in our hands alone."[1]

One of Ra-Sun's fellow Alabama inmates, writing in the same newspaper under the pseudonym "Swift Justice," called prisons "today's modern day plantations." Within them, the incarcerated "are still slaves, made applicable by the 13th Amendment to the United States Constitution," which excludes prison labor from the ban on slavery. Swift

Justice described the protests as a natural continuation of the freedom struggle waged by individuals from Harriet Tubman to Martin Luther King Jr., with "'modern-day' slavery" not really "all that modern" nor "named properly." "The correct term is industrial slavery, and industrial slavery was in full swing by the year 1866, hardly a year after the end of the Civil War." Replicating the essence of the analysis of both Ida B. Wells and W. E. B. Du Bois, the author recounts the history of convict labor in post–Civil War Alabama and across the South, describing it as the result of a successful campaign in which "every Southern state enacted an array of interlocking laws essentially intended to criminalize Black life." Swift Justice concludes, "nothing has changed today except the evolving of the prison industrial complex" and the evolution of "targeted individuals . . . from African Americans to impoverished Americans—albeit African Americans still feel the blunt end of this more than white Americans." Even after his release, Swift Justice writes, "I will always be branded and bear the marks of a slave, and I will remain in the capacity of a slave in the eyes of society due to the beliefs and propaganda that has been circulated throughout American history."[2]

In the words of Kevin Rashid Johnson, an incarcerated activist from Virginia and founder of the New African Black Panther Party, the clause of the Thirteenth Amendment permitting prison labor means that "slavery was not abolished, it was merely reformed." He writes in the *Guardian*, "Though I've always refused to engage in this modern slavery myself, I've witnessed plenty of examples of it. The most extreme were in Texas and Florida, where prisoners are forced to work in the fields for free, entirely unremunerated. They are cajoled into chain gangs and taken out to the fields where they are made to grow all the food that inmates eat: squash, greens, peas, okra. They are given primitive hand-held tools like wooden sticks and hoes and forced to till the soil, plant and harvest cotton." Participating means suffering enforcement through "coercion and violence." Refusal entails the "solitary confinement" Johnson has endured since 1994. Nationwide, there are hundreds of thousands of incarcerated men and women subject to what amounts to compulsory labor, some of it unpaid, as in Florida, some of it for a nominal wage of four cents per hour, as in Louisiana. As Swift Justice rightly notes, it is an institution that has become as multiracial as America itself. But as Johnson attests, "racial animus is always present," both in the societal justification and acceptance and in the inner workings of America's disproportionate incarceration of Black and brown people. Such critiques of the use of unpaid or extremely low-paid prison labor evince the continuing, active presence of postemancipation Black abolitionism.[3]

In a world built on and still featuring racial slavery, twentieth-century Black abolitionists' most important legacy was to keep the tradition of antiracist antislavery alive. They taught posterity that, in the absence of that alliance, varieties of racial slavery or its derivatives will escape detection. Abolitionists will find these hidden forms only if they look for them. In addition to manifesting all the hallmarks of what Wells called "civil and industrial slavery," they feature the world's "ultimate exploited" and display the same "color caste" that Du Bois identified as hereditary, historically entrenched, society-wide manifestations of oppression that often operate independent of the law. There endures the moral imperative to emancipate the victims of this "slavery in all but in name" or, as with prison activists, to support them in their struggle to free themselves. Even without providing a definitive standard, twentieth-century Black abolitionism may help expose what might otherwise be hidden from the standpoint of international law. Applying the intersectional Black abolitionist definition of slavery—using social difference as a basis for denying the rights and protections afforded other workers for purposes of exploitation beyond what is otherwise societally acceptable—provides a powerful tool to expose the new slavery that persists in our world.

The Continuing Role of Race

As in the American prison system, the racial basis of the new slavery is widespread in the twenty-first century. The *Guardian*, which was one of the few media outlets to chronicle the prison strike movement of 2018, must have counted on its ability to shock, if not dismay, its socially conscious readership when, some years earlier, it ran a story under the headline "Brazil's Ethanol Slaves." In this age of environmentalism, concern for the earth's fragile ecosystem is likely to be bundled with such worker-friendly practices as fair trade. Yet in a nation that is rapidly emerging, the paper declared, as "a global reference point on how to cut carbon emissions and oil imports at the same time," the "heart of Brazil's energy revolution" featured a scene right out of the continent's nefarious history of human bondage. The *Guardian* charged that "a destitute migrant workforce of about 200,000 men," housed in a "prison-like construction," "risk[ing] life and limb to provide the local factories with sugar cane," and "working 12-hour shifts in scorching heat," was helping to "prop up Brazil's ethanol industry." Scholars, government officials, and activists dispute the number of workers that should be classified as enslaved, based on various definitions of that status. But most agree that slavery exists in Brazil, including on sugar plantations, and is a function of recruitment methods, violations of minimum wage law, and "degrading conditions" of work. As Siobhán McGrath uncovered in extensive fieldwork, the workforce is intentionally racialized, with Black, or *pardo*, males preferred, even though an ample supply of willing workers exists locally. These practices are hidden by "a constructed silence around issues of race vis-à-vis slave labour" in Brazil.[4]

Across the Atlantic, such disturbing echoes of the past have also pricked the public conscience. CNN has reported on "chocolate's child slaves" employed in the West African cocoa industry, which produces most of the raw product that, when processed, feeds the world's chocolate addiction. In that industry, hundreds of thousands of workers are subject to bondage, and the principal victims of the rampant labor trafficking are children. The network charges that in Côte d'Ivoire and Ghana, "a team of CNN journalists found that child labor, trafficking and slavery are rife in an industry that produces some of the world's best-known brands." The International Institute for Tropical Agriculture concludes that perhaps 40 percent of the "child workers are recruited through intermediaries," and a quarter of them are "restricted to staying on the farms," where they work eleven-hour days, seven days a week, "under appalling conditions." Some of the children work for food only. The child laborers are often kept out of school, so illiteracy is not uncommon, especially among girls. Although the ILO concludes that "trafficked children . . . constituted a low percentage" of child laborers, the agency admits that this most vulnerable group might be difficult for "outsiders" to locate. In addition, as the *New York Times* observes, "the line between slave trading and the bondage of poverty is sometimes unclear."[5]

Awareness of the problem is not new. "International media attention at the beginning of the [last] decade on the use of child labour in cocoa farming in West Africa under appalling conditions," the ILO reports, "placed a glaring spotlight on just how harmful and hazardous agricultural work can be for children, particularly in areas of extreme rural poverty." "Glaring spotlight" might be something of an exaggeration, and the reverse is probably closer to the truth. The worst conditions of the derivatives of the new slavery, especially those involving children, generally take place in remote locations and attract little public notice, despite the recent upsurge in the global antislavery movement.[6]

There has been little investigation of cocoa, coffee, or tea production in Africa, and even less has been done about it. Negative publicity prompted an international boycott and efforts to pass legislation aimed at combating the use of coerced child labor, but the multibillion-dollar chocolate business successfully warded off regulation in favor of a voluntary protocol that seems to have had little effect. The experience of coffee cultivation is much the same, as Mark Pendergrast notes. "The vast majority" of producers "live in abject poverty without plumbing, electricity, medical care, or nutritious food. The coffee they prepare travels halfway around the world and lands on breakfast tables, offices, and upscale coffee bars of the United States, Europe, Japan and other developed countries, where cosmopolitan consumers routinely pay half a day's Third World wages for a good cup of coffee."[7]

These case studies demonstrate the continuation of the new slavery. In the United States and Brazil, Black and brown people are disproportionately victimized; on a global scale, they make up nearly the entirety of the enslaved. Yet the new antislavery's legacy of colorblind analysis continues to exert an impact. Kevin Bales has famously called the present-day bondage of children engaged in cocoa, coffee, tea, and tobacco production in Africa the "new slavery." He so named it on the grounds that it does not look all that much like the "old" slavery found especially in the Atlantic and Indian Ocean worlds. Bales, however, was not the first to use that term. His Black abolitionist forerunners and their turn-of-the-twentieth-century British antislavery allies coined it to describe European colonial labor systems taking shape across the Black world of the day. By the time Bales discovered the new slavery, it was no longer new. He simply ignored or was unaware of the history of twentieth-century Black abolitionism that, anticipating his usage by a hundred years, emphasized race as the inextricable link between the new slavery and the old.[8]

Bales inverts Black abolitionism's understanding, employing instead the colorblind analysis of the new antislavery, which views slavery in the abstract and then considers how race enters into it, if at all. Black abolitionists started with the observation that the new slavery perpetuated the old racial slavery and asked how it manifested, how it morphed from there, and how it impacted non-Black victims. They located its roots in race and saw its basis as global. In contrast, Bales writes in *Disposable People*, "in the new slavery race means little," adding that "caste and religion simply reflect [enslaved Black people's] vulnerability, it doesn't cause it." "The key difference" between those enslaved and those not "is not racial, but economic."[9]

Analyses like Bales's that deny the racial character of slavery today employ an ahistorical point of view that removes this bondage from its foundations in racism and colonialism. At the turn of the twentieth century, as Black abolitionism took shape in partnership with an antislavery that still harkened back to its nineteenth-century heyday, slavery above all brought race to mind. The reasons are readily apparent. The difference between trafficked white women and victims of the new slavery was all too real, a desideratum that became clear as soon as the scale of the respective scourges was examined. Despite similarly tragic and pitiable conditions, the slavery of Black people spanned—or threatened to span— a considerable part of three continents and affected millions of people, as it had in both the Atlantic and the Indian Ocean worlds. Like the earlier slavery in the Americas, it was rooted in the history and functioning of what Black abolitionists recognized as a purely racial system of colonialism, or what is sometimes called *racial colonialism* to distinguish it from other varieties. George Steinmetz defines that term as a "colonial situation . . . where political and social dominance was marked by the legal, social, and institutional division and segregation of colonizer and colonized, according to an officially sanctioned racial hierarchy." That racial organization was felt everywhere, including in the British antislavery movement, which is largely responsible for the definition of slavery now found in international treaties. Jean Allain reminds us, "There is no escaping the fact that the definition of slavery [in international law] emerged at the heights of European imperialism qua colonialism."[10]

The understanding put forward by twentieth-century Black abolitionism has very different implications for what the new slavery looks like in our world—and how to eradicate it—than that of the new antislavery. Black abolitionism recognized that to blame the new slavery on the effects of class and poverty conflates cause and effect. It is no coincidence that, using the World Bank's global standard of poverty, the proportion of white people in the world today who are middle class—and, conversely, the number of poor people who are nonwhite—asymptotically approaches 100 percent. This global relation between race and poverty is not a product of chance. The examination of global production reveals that these contours of class are expressed as a combination of the nature of the work involved in different branches of production, how much it is compensated, and who performs it. The categorical basis on which labor continues to be socially assigned is evinced in the perpetuation of unfree, often migratory labor in industries such as sugar and cocoa production, which bear the indelible imprint of a raced world economy.[11]

The end of European colonialism in the global South did not automatically mean the end of the new slavery as a racial system, any more than, as Frederick Douglass argued, emancipation guaranteed the termination of the old slavery. Just as African Americans could become the "slaves of society" even if they ceased to be chattel, global society's systemic racism and its effects can result in its own "slaves of society" where the colonial bonds have apparently been torn asunder. "Chocolate's child slaves," for instance, constitute the collective property of a structurally racist globalized society as much as, or perhaps more than, the individual property of their immediate employers. And they are far from alone. No one knows how many tens of billions of dollars are generated by the use of prison labor in the United States. At the same time, slave labor enters into the supply chain of global capitalism, known variously as the global production network or the global value chain. In addition to chocolate and sugar production, slave labor is involved in industries such as cutting and polishing diamonds; cutting and tanning leather; digging, loading, and crushing boulders at stone quarries; serving as porters in mines or even as silversmiths; and hundreds or perhaps thousands of other tasks spread across the world's slums that double as makeshift workplaces.[12]

In Africa's artisanal mining sector, a large if indefinite proportion of the million or so children employed are lone migrants; many of them are victims of trafficking, including those brought from Congo to

Angola to work in diamond mines. Mali estimates that 40 percent of child laborers between five and fourteen years old are performing *hazardous* labor, or 2.4 million of them. Children are favored workers in the West African cocoa industry and the East African tobacco, coffee, and tea industries for a number of interrelated reasons. First and foremost, they come cheaply: the forty thousand child laborers on the tea plantations of western Uganda, for instance, get thirty cents per day, slightly more than the twenty-five cents paid to the eighty thousand children working in the tobacco fields of Malawi. Just as important, children are readily controlled and exploited. In addition, employers claim that their size, energy, nimbleness, and dexterity make them particularly well suited to certain types of agrarian labor, such as picking tea leaves. One expert attests that "in any developing country where tobacco is grown, you find child labour starting at the age of five." The state makes little effort to protect children from the crassest forms of exploitation, so employers are subjected to little, if any, risk or potential inconvenience. Prosecutions in Malawi produce no more than a $34 fine.[13]

Reports of child labor on plantations and farms almost always include some variation of the phrase "long hours of unrelenting work," used by the *Guardian* to characterize the situation in the Malawian tobacco industry, which accounts for 70 percent of the nation's export income. The nongovernmental organization Plan International puts the average workday for children in the tobacco industry at twelve hours but admits that "some children work for much longer"—in fact, after working all day in the fields, "they go home and need to do household chores or work on the family farm." In the "picking season," according to the ILO, the workday can total eighteen to twenty hours between field work during the day and night work in the barns devoted to curing the leaves. A report by the US Department of Labor found that children employed on Kenyan coffee plantations who did not live on-site were "picked up by trucks between 05:30 and 06:30 and returned between 17:00 and 19:00."[14]

It is not just the long hours but the nature of the work itself and the conditions under which it is performed that mark this agrarian labor as the perpetuation of the new slavery. According to the ILO, "The problems related to agricultural child labour are particularly acute in sub-Saharan Africa, where nearly 30 per cent of all children under the age of 15 are thought to be working." In East African tobacco cultivation, children as young as five are put to a wide variety of tasks: clearing and digging fields prior to planting; weeding, picking leaves, and cutting down trees; carrying, sorting, bundling, and grading tobacco; and applying fertilizer and pesticides. Plan International conducted extensive interviews and concluded, "Children and adults we talked to were very clear that there is no differentiation between work done by adults and work done by children. Children do all the tasks even the heavy or dangerous ones." In the tobacco industry, as in many others, the dangers are not inconsiderable. Exposure to nicotine is a particular problem, with one study concluding that the average worker absorbs up to fifty-four milligrams per day, more than enough to induce nicotine poisoning and its considerable deleterious health effects. To all this are added the breathing difficulties and potential lung damage from inhaling tobacco dust, fumes, and smoke, as well as pesticides and fertilizers.[15]

These particular risks are compounded by the general effects of heavy labor, inducing nearly constant muscle and body pain, weakness, coughing (including coughing up blood), sleep deprivation, stunted growth, depression, and feelings of isolation. The weather, ranging from the cold dampness of the rainy season to the scorching sun and heat of the dry season, makes the labor more arduous and intensifies its physical toll. The work may be performed in what researchers describe as a "filthy environment," with squalid living quarters that offer no protection from the cold; nor are children provided with sufficient clothing or blankets. Drinking water is often contaminated, and diseases such as malaria, typhoid, and cholera are an incessant backdrop to plantation life. There are also environmental hazards, ranging from snake and insect bites to poisonous thorns. More potent is the danger from the human environment, which includes the omnipresent threat of punishment, beatings, psychological abuse, and the withholding of food. Girls on plantations are especially vulnerable to rape and the associated risk of sexually transmitted diseases (including HIV) and pregnancy. The work mangles children's bodies and ruins their health. In the mines of Africa, "children descend to the bowels of the earth to crawl through narrow, cramped, and poorly lit makeshift tunnels where the air is thick with dust." Children in the mines may work for up to twenty-four-hour shifts. Accidents are a constant menace. Mercury vapor takes an even greater toll, constituting an "invisible epidemic," according to Human Rights Watch (HRW). The adults in charge think nothing of inflicting these hazards and feel no obligation to ensure the proper care of these children, including providing something as basic as sufficient nourishment.[16]

The relationship between employers and child workers too often degenerates into pure coercion and ruthless exploitation. A striking paradox emerges from these conditions: the system traps children long enough for them to master what is often highly skilled labor. Given that there is little or no legal regulation of the hours of work for children, employers resort to the traditional means of controlling victims of unfree labor. Children are beaten for making mistakes or to promote docility. The US Department of Labor cites evidence of what it characterizes as "torture": "Cases have been documented where children trying to escape [from the factories or workshops where they were confined] were hung from trees, chained to looms, shot, or branded with a hot iron." Girls face the perpetual threat of sexual abuse or introduction to what international agencies call commercial sex work. Sometimes, as in gemstone brokering in Tanzania, such sex work is the only paid component of labor or the only means to obtain food.[17]

Toward an Intersectional Analysis of Present-Day Slavery

The true scale of exploitation becomes apparent only when we employ an intersectional Black abolitionist analysis. That vantage point reveals that the problem goes much deeper than is apparent from a survey of the conditions of child labor and that it centers on girls in particular. Human trafficking accounts for part of it. In its 2005 global survey, the United Nations identified three primary varieties in Africa: in order of prevalence, "trafficking in children primarily for farm labour and domestic work within and across countries; trafficking in women and young persons for sexual exploitation, mainly outside the region; and trafficking in women from outside the region for the sex industry of South Africa." These problems seemingly receive attention in inverse proportion to their pervasiveness. Cross-continental human trafficking in places like South Africa command much of the media coverage, even though local trafficking of girls is greater by orders of magnitude. Its dominance in the media notwithstanding, sex trafficking appears to constitute the smallest component of the reasons children are trafficked.

The largest is the least publicized: the traffic in child domestic workers. Each year, as many as 200,000 children are entrapped in this way in West and Central Africa alone.[18]

The case of fourteen-year-old "Susanne K," documented by HRW in 2007, illustrates the essential context of this exploitation of girls in particular. She describes how she became a "live-in" domestic worker in the Guinean capital. "I left [my] village after my parents died. I was about six or seven. I had no money and made my way to Conakry by going with truck drivers. First I tried to go by foot, but I was very hungry. So I was forced to go with men who wanted to have sex with me." That was only the beginning of Susanne K's ordeal. HRW sketches the conditions she met on arrival: "Child domestic workers rarely have any holidays, no weekly day off, and little rest during the day. They are made to work around the clock and are sometimes beaten when they try to rest or take a break." For the "live-out" domestic worker who resides with her family in rural areas, domestic labor typically involves a nine-hour workday and a six- to seven-day week. For migrant girls like Susanne K in cities, a fifteen- to seventeen-hour day is more common. The ILO finds that in Ghana, "many of them work for several years without taking any time off."[19]

"It has been established worldwide," the ILO concludes, that "domestic workers typically work in individual households where they are isolated and subject to the demands of the employer. Often, the conditions of their work are unregulated and prone to harassment (verbal, physical, and sexual), poor living conditions (small quarters and lack of adequate food), and little time off, if at all." A large number of child domestic workers like Susanne K work for room and board only, yet many report being given little food amounting to no more than two meals a day. As a result, they frequently experience weakness and illness. HRW discovered during its investigations in Guinea that "some girls are so hungry that they engage in sex for money or steal money from their host families to buy food." In general, the conditions of migrant domestic workers in urban areas are worse than those in rural areas, as "they leave their homes and live in with their employers with the risk of being physically or sexually abused." These girls may see their families no more than twice a year at most. Because they are often forced to perform onerous duties such as "carrying heavy weights at a young age," they can incur musculoskeletal deformation or other damage.[20]

Domestic servitude may involve relations of bondage, cash payments to parents for their children, and parents dealing with recruiters. As with sex trafficking, girls account for around 90 percent of trafficked domestic workers. In West Africa, where the problem is thought to be particularly rampant, girls working as migrants constitute the bulk of trafficking, much of it cross-border and even intercontinental. One estimate undertaken for the World Bank, now two decades old, put the number at more than fourteen million continent-wide in urban areas alone, meaning that the total was even greater. UNICEF acknowledges that the line between trafficking and legal "recruitment" is hazy, since "very little is known about recruitment processes and children's active involvement in these." Another UNICEF publication puts the proportion of child domestic workers subjected to trafficking or recruitment at four-fifths of the total in Ghana. A study for the United Nations found that "in Togo, for instance, child trafficking begins with a private arrangement between an intermediary and a family member, with promises for education, employment, or apprenticeship only to be turned to exploitative domestic workers." Facing little or no regulation, recruitment agencies have become notorious for their child trafficking activities.[21]

An ILO investigation reveals that the advent of "informal agents" has transformed "what used to be considered a system of traditional mutual assistance" into a crassly exploitative and overtly "commercial" practice. These agents may be relatives, friends, or neighbors, with payment rendered to the girls' parents. Debt bondage, however, need not involve payment to the parents of the child being trafficked. Desperately poor rural families may actually be charged a fee to place their children in employment, in which case the amount paid becomes the debt that binds the girl to the employer. Human rights workers suggest that these parents may never learn the actual fate of their children. According to the ILO, all too many "end up in conditions akin to slavery, where they perform extremely strenuous and dehumanizing work." Accounts broadly agree that, whatever its true extent, the trade in girls has risen dramatically over the past few decades. The urban affluent increasingly avail themselves of this cheap bonded (practically, if not legally) labor to relieve themselves of household duties.[22]

Domestic labor accounts for between one-third and two-thirds of "all working children" in the world—the vast majority of them girls—

according to a UNICEF study. International agencies and human rights groups testify that a substantial proportion of these girls face some of the most oppressive labor conditions in the world. However, the case of an anonymous twelve-year-old Malawian girl demonstrates that circumstances are no better in the agricultural sector. She told investigators for Plan International: "I went to work on the tobacco farm when the season had already started. It was the picking up time. We worked all day picking up the tobacco and then after 6 pm we would eat the supper and then start the bundling process again until 8 pm. After the bundling we would carry the tobacco to the pressing machine. When I did not manage 10 bundles per hour I would not be paid. I would just get food." All the elements of child exploitation seem present for this Malawian tobacco worker, just as they were for Susanne K. Reports of child labor on plantations and farms chronicle that the twelve-hour workdays endured by this anonymous twelve-year-old were widespread. Employers' ability to work these young girls so many hours speaks volumes.[23]

Under the 1956 Supplementary Slavery Convention, the state has an obligation to prevent what that international treaty designates *delivery into child exploitation*. This illegal practice is defined under the provision banning the employment of a "person of servile status," which also encompasses the bonded labor now widely labeled a form of modern slavery. Neither Susanne K nor the twelve-year-old Malawian girl fit the definitions of trafficking under existing international law. UNICEF recognizes the possibility of "recruiting" girls legally into child exploitation, but the line between legal recruitment and trafficking is unclear. Such a possibility can effectively disguise a market in girls. They are being delivered into child exploitation with such regularity and for such purposes that it amounts to nothing less than a trade in their bodies. Its scale is evidenced by the estimate that as many as fourteen million might be confined to domestic servitude in African cities alone.[24]

This present-day derivative of the slave trade is rooted in the demand for domestic servitude and sexual exploitation. Around the world, the consensus is that girls are being forced into prostitution at younger and younger ages. Over the last two decades, girls as young as ten have been trafficked in large numbers. In the much larger market for domestic servants, there is the same trend toward younger victims. An analysis by

Anti-Slavery International suggests that some incarnations of modern slavery preferentially target prepubescent girls, as much for their particular characteristics as for their special vulnerabilities. One reason that the youngest are preferred not only for sex trafficking but also as live-in domestics is that pregnancy is not an issue. Their lack of physical maturity gives their employers wide latitude for sexual abuse without unwanted consequences. Indeed, pregnancy can be grounds for return.[25]

Our tendency is to interpret so much of the world, and especially exploitation, in purely commercial terms. It might therefore be surprising to learn that the motivation behind girls' servitude is not profit but convenience and power. The virtual or actual enslavement of girls as domestics is tolerated not because it is profitable but because it is the only way for the urban affluent to obtain what they want from girls. Employers seek the subordination of girls' lives to expediency. There is both incentive and advantage. Although it shares many of the same essential conditions as sexual exploitation, trafficking for domestic servants is devoid of a profit motive for the employer. The trafficker may realize a profit, but the affluent household that hires the live-in domestic worker is engaging in a consumer transaction rather than a commercial operation. The buyer may save money but does not realize a profit on capital invested; this is purely the purchase of a service, even if it is still a form of economic exploitation.

The ramifications for girls at the bottom of the international labor hierarchy are profound. A report compiled for the World Bank, for instance, notes that while most trafficking of girls in Nigeria was for domestic labor, they were also taken for "sexual exploitation" and to "work in shops or on farms, to be scavengers or street hawkers." HRW found that, for West Africa as a whole, "children are trafficked for domestic labor, agricultural labor, market labor and street selling and begging," although "some children are also trafficked for prostitution and sexual exploitation." Girls are the usual victims because they are easily subjected to the total control of their de facto owners and confined to their houses, where they "may also be used for sex." The sexual exploitation of girls permeates their subjection to unfree labor today. Agrarian or mining labor can serve as an introduction to commercial sex work, or it may be the only means for girls so employed to obtain food. For girls especially, there is no clear demarcation between child exploitation and sexual servitude because the two are inextricably intertwined.[26]

Girls' participation in the workforce is necessarily coerced as a condition of forcing them to perform labor they do not want to engage in. They constitute a special category of worker, as the enslaved have since the institution's inception. There is preferential and even exclusive use of girls in entire industries, and they are almost uniquely subjected to child exploitation under the guise of family protection.[27] The exploitation of girls is distinguished by the following:

- The age at which it commences—as young as five
- The frequency of migration without a parent or guardian
- Low or no pay or being forced to resort to commercial sex work to survive
- The hours, place, and material circumstances of work
- The toxins to which they are exposed and the sicknesses they acquire
- The lack of state protections that most other workers claim as a right
- The amount of overt compulsion involved

Their oppression also includes systemic abuse—physical, emotional, and sexual. It is so pervasive that it almost seems to be a condition of girlhood itself. Human rights organizations report that employment for girls, as for no other workers, is the basis for forced prostitution and sex trafficking. There is an almost complete absence of the conditions of free labor as set down by the ILO.[28]

Kamala Kempadoo suggests that lessons from the history of slavery support "a move away from the conflation of slavery and human trafficking with all forced, bonded and migrant labour," especially on the grounds that slavery was a racial institution. The historiography of slavery, however, does not back up her contention that the term has been used only for the racial system found in the Americas, nor do historians use the word to describe only its chattel form. Rather, a historical vantage point shows that the institution of slavery has been notably diverse. Moreover, race itself is a form of *difference*, and not the only one that continues to be socially constructed or plays a vital role in determining social vulnerability today, although it is true that race remains central.[29]

Whatever their status under international law, the tens of millions of girls trapped in exploitative labor conditions meet the definition of the new slavery developed by twentieth-century Black abolitionism. As it did in the twentieth century, Black abolitionism offers an important analytical tool to identify the deeper and broader imprint of the new slavery today than is likely to be discerned without taking advantage of its explanatory power. Black abolitionist analysis penetrates beneath the outward forms to the underlying means and purposes that have always characterized the racial slavery built into the very structure of racial capitalism. The historical roots of this differential exploitation of Black and brown people lie deep in the colonial past, while the resultant slavery continues to serve neocolonial economic purposes as part of the global supply chain that enriches the global North at the expense of the South, even as it helps maintain the racialized wealth gap in the North. Making matters worse, it ramifies and morphs into other manifestations. Global society's need to profess ignorance of the racial foundations of the new slavery, despite being deeply implicated in it, leads to noncommercial practices that afflict even more people of color, while drawing on the same sources of victims using identical mechanisms.

The cause goes much deeper than class or poverty, as an intersectional analysis reveals. The interlocking systems of oppression that determine the social vulnerability of the girls who disproportionately make up the source population for modern slavery also include the following:

- Gender
- Social difference such as race, ethnicity, caste, indigeneity
- Rural birth
- Childhood

The girls marked by these social characteristics are often made vulnerable by the absence of three essential conditions: effective state protection, the security of urban citizenship, and meaningful education.

Girls like Susanne K who are subjected to the worst kind of child exploitation—especially in domestic and agricultural labor—come from distinct social groups. Girls of rural origin are a major source of unfree labor across much of the world. Annamarie Kiaga and Vicky Kanyoka describe the motivations of urban Tanzanians in preferring girls from rural areas: "The rural 'housegirl' is often perceived as timid, lacking the knowledge base and skills often associated with work in the urban space. . . . Migrants, due to their unfamiliarity of their new workplace, tend to accept, in the first instance, any rights offered to them, in a bid to survive the first few days, months or years of their migrancy." However they get to cities, most girls remain rural migrants in an alien and hostile urban world. In East Africa, according to Kiaga and Kanyoka's study for the ILO, few girls remain in towns and cities after their term of domestic servitude ends. A sizable portion are actually "escorted back to their rural villages." HRW finds that in Guinea, "Girls are expected to perform domestic work and then marry at a young age," having vacated the cities—where they were unwelcome migrants and, like African women under colonialism, lacked the rights and privileges of recognized urban citizens—and returned to the rural homes they came from. What the United Nations has called the unwanted "surplus population" of the cities includes girls of rural birth who work there.[30]

Joseph Miller notes that in early twentieth-century Africa and the Indian Ocean world, "Gender, in excluding women from participation in modern civic societies, became the equivalent of race in the Americas as an ideology." According to Orlando Patterson, the defining characteristic of persons subject to unfree labor has evolved from the racial "other" of the Atlantic slave trade to a primary focus on children. Just as crucial, he calculates that females today constitute a majority of the enslaved, as they have throughout history. Bales highlights the dangers to "children who are members of a group suffering from discrimination." In particular, he notes, "Without a birth certificate a child is a non-person." Even when their births are registered, impoverished girls of rural origin are often second-class citizens. What Bales does not acknowledge is that poverty now provides a pretext for this heritable social inferiority. What scholars of slavery call "social vulnerability" would not be preferentially attached to girls were it merely the reflection of poverty alone and not broader and interlocking systems of oppression. The plight of trafficked and exploited girls today is explained not by poverty but, in significant part, by global society's failure to protect them from delivery into child exploitation.[31]

The traffic in girls is tolerated because their migration occurs outside the state's purview. As the ILO puts it, "Society sees the children as the property of the employer, and 24 hours a day, 365 days a year, the domestic servant's status remains unchanged." Their right to education is denied because they are not deemed urban citizens entitled to attend local schools. The state refuses to uphold the Supplementary Slavery Convention with respect to girls like Susanne K because they are positioned outside its scope. That treaty, however, is applicable to all. To exclude anyone from its provisions is fundamentally to deny her humanity, with resonances of what Patterson famously described as a distinguishing feature of slavery: social death.[32]

Nevertheless, these girls do resist their subjection to ceaseless, brutalizing labor with no respite, let alone benefit. Their resistance to the violation of their bodily autonomy through sexual abuse is, ironically, reflected in the regimen of torture inflicted on those held in sexual servitude. Some of the cruelty exhibited by the employers of domestic workers is a response to the girls' refusal to submit to their conversion into either sex workers or domestic drudges in the households of strangers. As a result, nearly half the girls in one place investigated by Save the Children faced "severe abuse that left them with bodily injuries," as well as "emotional torture." Girls are isolated from their families and society to suppress their unwillingness to submit to exploitation. Child labor often comes to light only as a result of the abuse employers engage in to overcome the children's refusal to be compliant. Black abolitionism has always recognized the need to let the enslaved define what constitutes slavery. To understand unfree labor, we must make every effort to appreciate and comprehend the scope of resistance among child laborers, which suggests that they consider themselves unfree, if only in their determination to escape.[33]

The Ongoing Resistance of the Enslaved

The conditions of slavery that link incarcerated Black people in the United States, sugar plantation workers in Brazil, and children on cocoa plantations or in the homes of the affluent in Africa have everything to do with the systemic racism embedded in the world economy. Their bondage constitutes the perpetuation of the new slavery, which in no sense is an indigenous system in Africa or anywhere else. It is more continuity than legacy, the perpetuation into the twenty-first century of the ruthless exploitation of enslaved Black and brown people to supply the conveniences and extravagances of industrial societies. And that is not the only remnant of the previous century. Though they suck up a disproportionate share of attention and resources, the antislavery and antitrafficking movements have been insufficiently interested in and effective at combating the new slavery of Black and brown people in the twenty-first century.

The direct descendants of twentieth-century Black abolitionism, including movements like Black Lives Matter, take aim at systemic racism. Those descended from the colorblind new antislavery, in contrast, only ineffectively target symptoms of the much more deeply rooted problem of the racialized world economy, content to leave untouched the larger context in which slavery thrives, including racialized international labor law. To recapture its former transformative power, antislavery needs to reconnect directly and explicitly with antiracism, first and foremost in the movements growing out of the self-organization of the enslaved. The antislavery and antitrafficking movements should take their lead from these expressions of the enslaved for self-liberation.

Abolitionism has historically been unable to get to the heart of its chosen cause, except when grounded in the experiences of those whose cause it champions. The most consistent and advanced abolitionists have always been the enslaved or the formerly enslaved. Nineteenth-century abolitionism sprang from and was in constant contact with the enslaved. The most advanced nineteenth-century abolitionists, African Americans in particular, already understood that the racial slavery of the Americas would never be completely eradicated until the racism in which it took root was eliminated, a position confirmed by subsequent history. The abolition of slavery in the absence of the eradication of its underlying cause of racial oppression did more than leave African Americans in a predicament of second-class citizenship. That, on its own, was bad enough, permitting the persistence of slavery-like forms of tenancy and the violence and terrorism that kept it in place over the next hundred years. Worse yet, racial slavery recrossed the Atlantic to subjugate millions more Black people.

The problem of slavery today is not simply the large numbers—a Black abolitionist analysis uncovering the magnitude of the exploitation that remains. It also involves what links the present to the past—the same categorical nature of who is subject to enslavement found in the centuries-old racial slavery of the Americas and the new slavery of the twentieth century. Slavery on the mass scale that existed then and is still observed today requires a population of servile status to draw on. Eliminate that state-enforced servile status, and slavery must disappear. Colonial policy, with the complicity of international law, largely created these servile conditions, so we must now do everything in our power to eliminate those oppressive circumstances. That includes—but is by no means limited to—acknowledging the servile status that amounts to slavery and banning it. International law is not a sacred text; it is a mirror of the achievements but also the flaws and blind spots of contemporary society. The focus should not be on guarding legalistic or formalistic definitions of slavery. We do not need to protect the category—legal or otherwise—from its too broad application to conditions of human oppression. This argument applies whether we are considering US prison labor or global child exploitation. As "Swift Justice" recognizes, America's unpaid prison labor exploits a loophole in the Thirteenth Amendment. Similarly, the new slavery of girls, in particular, takes hold in the defective international conventions that are the legacy of the new antislavery.

The ILO's argument that child exploitation will be "progressively" eliminated through economic development, "with the eradication of the worst forms an urgent priority," is fundamentally flawed. Ending poverty is a noble and worthwhile goal, but it is not the means to end the enslavement of girls in our world, any more than America's general affluence has eliminated the prison-industrial complex. That task requires abolishing all systemic racism in the world economy and its ramifications, such as the second-class status of rural impoverished girls vis-à-vis the state. The state must provide equal protection and equal education to all children, not just those from affluent circumstances. Such a goal is immediately attainable and does not require a long-term "development strategy."[34]

A key lesson that emerges from the study of the abolitionism of both the nineteenth and twentieth centuries is that its most advanced forms emerged from the steadfast resistance of the enslaved to their bondage. That principle is at work in the activism of the incarcerated in the United States and in the struggle of Suzanne K and tens of millions of girls like her. What we might call their *resistance of unmet expectations* echoes what Frederick Douglass referenced in contrasting the difference between "a slave in form" and "a slave in fact," rooted in the former's determination to be free and refusal to succumb to a world that seemingly aspires to suppress that aim. Girls like Suzanne K embody that spirit. They clearly express before anything else their desire to go to school. And these girls do not want just the rudiments of education that UNESCO seeks to guarantee them, such as basic literacy, basic numeracy, and life skills. They want the same education provided to those who become doctors, lawyers, scientists, college professors, and antislavery activists. They understand that education alone is not enough. It must be education that breaks down the categorical basis of exclusion, education that ends the use of poverty as a pretext for their state-enforced servile status that enables their callous exploitation.[35]

That lesson must be applied to an intersectional analysis of all persons caught up in slavery today. The resistance of unmet expectations of rural impoverished girls is a clarion call, in David Walker's immortal words, "one continual cry" aimed at awakening the world's conscience. These girls themselves are doing the hardest part—fighting for the right to go to school and acquire an education in the most challenging circumstances imaginable. The urbanization following colonialism's demise has given way to another mass form of resistance by the girls caught on the bottom of the global social hierarchy that claims to be a regime of individual rights. Their quest for equal education—the irresistible and irrepressible process of their claiming it—embodies one of the most far-reaching and significant social justice movements of our time. Together with parallel movements of unpaid prison laborers, sugar plantation workers, and many others, it represents the self-liberation of the enslaved of this epoch. In a larger sense, it is the vindication of the human spirit, the striving after the intellectual, the spiritual, and the ethical that should define human society, rather than the material. The struggle of the enslaved everywhere, persevering in the face of a global society that turns its back on them, gives hope to a world that has lost its way and calls on us to refocus on what really matters. Given time, it will remake society, as movements of the oppressed always have.[36]

Appendix 1

Chronology of Important Events

1865   Emancipation; Frederick Douglass enunciates "four
            freedoms" in a speech to abolitionists
1885   Berlin conference—European powers divide Africa
1889   Henry Fox Bourne assumes leadership of Britain's
            Aborigines Protection Society
1890   Frederick Lugard commands British forces in conquest
            of East Africa
1893   Ida B. Wells takes her antilynching crusade to England
            and lays the groundwork for twentieth-century Black
            abolitionism
1896–1897   Alice Kinloch begins antislavery agitation in Britain;
            London-based African Association is created; W. E. B.
            Du Bois takes up a professorship at Atlanta University
            and begins studying the new slavery in the South
1900   Pan-African Conference
1903   Du Bois publishes *Souls of Black Folk*
1909   NAACP journal *The Crisis* is founded under Du Bois's
            editorship; Du Bois publishes *John Brown*; death of
            Henry Fox Bourne; merger of Aborigines Protection

	Society and Anti-Slavery Society, with John Harris as leader of the new organization
1912	Promulgation of the Cromer doctrine, underpinning the new antislavery
1919	Peace talks in Paris; Red Summer; First Pan-African Congress
1921	Second Pan-African Congress
1926	League of Nations' Slavery Convention ratified
1930	League of Nations' Forced Labour Convention ratified
1931	George Padmore publishes *The Life and Struggles of Negro Toilers*
1935	Du Bois publishes *Black Reconstruction*; Ella Baker publishes exposé of "slave market" for female African American domestic workers
1963	March on Washington; death of Du Bois in Accra, Ghana

Appendix 2

Organizations and Treaties

Aborigines Protection Society (APS). Founded initially as a committee of the British Parliament, it subsequently evolved into an independent membership organization that advocated better treatment of subjects of the British Empire. Under Henry Fox Bourne's leadership at the turn of the twentieth century, the APS became the leading abolitionist organization in Britain.

African Association. Formed in England in 1897 by South African journalist Alice Kinloch and Trinidadian law student Henry Sylvester Williams and their circle of associates to advance the political interests of Black people.

Anti-Slavery and Aborigines Protection Society. Created through the merger of the British and Foreign Anti-Slavery Society and the Aborigines Protection Society in 1909, following the death of Henry Fox Bourne. The group became the center of the new antislavery under the leadership of John Harris.

British and Foreign Anti-Slavery Society (BFASS). British abolitionist association founded in 1834 to aid the international antislavery movement after the abolition of slavery in British territories.

First Pan-African Congress. Called by W. E. B. Du Bois in 1919 to gather Black people and allies from around the world to place questions of African self-determination and Black freedom on the agenda of the peace talks ending World War I.

Forced Labour Convention of 1930. International treaty that obligated signatories to outlaw and suppress all forms of coerced labor, even if they did not fall under the definition of slavery in international law.

International Labor Organization (ILO). Post–World War I agency designed to bring together governments, employers, and workers to adopt and promulgate labor standards and other policies to improve working conditions globally. It was formed by a commission chaired by Samuel Gompers, president of the American Federation of Labor. In 1946 the ILO was attached to the United Nations.

League of Nations. First proposed by President Woodrow Wilson and founded by the victorious Allies in the aftermath of World War I—albeit without US participation—as a foundation for world governance. It became the model for the United Nations, which was created after World War II.

League of Nations Permanent Mandates Commission. Charged with overseeing the principally German colonies confiscated by and distributed among the Allies after World War I.

National Association for the Advancement of Colored People (NAACP). Interracial civil rights organization founded in 1909 to revive the politics of nineteenth-century abolitionism and pursue civil rights for African Americans. Du Bois was among its most prominent founders and one of its most important leaders through the mid-1930s; he edited its influential magazine *The Crisis*.

Pan-African Conference. Convened in London in 1900 by the African Association to discuss questions of importance to Africans and people of African descent across the Atlantic world and to develop a program of joint action. Du Bois attended and wrote its closing address "To the Nations of the World."

Second Pan-African Congress. Organized by Du Bois in 1921 to follow up on the first and form a permanent organization that he hoped would be a force in postwar international politics.

Slavery Convention of 1926. Treaty that developed the legal definition of slavery in international law and obligated its signatories to suppress slavery and the slave trade in territories under their control.

Appendix 3

Important Historical Figures

Ella Baker (1903–1986). Iconic civil rights leader who helped found both the Southern Christian Leadership Conference that catapulted Martin Luther King Jr. to national prominence and the Student Nonviolent Coordinating Committee that launched Black Power.

Cyril Briggs (1888–1966). Born in the British Caribbean territory of Nevis, Briggs was a Harlem-based political activist, founder of the African Blood Brotherhood, and editor of *The Crusader*.

Lord Cromer (1841–1917). Born Evelyn Baring, Cromer was a leading British imperial administrator who rose to the position of consul general of Egypt. He was an influential figure in the antislavery movement, particularly in delimiting the acceptable use of forced labor in the British Empire.

W. E. B. Du Bois (1868–1963). Political activist, scholar, leading figure in Pan-Africanism, principal founder of the NAACP, and author of *The Souls of Black Folk* and *Black Reconstruction*.

Henry Fox Bourne (1837–1909). Leading British abolitionist in the 1890s and early 1900s, when he served as secretary of the Aborigines

Protection Society. Fox Bourne worked closely with Alice Kinloch in reforging the long-dormant alliance of antiracism and antislavery and was a staunch critic of the new slavery in British territories.

Marcus Garvey (1887–1940). Influential Jamaican-born founder of the Universal Negro Improvement Association (UNIA), whose international membership in the 1920s surpassed that of all other Black political groups.

John H. Harris (1874–1940). Leading British abolitionist after the death of Henry Fox Bourne until his own death three decades leader. During that time, Harris helped formulate the principles and served as the organizational leader of the new antislavery in his role as secretary of the Anti-Slavery and Aborigines Protection Society.

Alice Kinloch (circa 1860–circa 1930). South African journalist who cofounded the African Association with Henry Sylvester Williams. Her speeches and writings in the late 1890s sparked an antislavery revival in Britain focused on the new slavery in the empire, and she worked with Henry Fox Bourne to revive the alliance of antiracism and antislavery.

Frederick Lugard (1858–1945). Britain's point man on the issue of slavery during the 1920s, when the foundations for international antislavery law were being developed. First Baron Lugard was a high-ranking imperial administrator, leader of British forces in East Africa in the early 1890s, and a key figure in the new antislavery.

Kwame Nkrumah (1909–1972). Pan-Africanist and anticolonial movement leader in Ghana. He served as the new nation's first prime minister in 1957, following its independence from Britain.

George Padmore (1903–1959). Born Malcolm Nurse in Trinidad, Padmore became a prominent Pan-Africanist in the 1930s and 1940s. In 1945 he took the lead in reviving the Pan-Africanist movement, which had been dormant for two decades, helping to galvanize the final push for African independence following World War II.

Ida B. Wells (1862–1931). Born into slavery, Wells garnered international attention when her antilynching crusade took her to England, where she helped spearhead the revival of the antislavery-antiracism alliance.

Henry Sylvester Williams (1867–1911). Trinidadian law student who worked with Alice Kinloch to found the African Association, which gave birth to the Pan-Africanist movement.

Notes

Preface

1. See, e.g., Manisha Sinha, *The Slave's Cause: A History of Abolition* (New Haven, CT: Yale University Press, 2016); Stanley Harrold, *American Abolitionism: Its Direct Impact from Colonial Times into Reconstruction* (Charlottesville: University of Virginia Press, 2019); Richard S. Newman, *Abolitionism: A Very Short Introduction* (New York: Oxford University Press, 2018); Christopher Leslie Brown, *Moral Capital: Foundations of British Abolitionism* (Chapel Hill: University of North Carolina Press, 2006); Paul Goodman, *Of One Blood: Abolitionism and the Origins of Racial Equality* (Berkeley: University of California Press, 1998); Eric Foner, *Politics and Ideology in the Age of the Civil War* (New York: Oxford University Press, 1980); Catherine Hall, *Civilising Subjects: Metropole and Colony in the English Imagination, 1830–1867* (Cambridge: Polity, 2002).

2. Joel Quirk, *The Anti-Slavery Project: From the Slave Trade to Human Trafficking* (Philadelphia: University of Pennsylvania Press, 2014); Suzanne Miers, *Slavery in the Twentieth Century: The Evolution of a Global Problem* (New York: AltaMira Press, 2003); Kevin Grant, *A Civilised Savagery: Britain and the New Slaveries in Africa, 1884–1926* (New York: Routledge, 2005).

3. On twentieth-century slavery, cf. Douglas Blackmon, *Slavery by Another Name: The Re-enslavement of Black Americans from the Civil War to World War Two* (New York: Anchor Books, 2008); Thomas C. Holt, *The Problem of Freedom: Race, Labor, and Politics in Jamaica and Britain, 1832–1938* (Baltimore: Johns Hopkins University Press, 1992); Frederick Cooper, Thomas C. Holt, and Rebecca J. Scott, *Beyond Slavery: Explorations of Race, Labor, and Citizenship in*

217

Postemancipation Societies (Chapel Hill: University of North Carolina Press, 2000); Miers, *Slavery in the Twentieth Century*; Grant, *Civilised Savagery*.

Introduction

1. Richard Luscombe, "Florida Prisoners Plan Martin Luther King Day Strike over 'Slavery,'" *Guardian*, January 15, 2018; Martin Luther King Jr., "Martin Luther King, Jr., Saw Three Evils in the World," *Atlantic*, February 2018. On the history of the freedom struggle of the incarcerated, see Robert Chase, *We Are Not Slaves: State Violence, Coerced Labor, and Prisoners' Rights in Postwar America* (Chapel Hill: University of North Carolina Press, 2019).

2. Ben Conarck, "Work Forced: A Century Later, Unpaid Prison Labor Continues to Power Florida," *Florida Times-Union*, May 25, 2019. On the prison-industrial complex and the history of mass incarceration, see Michelle Alexander, *The New Jim Crow: Mass Incarceration in the Age of Colorblindness* (New York: New Press, 2020); Elizabeth Hinton, *From the War on Poverty to the War on Crime: The Making of Mass Incarceration in America* (Boston: Harvard University Press, 2016). See also Clarence Lusane and Dennis Desmond, *Pipe Dream Blues: Racism and the War on Drugs* (Boston: South End Press, 1991).

3. Martin Luther King Jr., "Honoring Dr. Du Bois," W. E. B. Du Bois Papers (MS 312), Special Collections and University Archives, University of Massachusetts Amherst Libraries; Martin Luther King Jr., "I Have a Dream," address delivered at the March on Washington for Jobs and Freedom, Martin Luther King Papers, Martin Luther King Jr. Research and Education Institute, Stanford University. See also Robert W. Williams, "M. L. King's Abiding Tribute to W. E. B. Du Bois: Research, Activism, and the Unknowable," *Phylon* 56 (Summer 2019): 134–55; Charles Euchner, *Nobody Turn Me Around: A People's History of the 1963 March on Washington* (Boston: Beacon Press, 2010). On the history of the "long civil rights movement," see Nikhil Pal Singh, *Black Is a Country: Race and the Unfinished Struggle for Democracy* (Cambridge, MA: Harvard University Press, 2004).

4. Martin Luther King Jr. "Where Do We Go from Here?" address delivered at the Eleventh Annual SCLC Convention, Martin Luther King Papers, Martin Luther King Jr. Research and Education Institute, Stanford University; Martin Luther King Jr., "Martin Luther King Jr. Saw Three Evils in the World," *Atlantic*, February 2018, https://www.theatlantic.com/magazine/archive/2018/02/martin-luther-king-hungry-club-forum/552533/; Sylvie Laurent, *King and the Other America: The Poor People's Campaign and the Quest for Economic Equality* (Berkeley: University of California Press, 2018); Michael Honey, *Going down Jericho Road: The Memphis Strike, Martin Luther King's Last Campaign* (New York: Norton, 2011); Thomas F. Jackson, *From Civil Rights to Human Rights: Martin Luther King, Jr., and the Struggle for Economic Justice* (Philadelphia:

University of Pennsylvania Press, 2013); Bernard LaFayette Jr. et al., eds., *The Chicago Freedom Movement: Martin Luther King Jr. and Civil Rights Activism in the North* (Lexington: University Press of Kentucky, 2016). On the influence of the Black Power movement, see Peniel Joseph, *Waiting 'til the Midnight Hour: A Narrative History of Black Power in America* (New York: Holt, 2007).

5. Clarence B. Jones and Stuart Connelly, *Behind the Dream: The Making of the Speech that Transformed a Nation* (New York: St. Martin's Press, 2012), 145–49. For biographies of King and Du Bois, see David Levering Lewis, *King: A Biography* (Urbana: University of Illinois Press, 2013); David Levering Lewis, *W. E. B. Du Bois: Biography of a Race, 1868 to 1919* (New York: Holt, 1993); David Levering Lewis, *W. E. B. Du Bois, 1919–1963: The Fight for Equality and the American Century* (New York: Holt, 2001).

6. King, "Honoring Dr. Du Bois"; Martin Luther King Jr., "Dr. Martin Luther King, Jr.'s 1962 Speech in New York City," New York State Museum, www.nysm.nysed.gov/mlk-1962-address. See Heather Schoenfeld, *Building the Prison State: Race and the Politics of Mass Incarceration* (Chicago: University of Chicago Press, 2018).

7. W. E. Burghardt Du Bois, "The Spawn of Slavery: The Convict-Lease System in the South," *Missionary Review of the World* 14 (October 1901): 737, 738–40. For scholarly accounts, see Adelle Blackett and Alice Duquesnoy, "Slavery Is Not a Metaphor: U.S. Prison Labor and Racial Subordination through the Lens of the ILO's Abolition of Forced Labor Convention," *UCLA Law Review* 67, no. 6 (2021): 1504–35; Mary Rose Whitehouse, "Modern Prison Labor: A Reemergence of Convict Leasing under the Guise of Rehabilitation and Private Enterprises," *Loyola Journal of Public Interest Law* 18 (2017): 89; Neveen Hammad, "Shackled to Economic Appeal: How Prison Labor Facilitates Modern Slavery while Perpetuating Poverty in Black Communities," *Virginia Journal of Social Policy and the Law* 26, no. 2 (2019): 65–90; Jaron Brown, "Rooted in Slavery: Prison Labor Exploitation," *Race, Poverty and the Environment* 14, no. 1 (2007): 42–44. On the post–Civil War history, see Dan T. Carter, *Prisons, Politics and Business: The Convict Lease System in the Post–Civil War South* (Madison: University of Wisconsin Press, 1964); Douglas Blackmon, *Slavery by Another Name: The Re-enslavement of Black Americans from the Civil War to World War Two* (New York: Anchor Books, 2008).

8. Du Bois, "Spawn of Slavery," 745. On the ideological defense of slavery, see Larry Tise, *Proslavery: A History of the Defense of Slavery in America, 1701–1840* (Athens: University of Georgia Press, 1987).

9. Manisha Sinha, *The Slave's Cause: A History of Abolition* (New Haven, CT: Yale University Press, 2016), 338. See also Paul Goodman, *Of One Blood: Abolitionism and the Origins of Racial Equality* (Berkeley: University of California Press, 1998). On the tracing of modern antislavery's genealogy, see Joel

Quirk *The Anti-Slavery Project: From the Slave Trade to Human Trafficking* (Philadelphia: University of Pennsylvania Press, 2014).

10. Paul Lovejoy, *Transformations in Slavery: A History of Slavery in Africa*, 2nd ed. (New York: Cambridge University Press, 2000); Suzanne Miers and Richard L. Roberts, *The End of Slavery in Africa* (Madison: University of Wisconsin Press, 1988); Suzanne Miers and Martin A. Klein, introduction to *Slavery and Colonial Rule in Africa* (Portland, OR: Frank Cass, 1999); Gwynn Campbell, "Introduction: Slavery and Other Forms of Unfree Labour in the Indian Ocean World," in *The Structure of Slavery in Indian Ocean Africa and Asia*, ed. Gwynn Campbell (London: Frank Cass, 2004); Joseph Inikori, introduction to *Forced Migration: The Impact of the Export Slave Trade on African Societies*, ed. Joseph Inikori (London: Hutchinson University Library for Africa, 1982); Suzanne Miers, "Slavery to Freedom in Sub-Saharan Africa: Expectations and Reality," in *After Slavery: Emancipation and Its Discontents*, ed. Howard Temperley (London: Frank Cass, 2000); Ahmad Sikainga, *Slaves into Workers: Emancipation and Labor in Colonial Sudan* (Austin: University of Texas Press, 2010).

11. Lovejoy, *Transformations in Slavery*; Campbell, "Introduction: Slavery and Other Forms of Unfree Labour," xii–xxxii; Joseph Inikori, *Africans and the Industrial Revolution in England: A Study in International Trade and Development* (New York: Cambridge University Press, 2002); Inikori, introduction to *Forced Migration*. See also Joseph Miller, "A Theme in Variations: A Historical Schema of Slaving in the Atlantic and Indian Ocean Regions," in Inikori, *Forced Migration*, 169–94; Deryck Scarr, *Slaving and Slavery in the Indian Ocean* (New York: St. Martin's, 1998); John Wright, *The Trans-Saharan Slave Trade* (New York: Routledge, 2007); Paul Lovejoy, ed., *Slavery on Frontiers of Islam* (Princeton, NJ: Markus Wiener, 2004); Suzanne Miers and Igor Kopytoff, *Slavery in Africa: Historical and Anthropological Perspectives* (Madison: University of Wisconsin Press, 1977); Allan Fisher and Humphrey Fisher, *Slavery in Muslim Society in Africa* (New York: Doubleday, 1971); Abebe Zegeye and Shubi Ishemo, eds., *Forced Labour and Migration: Patterns of Movement within Africa* (New York: Hans Zell, 1989); Campbell, "Introduction: Slavery and Other Forms of Unfree Labour."

12. Blackett and Duquesnoy, "Slavery Is Not a Metaphor," 1512.

13. *International Conferences: White Slavery Traffic* (United Kingdom: n.p., 1905); Stephanie Limoncelli, *The Politics of Trafficking: The First International Movement to Combat the Sexual Exploitation of Women* (Palo Alto, CA: Stanford University Press, 2010), 22.

14. Levi Coffin, *Reminiscences of Levi Coffin, the Reputed President of the Underground Railroad* (Cincinnati: R. Clarke, 1880), 407–12. Cf. Richard Hildreth, *The White Slave: Another Picture of Slave Life in America* (London: Routledge, 1852).

15. Coffin, *Reminiscences*, 407–12.

16. See Limoncelli, *Politics of Trafficking*; Suzanne Miers, *Slavery in the Twentieth Century: The Evolution of a Global Problem* (New York: AltaMira Press, 2003).

17. Limoncelli, *Politics of Trafficking*.

18. "Teaching the natives to work" was used in 1901 in the House of Commons by Joseph Chamberlain, secretary of state for the colonies. George Padmore, *The Life and Struggles of Negro Toilers* (London: R. I. L. U. Magazine, 1931), 22. The notion of "a sacred trust of civilization" was included in article 22 of the Covenant of the League of Nations, April 28, 1919, http://www.unhcr.org/refworld/docid/3dd8b9854.html. See also Frederick Cooper, "Conditions Analogous to Slavery: Imperialism and Free Labor Ideology in Africa," in *Beyond Slavery: Explorations of Race, Labor, and Citizenship in Postemancipation Societies*, ed. Frederick Cooper, Thomas C. Holt, and Rebecca J. Scott (Chapel Hill: University of North Carolina Press, 2000), 113–20; Kathleen Harvey Simon, *Slavery* (London: Hodder and Stoughton, 1929), 142. On German and Portuguese colonies, see John Hobbis Harris, *Slavery or "Sacred Trust"?* (1926; reprint, New York: Negro Universities Press, 1969), 68; J. Tilley (Rio de Janeiro), No. 49, July 18, 1925, Colonial Office 323/936/19, National Archives, London; *Crusader*, June 1919, 13; Jacob Gould Schurman et al., *Report of the Philippine Commission to the President January 31, 1900[–December 20, 1900]*, vol. 2 (Washington, DC: Government Printing Office, 1900), 252. See also Frederick Cooper, *Decolonization and African Society: The Labor Question in French and British Africa* (Cambridge: Cambridge University Press, 1996); Kevin Grant, *A Civilised Savagery: Britain and the New Slaveries in Africa, 1884–1926* (New York: Routledge, 2005); Patrick Harries, *Work, Culture, and Identity: Migrant Laborers in Mozambique and South Africa, c. 1860–1910* (Portsmouth, NH: Heinemann, 1994); Paul E. Lovejoy and Jan S. Hogendorn, *Slow Death for Slavery: The Course of Abolition in Northern Nigeria, 1897–1936* (Cambridge: Cambridge University Press, 1993); David Northrup, *Indentured Labor in the Age of Imperialism, 1834–1922* (Cambridge: Cambridge University Press, 1995).

19. Sinha, *Slave's Cause*; David Geggus, *The Impact of the Haitian Revolution in the Atlantic World* (Columbia: University of South Carolina Press, 2001); Alfred Hunt, *Haiti's Influence on Antebellum America: Slumbering Volcano in the Caribbean* (Baton Rouge: LSU Press, 2006); Tom Zoellner, *Island on Fire: The Revolt that Ended Slavery in the British Empire* (Boston: Harvard University Press, 2020); Hannah-Rose Murray, *Advocates of Freedom: African American Transatlantic Abolitionism in the British Isles* (New York: Cambridge University Press, 2020); J. R. Oldfield, *The Ties that Bind: Transatlantic Abolitionism in the Age of Reform, c. 1820–1866* (New York: Oxford University Press, 2020); Aline Helg, *Slave No More: Self-Liberation before Abolitionism in the Americas* (Chapel

Hill: University of North Carolina Press, 2019); Jane Landers, ed., *Slavery and Abolition in the Atlantic World: New Sources and New Findings* (New York: Taylor and Francis, 2017); Seymour Drescher, *Pathways from Slavery: British and Colonial Mobilizations in Global Perspective* (New York: Taylor and Francis, 2017); Carol Anderson, *Bourgeois Radicals: The NAACP and the Struggle for Colonial Liberation, 1941–1960* (New York: Cambridge University Press, 2015); Penny Von Eschen, *Race against Empire: Black Americans and Anticolonialism, 1937–1957* (Ithaca, NY: Cornell University Press, 1997).

20. See, especially, Miers, *Slavery in the Twentieth Century*; Grant, *Civilised Savagery*; Blackmon, *Slavery by Another Name*; Carter, *Prisons, Politics and Business*.

1. The Origins and Launch of Twentieth-Century Black Abolitionism

1. Dan Carter, *When the War Was Over: The Failure of Self-Reconstruction in the South, 1865–1867* (Baton Rouge: LSU Press, 1985); Peyton McCrary, *Abraham Lincoln and Reconstruction: The Louisiana Experiment* (Princeton, NJ: Princeton University Press, 2015); David Williams, *I Freed Myself: African American Self-Emancipation in the Civil War Era* (New York: Cambridge University Press, 2014); Thavolia Glymph, "Du Bois's Black Reconstruction and Slave Women's War for Freedom," *South Atlantic Quarterly* 112, no. 3 (2013).

2. Carter, *When the War Was Over*, 178.

3. Carter, 178. See also McCrary, *Lincoln and Reconstruction*.

4. Stephen Tuck, *We Ain't What We Ought to Be: The Black Freedom Struggle from Emancipation to Obama* (Boston: Harvard University Press, 2010), 27–31; Carter, *When the War Was Over*; McCrary, *Lincoln and Reconstruction*. See also Willie Lee Rose, *Rehearsal for Reconstruction: The Port Royal Experiment* (Athens: University of Georgia Press, 1999); Kevin Dougherty, *The Port Royal Experiment: A Case Study in Development* (Jackson: University of Mississippi Press, 2014).

5. C. L. R. James, *Black Jacobins: Toussaint L'Ouverture and the San Domingo Revolution* (1938; reprint, New York: Penguin, 2001); Laurent Du Bois, *Avengers of the New World: The Story of the Haitian Revolution* (Boston: Harvard University Press, 2009); David Geggus, "Toussaint's Labor Decree," in *The Haitian Revolution: A Documentary History* (Indianapolis: Hackett, 2014).

6. Frederick Douglass, "What the Black Man Wants: An Address Delivered in Boston, Massachusetts, on 26 January 1865," in *The Frederick Douglass Papers: Series One, Speeches, Debates, and Interviews*, ed. John W. Blassingame and John R. McKivigan, 5 vols. (New Haven, CT: Yale University Press, 1979), 4:59–69. See David Blight, *Frederick Douglass: Prophet of Freedom* (New York: Simon and Schuster, 2018); Stephen G. Hall, *A Faithful Account of the Race: African American Historical Writing in Nineteenth-Century America* (Chapel Hill: University of North Carolina Press, 2009), 125.

7. Douglass, "What the Black Man Wants," 59–69.

8. Thaddeus Stevens, "Speech of Hon. T. Stevens, of Pennsylvania, Delivered in the House of Representatives, March 19, 1867 on the Bill (H.R. no. 20) Relative to Damages to Loyal Men, and for Other Purposes" (Washington, DC: Republican Congressional Executive Committee, 1867); Eric Foner, *Reconstruction: America's Unfinished Revolution, 1863–1877* (New York: HarperCollins, 1988); Bruce Levine, *Thaddeus Stevens: Civil War Revolutionary, Fighter for Racial Justice* (New York: Simon and Schuster, 2021); Hans Trefousse, *Thaddeus Stevens: Nineteenth Century Egalitarian* (Chapel Hill: University of North Carolina Press, 1997).

9. Stevens, "Speech of Hon. T. Stevens."

10. Martin Luther King Jr., "Martin Luther King, Jr., Saw Three Evils in the World," *Atlantic*, February 2018; Martin Luther King, "Dr. Martin Luther King, Jr.'s 1962 Speech in New York City," New York State Museum, www.nysm.nysed.gov/mlk-1962-address.

11. Douglass, "What the Black Man Wants," 59–69; Blight, *Frederick Douglass*. On master-slave relationships, see Ira Berlin, *Many Thousands Gone: The First Two Centuries of Slavery in North America* (Cambridge, MA: Belknap Press of Harvard University Press, 1998).

12. Leslie G. Carr, *"Colorblind" Racism* (London: Sage, 1997).

13. Frederick Douglass, "What to the Slave Is the Fourth of July?" in *Great Speeches by African Americans*, ed. James Daley (Mineola, NY: Courier, 2012), 23.

14. Jeremiah Eames Rankin, "Introductory Sketch," in John Mercer Langston, *Freedom and Citizenship* (Washington, DC: Rufus H. Darby, 1883), 15, 18.

15. Frederick Douglass, *The Life and Times of Frederick Douglass* (Hartford, CT: Park Publishing, 1882), 77, 85, 92, 375; Blight, *Frederick Douglass*.

16. Keith Griffler, *Front Line of Freedom: African Americans and the Forging of the Underground Railroad in the Ohio Valley* (Lexington: University Press of Kentucky, 2004); Keith Griffler, "On Egypt's Border: The Underground Railroad in Antebellum America," in *Passage on the Underground Railroad*, ed. Stephen Marc Smith (Jackson: University of Mississippi Press, 2009), 10–28. On underground movements in Europe, see Matthew Cobb, *The Resistance: The French Fight against the Nazis* (London: Simon and Schuster, 2009); David Schoenbrun, *Soldiers of the Night: The Story of the French Resistance* (New York: Dutton, 1980).

17. Stephen B. Oates, *To Purge This Land with Blood: A Biography of John Brown* (Amherst: University of Massachusetts Press, 1984), 227; F. B. Sanborn and William Ellery Channing, *Memoirs of John Brown, Written for Rev. Samuel Orcutt's History of Torrington, Ct.* (Concord, MA: J. Munsell, 1878), 56; Douglass, *Life and Times*, 375.

18. Henry Mayer, *All on Fire: William Lloyd Garrison and the Abolition of Slavery* (New York: Norton, 2008), 313; Keith Griffler, "Come Together: The Underground Railroad and the Project for the New American Century," in *The American Uses of History: Essays on Public Memory*, ed. Tomasz Basiuk, Sylwia Kuźma-Markowska, and Krystyna Mazur (Frankfurt: Peter Lang, 2011), 89–101; R. J. M. Blackett, The *Captive's Quest for Freedom: Fugitive Slaves, the 1850 Fugitive Slave Law, and the Politics of Slavery* (New York: Cambridge University Press, 2018).

19. Robin Blackburn, *The Making of New World Slavery: From the Baroque to the Modern 1492–1800* (London: Verso, 1997), 3, 5.

20. Douglass, "What the Black Man Wants"; Joseph Inikori, *Africans and the Industrial Revolution in England: A Study in International Trade and Development* (New York: Cambridge University Press, 2002), 404. Cf. Ira Berlin, *The Making of African America: The Four Great Migrations* (New York: Viking, 2010).

21. Douglass, "What the Black Man Wants"; Foner, *Reconstruction*. On the aftermath of emancipation, see Thomas C. Holt, *The Problem of Freedom: Race, Labor, and Politics in Jamaica and Britain, 1832–1938* (Baltimore: Johns Hopkins University Press, 1992); Jeremy Adelman, *Sovereignty and Revolution in the Iberian Atlantic* (Princeton, NJ: Princeton University Press, 2006); Robin Blackburn, *The Overthrow of Colonial Slavery, 1776–1848* (London: Verso, 1988); Christopher Leslie Brown, *Moral Capital: Foundations of British Abolitionism* (Chapel Hill: University of North Carolina Press, 2006); Rebecca J. Scott, *Slave Emancipation in Cuba: The Transition to Free Labor, 1860–1899* (Pittsburgh: University of Pittsburgh Press, 2000).

22. David Levering Lewis, *W. E. B. Du Bois: Biography of a Race, 1868 to 1919* (New York: Holt, 1993); Mia Bey, *To Tell the Truth Freely: The Life of Ida B. Wells* (New York: Hill and Wang, 2009); Foner, *Reconstruction*.

23. Plessy vs. Ferguson Judgement, Decided May 18, 1896, Records of the Supreme Court of the United States, Record Group 267, *Plessy v. Ferguson*, 163, #15248, National Archives; W. E. Burghardt Du Bois, "The Spawn of Slavery: The Convict-Lease System in the South," *Missionary Review of the World* 14 (October 1901): 739; Lewis, *Du Bois: Biography of a Race*; Aldon Morris, *The Scholar Denied: W. E. B. Du Bois and the Birth of Modern Sociology* (Berkeley: University of California Press, 2015); William James Hoffer, *Plessy v. Ferguson: Race and Inequality in Jim Crow America* (Lawrence: University Press of Kansas, 2012); Don Fehrenbacher, *The Dred Scott Case: Its Significance in American Law and Politics* (New York: Oxford University Press, 2001); Davison Douglas, *Jim Crow Moves North: The Battle over Northern School Segregation, 1865–1954* (New York: Cambridge University Press, 2005); Thomas Dyer, *Theodore Roosevelt and the Idea of Race* (Baton Rouge: LSU Press, 1992).

24. Ida B. Wells-Barnett, *Southern Horrors: Lynch Law in All Its Phases* (New York: Outlook Verlag, 2018), 4; Ida B. Wells, *Crusade for Justice: The Autobiography of Ida B. Wells* (Chicago: University of Chicago Press, 2020), 86.

25. Blight, *Frederick Douglass*; Douglass, *Life and Times*, 300–301, 393.

26. William Wells Brown, *The American Fugitive in Europe* (Boston: Jewett, 1855), 29–33, 215–22. See also Manisha Sinha, *The Slave's Cause: A History of Abolition* (New Haven, CT: Yale University Press, 2016). For a biography of Brown, see Ezra Greenspan, *William Wells Brown: An African American Life* (New York: Norton, 2014).

27. Brown, *American Fugitive in Europe*, 29–33, 215–22; Hall, *Faithful Account of Race*, 2.

28. Wells-Barnett, *Southern Horrors*, 4; Bey, *To Tell the Truth*, 144; "The Society for the Recognition of the Brotherhood of Man," *Bond of Brotherhood* 1 (April 1895): 41–47.

29. Bey, *To Tell the Truth*, 182; Wells, *Crusade for Justice*, 86; "The Honorable Frederick Douglass," *Anti-Slavery Reporter*, May–June 1894, 165–67; "The Treatment of Negroes in America," *Anti-Slavery Reporter*, May–June 1894, 168–70.

30. Lawrence S. Little, *Disciples of Liberty: The African Methodist Episcopal Church in the Age of Imperialism, 1884–1916* (Knoxville: University of Tennessee Press, 2000), 148; Lewis, *Du Bois: Biography of a Race*.

31. W. E. B. Du Bois, *The Souls of Black Folk: Essays and Sketches* (Chicago: McClurg, 1903), 116, 126, 127. On *Souls*, see Stephanie Shaw, *W. E. B. Du Bois and The Souls of Black Folk* (Chapel Hill: University of North Carolina Press, 2013).

32. Du Bois, *Souls of Black Folk*, 116, 126, 127; Du Bois, "Spawn of Slavery," 739.

33. W. E. Burghardt Du Bois, "The Negro in the Black Belt: Some Social Sketches," *Bulletin of the United States Bureau of Labor* 4 (May 1899): 401–17. See also Lewis, *Du Bois: Biography of a Race*; Morris, *Scholar Denied*.

34. Du Bois, "Spawn of Slavery," 740, 741; Ben Conarck, "Work Forced: A Century Later, Unpaid Prison Labor Continues to Power Florida," *Florida Times-Union*, May 25, 2019. On the history of the chain gang, see Alexander Lichtenstein, *Twice the Work of Free Labor: The Political Economy of Convict Labor in the New South* (London: Verso, 1996).

1 Du Bois, "Spawn of Slavery," 745. On the ideological defense of slavery, see Larry Tise, *Proslavery: A History of the Defense of Slavery in America, 1701–1840* (Athens: University of Georgia Press, 1987).

35. Du Bois, *Souls*, vii, 13, 56, 117, 120, 127; Du Bois, "Spawn of Slavery," 739. On African American migration, see Nell Painter, *Exodusters: Black Migration to Kansas after Reconstruction* (New York: Norton, 1992); Carole Marks, *Farewell, We're Good and Gone: The Great Black Migration* (Bloomington:

Indiana University Press, 1989). On sharecropping, see Gerald Jaynes, *Branches without Roots: Genesis of the Black Working Class in the American South, 1862–1882* (New York: Oxford University Press, 1986).

36. Du Bois, *Souls*, vii, 13, 117, 120, 127.

37. Tembeka Ngcukaitobi, *The Land Is Ours: Black Lawyers and the Birth of Constitutionalism in South Africa* (Johannesburg, South Africa: Penguin, 2018); David Killingray, "Significant Black South Africans in Britain before 1912: Pan-African Organisations and the Emergence of South Africa's First Black Lawyers," *South African Historical Journal* 64, no. 3 (2012): 393–417. See Marika Sherwood, *Origins of Pan-Africanism: Henry Sylvester Williams, Africa, and the African Diaspora* (London: Routledge, 2012).

38. Killingray, "Significant Black South Africans in Britain," 401–4; Ngcukaitobi, *The Land Is Ours*.

39. "Natives in the Diamond Mines" and "The African Association," *Aborigines' Friend*, November 1897, 297–98; Killingray, "Significant Black South Africans in Britain," 401–4; Ngcukaitobi, *The Land Is Ours*.

40. Charles van Onselen, *Chibaro: African Mine Labour in Southern Rhodesia, 1900–1933* (Bloomington: Indiana University Press, 1980), 98–99; "Report of the Commission Appointed to Inquire into the Disturbances in the Copperbelt, Northern Rhodesia," July 1940, 63, 64, Colonial Office (hereafter CO) 795/122/19, National Archives, London.

41. Frederick Cooper, *Decolonization and African Society: The Labor Question in French and British Africa* (Cambridge: Cambridge University Press, 1996), 24.

42. Earl of Lytton, *The Parliamentary Debates in the Fifth Session of the Twenty-Seventh Parliament of the United Kingdom of Great Britain and Ireland* (London: Wyman, 1904), 128, 204; Minute by J. Fredk. N. Green, January 2, 1930, CO 795/33/15; *Transvaal: Further Correspondence Relating to Labour in the Transvaal Mines* (London: Colonial Office, December 1905), nos. 25, 24; J. C. Maxwell, governor, Northern Rhodesia, to Lord Passfield, November 21, 1929, CO 795/33/15; "Observations on Labour Conditions on Mines on the Rand," 1930, 5, CO 795/39/17; J. A. Hobson, *The War in South Africa: Its Causes and Effects* (London: Nisbet, 1900), 237; A. W., "Yellow Slavery—and White!" *Westminster Review* 161, nos. 5–6 (1904): 480. On compounds, see van Onselen, *Chibaro*, 34–74; Patrick Harries, *Work, Culture, and Identity: Migrant Laborers in Mozambique and South Africa, c. 1860–1910* (Portsmouth, NH: Heinemann, 1994), 66–71, 195–200.

43. A. Lynn Saffery, *A Report on Some Aspects of African Living Conditions on the Copper Belt of Northern Rhodesia* (Lusaka: Government Printer, 1943), 52, CO 795/128/12; Granville St. John Orde-Browne. *Report upon Labour in the Tanganyika Territory* (London: H. M. Stat. Off., 1926); memorandum by C. G. Eastwood, July 6, 1931, CO 822/37/9; New Reform Club, *British Workmen or Chinese Slaves* (London: New Reform Club, 1904), 5.

44. William Beinart, *The Political Economy of Pondoland 1860–1930* (New York: Cambridge, 2009), 60; van Onselen, *Chibaro*, 135. On pass laws under slavery, see Sally E. Hadden, *Slave Patrols: Law and Violence in Virginia and the Carolinas* (Cambridge, MA: Harvard University Press, 2001).

45. *Transvaal: Further Correspondence Relating to Labour in the Transvaal Mines* (London: Colonial Office, January 1906), 24, 48; *John Burns, Bondage for Black* (London: Simpkin, 1904), 6.

46. Van Onselen, *Chibaro*, 156–57; Raymond Leslie Buell, *The Native Problem in Africa*, 2 vols. (New York: Macmillan, 1928), 1:49.

47. Report of the Native Labour Sub-Committee of the Economic Council, October 16, 1939, CO 525/178/13. Capt. G. N. Burden, "Nyasaland Native Labour in Southern Rhodesia," 1938, 15, CO 525/173/11; Mary Turner, *From Chattel Slaves to Wage Slaves: The Dynamics of Labour Bargaining in the Americas* (Bloomington: Indiana University Press, 1995). On the Caribbean, see Roseanne Adderley, "'A Most Useful and Valuable People?' Cultural, Moral and Practical Dilemmas in the Use of Liberated African Labor in the Nineteenth-Century Caribbean," in *From Slavery to Emancipation in the Atlantic World*, ed. Sylvia R. Frey and Betty Wood (New York: Routledge, 2013), 59–80; Mary Turner, "The 11 O'clock Flog: Women, Work and Labour Law in the British Caribbean," in Frey and Wood, 38–58.

48. On the use of the term *new slavery*, see Liberal League, *The New Slavery: The Case against Chinese Labour for the Transvaal* (London: Liberal League, [1904]); Kevin Grant, *A Civilised Savagery: Britain and the New Slaveries in Africa, 1884–1926* (New York: Routledge, 2005), 91; E. D. Morel, *The Congo Slave State: A Protest against the New African Slavery and an Appeal to the Public of Great Britain, of the United States, and of the Continent of Europe* (Liverpool: J. Richardson and Sons, 1903), 7; Henry Woodd Nevinson, *A Modern Slavery* (London: Harper and Brothers, 1906), 17; Suzanne Miers, *Slavery in the Twentieth Century: The Evolution of a Global Problem* (New York: AltaMira Press, 2003); Suzanne Miers, "Slavery and the Slave Trade as International Issues 1890–1939," *Slavery and Abolition* 19, no. 2 (1998); Joel Quirk, *The Anti-Slavery Project: From the Slave Trade to Human Trafficking* (Philadelphia: University of Pennsylvania Press, 2014).

49. Pan-African Association, "Report of the Pan-African Conference," ca. 1900, 3, W. E. B. Du Bois Papers (MS 312), Special Collections and University Archives, University of Massachusetts Amherst Libraries; Killingray, "Significant Black South Africans in Britain," 403; Sherwood, *Origins of Pan-Africanism*, 41–42; Ngcukaitobi, *The Land Is Ours*.

50. Lewis, *Du Bois: Biography of a Race*, 248–51. See Vivian M. May, *Anna Julia Cooper, Visionary Black Feminist: A Critical Introduction* (New York: Taylor and Francis, 2007).

51. Pan-African Association, "Report of the Pan-African Conference," 11–12.

52. Pan-African Association, 12–15; Du Bois, "Negro in the Black Belt"; Du Bois, "Spawn of Slavery"; W. E. Burghardt Du Bois, "The Negro as He Really Is," *World's Work* 2 (May 1901): 848–66; Du Bois, *Souls*; Lewis, *Du Bois: Biography of a Race.*

53. Pan-African Association, "Report of the Pan-African Conference," 13. See also W. E. B. Du Bois, *Darkwater: Voices from within the Veil* (New York: Harcourt, Brace and Howe, 1920), 44–45; Du Bois, *Souls*, 79–80; Tony Martin, *Race First: The Ideological and Organizational Struggles of Marcus Garvey and the Universal Negro Improvement Association* (Dover, DE: Majority Press, 1986), 10; Paul Gilroy, *The Black Atlantic: Modernity and Double Consciousness* (Cambridge, MA: Harvard University Press, 1993); Lisa Brock, Robin Kelley, and Karen Sotiropoulos, eds., *Transnational Black Studies* (Durham, NC: Duke University Press, 2003); Manning Marable and Vanessa Agard-Jones, eds., *Transnational Blackness: Navigating the Global Color Line* (New York: Palgrave Macmillan, 2008); Isidore Okpewho, Carole Boyce Davies, and Ali Al'Amin Mazrui, eds., *The African Diaspora: African Origins and New World Identities* (Bloomington: Indiana University Press, 1999). For Braudel's use of "world," see Fernand Braudel, *A History of Civilizations*, trans. Richard Mayne (New York: Penguin Books, 1995), 120. See also Fernand Braudel, *Civilization and Capitalism, 15th–18th Century*, 3 vols. (Berkeley: University of California Press, 1992).

54. Pan-African Association, "Report of the Pan-African Conference," 13–14.

55. Du Bois, "Spawn of Slavery"; Du Bois, "Negro as He Really Is"; Du Bois, *Souls*; Shaw, *Du Bois and The Souls.*

56. Du Bois, "Spawn of Slavery," 737–8, 742; Lewis, *Du Bois: Biography of a Race.*

57. Du Bois, *Souls*, 13.

58. W. E. B. Du Bois, *The Suppression of the African Slave-Trade to the United States of America, 1638–1870* (London: Longmans, Green. 1896), v, 6, 70.

59. Du Bois, 70, 132.

60. Lewis, *Du Bois: Biography of a Race,* 356.

61. W. E. B. Du Bois, *John Brown* (Philadelphia: George W. Jacobs, 1909), 7–8. On *John Brown*, see William Cain, "Violence, Revolution, and the Cost of Freedom: John Brown and W. E. B. DuBois," *Boundary 2* 17, no. 1 (1990): 305–30. On John Brown, see Oates, *To Purge This Land*; Franny Nudelman, *John Brown's Body: Slavery, Violence & the Culture of War* (Chapel Hill: University of North Carolina Press, 2004); Tony Horwitz, *Midnight Rising: John Brown and the Raid that Sparked the Civil War* (New York: Henry Holt, 2011).

62. Du Bois, *John Brown*; Shaw, *Du Bois and The Souls*; Edward Baptist, *The Half Has Never Been Told: Slavery and the Making of American Capitalism* (New

York: Basic Books, 2016); Joseph Wilson, *The Black Phalanx: A History of the Negro Soldiers of the United States in the Wars of 1775–1812, 1861–'65* (Hartford, CT: American Publishing Co., 1890), 200. On Wilson, see Hall, *Faithful Account of Race*, 159–66. On the Egyptian origins of the phalanx, see Christelle Fischer-Bovet, *Army and Society in Ptolemaic Egypt* (New York: Cambridge University Press, 2014).

63. Du Bois, *John Brown*, 82; George Washington Williams, *History of the Negro Race in America, from 1619 to 1880*, vol. 2, *Negroes as Slaves, as Soldiers, and as Citizens* (New York: G. P. Putnam's Sons, 1883), 59. On Williams, see Hall, *Faithful Account of Race*, 160.

64. Du Bois, *John Brown*. See also Sinha, *Slave's Cause*.

65. Du Bois, *John Brown*, 101, 110, 280, 346–47. On Shields Green, see Douglass, *Life and Times*, 387–92; William C. Nell, "Biographies of John Brown's Men," *Pine and Palm*, June 22, 1861; "The Harper's Ferry Insurrection," *Rochester Democrat*, October 21, 1859.

66. Du Bois, *John Brown*, 101, 110, 280, 346–47.

67. W. E. B. Du Bois, *Black Reconstruction; An Essay toward a History of the Part which Black Folk Played in the Attempt to Reconstruct Democracy in America, 1860–1880* (1935; reprint, New York: Atheneum, 1985). On Du Bois's thesis of African American self-liberation, see Williams, *I Freed Myself*; Glymph, "Du Bois's Black Reconstruction."

68. Du Bois, *Souls*, 129; Larry Gara, *The Liberty Line: The Legend of the Underground Railroad* (Lexington: University Press of Kentucky, 1961).

69. Benjamin Quarles, *Allies for Freedom: Blacks and John Brown* (New York: Oxford University Press, 1974), 85–89.

70. Holt, *Problem of Freedom*; Tom Zoellner, *Island on Fire: The Revolt that Ended Slavery in the British Empire* (Boston: Harvard University Press, 2020); David Walker, *David Walker's Appeal* (New York: Black Classic Press, 1997).

71. Nell, "Biographies"; Peter H. Wood, *Black Majority: Negroes in Colonial South Carolina, from 1670 through the Stono Rebellion* (New York: Knopf Doubleday, 1974); Judith A. Carney, *Black Rice: The African Origins of Rice Cultivation in the Americas* (Boston: Harvard University Press, 2009); Daniel Littlefield, *Rice and Slaves: Ethnicity and the Slave Trade in Colonial South Carolina* (Chicago: University of Illinois Press, 1991).

72. Peter Hoffer, *Cry Liberty: The Great Stono River Slave Rebellion of 1739* (New York: Oxford University Press, 2010); Jack Shuler, *Calling out Liberty: The Stono Rebellion and the Universal Struggle for Human Rights* (Oxford: University Press of Mississippi, 2010); David M. Robertson, *Denmark Vesey: The Buried Story of America's Largest Slave Rebellion and the Man Who Led It* (New York: Knopf Doubleday, 2009).

73. Du Bois, *John Brown*, 390, 393.

2. Reactivating the Antislavery-Antiracism
Alliance for a New Century

1. Historians of the abolitionist movement have ignored Kinloch and Pan-Africanism. See, e.g., Joel Quirk, *The Anti-Slavery Project: From the Slave Trade to Human Trafficking* (Philadelphia: University of Pennsylvania Press, 2014); Suzanne Miers, *Slavery in the Twentieth Century: The Evolution of a Global Problem* (New York: AltaMira Press, 2003); Kevin Grant, *A Civilised Savagery: Britain and the New Slaveries in Africa, 1884–1926* (New York: Routledge, 2005); "Natives under British Rule in Africa," *Aborigines' Friend*, December 1896, 96, 100–101.

2. David Levering Lewis, *W. E. B. Du Bois: Biography of a Race, 1868 to 1919* (New York: Holt, 1993), 386–407; [W. E. B. Du Bois], "Opportunity," *The Crisis*, January 1911, 17. Cf. Patricia Sullivan, *Lift Every Voice and Sing: The NAACP and the Making of the Civil Rights Movement* (New York: New Press, 2009); George Hutchinson, *The Harlem Renaissance in Black and White* (Boston: Harvard University Press, 1995), 167–73; Flint Kellogg, "Oswald Villard, the NAACP and the Nation," *Nation*, July 2, 2009.

3. "The African Association," *Anti-Slavery Reporter*, March–May 1899, 112; G. R. Searle, *A New England? Peace and War, 1886–1918* (Oxford: Clarendon Press, 2005), 292; Marika Sherwood, *Origins of Pan-Africanism: Henry Sylvester Williams, Africa, and the African Diaspora* (London: Routledge, 2012), 43.

4. Henry Fox Bourne, *The Aborigines Protection Society: Chapters in Its History* (London: P. S. King and Son, 1899), 3; "Natives in the Diamond Mines," *Aborigines' Friend*, November 1897, 297; David Killingray, "Significant Black South Africans in Britain before 1912: Pan-African Organisations and the Emergence of South Africa's First Black Lawyers," *South African Historical Journal* 64, no. 3 (2012): 402. Cf. Kenneth D. Nworah, "The Aborigines' Protection Society, 1889–1909: A Pressure-Group in Colonial Policy," *Canadian Journal of African Studies* 5, no. 1 (1971); Reginald Coupland, *The British Anti-Slavery Movement* (London: T. Butterworth, 1933); Howard Temperley, *British Antislavery, 1833–1870* (London: Longman, 1972); David Turley, *The Culture of English Antislavery, 1780–1860* (London: Routledge, 1991).

5. "Annual Meeting of the Society," *Anti-Slavery Reporter* 23 (June–July 1903): 80; Killingray, "Significant Black South Africans in Britain," 403; "The African Association," *Aborigines' Friend*, November 1897, 297; Sherwood, *Origins of Pan-Africanism*, 42; "The African Association: Its Aims and Objects," *Anti-Slavery Reporter*, July–August 1898, 182; "The African Association," *Anti-Slavery Reporter*, March–May 1899, 112; "Annual Meeting of the Society," *Anti-Slavery Reporter*, March–May 1900, 75; "The Annual Meeting, 1899," *Aborigines' Friend*, November 1899, 448–52.

6. Pan-African Association, "Report of the Pan-African Conference," ca. 1900, 9–12, W. E. B. Du Bois Papers (MS 312), Special Collections and University Archives, University of Massachusetts Amherst Libraries; Killingray, "Significant Black South Africans in Britain," 404.

7. "Review: The Souls of Black Folk," *Anti-Slavery Reporter*, March–May 1904, 69–72; *Anti-Slavery Reporter*, August–October 1900, 139–41.

8. "H. R. Fox Bourne," *Aborigines' Friend*, May 1909, 245–54; H. R. Fox Bourne, *English Newspapers: Chapters in the History of Journalism*, 2 vols. (London: Chatto and Windus, 1887), 2:289, 349–53. Cf. H. C. Swaisland, "Bourne, Henry Richard Fox (1837–1909)," in *Oxford Dictionary of National Biography* (Oxford University Press, 2004), http://www.oxforddnb.com/view/article /31993; Grant, *Civilised Savagery*, 32–33, 63; Nworah, "Aborigines' Protection Society," 81–89; Charles Swaisland, "The Aborigines Protection Society, 1837–1909," in *After Slavery: Emancipation and Its Discontents*, ed. Howard Temperley (London: Frank Cass, 2000), 265–75.

9. Henry Fox Bourne, "The Duty of Civilised States to Weaker Races," *Aborigines' Friend*, April 1891, 173–75; Henry Fox Bourne, *The Aborigines Protection Society: Its Aims and Methods* (London: APS, 1900).

10. "The Aborigines Protection Society," *Aborigines' Friend*, March 1889, 511–12; "H. R. Fox Bourne," 245–54.

11. "Earl Grey on African Affairs," *Aborigines' Friend*, February 1890, 35, 37; "Cecil Rhodes and the Native Races," *Anti-Slavery Reporter*, January–March 1897, 59; "Coloured British Subjects in the Transvaal," *Aborigines' Friend*, April 1891, 149.

12. "The Glen Grey Act," *Aborigines' Friend*, January 1895, 442–50; "The Native Question in South Africa," *Anti-Slavery Reporter* 21 (March–May 1901):, 51; "Natives under British Rule in Africa," *Aborigines' Friend*, December 1896, 96, 100–101; "Abolition of the Status of Slavery in Zanzibar," *Anti-Slavery Reporter* 10 (July–August 1890): 140–43; "Slavery in Tunis and Algiers," *Anti-Slavery Reporter* 11 (March–April 1891): 53–54; "Slavery in Western Australia," *Anti-Slavery Reporter* 12 (July–August 1892): 215; "The Slave-Trade in Central Africa," *Anti-Slavery Reporter* 13 (September–October 1893): 267–73; "Morocco: Further Mohammedan Massacres; Activity of the Slave Trade," *Anti-Slavery Reporter* 16 (May–July 1896): 154–56; "West Africa: Is Slavery Essential to the Wellbeing of Africa?" *Anti-Slavery Reporter* 17 (January–March 1897): 55–57; "Slavery under the British Flag," *Anti-Slavery Reporter* 18 (January–February 1898): 54–57; "Slavery in Persia," *Anti-Slavery Reporter* 18 (January–February 1898): 57–58.

13. Joseph A. Pease, speech to the House of Commons, June 1, 1894, Parliamentary Debates, Commons, 4th ser., vol. 25, cols. 236–38; "South African Native Questions," *Aborigines' Friend*, May 1904, 101; APS to Colonial Office, September 15 and 28, 1897, in Colonial Office Great Britain, "Correspondence

Relating to Native Disturbances in Bechuanaland," in *Miscellaneous Pamphlets on South Africa*, vol. 1 (London: Printed for His Majesty's Stationery Office, 1872–1898), 21, 24; *Further Correspondence Relating to Affairs in South Africa (in Continuation of [Cd. 43] January, 1900)* (London: Darling and Son, 1900), 34; H. R. Fox Bourne, *Blacks and Whites in South Africa: An Account of the Past Treatment and Present Condition of South African Natives under British and Boer Control* (London: P. S. King and Son, 1900), 88, 90; APS to Colonial Office, January 11, 1901, in *Transvaal: Papers Relating to Legislation Affecting Natives in the Transvaal (In Continuation of [Cd. 714], July, 1901, Presented to Both Houses of Parliament by Command of His Majesty, January, 1902* (London: Printed for His Majesty's Stationery Office by Darling and Son, 1902), 4–5; "What Is to Be Done for the South African Natives?" *Speaker*, June 2, 1900, 237; "The Native Question in South Africa," *Anti-Slavery Reporter* 21 (March–May 1901): 51; "The Native Question in South Africa," *Anti-Slavery Reporter* 21 (June–July 1901): 111; "Annual Meeting of the Society," *Anti-Slavery Reporter* 23 (June–July 1903): 79–80; Sir Charles Dilke, speech to the House of Commons, June 1, 1894, Parliamentary Debates, Commons, 4th ser., vol. 25, cols. 195–96; *The Annual Report of the Aborigines Protection Society, 1898* (London: APS, 1898), 12.

14. "South African Questions," *Aborigines' Friend*, March 1905, 270–71. See also Grant, *Civilised Savagery*, 91; Swaisland, "Aborigines Protection Society," 274; John Stauffer, *The Black Hearts of Men: Radical Abolitionists and the Transformation of Race* (Cambridge, MA: Harvard University Press, 2002); Keith Griffler, *Front Line of Freedom: African Americans and the Forging of the Underground Railroad in the Ohio Valley* (Lexington: University Press of Kentucky, 2004); H. R. Fox Bourne, *Forced Labour in British South Africa: Notes on the Condition and Prospects of South African Natives under British Control* (London: P. S. King and Son, [1903]), 21; W. E. B. Du Bois, *The Souls of Black Folk: Essays and Sketches* (Chicago: A. C. McClurg, 1903); "The Souls of Black Folk," *Aborigines' Friend*, June 1904, 122–28; Fox Bourne, *Blacks and Whites in South Africa*; H. R. Fox Bourne, *Native Labour Question in the Transvaal* (London: APS, 1901).

15. "Annual Meeting of the Society," *Anti-Slavery Reporter* 23 (June–July 1903): 80.

16. Griffler, *Front Line of Freedom*; Keith Griffler, "Beyond the Quest for the 'Real Eliza Harris': Fugitive Slave Women in the Ohio Valley," *Ohio Valley History* 3, no. 2 (2003). Cf. Eric Eustace Williams, *Capitalism & Slavery* (1944; reprint, Chapel Hill: University of North Carolina Press, 1994); Seymour Drescher, *Econocide: British Slavery in the Era of Abolition* (Pittsburgh: University of Pittsburgh Press, 1977); David Eltis, *Economic Growth and the Ending of the Transatlantic Slave Trade* (New York: Oxford University Press, 1987); Thomas L. Haskell, "Capitalism and the Origins of the Humanitarian Sensibility, Part 1," *American Historical Review* 90, no. 2 (1985); David Brion Davis, *The Problem*

of Slavery in the Age of Revolution, 1770–1823 (Ithaca, NY: Cornell University Press, 1975); Christopher Leslie Brown, *Moral Capital: Foundations of British Abolitionism* (Chapel Hill: University of North Carolina Press, 2006).

17. David Walker, *David Walker's Appeal* (New York: Black Classic Press, 1997). On the nineteenth-century roots of missionary abolitionism in Africa and its relation to women's resistance, see, e.g., Edward A. Alpers, "The Story of Swema: Female Vulnerability in Nineteenth-Century East Africa," in *Women and Slavery in Africa*, ed. Claire Robertson and Martin Klein (Madison: University of Wisconsin Press, 1983), 185–219. Seeking the protection of the colonial state was a common strategy for enslaved women. See, e.g., Joseph Miller, "Women as Slaves and Owners of Slaves," in *Women and Slavery: Africa, the Indian Ocean World, and the Medieval North Atlantic*, ed. Gwyn Campbell, Suzanne Miers, and Joseph Calder Miller, 2 vols. (Athens: Ohio University Press, 2007), 1:31. On the reliability of missionary testimony, see Catherine Coquery-Vidrovitch, "Women, Marriage, and Slavery in Sub-Saharan Africa in the Nineteenth Century," in Campbell, Miers, and Miller, *Women and Slavery*, 1:45–47. On the role of missionaries, see also Miller, "Women as Slaves and Owners of Slaves," 31.

18. Frederick Lugard, *The Rise of Our East African Empire*, 2 vols. (London: Blackwood, 1893), 2:55–58. For other accounts of women seeking to escape slavery after its abolition, see Coquery-Vidrovitch, "Women, Marriage, and Slavery," 56; Marcia Wright, "Bwanikwa: Consciousness and Protest among Slave Women in Central Africa, 1886–1911," in Robertson and Klein, *Women and Slavery in Africa*, 249; Richard Roberts, "Women, Household Instability, and the End of Slavery in Banamba and Gumbu, French Soudan, 1905–1912," in Campbell, Miers, and Miller, *Women and Slavery*, 1:281–305; Marie Rodet "'Under the Guise of Guardianship and Marriage': Mobilizing Juvenile and Female Labor in the Aftermath of Slavery in Kayes, French Soudan, 1900–1939," in *Trafficking in Slavery's Wake: Law and the Experience of Women and Children*, ed. Benjamin N. Lawrance and Richard L. Roberts (Athens: Ohio University Press, 2012), 86–100.

19. Frederick Douglass, "What the Black Man Wants," in *Let Nobody Turn Us Around: Voices of Resistance, Reform, and Renewal*, ed. Manning Marable and Leith Mullings (Lanham, MD: Rowman and Littlefield, 2009), 125; W. E. B. Du Bois, *Black Reconstruction; An Essay toward a History of the Part which Black Folk Played in the Attempt to Reconstruct Democracy in America, 1860–1880* (1935; reprint, New York: Atheneum, 1985); David W. Blight, *Beyond the Battlefield: Race, Memory & the American Civil War* (Amherst: University of Massachusetts Press, 2002); Griffler, *Front Line of Freedom*; Eric Foner, *The Fiery Trial: Abraham Lincoln and American Slavery*, 1st ed. (New York: W. W. Norton, 2010); Eric Foner and Joshua Brown, *Forever Free: The Story of Emancipation and Reconstruction* (New York: Knopf, 2005).

20. "The Glen Grey Act: An Adverse Opinion" and "Another View of the Act," *Anti-Slavery Reporter* 14 (September–October 1894): 292–97; *The Annual Report of the Aborigines Protection Society, 1903* (London: APS, 1900), 2; "The Native Question in South Africa," *Aborigines' Friend*, August 1900, 531; "The Native Question in South Africa," *Anti-Slavery Reporter* 21 (January–February 1901): 7, 11–12; "The Native Question in South Africa," *Anti-Slavery Reporter* 21 (June–July 1901): 112; APS to Colonial Office, October 23, 1889, in *South Africa: Further Correspondence Respecting the Affairs of Swaziland and Tongaland, June 1887* (London: Eyre and Spottiswoods, 1890), 207–8; APS to Colonial Office, December 8, 1900, January 11, 1901, February 22, 1901 in *Transvaal: Papers Relating to Legislation Affecting Natives*, 2–3, 3–5, 7–8; "The Native Question in South Africa," *Anti-Slavery Reporter* 20 (June–July 1900): 100–101; "The Native Question in South Africa," *Anti-Slavery Reporter* 21 (March–May 1901): 51; "Annual Meeting of the Society," *Anti-Slavery Reporter* 23 (June–July 1903): 79; Aborigines Protection Society, *The Native Question in South Africa: Outlines of a Suggested Charter for Natives under British Rule in South Africa* (London: P. S. King and Son, 1900); Fox Bourne, *Blacks and Whites in South Africa*; Thomas Fowell Buxton and Travers Buxton to Colonial Office, November 9, 1900, in *Transvaal: Papers Relating to Legislation Affecting Natives*, 1–2.

21. "Joint Public Meeting," *Anti-Slavery Reporter* 23 (March–May 1903): 41–42; *Native Labour in South Africa: Report of a Public Meeting, 29th April, 1903* (London: P. S. King and Son, 1903), 2–4; "Annual Meeting of the Society," *Anti-Slavery Reporter* 23 (June–July 1903): 76–77, 79.

22. "The Recruiting of Labour in the Colonies and in Other Territories with Analogous Labour Conditions," 1933, 6, Colonial Office (hereafter CO) 323/1212/6, National Archives, London; League of Nations, *Permanent Mandates Commission, Minutes of the Sixth Session* (Geneva: League of Nations Publications, 1925), 17; Great Britain, Colonial Office, *Correspondence Relating to the Recruitment of Labour in the British Central Africa Protectorate for Employment in the Transvaal* (African No. 2, 1903) (London: His Majesty's Stationery Office, 1903), 18. See also *Report of the Committee Appointed to Consider and Advise on Questions Relating to the Supply and Welfare of Native Labour in the Tanganyika Territory* (Dar es Salaam: Government Printer, 1938), 23, CO 691/166/8. Cf. William Beinart, *The Political Economy of Pondoland 1860–1930* (New York: Cambridge University Press, 2009), chap. 2; Charles van Onselen, *Chibaro: African Mine Labour in Southern Rhodesia, 1900–1933* (Bloomington: Indiana University Press, 1980), 74–115. The recruited workers were referred to as *chibaro* (slave) labor, "the most exploited group of an exploited class," since direct coercion was sometimes used to "round [them] up" (van Onselen, 104–5, 112).

23. Great Britain, Colonial Office, *Nyasaland Labor Recruitment for the Transvaal, Summary of Correspondence Relating to the Recruitment of Labor* (African No. 2, 1903) (London: His Majesty's Stationery Office, 1903), 32;

Lyttelton to Milner, no. 3, in *Transvaal: Further Correspondence Relating to Labour in the Transvaal Mines* (London: Colonial Office, Transvaal, August 1904), 2; Milner to Lyttelton, no. 7 and enclosure in no. 7, in *Transvaal: Further Correspondence*, 20. On death rates, see memorandum, "Chinese Labour in the Transvaal: The Question of Its Continuance. Prepared for Lord Elgin," December 1905, 4, CO 879/89/10; Colonial Office, "Chinese Labour in the Transvaal," January 2, 1906, 6, CO 879/89/11; Herbert S. Klein, *African Slavery in Latin America and the Caribbean* (New York: Oxford University Press, 1986), 160–61; van Onselen, *Chibaro*, 48–57, 109; League of Nations, *Permanent Mandates Commission, Minutes of the Sixth Session*, 47. The high death rate was still a concern in 1938, according to Northern Rhodesia's Native Industrial Labour Advisory Board, minutes of the meeting, October 4, 1938, 4, CO 795/109/3. On Northern Rhodesia, see minute by H. F. Downie, June 9, 1931, CO 795/47/3. On Chinese indentured workers, see *Transvaal: Further Correspondence Relating to Labour in the Transvaal Mines* (London: Colonial Office, Transvaal, December 1905), no. 15, 8.

24. League of Nations, *Permanent Mandates Commission, Minutes of the Sixth Session*, 47; *Report of the Committee . . . on . . . the Supply and Welfare of Native Labour in the Tanganyika Territory*, 27; Edward B. Rose, *Uncle Tom's Cabin Up-to-Date or Chinese Slavery in South Africa*(London: South African Free Press Committee and Morning Leader, 1904). A similar claim was reported in 1952 by a visitor to French West Africa. See extract from [D. Pirie], "Tour of Parts of British, French, and Portuguese West Africa. November 29th, 1951–February 29th, 1952," CO 554/510. On conditions in the mines see, e.g., "Observations on Labour Conditions on Mines on the Rand at the Municipal Area of Johannesburg," 1930, 8–9, CO 795/39/17; minute by G. F. Seel, May 15, 1939; minute by Pritchard, May 18, 1939; minute by G. J. Orde Browne, May 25, 1939; memorandum on the recruitment of natives of Nyasaland and Northern Rhodesia by the Witwatersrand Native Labour Association, June 1939, CO 525/178/12. Cf. van Onselen, *Chibaro*.

25. Joseph Inikori, *Africans and the Industrial Revolution in England: A Study in International Trade and Development* (New York: Cambridge University Press, 2002), 392. See also Joseph Inikori, introduction to *Forced Migration: The Impact of the Export Slave Trade on African Societies*, ed. Joseph Inikori (London: Hutchinson University Library for Africa, 1982); "Annual Meeting of the Society," *Anti-Slavery Reporter* 23 (June–July 1903): 76–77, 79.

26. "The Native Question in South Africa," *Aborigines' Friend*, April 1901, 1; "Sir Alfred Milner," *Aborigines' Friend*, May 1897, 184; "Natives in the Diamond Mines," *Aborigines' Friend*, November 1897, 297; Alfred E. Pease and Henry Fox Bourne, *The Native Question in South Africa: Outlines of a Suggested Charter for Natives under British Rule in South Africa* (London: APS, 1900), 18; "The Native Question in South Africa," *Aborigines' Friend*, August 1900, 545.

27. Henry Fox Bourne, *The Claims of Uncivilised Races* (London: APS, 1900), 11; Henry Fox Bourne, *APS Notes* (London: APS [1897]); Henry Fox Bourne, *The Bechuana Troubles: A Story of Pledge-Breaking, Rebel-Making and Slave-Making in a British Colony* (London: APS, [1898]); Henry Fox Bourne, "Slavery and Its Substitutes in Africa. A Paper Submitted to the Anti-Slavery Conference, Held in Paris in August 1900," 14; Kevin Bales, *Disposable People: New Slavery in the Global Economy* (Berkeley: University of California Press, 1999).

28. Minute by W. C. B. [Bottomley] to C. Parkinson, February 21, 1938; O. G. R. Williams to the Undersecretary of State, Foreign Office, March 7, 1938, CO 583/231/1. Cf. J. C. Abraham, *Report on Nyasaland Natives in the Union of South Africa and in Southern Rhodesia* (Zomba, Nyasaland: Government Printer, 1937), 18, 45, CO 525/167/2; *Report of the Committee of Enquiry into the Labour Situation in the Uganda Protectorate, 1938* (Government Printer, Uganda, 1938), 27, CO 536/200/3; "Observations on Labour Conditions on Mines on the Rand at the Municipal Area of Johannesburg," 1930, 6, CO 795/39/17; W. Gemmill to Chief Secretary to the Government, Nyasaland, February 20, 1951, 4, CO 525/220/13; [Annual Report on Native Affairs, 1930], 58, CO 795/47/3; Cf. van Onselen, *Chibaro*, 40–48; Earl of Selborne to Lyttelton, no. 25, in *Transvaal: Further Correspondence* (December 1905), 25. On Uganda, see appendix III: J. C. Earl and R. L. Hett, Entebbe, October 8, 1942, in R. E. Barrett, *Second Report of the Advisory Labour Committee: Organization of the South-Western Labour Migration Routes* (Entebbe, Uganda: Government Printer, 1943), 27, CO 536/209/6; minute by Orde-Browne, January 23, 1942, CO 533/525/12; minute by S. M. [?] Culwick [on Kakira and Budongo Ration], March 13, 1944, CO 536/213/4; Savingram no. 901, Officer Administering the Government of Nigeria to Secretary of State for the Colonies, London, October 30, 1943, CO 536/213/4. On slave nutrition, see Robert William Fogel and Stanley L. Engerman, *Time on the Cross: The Economics of American Negro Slavery* (Boston: Little, 1974), 109–13; Eugene D. Genovese, *Roll, Jordan, Roll: The World the Slaves Made* (New York: Pantheon Books, 1974), 62; Herbert George Gutman, *Slavery and the Numbers Game: A Critique of Time on the Cross* (Urbana: University of Illinois Press, 1975), 38; William Dosite Postell, *The Health of Slaves on Southern Plantations* (1951; reprint, Baton Rouge: Louisiana State Universiy Press, 1970), 31; Kenneth M. Stampp, *The Peculiar Institution: Slavery in the Ante-Bellum South* (1956, reprint, New York: Knopf, 1972), 282; Richard Sutch, "The Care and Feeding of Slaves," in *Reckoning with Slavery: A Critical Study in the Quantitative History of American Negro Slavery*, ed. Paul A. David (New York: Oxford University Press, 1976), 234; Michael Tadman, "The Demographic Cost of Sugar: Debates on Slave Societies and Natural Increase in the Americas," *American Historical Review* 105, no. 5 (2000): 59; Hilary Beckles, *Natural Rebels: A Social History of Enslaved*

Black Women in Barbados (New Brunswick, NJ: Rutgers University Press, 1989), 47; Barbara Bush, *Slave Women in Caribbean Society, 1650–1838* (Bloomington: Indiana University Press, 1990), 48, 132; B. W. Higman, *Slave Populations of the British Caribbean, 1807–1834* (Baltimore: Johns Hopkins University Press, 1984), 205, 17–18; Kenneth F. Kiple and Virginia H. Kiple, "Deficiency Diseases in the Caribbean," *Journal of Interdisciplinary History* 11, no. 2 (1980): 197–215; Richard B. Sheridan, *Sugar and Slavery: An Economic History of the British West Indies, 1623–1775* (Baltimore: Johns Hopkins University Press, 1974), 242; Laird Bergad, *The Comparative Histories of Slavery in Brazil, Cuba, and the United States* (Cambridge: Cambridge University Press, 2007), 99; Frederick P. Bowser, *The African Slave in Colonial Peru, 1524–1650* (Stanford, CA: Stanford University Press, 1974), 224–26; C. R. Boxer, *The Golden Age of Brazil, 1695–1750: Growing Pains of a Colonial Society* (Berkeley: University of California Press, 1962), 173; Kenneth F. Kiple, "The Nutritional Link with Slave Infant and Child Mortality in Brazil," *Hispanic American Historical Review* 69, no. 4 (1989): 677–90. On the Sunday procurement of food, see Beckles, *Natural Rebels*, 46; Daina Berry, *"Swing the Sickle for the Harvest Is Ripe": Gender and Slavery in Antebellum Georgia* (Urbana: University of Illinois Press, 2007), 112; Bush, *Slave Women in Caribbean Society*, 47; Sam Hilliard, *Hog Meat and Hoecake: Food Supply in the Old South, 1840–1860* (Carbondale: Southern Illinois University Press, 1972), 56, 182–85; Rebecca Scott, *Slave Emancipation in Cuba: The Transition to Free Labor, 1860–1899* (Pittsburgh: University of Pittsburgh Press, 2000), 246.

29. Appendix III: Earl and Hett to Secretary, Labour Advisory Committee, in Barrett, *Second Report of the Advisory Labour Committee*, 26–27, CO 536/209/6; J. R. McD. Elliot, *Report on the Investigation into Conditions Affecting Unskilled Labour, and the Supply of Thereof, within the Protectorate* (Entebbe, Uganda: Government Printer, 1937), 11, CO 323/1429/9; appendix A, "Wages and the Cost of Living," [1938], CO 96/752/5. Cf. Hill Carter, "On the Management of Negroes: Addressed to the Farmers and Overseers of Virginia," *Farmers' Register* 1, no. 9 (February 1834): 564–65; John Hume Simons, *The Planter's Guide and Family Book of Medicine: For the Instruction and Use of Planters, Families, Country People and All Others Who May Be out of the Reach of Physicians, or Unable to Employ Them* (Charleston, SC: J. B. Nixon, 1848); Frederick Law Olmsted, *A Journey in the Seaboard Slave States: With Remarks on Their Economy* (New York: Dix and Edwards; Sampson Low, Son and Co., 1856), 108–10; John S. Wilson, "The Negro— His Diet, Clothing, Etc.," *American Cotton Planter and Soil of the South* 3 (1859): 197–98. See also James O. Breeden, ed., *Advice among Masters: The Ideal in Slave Management in the Old South* (Westport, CT: Greenwood Press, 1980). On health of the enslaved, see, e.g., David Lee Chandler, *Health and Slavery in Colonial Colombia* (New York: Arno

Press, 1981); Kenneth F. Kiple, *The Caribbean Slave: A Biological History* (Cambridge: Cambridge University Press, 1984); Postell, *Health of Slaves on Southern Plantations*; Todd Lee Savitt, *Medicine and Slavery: The Diseases and Health Care of Blacks in Antebellum Virginia* (Urbana: University of Illinois Press, 1978).

30. Fox Bourne, *Claims of Uncivilised Races*, 11; Fox Bourne, *APS Notes*; Pease and Fox Bourne, *Native Question in South Africa*.

31. Lewis, *Du Bois: Biography of a Race*, 386–407; [Du Bois], "Opportunity," *The Crisis*, January 1911, 17. On the post–Civil War history of abolitionism, see James McPherson, *The Abolitionist Legacy: From Reconstruction to the NAACP* (Princeton, NJ: Princeton University Press, 1976).

32. [Du Bois], "From the South," *The Crisis*, August 1911, 166; Pete Daniel, "Up from Slavery and down to Peonage: The Alonzo Bailey Case," *Journal of American History* 57 (December 1970): 654–70; Pete Daniel, *The Shadow of Slavery: Peonage in the South, 1901–1969* (Urbana: University of Illinois Press, 1972); [Du Bois], "Along the Color Line" and "The Christmas Reckoning," *The Crisis*, December 1910, 7, 19; [Du Bois], "Peonage" and "The Courts," *The Crisis*, February 1911, 6, 11; Jessie Fauset, "What to Read," *The Crisis*, April 1912, 261–62; [Du Bois], "Courts" and "The Black Folks of America in Account with the Year of Grace, 1911," *The Crisis*, January 1912, 100–101; William English Walling, "A Minimum Program of Negro Advancement," *The Crisis*, May 1913, 31–33; "The Negro and the Unions," *The Crisis*, November 1912, 20; "The Election," *The Crisis*, December 1912, 70; [Du Bois], "The Democrats," *The Crisis*, June 1913, 79; Du Bois, "Free, White and Twenty-One," *The Crisis*, January 1914, 134; Du Bois, "50,000," *The Crisis*, February 1914, 186; Du Bois, "The Immediate Program of the American Negro," *The Crisis*, April 1915, 310; [Du Bois], "Peonage," April 1916, 302–5; "National Association for the Advancement of Colored People, Sixth Annual Report, 1915," *The Crisis*, March 1916, 245; "Meetings," *The Crisis*, November 1916, 32; John Hope, "Letter," *The Crisis*, January 1918, 127; Du Bois, "Crime," *The Crisis*, February 1920, 173; "National Association for the Advancement of Colored People," *The Crisis*, August 1921, 161–62; "National Association for the Advancement of Colored People," *The Crisis*, August 1922, 164–67; [Du Bois], "Peonage," *The Crisis*, June 1921, 68; [Du Bois], "Peonage," *The Crisis*, July 1923, 128; [Du Bois], "Victory in Arkansas," *The Crisis*, August 1923, 163–64.

33. Du Bois, "World War and the Color Line," *The Crisis*, November 1914, 28; [Du Bois], "Slavery," *The Crisis*, August 1913, 186; [Du Bois], "Foreign," *The Crisis*, May 1914, 11; Du Bois, "Does Race Antagonism Serve Any Good Purpose," *The Crisis*, September 1914, 233; [Du Bois], "The Looking Glass" and "Meetings," *The Crisis*, February 1917, 177, 194. Du Bois also chronicled, to a lesser extent, conditions of the new slavery in the Caribbean. See, e.g., Du Bois, "Lead, Kindly Light," *The Crisis*, April 1918, 267.

34. [Du Bois], "Social Uplift," *The Crisis*, November 1910, 5; "Politics," *The Crisis*, August 1912, 180–81; [Du Bois], "Foreign," *The Crisis*, August 1913, 186; Carole Marks, *Farewell—We're Good and Gone: The Great Black Migration* (Bloomington: Indiana University Press, 1989); Lewis, *Du Bois: Biography of a Race*; Barbara Ross, *J. E. Spingarn and the Rise of the NAACP, 1911–1939* (New York: Atheneum, 1972), 26; Sullivan, *Lift Every Voice*.

35. Lewis, *Du Bois: Biography of a Race*, 423, 555; Eric Yellin, *Racism in the Nation's Service: Government Workers and the Color Line in Woodrow Wilson's America* (Chapel Hill: University of North Carolina Press, 2013); Nicholas Patler, *Jim Crow and the Wilson Administration: Protesting Federal Segregation in the Early Twentieth Century* (Boulder: University Press of Colorado, 2007).

36. [Du Bois], "The Real Causes of Two Races Riots," *The Crisis*, December 1919, 56; Lewis, *Du Bois: Biography of a Race*, 423, 555; Cameron McWhirter, *Red Summer: The Summer of 1919 and the Awakening of Black America* (New York: Henry Holt, 2011); Scott Ellsworth, *Death in a Promised Land: The Tulsa Race Riot of 1921* (Baton Rouge: LSU Press, 1992); Kenneth Janken, *Walter White: Mr. NAACP* (Chapel Hill: University of North Carolina Press, 2006); Felton O. Best, ed., *Black Resistance Movements in the United States and Africa, 1800–1993: Oppression and Retaliation* (New York: Edwin Mellon Press, 1995).

37. Lewis, *Du Bois: Biography of a Race*, 423, 555; Adriana Lentz-Smith, *Freedom Struggles: African Americans and World War I* (Boston: Harvard University Press, 2009).

38. Moorfield Storey, "An Open Letter to the People of the United States," *The Crisis*, June 1915, 78–80; Du Bois, "Approval," *The Crisis*, June 1914, 77; Du Bois, "The Supreme Court," *The Crisis*, December 1914, 77; Daniel, "Up from Slavery and down to Peonage."

39. "Review: The Souls of Black Folk," *Anti-Slavery Reporter*, March–May 1904, 69–72; T. Fisher Unwin, "Review: The American Negro," *Anti-Slavery Reporter and Aborigines' Friend*, January 1910, 74–77.

40. *Anti-Slavery Reporter and Aborigines' Friend*, January 1911, 196–97; "The Universal Races Congress," *Anti-Slavery Reporter and Aborigines' Friend*, October 1911, 109–10; Lentz-Smith, *Freedom Struggles*; W. E. B. Du Bois, *Dusk of Dawn: An Essay toward an Autobiography of a Race Concept* (New York: Oxford University Press, 2014), 115; Lewis, *Du Bois: Biography of a Race*, 438–44.

41. W. E. B. Du Bois, "The Black Man in the Revolution of 1914–1918," *The Crisis*, March 1919, 218; [Du Bois], "Africa," *The Crisis*, April 1918, 290; Du Bois, "League of Nations," *The Crisis*, May 1919, 10–11; [Du Bois], "The World in Council," *The Crisis*, September 1911, 196; [Du Bois], "The Races Congress," *The Crisis*, September 1911, 200–202; [Du Bois], "A Plank," *The Crisis*, July 1916, 135; [Du Bois], "The Attitude of Candidates," *The Crisis*,

November 1916, 18; Michael Neiberg, *The Treaty of Versailles: A Very Short Introduction* (New York: Oxford University Press, 2017).

42. W. E. B. Du Bois, "Close Ranks," *The Crisis*, July 1918, 111; [Du Bois], "Africa," *The Crisis*, April 1918, 290; Du Bois, "Easter, 1919," *The Crisis*, April 1919, 267; Chad Williams, *Torchbearers of Democracy: African American Soldiers in the World War I Era* (Chapel Hill: University of North Carolina Press, 2010).

43. Du Bois, *Black Reconstruction*.

44. Stephanie M. H. Camp, *Closer to Freedom: Enslaved Women and Everyday Resistance in the Plantation South* (Chapel Hill: University of North Carolina Press, 2004), 117; Isabel Wilkerson, *The Warmth of Other Suns: The Epic Story of America's Great Migration* (New York: Random House, 2010), 10. See also Ira Berlin, *The Making of African America: The Four Great Migrations* (New York: Viking, 2010). On marronage, see, e.g., Gad J. Heuman, ed., *Out of the House of Bondage: Runaways, Resistance and Marronage in Africa and the New World* (London: Frank Cass, 1986); Barbara Klamon Kopytoff, "The Early Political Development of Jamaican Maroon Societies," *William and Mary Quarterly* 35, no. 2 (1978): 287–307; Richard Price, *Maroon Societies: Rebel Slave Communities in the Americas*, 3rd ed. (Baltimore: Johns Hopkins University Press, 1996).

45. Alain Locke, "The New Negro," in *The New Negro: An Interpretation* (New York: Albert and Charles Boni, 1925), 7. On Locke, see Leonard Harris, introduction to *The Philosophy of Alain Locke: Harlem Renaissance and Beyond* (Philadelphia: Temple University Press, 1989). On the two-stage migration, see Marks, *Farewell*.

46. Locke, "New Negro," 7–8.

47. Alaine Locke, "Harlem," *Survey Graphic* 6 (March 1925): 630; James Weldon Johnson, "The Making of Harlem," *Survey Graphic* 6 (March 1925): 638–39; James Weldon Johnson, *Black Manhattan* (New York: Alfred A. Knopf, 1930); Gilbert Osofsky, *Harlem: The Making of a Ghetto, Negro New York, 1890–1930* (New York: Harper and Row, 1963); Jervis Anderson, *This Was Harlem: A Cultural Portrait, 1900–1950* (New York: Farrar Straus Giroux, 1981); Cheryl Lynn Greenburg, *"Or Does It Explode?" Black Harlem in the Great Depression* (New York: Oxford University Press, 1991).

48. Locke, "New Negro," 7–8.

49. Amy Jacques Garvey, ed., *Philosophy and Opinions of Marcus A. Garvey*, vol. 1 (New York: Atheneum, 1969), 38–39; Walter White, *A Man Called White: The Autobiography of Walter White* (Athens: University of Georgia Press, 1995), 60. For more on Garvey, see Theodore Vincent, *Black Power and the Garvey Movement* (Berkeley: University of California Press, 1972); Tony Martin, *Race First: The Ideological and Organizational Struggles of Marcus Garvey and the Universal Negro Improvement Association* (New York: Majority Press, 1986); Judith Stein, *The World of Marcus Garvey: Race and Class in Modern Society* (Baton Rouge: Louisiana State University Press, 1986); Colin Grant, *Negro with a Hat:*

The Rise and Fall of Marcus Garvey (New York: Oxford University Press, 2010); Robert Hill, ed., *The Marcus Garvey and Universal Negro Improvement Association Papers* (Berkeley: University of California Press, 1983).

50. Du Bois, *Dusk of Dawn*, 139; A. Philip Randolph, "Garveyism" *Messenger* 3 (September 1921): 248–52.

51. Arna Bontemps, "The Awakening: A Memoir," in *The Harlem Renaissance Remembered*, ed. Arna Bontemps (New York: Dodd, Mead, 1972), 6, 8–9; Claude McKay, *Harlem: Negro Metropolis* (New York: E. P. Dutton, 1940), 177; Johnson, *Black Manhattan*, 179.

52. James Jackson [Fort-Whiteman], "The Negroes in America," *Communist International* 8 (1925): 96; Walker, *David Walker's Appeal*; Pan-African Association, "Report of the Pan-African Conference," ca. 1900, 11, W. E. B. Du Bois Papers (MS 312), Special Collections and University Archives, University of Massachusetts Amherst Libraries. On Delany and Black nationalism, see Wilson Jeremiah Moses, *Liberian Dreams: Back-to-Africa Narratives from the 1850s* (State College: Pennsylvania State University Press, 1998). See also Manisha Sinha, *The Slave's Cause: A History of Abolition* (New Haven, CT: Yale University Press, 2016).

53. W. E. B. Du Bois, *The Souls of Black Folk: Essays and Sketches* (Chicago: McClurg, 1903), 13; Du Bois, *Dusk of Dawn*, 138–39. Cf. Anna Pochmara, *The Making of the New Negro: Black Authorship, Masculinity, and Sexuality in the Harlem Renaissance* (Amsterdam: Amsterdam University Press, 2011).

54. [Du Bois], "The Races Congress," *The Crisis*, September 1911, 200; "History," *The Crisis*, May 1919, 11; [Du Bois], "Africa," *The Crisis*, February 1919, 164–65; "Letters from Dr. Du Bois" *The Crisis*, February 1919; "The Peace Conference," *The Crisis*, January 1919, 112; "Africa and the World Democracy: A Report," *The Crisis*, February 1919.

55. [Du Bois], "The League of Nations," *The Crisis*, March 1921, 199–200; [Du Bois], "Pan-Africa," *The Crisis*, January 1921, 101.

56. Du Bois, "Pan-Africa," *The Crisis*, March 1921, 198; Lewis, *Du Bois: Biography of a Race*.

57. "Peace Conference," *The Crisis*, January 1919, 112; Du Bois, "The Pan-African Congress," *The Crisis*, April 1919, 271–75; Du Bois, "Memorandum to M. Diagne and Others on a Pan-African Congress to Be Held in Paris in February, 1919," *The Crisis*, March 1919, 224.

58. "Two Points of View," *The Crisis*, September 1917, 245; Du Bois, "My Mission," *The Crisis*, May 1919, 7–9; Du Bois, "League of Nations," *The Crisis*, May 1919, 11; Du Bois, "Pan-African Congress," *The Crisis*, April 1919, 273; Du Bois, "Memorandum to M. Diagne," *The Crisis*, March 1919, 224; "The Denial of Passports," *The Crisis*, March 1919, 237.

59. Du Bois, "My Mission," *The Crisis*, May 1919, 7–9; Du Bois, "Pan-African Congress," *The Crisis*, April 1919, 273; "Denial of Passports," *The Crisis*,

March 1919, 237; Du Bois, "League of Nations," *The Crisis*, May 1919, 10–11; A'Lelia Bundles, *On Her Own Ground: The Life and Times of Madam C. J. Walker* (New York: Scribner, 2001); Kerri K. Greenidge, *Black Radical: The Life and Times of William Monroe Trotter* (New York: Liveright, 2019).

60. "The African Mandates," *The Crisis*, August 1921; Du Bois, "Pan-Africa," *The Crisis*, March 1921, 198–99; Du Bois, "Why a Pan-African Congress," *The Crisis*, September 1921, 221.

61. [Du Bois], "Foreign," *The Crisis*, September 1915, 219; [Du Bois], "A Library," *The Crisis*, February 1916, 187; [Du Bois], "A Noble Family," *The Crisis*, May 1916, 16; [Du Bois], "The Negro Library," *The Crisis*, May 1916, 32; "The Birth of a Nation," *The Crisis*, December 1915, 85–86; W. E. B. Du Bois, *Darkwater: Voices from within the Veil* (New York: Harcourt, Brace and Howe, 1920), 66; [Du Bois], "Foreign," *The Crisis*, March 1918, 249; [Du Bois], "Africans, Asiatics and Anglo-Saxons," *The Crisis*, December 1920, 74.

62. Du Bois, *Darkwater*, 69; "Forced Labour: 14th International Labour Conference, Geneva, 10th–28th June, 1930: Report of the Colonial Office Members of the Delegation of His Majesty's Government in the United Kingdom," July 1, 1930, 7, CO 323/1076/1.

63. Sidney Webb's works include *Socialism: True and False* (London: Fabian Society, 1894); *Labour in the Longest Reign, 1837–1897* (London: Fabian Society, 1897); *Twentieth Century Politics: A Policy of National Efficiency* (London: Fabian Society, 1901); *The Necessary Basis of Society* (London: Fabian Society, 1911); *The Labour Party on the Threshold* (Westminster [London]: Fabian Society, 1923); *What Happened in 1931: A Record* (London: Fabian Society, 1932).

64. On the Fabian Society, see G. D. H. Cole, *The Fabian Society, Past and Present* (London: Fabian Society, 1942); Edward R. Pease, *The History of the Fabian Society*, 3rd ed. (New York: Barnes and Noble, 1963); A. M. McBriar, *Fabian Socialism and English Politics, 1884–1918* (Cambridge: Cambridge University Press, 1962). On the history of the Labour Party, see David Coates, *The Labour Party and the Struggle for Socialism* (London: Cambridge University Press, 1975); H. M. Drucker, *Doctrine and Ethos in the Labour Party* (London: G. Allen and Unwin, 1979).

65. Sidney Webb, *The New Constitution of the Labour Party* (London: Labour Party, 1917), 3.

66. Webb, *Labour Party on the Threshold*, 13; Ramsey MacDonald, *Labour and the Empire* (London: George Allen, 1907), 42; Du Bois, "Why a Pan-African Congress," *The Crisis*, September 1921, 221.

67. Mia Bey, *To Tell the Truth Freely: The Life of Ida B. Wells* (New York: Hill and Wang, 2009), 180; "The Society for the Recognition of the Brotherhood of Man," *Bond of Brotherhood* 1 (April 1895): 41–47.

68. "Recent Pamphlets on Social Reform," in *The Labour Annual, 1898* (London: William Glaisher, 1898); 172; Tembeka Ngcukaitobi, *The Land Is Ours: Black Lawyers and the Birth of Constitutionalism in South Africa* (Johannesburg, South Africa: Penguin, 2018); Killingray, "Significant Black South Africans in Britain," 403–4; Marika Sherwood, *Origins of Pan-Africanism: Henry Sylvester Williams, Africa, and the African Diaspora* (London: Routledge, 2012).

69. T. Fisher Unwin, "Review: The American Negro," *Anti-Slavery Reporter and Aborigines' Friend*, January 1910, 74–77.

70. "The Annual Meeting, 1899," *Aborigines' Friend*, November 1899, 448–52; Du Bois, *Dusk of Dawn*, 115.

3. The Rise of a New Antislavery

1. W. E. B. Du Bois, "The Pan-African Congress," *The Crisis*, April 1919, 273.

2. For a biography of Lugard, see Margery Perham, *Lugard*, 2 vols. (London: Collins, 1956). On the conventions Lugard authored, see Jean Allain, *The Slavery Conventions: The Travaux Préparatoires of the 1926 League of Nations Convention and the 1956 United Nations Convention, The Travaux Préparatoires of Multilateral Treaties* (Leiden, the Netherlands: Martinus Nijhoff, 2008), 31–166; Jean Allain, *The Legal Understanding of Slavery: From the Historical to the Contemporary*, 1st ed. (Oxford: Oxford University Press, 2012); Jean Allain, *Slavery in International Law: Of Human Exploitation and Trafficking* (Leiden, the Netherlands: Martinus Nijhoff, 2013); Joel Quirk, *The Anti-Slavery Project: From the Slave Trade to Human Trafficking* (Philadelphia: University of Pennsylvania Press, 2014). On the Anti-Slavery Society's support for the military expedition in East Africa, see British and Foreign Anti-Slavery Society, *Resignation of Chas. H. Allen, Honorary Secretary, and Joseph Allen, Treasurer: Address to Members of Committee* (London: Newnham and Cowell, 1902); Joseph A. Pease, speech to the House of Commons, June 1, 1894, Parliamentary Debates, Commons, 4th ser., vol. 25, cols. 236–38. On early British East Africa, see Anthony Clayton and Donald Cockfield Savage, *Government and Labour in Kenya 1895–1963* (New York: Routledge, 2012). Cf. Suzanne Miers, "Slavery and the Slave Trade as International Issues, 1890–1939," in Suzanne Miers and Martin A. Klein, *Slavery and Colonial Rule in Africa* (Portland, OR: Frank Cass, 1999); Elisabeth McMahon, *Slavery and Emancipation in Islamic East Africa: From Honor to Respectability* (Cambridge: Cambridge University Press, 2013); Elisabeth McMahon, "Trafficking and Reenslavement: The Social Vulnerability of Women and Children in Nineteenth-Century East Africa," in *Trafficking in Slavery's Wake: Law and the Experience of Women and Children*, ed. Benjamin N. Lawrance and Richard L. Roberts (Athens: Ohio University Press, 2012).

3. Frederick John Dealtry Lugard, *The Rise of Our East African Empire*, 2 vols. (Edinburgh: W. Blackwood and Sons, 1893), 1:56–58; *General Act of the Conference of Berlin: Signed February 26, 1885* (London: Harrison, 1886), article 6; *General Act of the Brussels Conference, 1889–90, with Annexed Declaration, Etc.* (London: Her Majesty's Stationery Office, [1890]); "Convention Revising the General Act of Berlin, February 26, 1885, and the General Act and Declaration of Brussels, July 2, 1890," *American Journal of International Law* 15, no. 4 (October 1921): article 11. Writing about Lugard's British East Africa, Elisabeth McMahon concludes, "While colonial officials asserted a desire to emancipate slaves, in reality they wanted to emancipate male slaves only, not women." McMahon, "Trafficking and Reenslavement," 30. Benjamin Lawrance and Richard Roberts observe, "Whereas most colonial powers formally abolished slavery, they often did little to enforce their decrees." Benjamin Lawrance and Richard Roberts, "Contextualizing Trafficking in Women and Children in Africa," in *Trafficking in Slavery's Wake*, 7. See also Miers and Klein, *Slavery and Colonial Rule in Africa.* On the general indifference of the British colonial authorities to the freeing of enslaved women, see Claire Robertson, "Post-Proclamation Slavery in Accra: A Female Affair?" in *Women and Slavery in Africa*, ed. Claire Robertson and Martin Klein (Madison: University of Wisconsin Press, 1983), 220–45; Kristin Mann, *Slavery and the Birth of an African City: Lagos, 1760–1900* (Bloomington: Indiana University Press, 2007); Paul E. Lovejoy and Jan S. Hogendorn, *Slow Death for Slavery: The Course of Abolition in Northern Nigeria, 1897–1936* (Cambridge: Cambridge University Press, 1993).

4. On Britain's suppression of slavery in East Africa, see Richard Roberts and Suzanne Miers, "The End of Slavery in Africa," in Suzanne Miers and Richard L. Roberts, *The End of Slavery in Africa* (Madison,: University of Wisconsin Press, 1988). On the parallel process in French colonial Africa, see, e.g., Martin A. Klein, *Slavery and Colonial Rule in French West Africa*, African Studies Series (Cambridge: Cambridge University Press, 1998). On slave resistance and escape, see Fred Morton, *Children of Ham: Freed Slaves and Fugitive Slaves on the Kenya Coast, 1873 to 1907* (Boulder, CO: Westview Press, 1990).

5. Lugard, *Rise of Our East African Empire*, 1:80–82. On the criticism of Lugard and British labor policy in East Africa, see Henry Fox Bourne, "The Duty of Civilised States to Weaker Races," *Aborigines' Friend*, April 1891, 173–75; "The Treatment of Native Races: Meeting at Westminster Palace Hotel," *Aborigines' Friend*, April 1897, 155; Sir Charles Dilke, speech to the House of Commons, June 1, 1894, Parliamentary Debates, Commons, 4th ser., vol. 25, cols. 195–96; Sir J. Swinburne, speech to the House of Commons, April 22, 1890, Parliamentary Debates, Commons, 4th ser., vol. 343, col. 1130; Samuel Storey, speech to the House of Commons, April 22, 1890, Parliamentary Debates, Commons, 4th ser., vol. 343, col. 1131; John Dillon, speech to the House of Commons, April 25, 1890, Parliamentary Debates, Commons, 4th

ser., vol. 343, col. 1443; Henry Labouchere, speech to the House of Commons, March 4, 1892, Parliamentary Debates, Commons, 4th ser., vol. 2, col. 56; H. R. Fox Bourne, *Slavery and Its Substitutes in Africa: A Paper Submitted to the Anti-Slavery Conference, Held in Paris in August 1900* (London: Aborigines Protection Society, 1900), 4.

6. Lugard, *Rise of Our East African Empire*, 1:480–87; Pease, speech to the House of Commons, June 1, 1894.

7. Lugard, *Rise of Our East African Empire*, 1:484–87; Miers and Klein, introduction to *Slavery and Colonial Rule in Africa*, 2; H. R. Fox Bourne, *Forced Labour in British South Africa* (London: P. S. King and Son, [1903]), 21; "Native Questions in South Africa," *Aborigines' Friend*, January 1902, 127; "Native Questions in South Africa," *Aborigines' Friend*, April 1903, 336; "Native Questions in South Africa," *Aborigines' Friend*, October 1901, 86–87. On Chamberlain, see Harry Browne, *Joseph Chamberlain, Radical and Imperialist* (London: Longman, 1974); Robert V. Kubicek, *The Administration of Imperialism: Joseph Chamberlain at the Colonial Office* (Durham, NC: Duke University Press, 1969).

8. "The Glen Grey Act," *Aborigines' Friend*, January 1895, 442–50; "The Native Question in South Africa," *Anti-Slavery Reporter* 21 (March–May 1901): 51; H. R. Fox Bourne, *Forced Labour in British South Africa: Notes on the Condition and Prospects of South African Natives under British Control* (London: P. S. King and Son, [1903]), 17; H. R. Fox Bourne, *Blacks and Whites in South Africa: An Account of the Past Treatment and Present Condition of South African Natives under British and Boer Control* (London: P. S. King and Son, 1900), 88–89; H. J. Ogden, *The War against the Dutch Republics in South Africa: Its Origin, Progress and Results* (Manchester, UK: National Reform Union, 1901), 79; Raymond Buell, *The Native Problem in Africa*, 2 vols. (New York: Macmillan, 1928), 1: 229.

9. Fourth Earl Albert Henry George Grey, *Native Labour in South Africa* (London: Imperial South African Association, 1903), 5.

10. Catherine Ann Cline, *E. D. Morel, 1873–1924: The Strategies of Protest* (Belfast: Blackstaff, 1980), 27, 30, 43, 57; Kevin Grant, *A Civilised Savagery: Britain and the New Slaveries in Africa, 1884–1926* (New York: Routledge, 2005), 41, 59–60, 77; Edward Grey, speech to the House of Commons, in *The Parliamentary Debates*, vol. 179 (from Thursday, July 25, to Tuesday, August 6, 1907), 407. See also "The Congo Question," *Anti-Slavery Reporter* 26 (June–July 1906): 61, 63; "Parliamentary (House of Commons)," *Anti-Slavery Reporter* 26 (June–July 1906): 66; "The Congo Question," *Anti-Slavery Reporter* 26 (November–December 1906): 125; "The Congo Question," *Anti-Slavery Reporter* 28 (June–July 1908): 91–92; *Parliamentary Debates*, vol. 174 (from Wednesday, February 12, to Wednesday, February 26, 1908), 1870–74, 1875–81; "The Annexation of the Congo State," *Spectator*, August 29, 1908, 285. Cf. K. G. Robbins, "Public Opinion, the Press and Pressure Groups," in *British Foreign Policy under Sir Edward Grey*, ed. F. H. Hinsley (Cambridge: Cambridge

University Press, 1977), 86; "The Congo Question: Parliamentary Papers," *Anti-Slavery Reporter* 28 (June–July 1908): 91, 93; Edward Grey, speech to the House of Commons, in *Parliamentary Debates*, vol. 179, 317.

11. Grey, speech to the House of Commons, 407; "Earl Grey on African Affairs," *Aborigines' Friend*, February 1890, 37.

12. Lord Cromer, "What Is Slavery?" *Spectator*, January 17, 1914, 6; John Harris, *Africa: Slave or Free?* (New York: Negro Universities Press, 1969), viii, xxiv, 43, 114.

13. League of Nations, *Permanent Mandates Commission, Minutes of the Seventh Session* (Geneva: League of Nations Publications, 1925), 207; Chairman of the Tanganyika Sisal Growers Association to the Chief Secretary, Dar es Salaam, October 18, 1932, Colonial Office (hereafter CO) 691/158/6, National Archives, London. On the widespread acceptance of Cromer's position, see, e.g., T. F. Victor Buxton, "Letter to Editor," *Spectator*, August 23, 1918, 12; "Memorial to the International Labour Office of the League of Nations," *Anti-Slavery Reporter* 17 (July 1927): 57–58; Kathleen Harvey Simon, *Slavery* (London: Hodder and Stoughton, 1929), 174–75; British Anti-Slavery and Aborigines Protection Society and British League of Nations Union to Albert Thomas, International Labour Office, Geneva, April 30, 1927, CO 822/5/1; "III. Native Labour," [1927], CO 323/972/13; "Forced Labour, Report of Colonial Office Committee, May 1929, Twelfth International Labour Conference, Geneva, 30th May–22nd June, 1929," June 29, 1929, 33, CO 885/31/7; International Labour Office, "International Labour Conference, Twelfth Session, Geneva, 1929, Forced Labour, Report and Draft Questionnaire," 193, CO 323/1027/1; International Labour Office, "International Labour Conference, Fourteenth Session, Geneva, 1930, Forced Labour," 41, CO 323/1075/2.

14. *Compulsory Native Labour (Colonies), Parliamentary Return* (London: HMSO, 1908), 4–6, 20–22, 27–28; *Anti-Slavery Reporter* 30 (1910): 103; "Employment of Girls (Central Kavirondo)," n.d., "Report on the Allegations Made by Archdeacon W. E. Owen in the Article of December 6, [1929]," CO 533/386/12; "Correspondence Relating to the Question of the Employment of Women on Compulsory Labour in the Colonies, Protectorates, and Mandated Territories, 1926–1928," 5, CO 885/31/1. See also J. W. Barth, Acting Governor of Kenya, to L. C. M. S. Amery, Secretary of State for the Colonies, March 9, 1929; W. E. Owen to District Commissioner, North Kavirondo, "Forced Unpaid Labour on Roads," May 6, 1929; Will Lunn to A. Fenner Brockway, July 19 1929, CO 533/386/12.

15. Charles William James Orr, *The Making of Northern Nigeria* (1911; reprint, London: Frank Cass, 1965, 116, 210, 188; A. Bonar Law, "Memorandum on Steps Taken to Increase a Supply of (a) Coloured Troops, (b) Coloured Labour," January 1917, CO 885/25/11; Buell, *Native Problem in Africa*, 1:465;

Granville St. John Orde-Browne, *Report upon Labour in the Tanganyika Territory* (London: HMSO, 1926), 37; "Debate in the House of Commons," *Anti-Slavery Reporter* 19 (October 1929): 105. Cf. Charles William Hobley, *Kenya, from Chartered Company to Crown Colony: Thirty Years of Exploration and Administration in British East Africa* (London: H. F. and G. Witherby, 1929), 13; Isaias Chaves, Stanley Engerman, and James Robinson, "Reinventing the Wheel: The Economic Benefits of Wheeled Transportation in Early Colonial British West Africa," in *Africa's Development in Historical Perspective*, ed. Emmanuel Akyeampong, Robert Bates, Nathan Nunn, and James Robinson (New York: Cambridge University Press, 2014), 321–65.

16. W. Ormsby-Gore to J. H. Harris, April 29, 1927, CO 822/5/1; Alexander Ransford Slater to Lord Passfield, January 13, 1930, 3, CO 323/1032/2/02; R. Rankurl to Secretary of State for the Colonies, December 20, 1929, CO 323/1032/2/02; W. E. Owen, "Forced Labour in Uganda," *Manchester Guardian*, December 27, 1929, CO 536/157/5; League of Nations, *Permanent Mandates Commission, Minutes of the Sixth Session* (Geneva: League of Nations Publications, 1925), 41.

17. League of Nations, *Permanent Mandates Commission, Minutes of the Sixth Session*, 18, 41–42.

18. League of Nations, *Permanent Mandates Commission, Minutes of the Sixth Session*, 18; League of Nations, *Permanent Mandates Commission, Minutes of the Seventh Session*, 155, 202; P. E. Mitchell, Conference of Governors of British East African Territories, February 1933, "Native Policy: Marketing of Produce of Native Reserves," memorandum by government of Tanganyika Territory, March 21, 1932, CO 822/55/10; Robert Service, *Stalin: A Biography* (Cambridge, MA: Belknap Press of Harvard University Press, 2005). For British condemnation of forced labor in the Soviet bloc, see Emrys Hughes, draft reply to Parliamentary question no. 74. July 11, [1952]; extract from official report on forced labor, United Nations inquiry, September 14, 1952; "Reply by the United Kingdom to the United Nations Questionnaire on Forced Labour," [1952], CO 859/284; "Summary of Allegations and of the Material Available to the Committee," November 1952; "Slave Labor Rising U.N. Inquiry Is Told," *New York Times*, October 25, 1952, CO 859/285.

19. W. Ormsby-Gore to J. H. Harris, April 29, 1927, CO 822/5/1; Alexander Ransford Slater to Lord Passfield, January 13, 1930, 3, CO 323/1032/2/02; R. Rankurl to Secretary of State for the Colonies, December 20, 1929, CO 323/1032/2/02; "Convention Concerning Forced or Compulsory Labour: Note of Discussion Held on the 19th July, 1932," CO 323/1069/15; Neville Bland to Arthur Henderson, July 1, 1930, CO 822/26/2. A Colonial Office staffer said of a request by the League of Nations Permanent Mandates Commission for information about a colony the British had controlled for two

decades: "the demand for light on the Administration's 'wage policy' may be a little embarrassing to meet." Minute by F. G. Lee, June 25, 1937, CO 691/153/4. J. C. Maxwell to Lord Passfield, December 31, 1929, CO 323/1032/2/02; League of Nations, *Permanent Mandates Commission, Minutes of the Sixth Session*, 18; League of Nations, *Permanent Mandates Commission, Minutes of the Seventh Session*, 155, 202. "Forced Labour: Second Report of the Colonial Office Committee, 1st October, 1929," CO 323/1032/2/02; Ransford Slater to Lord Passfield, January 13, 1930, 2, 5.

20. Maxwell to Lord Passfield, December 31, 1929; League of Nations, *Permanent Mandates Commission, Minutes of the Sixth Session*, 18; League of Nations, *Permanent Mandates Commission, Minutes of the Seventh Session*, 155, 202; "Memorandum on the Rates of Wages of Skilled, Semi-Skilled, and Unskilled Labour in the Gold Coast," August 17, 1938, 3, CO 96/752/5; International Labour Office, *Annual Review 1930* (Geneva: ILO, 1931), 419.

21. *The Anti-Slavery and Aborigines Protection Society: Being the Amalgamation. Effected on 1st July, 1909, of the British and Foreign Anti-Slavery Society and the Aborigines Protection Society* (London: ASAPS, 1909); "Amalgamation of the Aborigines Protection Society and the British and Foreign Anti-Slavery Society," *Aborigines' Friend*, May 1909, 255–56; "H. R. Fox Bourne," *Aborigines' Friend*, May 1909, 245–54; Harris, *Africa: Slave or Free?*

22. Harris, *Africa: Slave or Free?* viii, xii, xxiv, 43, 114. On Harris, see Grant, *Civilised Savagery*; Suzanne Miers, "The Anti-Slavery Game: Britain and the Suppression of Slavery in Africa and Arabia, 1890–1975," in *Slavery, Diplomacy and Empire: Britain and the Suppression of the Slave Trade, 1807–1975*, ed. Keith Hamilton and Patrick Salmon (Portland, OR: Sussex Academic Press, 2009), 196–214. The account that follows is a reappraisal of both Harris and British antislavery from the standpoint of their shared opposition to Black abolitionism and antiracism in general.

23. *Anti-Slavery Reporter* 26 (January–February 1906): 18. In 1904 the *Anti-Slavery Reporter* criticized the "experiment" of bringing workers from Nyasaland to the Transvaal mines, calling it "a failure" and noting the horrific conditions experienced by the migrant workers. "The Importation of Central Africa Natives," *Anti-Slavery Reporter* 24 (January–February 1904): 7–8. In 1908 it reversed itself on the dubious grounds that conditions had improved. "Central Africa Natives in the Mines," *Anti-Slavery Reporter* 23 (March–May 1908): 59–62. See also "Nyasaland Natives," *Anti-Slavery Reporter* 30 (January 1910): 72. For a critique of Portugal, France, and Germany see, e.g., "The Abuses in French Congo," *Anti-Slavery Reporter* 25 (August–October 1905): 111; "Annual Report 1905," *Anti-Slavery Reporter* 25 (November–December 1905): 10–11; Travers Buxton to the Undersecretary of the State, June 11, 1908, *Anti-Slavery Reporter* 28 (June–July 1908): 76–77; "Slave Trade Papers," *Anti-Slavery Reporter* 28 (June–July 1908): 81–84; "Slave Labour in Portu-

guese West Africa," *Anti-Slavery Reporter* 28 (August–October 1908): 99–101; "Slave Trade in Central Africa," *Anti-Slavery Reporter* 28 (August–October 1908): 102–3; "Portuguese Slave Labour," *Anti-Slavery Reporter* 29 (January–February 1909): 3–9.

24. Harris, *Africa: Slave or Free?* iii, vii, 61, 72, 78, 118, 153, 248.

25. Harris, iii, vii, 61, 72, 78, 118, 153, 248; Peggy Pascoe, *What Comes Naturally: Miscegenation Law and the Making of Race in America* (New York: Oxford University Press, 2009).

26. Lord Cromer, "Portuguese Slavery—I," *Spectator*, January 16, 1913, 7.

27. "Indian Coolie Emigrants," *Anti-Slavery Reporter* 25 (November–December 1905): 143; "The Transvaal Labor Question: Parliamentary Papers," *Anti-Slavery Reporter* 24 (November–December 1904): 141. See also "Native Labour in South Africa," *Anti-Slavery Reporter* 23 (January–February 1903): 18; "South African Native Labour," *Anti-Slavery Reporter* 23 (November–December 1903): 132–34; "Annual Meeting of the Society," *Anti-Slavery Reporter* 24 (March–May 1904): 44–51; "Chinese Labour on the Rand: Parliamentary Papers," *Anti-Slavery Reporter* 24 (March–May 1904): 51–54; "The Transvaal Labour Question: Parliamentary Paper," *Anti-Slavery Reporter* 25 (March–May 1905): 33–38; "Chinese Labour on the Rand: Parliamentary Papers," *Anti-Slavery Reporter* 26 (January–February 1906): 9–15; "The Native Problem in the United States," *Anti-Slavery Reporter* 26 (June–July 1906): 80; "The Race Problem in the United States," *Anti-Slavery Reporter* 21 (October–December 1901): 168–71; "Annual Report 1902," *Anti-Slavery Reporter* 22 (November–December 1902): 8; "The Race Question in America," *Anti-Slavery Reporter* 25 (August–October 1905): 110–11; "The Race Question in America," *Anti-Slavery Reporter* 25 (November–December 1905): 144; "The Negro Problem in America," *Anti-Slavery Reporter* 29 (March–May 1909): 59–62. For earlier examples of the denunciation of the legacy of slavery, see, e.g., "The Treatment of Negroes in America," *Anti-Slavery Reporter* 14 (May–June 1894): 168–71; "The Convict-Leasing System in the United States," *Anti-Slavery Reporter* 18 (January–February 1899): 42–44; "Review of *The Souls of Black Folk* by W. E. B. Du Bois," *Anti-Slavery Reporter* 24 (March–May 1904): 69–72. On the Liberal Party, see David Dutton, *A History of the Liberal Party since 1900*, 2nd ed. (New York: Palgrave Macmillan, 2013), chap. 1; Duncan Tanner, *Political Change and the Labour Party, 1900–1918* (Cambridge: Cambridge University Press, 1990).

28. Harris, *Africa: Slave or Free?* xii; "Blacks and Whites in America and Elsewhere," *Anti-Slavery Reporter* 26 (November–December 1906): 130–31; Josiah Royce, *Race Questions, Provincialism, and Other American Problems* (New York: Macmillan, 1908), 16, 19; "Two Points of View," *The Crisis*, September 1917, 245–46; Paul A. Kramer, "Empires, Exceptions, and Anglo-Saxons: Race and Rule between the British and United States Empires, 1880–1910," *Journal*

of American History 88, no. 4 (2002): 1315–53; Reginald Horsman, "Origins of Racial Anglo-Saxonism in Great Britain before 1850," *Journal of the History of Ideas* 37, no. 3 (1976): 387–89.

29. "Darkwater: Voices from within the Veil," *Anti-Slavery Reporter and Aborigines' Friend*, April 1921, 29–31; "The Looking Glass," *The Crisis*, December 1920, 68; Du Bois, "On the Book Shelf," *The Crisis*, June 1921, 61–62.

30. "The Pan-African Congress," *Anti-Slavery Reporter and Aborigines' Friend*, December 1921, 106; Jessie Fauset, "Impressions of the Second Pan-African Congress," *The Crisis*, November 1921, 12–18; "Second Pan-African Congress," *The Crisis*, March 1922, 214; "Manifesto to the League of Nations," *The Crisis*, November 1921, 18; "110 Delegates to the Pan-African Congress by Countries," *The Crisis*, December 1921, 68–69; "To the World (Manifesto of the Second Pan-African Congress)," *The Crisis*, November 1921, 5–10; Walter White, *A Man Called White: The Autobiography of Walter White* (Athens: University of Georgia Press, 1995), 61; Kenneth Janken, *Walter White: Mr. NAACP* (Chapel Hill: University of North Carolina Press, 2006) 65, 66.

31. Janken, *Walter White*, 66; White, *Man Called White*, 140.

32. Janken, *Walter White*, 66; White, *Man Called White*, 140. On Tuskegee, see Trevor Thompson, *Booker T. Washington: The Building of the "Tuskegee Machine"* (Jackson: University of Mississippi Press, 1994).

33. [Oswald Garrison Villard], "Harpers Ferry and Gettysburg," *Nation* 89 (October 28, 1909): 405; W. E. B. Du Bois, *John Brown* (Philadelphia: George W. Jacobs, 1909); Oswald Garrison Villard, *John Brown, 1800–1859: A Biography after Fifty Years* (Boston: Houghton Mifflin, 1910).

34. *Anti-Slavery Reporter and Aborigines' Friend*, January 1922, 135.

35. White, *Man Called White*, 62; David Levering Lewis, *W. E. B. Du Bois: The Fight for Equality and the American Century, 1919–1963* (New York: Holt, 2001), 208–11. On transatlantic racism, see Kramer, "Empires, Exceptions, and Anglo-Saxons"; Paul Lauren, *Power and Prejudice: The Politics and Diplomacy of Racial Discrimination* (New York: Taylor and Francis, 2018). On antebellum abolitionists' recognition of the racial character of slavery, see Paul Goodman, *Of One Blood: Abolitionism and the Origins of Racial Equality* (Berkeley: University of California Press, 1998); J. R. Oldfield, *Popular Politics and British Anti-Slavery: The Mobilisation of Public Opinion against the Slave Trade, 1787–1807* (Manchester, UK: Manchester University Press, 1995), 20–24, 144–46; Carolyn Williams, "The Female Antislavery Movement: Fighting against Racial Prejudice and Promoting Women's Rights in Antebellum America," in *The Abolitionist Sisterhood: Women's Political Culture in Antebellum America*, ed. Jean Fagan Yellin and John C. Van Horne (Ithaca, NY: Cornell University Press, 1994), 159–77; Keith Griffler, *Front Line of Freedom: African Americans and the Forging of the Underground Railroad in the Ohio Valley* (Lexington: University Press of Kentucky, 2004).

36. Du Bois, "Pan-African Congress," *The Crisis*, April 1919, 273. For background on the League of Nations and the Permanent Mandates Commission, see Leonard Smith, *Sovereignty at the Paris Peace Conference of 1919* (New York: Oxford University Press, 2018).

37. League of Nations, *Permanent Mandates Commission, Minutes of the Sixth Session*, 47–48; League of Nations, *Permanent Mandates Commission, Minutes of the Seventh Session*, 195, 200.

38. Du Bois, "Pan-African Congress," *The Crisis*, April 1919, 273; League of Nations, *Permanent Mandates Commission, Minutes of the Sixth Session*, 50; League of Nations, *Permanent Mandates Commission, Minutes of the Seventh Session*, 196. See also League of Nations, *Permanent Mandates Commission, Minutes of the Third Session* (Geneva: League of Nations Publications, 1923), 268. For mortality rates, see International Labour Office, *The I.L.O. Year Book, 1930* (Geneva: ILO, 1931), 429; League of Nations, *Permanent Mandates Commission, Minutes of the Sixth Session*, 47.

39. Colonial Office memorandum, "Direction of Labour," [1951], CO 96/826/8; Robert Service, *Lenin: A Biography* (Cambridge, MA: Harvard University Press, 2000).

40. League of Nations, *Permanent Mandates Commission, Minutes of the Sixth Session*, 16; League of Nations, *Permanent Mandates Commission, Minutes of the Seventh Session*, 207; International Labour Office, "Investigation of Forced Labour," 1927, CO 323/988/2.

41. W. E. B. Du Bois, *Dusk of Dawn: An Essay toward an Autobiography of a Race Concept* (New York: Oxford University Press, 2014), 116; David Levering Lewis, *W. E. B. Du Bois: Biography of a Race, 1868 to 1919* (New York: Holt, 1993); Aldon Morris, *The Scholar Denied: W. E. B. Du Bois and the Birth of Modern Sociology* (Berkeley: University of California Press, 2015).

42. League of Nations, *Slavery Convention, Geneva, September 25th 1926* (Geneva: League of Nations, 1926), article 5; Allain, *Slavery Conventions*; Allain, *Legal Understanding of Slavery*.

43. International Labour Office, *I.L.O. Year Book, 1930*, 442.

44. International Labour Office, *C29 Forced Labour Convention, 1930: Convention Concerning Forced or Compulsory Labour* (Geneva: ILO, 1930); Allain, *Slavery Conventions*; Roger Maul, "The International Labour Organization and the Struggle against Forced Labour from 1919 to the Present," *Labor History* 48, no. 4 (2007): 477–500.

45. "Quarterly Notes," *Anti-Slavery Reporter* 19 (October 1929): 78; "Quarterly Notes," *Anti-Slavery Reporter* 19 (April 1929): 2; "The East African Commission," *Anti-Slavery Reporter* 19 (April 1929): 9; Suzanne Miers, *Slavery in the Twentieth Century: The Evolution of a Global Problem* (New York: AltaMira Press, 2003); Miers, "Anti-Slavery Game," 202, 206.

46. "Annual Meeting," *Anti-Slavery Reporter* 21 (July 1931): 77; "Annual Report, 1931," *Anti-Slavery Reporter* 22 (April 1932): 44; "Annual Report, 1930," *Anti-Slavery Reporter* 21 (April 1931): 59;

47. League of Nations, *Report of the Committee of Experts on Slavery Provided for by the Assembly Resolution of September 25th, 1931* (Geneva: League of Nations, 1932), 17; League of Nations, *Report of the Advisory Committee of Experts, Second Session of the Committee Held in Geneva, April 1st to 10th, 1935* (Geneva: League of Nations, 1935), 17; League of Nations, *Report of the Advisory Committee of Experts, Fifth (Extraordinary) Session of the Committee Held in Geneva, March 31st to April 5th, 1938* (Geneva: League of Nations, 1938), 9; minute by J. A. Calder, March 13, 1939, CO 533/497/6; note by Sheila Ann Ogilvie, June 25, 1952, CO 859/282; "Compulsory Labour in Tanganyika," n.d., CO 859/282; R. V. Vernon and J. J. Paskin, "Forced Labour: 14th International Labour Conference, Geneva, 10th–28th June, 1930, Report of the Colonial Office Members of the Delegation of His Majesty's Government in the United Kingdom," July 1, 1930, 9, CO 323/1076/1; minute by J. J. Paskin, March 9, 1939, CO 533/497/6. On the legislation's inconsistency with Britain's public pronouncements, see minutes by J. J. Paskin, July 16, 1938; J. A. Calder, August 12, 1938; Malcolm MacDonald, October 3, 1938, CO 533/497/6; Vernon and Paskin, "Forced Labour"; minute by J. J. Paskin, March 9, 1939, CO 533/497/6; minute by J. A. Calder, March 13, 1939, CO 533/497/6. See also International Labour Office, *C105 Abolition of Forced Labour Convention, 1957: Convention Concerning the Abolition of Forced Labour* (Geneva: ILO, 1957).

48. Note by Ogilvie, June 25, 1952; note by [initials unreadable] to Watson, June 30, 1952, CO 859/282; "Compulsory Labour in Tanganyika," n.d. See also minutes by Paskin, July 16, 1938; Calder, August 12, 1938; MacDonald, October 3, 1938; ILO, *C105 Abolition of Forced Labour Convention*; Maul, "International Labour Organization and Struggle against Forced Labour"; "Forced Labour, Report of Colonial Office Committee, May 1929, Twelfth International Labour Conference, 33; Vernon and Paskin, "Forced Labour," 5–6, CO 885/32/9.

49. Bailey v. State of Alabama, 219 U.S. 241, 244 (1911).

50. Minute by R. V. Vernon, February 6, 1929; minute by J. E. W. Flood, February 16, 1929; minute by G. G. [Grindle], February 6, 1929; minute by A. C. C. Parkinson, February 15, 1929, CO 323/1027/6; Vernon and Paskin, "Forced Labour." The Colonial Office hoped to limit the discussion to "representatives of the Colonial Powers" and their lieutenants in the field "who are conversant with native labour problems" and from whom they expected a sympathetic hearing. Minute by J. J. Paskin, October 9, 1933, CO 323/1212/6.

51. Minute by J. J. Paskin, March 9. 1939; minute by J. A. Calder, March 13, 1939, CO 533/497/6.

52. "Tax-Resistance by Kenyan Natives," *Times*, January 16 1936, CO 533/466/6; "Council Debates Labour Position," *East African Standard*, April 29, 1935, CO 533/497/6; W. E. Owen, "Taxation in Boys in Kenya," *Manchester Guardian*, September 20, 1931, CO 533/425/4; "Re Native Hut and Poll Tax," January 9, 1936, CO 533/466/5. The convention did, however, ban private prison labor arrangements, leading to the United States' refusal to sign on. Adelle Blackett and Alice Duquesnoy, "Slavery Is Not a Metaphor: U.S. Prison Labor and Racial Subordination through the Lens of the ILO's Abolition of Forced Labor Convention," *UCLA Law Review* 67, no. 6 (2021): 1513–14.

53. [Position on imprisonment in default of payment of native hut and poll tax], n.d., [ca. 1931], CO 533/425/4; Colony and Protectorate of Kenya, "Report of the Commission Appointed to Inquire into and Report upon Allegations of Abuse and Hardships in the Collection of Non-Native Graduated Poll Tax and of Native Poll and Hut Tax," 1936, 17, CO 533/480/11; extracts from records of debates in the Kenya Legislative Council, November 1936, 423, CO 533/480/11; minute by C. A. Grossmith, April 20, 1937, CO 533/480/11; A. W., "Yellow Slavery—and White!" *Westminster Review* 161, nos. 5–6 (1904): 480; J. A. Hobson, *The War in South Africa: Its Causes and Effects* (New York: H. Fertig, 1969), 237. On penal sanctions, see African (South), no. 820, "South Africa, Secret Papers [1906 and 1907] Relating to Affairs in South Africa," April 1908, 94, CO 879/106/2. On Uganda, see Uganda Protectorate, "Report of the Committee of Enquiry into the Labour Situation in the Uganda Protectorate, 1938," 1938, 56, CO 536 200/3. On Kenya, see A. de V. Wade, Governor of Kenya, "Memorandum on Certain Questions in the 'Red Report,'" November 2, 1938, 3, CO 533/497/6. For a history of penal sanctions, see Douglas Hay and Paul Craven, eds., *Masters, Servants, and Magistrates in Britain and the Empire, 1562–1955* (Chapel Hill: University of North Carolina Press, 2005); David Anderson, "Master and Servant in Colonial Kenya, 1895–1939," *Journal of African History* 41, no. 3 (2000): 459–85.

54. Minute to Watson, June 30, 1952, CO 859/282; League of Nations, *Permanent Mandates Commission, Minutes of the Twenty-Sixth Session* (Geneva: League of Nations, 1934), 17–18; League of Nations, *Permanent Mandates Commission, Minutes of the Seventh Session*, 196.

55. J. C. Maxwell to Lord Passfield, December 31, 1929, CO 323/1032/2/02; "Memorandum on Forced Labour," May 23, 1929, CO 822/17/7; International Labour Office, *Annual Review 1930*, 419.

56. League of Nations, Permanent Mandates Commission, Minutes of the Thirty-First Session Held at Geneva from May 31st to June 15th, 1937, 46, CO 691/153/4; memorandum, "Native Taxation—Tax Defaulters and Forced Labour," n.d., CO 533/425/4; minute by F. G. Lee, November 6, 1935, CO 822/69/7.

57. Memorandum by Lloyd-Blood, acting attorney-general, Nyasaland Protectorate, [1926], CO 525/116/1. Nyasaland's governor commented on the "large number of men who were in prison as Hut Tax defaulters." Circular no. 1 of 1935 to Provincial Commissioners and District Commissioners, "Hut Tax Defaulters," Zomba, Nyasaland, January 3, 1935, CO 822/69/7; minute by H. F. Downie, July 28, 1926; minute by H. F. Downie to Ehrhardt, Green, and Strachey, December 11, 1926, CO 525/116/1; P. Cunliffe-Lister to Governor of Tanganyika Territory, August 21, 1934, CO 691/138/13; Northern Rhodesia, "Report of the Taxation Committee," April 1934, 1934, 14, CO 795/69/8; minutes of the meeting of the Native Industrial Labour Advisory Board held at Ndola on 22nd and 23rd April, 1936, CO 795/83/3; "Native Tax Collection in Kenya: Inquiry into Abuses," extract from *Times*, November 6, 1936; "Tribesmen Tortured for Taxes," extract from *Daily Herald*, November 6, 1936; "Kenya Native Tax Collection: Archdeacon Burns's Allegations," *Times*, December 28, 1935, clippings in CO 533/466/5; Kenya Legislative Council, January 9, 1936, 1156–63; J. Byrne to J. H. Thomas, Secretary of State for the Colonies, January 31, 1936, CO 533/466/6; Colony and Protectorate of Kenya, "Report of the Commission Appointed to Inquire into and Report upon Allegations of Abuse and Hardships," 1936, 7; extracts from records of debates in the Kenya Legislative Council, November 1936, 420; note of a meeting held in Sir C. Bottomley's room on Wednesday, November 27, 1935, CO 822/69/7; minute by J. E. W. Flood, November 21, 1935, CO 822/69/7; minute by K. O. Roberts-Wray, August 11, 1934, CO 691/138/13; P. Cunliffe-Lister to Governor of Tanganyika, August 21, 1934, CO 691/138/13; Governor of Kenya, note [unsigned] to R. W. Sorensen, House of Commons, [August 16, 1957]; Governor of Kenya to Secretary of State for the Colonies, August 8, 1957, CO 822/1296. See also J. E. W. Flood to Secretary, East African Governors' Conference, July 20, 1936, CO 822/69/7; memorandum, "Native Taxation—Tax Defaulters and Forced Labour," n.d.; Native Affairs Department, "Native Hut and Poll Tax," August 9, 1932, CO 533/425/4. Kenya also "freely used" detention camps to get around any legal obstacles to imprisonment for tax default. [Position on imprisonment in default of payment of native hut and poll tax], n.d. The Colonial Office reported that the number of such detention camps for roadwork was increasing. Minute by C. A. Grossmith, April 20, 1937, CO 533/480/11.

58. R. V. Vernon to Ellis and Grindle, January 31, 1930, CO 323/1066/14; note by T. D. S., April 29, 1930; Lord Passfield to Governor Thomas, Nyasaland, June 18, 1930, CO 525/137/11; T. S. W. Thomas to Lord Passfield, January 11, 1930, 2, CO 525/137/8; "Forced Labour: Second Report of the Colonial Office Committee, 1st October, 1929," CO 323/1032/2/02; Alexander Ransford Slater to Lord Passfield, January 13, 1930, 2, 5, CO 323/1032/2/02.

59. Labour Research Department, "British Imperialism in East Africa" 1926, 3, CO 323/954/39; minute by A. J. D. to George Gater, July 17, 1943, CO 691/184/6.

60. Leslie G. Carr, *"Colorblind" Racism* (London: Sage, 1997). See also Eduardo Bonilla-Silva, *Racism without Racists: Color-Blind Racism and the Persistence of Racial Inequality in the United States* (New York: Rowman, 2006); Meghan Burke, *Colorblind Racism* (New York: Polity Press, 2018).

61. Memorandum by C. G. Eastwood, July 5, 1931, 1, CO 822/37/9; Office of the High Commissioner for Human Rights, "Convention (No. 29) Concerning Forced Labour, Adopted on 28 June 1930 by the General Conference of the International Labour Organisation at Its Fourteenth Session"; Committee on Forced Labour, June 1, 1929, 3, CO 323/1031/8; R. V. Vernon to Mr. Ellis and G. Grindle, January 31, 1930, CO 323/1066/14; memorandum, "International Labour Conventions. Application to Colonies, Etc.," 1930, 1–2, CO 323/1066/14.

62. "The Annual Meeting," *Anti-Slavery Reporter* 22 (July 1932): 61. Cf. Blackett and Duquesnoy, "Slavery Is Not a Metaphor," 1512.

63. "Native Health and Progress in East Africa," *Anti-Slavery Reporter* 22 (April 1932):, 35; "The Centenary of 1833–4," *Anti-Slavery Reporter* 23 (July 1933): 53; *Anti-Slavery Reporter* 23 (July 1933): 1. On the racial justification for slavery in North America, see, e.g., Winthrop D. Jordan, *White over Black: American Attitudes toward the Negro, 1550–1812,* 2nd ed. (Chapel Hill: University of North Carolina Press, 2012).

64. Du Bois, "Slavery," *The Crisis*, May 1921, 6.

65. Lewis, *Du Bois: Fight for Equality*, 208–11; "The Looking Glass," *The Crisis*, March 1922, 228; Du Bois, "Slavery"; "The Third Pan-African Congress," *The Crisis*, July 1923, 103; "The Third Pan-African Congress," *The Crisis*, January 1924, 120–22; Frank L. Schoell, "La Question des Noirs Aux Etats-Unis," *The Crisis*, June 1924, 83–86.

66. W. E. B. Du Bois, *Black Reconstruction; An Essay toward a History of the Part which Black Folk Played in the Attempt to Reconstruct Democracy in America, 1860–1880* (1935; reprint, New York: Atheneum, 1985). Cf. Frederick Cooper, "Conditions Analogous to Slavery: Imperialism and Free Labor Ideology in Africa," in *Beyond Slavery: Explorations of Race, Labor, and Citizenship in Postemancipation Societies*, ed. Frederick Cooper, Thomas C. Holt, and Rebecca J. Scott (Chapel Hill: University of North Carolina Press, 2000), 113–20.

4. "The Emancipation of Man"

1. Robert Hill, introduction to *Crusader* (New York: Garland, 1987); "Program of the African Blood Brotherhood," in *American Communism and Black Americans: A Documentary History, 1919–1929*, ed. Philip Foner and James S.

Allen (Philadelphia: Temple University Press, 1987); [Cyril Briggs], "A Discredited Man," *Crusader Magazine*, April 1919, 8–9; Cyril Briggs, "Africa and World Democracy," *Crusader Magazine*, January 1919, 3. See also Erez Manela, *The Wilsonian Moment: Self-Determination and the International Origins of Anticolonial Nationalism* (New York: Oxford University Press, 2007); Adom Getachew, *Worldmaking after Empire: The Rise and Fall of Self-Determination* (Princeton, NJ: Princeton University Press, 2019).

2. Nikki Taylor, *America's First Black Socialist: The Radical Life of Peter H. Clark* (Lexington: University Press of Kentucky, 2012); Cyril Briggs, "The Call for Unity," *Crusader* 1 (June 1919): 6–7; Briggs, "West Indian American Trade Opportunities," *Crusader* 1 (June 1919): 16; Briggs, "A Negro Bank for Harlem," *Crusader* 1 (March 1919): 10; Briggs, "A Harlem Negro Chamber of Commerce," *Crusader* 2 (April 1920): 9–10; A. Philip Randolph, "The Crisis in Negro Business," *Messenger* 4 (March 1922): 373; "Co-operative Business" [unsigned editorial], *Messenger* 3 (March 1920): 6–7; Marcus Garvey, "The Future as I See It," in *Philosophy and Opinions of Marcus A. Garvey*, vol. 1, ed. Amy Jacques Garvey (New York: Atheneum, 1969), 38–39; [Cyril Briggs], "Restore Africa to the Africans," *Crusader Magazine*, December 1918, 13; [Briggs], "Slavery in the South," *Crusader Magazine*, May 1919, 6; [Briggs], "Southern Atrocities," *Crusader Magazine*, August 1919, 31–32.

3. [Cyril Briggs], "Make Their Cause Your Own," *Crusader Magazine*, July 1919, 6; [Briggs], "The Lusk Committee Makes a Discovery," *Crusader Magazine*, August 1919, 6; [Briggs], "Wage Slavery in the West Indies," *Crusader Magazine*, September 1919, 9; Keith P. Griffler, *What Price Alliance? Black Radicals Confront White Labor, 1918–1938* (New York: Garland, 1995).

4. George Padmore, *The Life and Struggles of Negro Toilers* (London: R. I. L. U. Magazine, 1931); note by J. E. W. Flood, July 4, 1933, Colonial Office (hereafter CO) 533/437/16, National Archives, London; Rodney Worrell, *George Padmore's Black Internationalism* (Kingston, Jamaica: University of the West Indies Press, 2020); "A Resolution Passed at the Glover Memorial Hall in Lagos, 19 May 1945," in *The Voice of Coloured Labour: Speeches and Reports of Colonial Delegates to the World Trade Union Conference, 1945*, ed. George Padmore (London: Panaf Service, 1945); Griffler, *What Price Alliance*. On Padmore, see Leslie James, *George Padmore and Decolonization from Below: Pan-Africanism, the Cold War, and the End of Empire* (New York: Palgrave, 2014).

5. Padmore, *Life and Struggles*, 5, 48–49.

6. Padmore, 5, 13, 62, 111, 122. On labor conditions in the Caribbean, see Michael L. Conniff, *Black Labor on a White Canal: Panama, 1904–1981* (Pittsburgh: University of Pittsburgh Press, 1985); Mary Chamberlain, ed., *Caribbean Migration: Globalised Identities* (London: Routledge, 1998); Walton Look Lai, *Indentured Labor, Caribbean Sugar: Chinese and Indian Migrants to the Brit-*

ish West Indies, 1838–1918 (Baltimore: Johns Hopkins University Press, 1993); Samuel Martínez, *Peripheral Migrants: Haitians and Dominican Republic Sugar Plantations* (Knoxville: University of Tennessee Press, 1995).

7. Griffler, *What Price Alliance*, 104; note by Flood, July 4, 1933; Worrell, *George Padmore's Black Internationalism*; "Resolution Passed at Glover Memorial Hall."

8. Langston Hughes, *The Big Sea* (New York: Hill and Wang, 1940), 228; Claude McKay, *Harlem: Negro Metropolis* (New York: E. P. Dutton, 1940), 27; Alain Locke, "Spiritual Truancy," *New Challenge* 2 (1937): 81–85; Cheryl Greenberg, *To Ask for an Equal Chance: African Americans in the Great Depression* (New York: Rowman and Littlefield, 2009).

9. Griffler, *What Price Alliance*; Jonathan Scott Holloway, *Confronting the Veil: Abram Harris, Jr., E. Franklin Frazier, and Ralph Bunche, 1919–1941* (Chapel Hill: University of North Carolina Press, 2002); William A. Darity and Abram L. Harris, *Race, Radicalism and Reform: Selected Papers* (New York: Transaction, 1989); Herbert Hill, "Black Workers, Organized Labor, and Title VII of the 1964 Civil Rights Act: Legislative History and Litigation Record," in *Race in America: The Struggle for Equality*, ed. Herbert Hill and James E. Jones (Madison: University of Wisconsin Press, 1993), 263–344.

10. Ralph Bunche, *A World View of Race* (New York: Associates in Negro Folk Education, 1936), 32, 35, 43–47.

11. Abram Harris to W. E. B. Du Bois, January 6, 1934; Du Bois to Harris, January 6, 1933; Harris to Du Bois, January 7, 1933; Harris to Du Bois, March 13, 1933; Du Bois to Harris, January 3, 1934; Du Bois to Harris, January 16, 1934; Du Bois to Harris, February 1, 1934, W. E. B. Du Bois Papers (MS 312), Special Collections and University Archives, University of Massachusetts–Amherst Libraries.

12. George Padmore to W. E. B. Du Bois, February 17, 1934; Du Bois to Padmore, May 29, 1936; Tracy Phillips to Du Bois, March 29, 1932, Du Bois Papers; W. E. B. Du Bois, *Black Reconstruction; An Essay toward a History of the Part which Black Folk Played in the Attempt to Reconstruct Democracy in America, 1860–1880* (1935; reprint, New York: Atheneum, 1985); Griffler, *What Price Alliance*; Manning Marable, *W. E. B. Du Bois: Black Radical Democrat* (New York: Paradigm, 2005); David Levering Lewis, *W. E. B. Du Bois, 1919–1963: The Fight for Equality and the American Century* (New York: Holt, 2001).

13. Griffler, *What Price Alliance*; Holloway, *Confronting the Veil*.

14. Abram L. Harris, "Reconstruction and the Negro," *New Republic*, August 7, 1935.

15. Glenda Elizabeth Gilmore, *Defying Dixie: The Radical Roots of Civil Rights, 1919–1950* (New York: W. W. Norton, 2008); Griffler, *What Price Alliance*; Holloway, *Confronting the Veil*; Robin D. G. Kelley, *Freedom Dreams: The*

Black Radical Imagination (Boston: Beacon Press, 2002); Robin D. G. Kelley, *Hammer and Hoe: Alabama Communists during the Great Depression* (Chapel Hill: University of North Carolina Press, 1990); Mark Naison, *Communists in Harlem during the Depression* (Urbana: University of Illinois Press, 1983); Cedric J. Robinson, *Black Marxism: The Making of the Black Radical Tradition* (London: Zed Press, 1983); Cedric J. Robinson, *Black Movements in America* (New York: Routledge, 1997).

16. Bunche, *World View of Race*, 43–47. Cf. Aldon Morris, *Origins of the Civil Rights Movement: Black Communities Organizing for Change* (New York: Free Press, 1986).

17. Karl Marx, "The International Workingmen's Association 1864 Address . . . to Abraham Lincoln, President of the United States of America, Presented to U.S. Ambassador Charles Francis Adams January 28, 1865," Marx & Engels Internet Archive, http://www.marxists.org/history/international/iwma/documents/1864/lincoln-letter.htm.

18. Du Bois, *Black Reconstruction*, 6, 12.

19. Du Bois, 15–16.

20. Patrick O'Brien, "European Economic Development: The Contribution of the Periphery," *Economic History Review* 35, no. 1 (1982): 1–18; Patrick O'Brien, "European Industrialization: From the Voyages of Discovery to the Industrial Revolution," in *The European Discovery of the World and Its Economic Effects on Pre-Industrial Society, 1500–1800*, ed. Hans Pohl (Stuttgart: Franz Steiner Verlag, 1990), 154–77; Brian William Cowan, *The Social Life of Coffee: The Emergence of the British Coffeehouse* (New Haven, CT: Yale University Press, 2005); Craig Koslofsky, *Evening's Empire: A History of the Night in Early Modern Europe* (Cambridge: Cambridge University Press, 2011); Sidney Wilfred Mintz, *Sweetness and Power: The Place of Sugar in Modern History* (New York: Viking, 1985); Woodruff D. Smith, "Complications of the Commonplace: Tea, Sugar, and Imperialism," *Journal of Interdisciplinary History* 23, no. 2 (1992): 259–79.

21. Raymond Buell, *The Native Problem in Africa*, 2 vols. (New York: Macmillan, 1928), 1:772.

22. Nayan Chanda, *Bound Together: How Traders, Preachers, Adventurers, and Warriors Shaped Globalization* (New Haven, CT: Yale University Press, 2007), 207, 219; Orlando Patterson, *Slavery and Social Death: A Comparative Study* (Cambridge, MA: Harvard University Press, 1982), 152; Robinson, *Black Marxism*, 16; Barbara L. Solow, "Capitalism and Slavery in the Exceedingly Long Run," *Journal of Interdisciplinary History* 17, no. 4 (1987): 712–15; Charles Verlinden, *The Beginnings of Modern Colonization* (Ithaca, NY: Cornell University Press, 1970), 31–32; Michael Tadman, "The Demographic Cost of Sugar: Debates on Slave Societies and Natural Increase in the Americas," *American Historical Review* 105, no. 5 (2000): 1534–75.

23. O. Nigel Bolland, "Systems of Domination after Slavery: The Control of Land and Labor in the British West Indies after 1838," *Comparative Studies in Society and History* 23, no. 4 (1981): 591–619; Pete Daniel, "The Metamorphosis of Slavery, 1865–1900," *Journal of American History* 66, no. 1 (1979): 88–99; Ronald L. F. Davis, *Good and Faithful Labor: From Slavery to Sharecropping in the Natchez District, 1860–1890* (Westport, CT: Greenwood Press, 1982); Howard Johnson, "The Share System in the Bahamas in the Nineteenth and Early Twentieth Centuries," *Slavery and Abolition* 5, no. 2 (1984): 141–53; Howard Johnson, *The Bahamas in Slavery and Freedom* (Kingston, Jamaica: Ian Randle Publishers, 1991); Woodville K. Marshall, "Metayage in the Sugar Industry of the British Windward Islands, 1838–1865," *Jamaican Historical Review* 5 (1965): 28–55; Brian L. Moore, *Race, Power, and Social Segmentation in Colonial Society: Guyana after Slavery, 1838–1891* (New York: Gordon and Breach Science Publishers, 1987); Monica Schuler, *"Alas, Alas, Kongo": A Social History of Indentured African Immigration into Jamaica, 1841–1865* (Baltimore: Johns Hopkins University Press, 1980); Robin Blackburn, *The Making of New World Slavery: From the Baroque to the Modern 1492–1800* (London: Verso, 1997); M. L. Bush, *Servitude in Modern Times* (Cambridge: Polity Press, 2000); David Brion Davis, *Inhuman Bondage: The Rise and Fall of Slavery in the New World* (Oxford: Oxford University Press, 2006); Herbert Klein, *African Slavery in Latin America and the Caribbean* (New York: Oxford University Press, 1986); David Northrup, *Indentured Labor in the Age of Imperialism, 1834–1922* (Cambridge: Cambridge University Press, 1995); Moses Finley, *The Ancient Economy* (Berkeley: University of California Press, 1973); Bernard Lewis, *Race and Slavery in the Middle East: An Historical Enquiry* (New York: Oxford University Press, 1990); William Phillips, *Slavery from Roman Times to the Early Transatlantic Trade* (Minneapolis: University of Minnesota Press, 1985); Ehud Toledano, *Slavery and Abolition in the Ottoman Middle East* (Seattle: University of Washington Press, 1998).

24. Klein, *African Slavery in Latin America and the Caribbean*, 68, 81, 84. Joel Quirk cites mining as among the most common "slave roles" across history, from "Ancient Athens to early modern Brazil." Joel Quirk, *Unfinished Business: A Comparative Survey of Historical and Contemporary Slavery* (Paris: UNESCO, 2009), 60. See also Gregory Chirichigno, *Debt-Slavery in Israel and the Ancient Near East* (Sheffield, UK: JSOT Press, 1993); Finley, *Ancient Economy*; Moses Finley, *Ancient Slavery and Modern Ideology* (New York: Viking Press, 1980); Yvon Garlan, *Slavery in Ancient Greece*, rev. ed. (Ithaca, NY: Cornell University Press, 1988); Catherine Hezser, *Jewish Slavery in Antiquity* (Oxford: Oxford University Press, 2005); Keith Hopkins, "Novel Evidence for Roman Slavery," *Past and Present* 138, no. 1 (1993): 3–27; Zvi Yavetz, *Slaves and Slavery in Ancient Rome* (New Brunswick, NJ: Transaction Books, 1988); E. G. Pulleyblank, "The

Origins and Nature of Chattel Slavery in China," *Journal of the Economic and Social History of the Orient* 1, no. 2 (1958): 185–220; G. K. Rai, *Involuntary Labour in Ancient India* (Allahabad, India: Chaitanya, 1981); Ram Sharan Sharma, *Sudras in Ancient India: A Social History of the Lower Order down to Circa A.D. 600*, 2nd rev. ed. (Delhi: Motilal Banarsidass, 1980); Joseph Vogt, *Ancient Slavery and the Ideal of Man* (Oxford: B. Blackwell, 1974); Laird Bergad, *The Comparative Histories of Slavery in Brazil, Cuba, and the United States* (Cambridge: Cambridge University Press, 2007), 194; Jonathan Daniel Wells, *The Origins of the Southern Middle Class, 1800–1861* (Chapel Hill: University of North Carolina Press, 2004), 186–91; Robert S. Starobin, *Industrial Slavery in the Old South* (New York: Oxford University Press, 1970).

25. Klein, *African Slavery in Latin America and the Caribbean*, 68, 81, 84; Joan Casanovas, *Bread or Bullets! Urban Labor and Spanish Colonialism in Cuba, 1850–1898* (Pittsburgh: University of Pittsburgh Press, 1998), 5; Ira Berlin, *Many Thousands Gone: The First Two Centuries of Slavery in North America* (Cambridge, MA: Belknap Press of Harvard University Press, 1998), 269–70, 75; Jacqueline Jones, *Labor of Love, Labor of Sorrow: Black Women, Work and the Family, from Slavery to the Present* (New York: Basic Books, 2010), 12, 15; Rebecca J. Scott, *Slave Emancipation in Cuba: The Transition to Free Labor, 1860–1899* (Pittsburgh: University of Pittsburgh Press, 2000), 28.

26. Bailey v. State of Alabama, 219 U.S. 246 (1911).

27. Du Bois, *Black Reconstruction*, 6; League of Nations, *Slavery Convention, Geneva, September 25th 1926* (Geneva: League of Nations, 1926), 1.

28. Frederick Engels, *The Condition of the Working-Class in England in 1844* (London: Swan Sonnenschein, 1892), 134–87. On white sharecropping, see, e.g., Wayne Flynt, *Dixie's Forgotten People: The South's Poor Whites* (Bloomington: Indiana University Press, 1979); Jacqueline Jones, *The Dispossessed: America's Underclasses from the Civil War to the Present* (New York: Basic Books, 1992); Mark Schultz, *The Rural Face of White Supremacy: Beyond Jim Crow* (Urbana: University of Illinois Press, 2005).

29. Du Bois, *Black Reconstruction*, 6; Davis, *Inhuman Bondage*, 3; David Brion Davis, *The Problem of Slavery in the Age of Revolution, 1770–1823* (Ithaca, NY: Cornell University Press, 1975), 164; David Brion Davis, *The Problem of Slavery in Western Culture* (Ithaca, NY: Cornell University Press, 1966), vii.

30. Du Bois, *Black Reconstruction*, 26.

31. John Higham, *Strangers in the Land: Patterns of American Nativism, 1860–1925* (New Brunswick, NJ: Rutgers University Press, 1955); James R. Barrett and David Roediger, "Inbetween Peoples: Race, Nationality and the 'New Immigrant' Working Class," *Journal of American Ethnic History* 16, no. 3 (1997): 3-44; David R. Roediger, *Working toward Whiteness: How America's Immigrants Became White; the Strange Journey from Ellis Island to the Suburbs* (New York: Basic Books, 2005).

32. "Report of the Commission Appointed to Inquire into the Disturbances in the Copperbelt, Northern Rhodesia," July 1940, 8, 196, CO 795/122/19. Cf. Barbara Bush, *Imperialism, Race, and Resistance: Africa and Britain, 1919–1945* (London: Routledge, 1999); P. J. Cain and A. G. Hopkins, *British Imperialism, 1688–2000*, 2nd ed. (New York: Longman, 2001); Muriel Evelyn Chamberlain, *The Scramble for Africa* (New York: Longman, 2010); Mahmood Mamdani, *Citizen and Subject: Contemporary Africa and the Legacy of Late Colonialism* (Princeton, NJ: Princeton University Press, 1996).

33. Native Reserves Commission, Report to the Officer Administering the Government, signed by P. J. Macdonell, H. P. Hart, and J. Moffat Thomson, January 25, 1927, 56, CO 795/17/1; "Report of the Commission Appointed to Inquire into the Disturbances in the Copperbelt," 195, CO 795/122/19; Peter Koinange, "The Agrarian Problem in Kenya," Ohio Wesleyan University, [1933], 4, CO 533/437/16; R. S. Hudson, "Extension of Opportunities for African Workers on the Copperbelt," November 1941, 2–3, CO 795/122/17.

34. George Farrar, *Transvaal Labour Importation Ordinance* (Johannesburg: Transvaal Leader Office, 1904), 12–22; Joseph Miller, "Retention, Reinvention, and Remembering: Restoring Identities through Enslavement in Africa and under Slavery in Brazil," in *Enslaving Connections: Changing Cultures of Africa and Brazil during the Era of Slavery*, ed. Jose Curto and Paul Lovejoy (Amherst, NY: Humanity Books, 2004), 89; Frederick C. Knight, *Working the Diaspora: The Impact of African Labor on the Anglo-American World, 1650–1850* (New York: New York University Press, 2010), 1–2.

35. Farrar, *Transvaal Labour Importation Ordinance*, 12–22; Tadman, "Demographic Cost of Sugar"; Charles van Onselen, *Chibaro: African Mine Labour in Southern Rhodesia, 1900–1933* (Bloomington: Indiana University Press, 1980).

36. Uganda Protectorate, *Report of the Committee of Enquiry into the Labour Situation in the Uganda Protectorate, 1938* (Uganda: Government Printer, 1938), 23, CO 536/200/3.

37. Joseph Inikori, *Africans and the Industrial Revolution in England: A Study in International Trade and Development* (New York: Cambridge University Press, 2002), 382. On the agricultural knowledge of Africans, see, e.g., Tirfe Mammo, *The Paradox of Africa's Poverty: The Role of Indigenous Knowledge, Traditional Practices and Local Institutions—the Case of Ethiopia* (Trenton, NJ: Red Sea Press, 1999); Netsayi Noris Mudege, *An Ethnography of Knowledge: The Production of Knowledge in Mupfurudzi Resettlement Scheme, Zimbabwe* (Leiden, Netherlands: Brill, 2008); Saul Dubow, *Science and Society in Southern Africa* (Manchester, UK: Manchester University Press, 2000); Ali Al'Amin Mazrui, *Africa since 1935* (Berkeley: University of California Press, 1993), 635–38; Fiona Mackenzie *Land, Ecology and Resistance in Kenya, 1880–1952* (Edinburgh: Edinburgh University Press for the International African Institute, 1998). On

the African knowledge at the root of rice production, see Judith A. Carney, *Black Rice: The African Origins of Rice Cultivation in the Americas* (Cambridge, MA: Harvard University Press, 2001); Judith A. Carney, "From Hands to Tutors: African Expertise in the South Carolina Rice Economy," *Agricultural History* 67, no. 3 (1993): 1–30; Judith Ann Carney and Richard Nicholas Rosomoff, *In the Shadow of Slavery: Africa's Botanical Legacy in the Atlantic World* (Berkeley: University of California Press, 2009); Edda L. Fields-Black, *Deep Roots: Rice Farmers in West Africa and the African Diaspora* (Bloomington: Indiana University Press, 2008); Daniel C. Littlefield, *Rice and Slaves: Ethnicity and the Slave Trade in Colonial South Carolina* (Baton Rouge: Louisiana State University Press, 1981); Peter H. Wood, *Black Majority: Negroes in Colonial South Carolina from 1670 through the Stono Rebellion* (New York: Knopf, 1974); Peter H. Wood, "'It Was a Negro Taught Them': A New Look at African Labor in Early South Carolina," *Journal of Asian and African Studies* 9, no. 3–4 (1974): 160–79.

38. Carmen Diana Deere, "Rural Women's Subsistence Production in the Capitalist Periphery," *Review of Radical Political Economics* 8, no. 1 (1976): 9–17; Harold Wolpe, "Capitalism and Cheap Labour-Power in South Africa: From Segregation to Apartheid," *Economy and Society* 1, no. 4 (1972): 425–56.

39. Uganda Protectorate, *Report of the Committee of Enquiry*," 48–49, 22–23.

40. Davis, *Inhuman Bondage*, 3; Blackburn, *Making of New World Slavery*, 3; Patterson, *Slavery and Social Death*, 134–47.

41. Inikori, *Africans and the Industrial Revolution in England*, 392. On settler colonialism, see, e.g., Patrick Wolfe, *Settler Colonialism* (London: Bloomsbury Academic, 1999); Lorenzo Veracini, *Settler Colonialism: A Theoretical Overview* (New York: Palgrave, 2010).

42. Peter Koinange to Ramsay MacDonald, June 12, 1933, CO 533/437/16; Koinange, "Agrarian Problem in Kenya," 3–4; note to Sir S. Wilson, July 7, 1933, CO 533/437/16; Ramsay MacDonald, *Labour and the Empire* (London: George Allen, 1907), 52, 49, 50. On the rise of the social welfare state, see Peter Baldwin, *The Politics of Social Solidarity: Class Bases of the European Welfare State, 1875–1975* (Cambridge: Cambridge University Press, 1990); Derek Fraser, *The Evolution of the British Welfare State: A History of Social Policy since the Industrial Revolution* (London: Macmillan, 1973).

43. Koinange, "Agrarian Problem in Kenya"; Koinange to MacDonald, June 12, 1933; note by Flood, July 4, 1933; J. S. Crush, *The Struggle for Swazi Labour, 1890–1920* (Kingston, ON: McGill-Queen's University Press, 1987), 146; Mbiyu Koinange, *The People of Kenya Speak for Themselves* (Detroit: Kenya Publishing House, 1955).

44. [Frederick Lugard], Confidential Note in the Kenya Land Commission Report, September 1935, 2, 23, CO 533/453/10; [revised memo by Sir

Donald Cameron], "Federation," May 22, 1927, CO 822/4/19; Labour Party, Advisory Committee on Imperial Questions, "Memorandum on Land Utilisation and Settlement in Kenya," April 1946, CO 533/556/7.

45. Northern Rhodesia, Native Reserves Commission Report, 1926, vol. 1, 59, CO 795/17/1; minute by J. J. Paskin, June 9, 1938, CO 533/497/6; Labour Party, "Memorandum on Land Utilisation and Settlement in Kenya," April 1946.

46. Native Reserves Commission, Report to the Officer Administering the Government, January 25, 1927, 10. Cf. George M. Fredrickson, *White Supremacy: A Comparative Study in American and South African History* (New York: Oxford University Press, 1981); Mamdani, *Citizen and Subject*; William Beinart and Saul Dubow, eds., *Segregation and Apartheid in Twentieth-Century South Africa* (London: Routledge, 1995); Owen Crankshaw, *Race, Class, and the Changing Division of Labour under Apartheid* (London: Routledge, 1997); Adrian Guelke, *Rethinking the Rise and Fall of Apartheid: South Africa and World Politics* (New York: Palgrave Macmillan, 2005); P. Eric Louw, *The Rise, Fall, and Legacy of Apartheid* (Westport, CT: Praeger, 2004). On the British roots of apartheid, see Robert Magubane, *The Making of a Racist State: British Imperialism and the Union of South Africa, 1875–1910* (Trenton, NJ: Africa World Press, 1996). On land policy, see Sam Moyo, *African Land Questions, Agrarian Transitions and the State: Contradictions of Neo-liberal Land Reforms* (Oxford: African Books Collective, 2008); Lungisile Ntsebeza and Ruth Hall, *The Land Question in South Africa: The Challenge of Transformation and Redistribution* (Cape Town, South Africa: HSRC Press, 2007); Mwangi Wa-Githumo, *Land and Nationalism: The Impact of Land Expropriation and Land Grievances upon the Rise and Development of Nationalist Movements in Kenya, 1885–1939* (Lanham, MD: University Press of America, 1981); Robert Home, ed., *Essays in African Land Law* (Pretoria, South Africa: Pretoria University Law Press, 2011); Carlos Nunes Silva, ed., *Urban Planning in Sub-Saharan Africa: Colonial and Post-Colonial Planning Cultures* (New York: Routledge, 2013); Ambe Njoh, *Planning Power: Town Planning and Social Control in Colonial Africa* (London: Taylor and Francis, 2007).

47. Crush, *Struggle for Swazi Labour*, 140–79; Nyasaland Commission to Enquire into and Report upon the Occupation of Land, *Report of a Commission to Enquire into and Report upon Certain Matters Connected with the Occupation of Land in Nyasaland Protectorate* (Zomba: Government Printer, [1920]), 12, 14–17; memorandum by R. Rankine, Chief Secretary, Nyasaland, January 28, 1927, 3–4, CO 525/119/2; memorandum, "Native Tenants on Private Estates," December 28, 1926, CO 525/116/14; Nyasaland Native Rising Commission, *Report of the Commission Appointed by His Excellency the Governor to Inquire into Various Matters and Questions Concerned with the Native Rising within the Nyasaland Protectorate*

(Zomba: Government Printer, [1916]), 5–6; Nyasaland Chamber of Agriculture and Commerce, memorandum, "Native Tenants on Private Estates," n.d., CO 525/119/2; memorandum [on Sir Barlow's interview], n.d., CO 525/160/1.

48. Martin Chanock, "South Africa, 1841–1924: Race, Contract, and Coercion" in *Masters, Servants, and Magistrates in Britain and the Empire, 1562–1955*, ed. Douglas Hay and Paul Craven (Chapel Hill: University of North Carolina Press, 2005), 338; Teresa Barnes, "'Am I a Man?' Gender and the Pass Laws in Urban Colonial Zimbabwe, 1930–1980," *African Studies Review* 40, no. 1 (1995): 59–81; David Anderson, "Master and Servant in Colonial Kenya, 1895–1939," *Journal of African History* 41, no. 3 (2000): 459–85; New Reform Club, *British Workmen or Chinese Slaves* (London: New Reform Club, 1904), 5; William Beinart, *The Political Economy of Pondoland 1860–1930* (New York: Cambridge University Press, 2009), 60; van Onselen, *Chibaro*, 135.

49. Extract from a report by Colonel Watkins, March 9, 1927, CO 533/698; memorandum by C. G. Eastwood, July 6, 1931, CO 822/37/9.

50. "Labour Conditions in North," *Bulawayo Chronicle*, December 20, 1938, CO 795/109/1; W. B. Davidson-Houston, Acting Governor of Nyasaland, to Lord Passfield, Secretary of State for the Colonies, March 15, 1930, CO 525/137/11; Edward Denham, Governor of Kenya, to L. C. M. S. Amery, Secretary of State for the Colonies, July 8, 1927, CO 533/716.

51. Fredrickson, *White Supremacy*, xi.

52. Patterson, *Slavery and Social Death*; Austin Allen, *Origins of the Dred Scott Case: Jacksonian Jurisprudence and the Supreme Court, 1837–1857* (Athens: University of Georgia Press, 2006).

53. Nyasaland, *Report of Commission to Enquire into Occupation of Land*, 41; Granville St. John Orde-Browne, *Report upon Labour in the Tanganyika Territory, with a Covering Despatch from the Governor* (London: HMSO, 1926), 45, 59; A. Lynn Saffery, *A Report on Some Aspects of African Living Conditions on the Copper Belt of Northern Rhodesia* (Lusaka: Government Printer, 1943), 52, CO 795/128/12; T. F. Sandford, minutes of Native Industrial Labour Advisory Board meeting, Ndola, April 22–23, 1936, 8, CO 795/83/3. Cf. Robert Home, "Colonial Urban Planning in Anglophone Africa," in Silva, *Urban Planning in Sub-Saharan Africa*, 53–66; Njoh, *Planning Power*.

54. Saffery, *Report on Living Conditions on the Copper Belt*, 59; minute by G. J. Orde Browne, May 25, 1939, CO 525/178/12; Godfrey Wilson, *An Essay on the Economics of Detribalization in Northern Rhodesia*, 2 vols. (Livingstone, Northern Rhodesia: Rhodes-Livingstone Institute, 1941), 1:48.

55. Orde-Browne, *Report upon Labour in the Tanganyika Territory*; minute by J. Fredk. N. Green, April 13, 1932, CO 822/37/9; Colonial Office to Sir Ronald Storrs, July 1, 1933, CO 822/37/9; Mr. Roger to B. Hobson, June 19,

1951, CO 533/564/6; Thomas Ellis Naylor, *Yellow Labour: The Truth about the Chinese in the Transvaal* (London: Daily Chronicle Office, 1904), 7.

56. Patterson, *Slavery and Social Death*; Native Reserves Commission Report to the Officer Administering the Government, January 25, 1927, 10. Cf. Fredrickson, *White Supremacy*; Mamdani, *Citizen and Subject*; Beinart and Dubow, *Segregation and Apartheid in Twentieth-Century South Africa*; Crankshaw, *Race, Class, and the Changing Division of Labour under Apartheid*; Guelke, *Rethinking the Rise and Fall of Apartheid*; Louw, *Rise, Fall, and Legacy of Apartheid*.

57. Du Bois, *Black Reconstruction*, 15–16.

58. See Keeanga-Yamahtta Taylor, *From #BlackLivesMatter to Black Liberation* (New York: Haymarket Books, 2016); Rinaldo Walcott, *The Long Emancipation: Moving toward Black Freedom* (Durham, NC: Duke University Press, 2021).

59. Virginia Whatley Smith, ed., *Richard Wright's Travel Writings: New Reflections* (Oxford: University of Mississippi, 2012); W. Burghardt Turner and Joyce Moore Turner, *Richard B. Moore, Caribbean Militant in Harlem: Collected Writings, 1920–1972* (Bloomington: Indiana University Press, 1988), 193; Kwame Nkrumah, *Africa Must Unite* (New York: International Publishers, 1970), ix; George Padmore, *History of the Pan-African Congress: Colonial and Coloured Unity, a Programme of Action* (London: Hammersmith Bookshop, 1947); Hakim Adi, *Pan-Africanism: A History* (London: Bloomsbury, 2018).

60. Nkrumah, *Africa Must Unite*, ix, xv, 135, 180.

61. Frantz Fanon, *The Wretched of the Earth* (New York: Grove Atlantic, 2007), 5, 34, 53–54, 57–58; David Macey, *Frantz Fanon: A Biography* (London: Verso, 2000); Leo Zeilig, *Frantz Fanon: A Political Biography* (London: Bloomsbury, 2021).

62. Fanon, *Wretched of the Earth*, 5, 34, 53–54, 57–58.

63. Stokely Carmichael and Charles V. Hamilton, *Black Power: The Politics of Liberation* (New York: Knopf Doubleday, 2011), 4–6; Peniel Joseph, *Stokely: A Life* (New York: Basic Books, 2014).

64. Carmichael and Hamilton, *Black Power*, 6, 10, 17, 23.

65. Pete Daniel, *The Shadow of Slavery: Peonage in the South, 1901–1969* (Urbana: University of Illinois Press, 1972); Vijay Prashad, *The Darker Nations: A People's History of the Third World* (New York: New Press, 2007); Adi, *Pan-Africanism*; Kimberle Crenshaw, "Beyond Racism and Misogyny: Black Feminism and 2 Live Crew," in *Words that Wound: Critical Race Theory, Assaultive Speech and the First Amendment*, ed. Mari Matsuda et al. (Boulder, CO: Westview Press, 1993), 112–13; Kimberlé Crenshaw, *On Intersectionality: Essential Writings* (New York: New Press, 2019).

5. The Emancipation of Women

1. Ella Baker and Marvel Cooke, "The Bronx Slave Market," *The Crisis* 42 (November 1935): 329–30, 340; Barbara Ransby, *Ella Baker and the Black Freedom Movement* (Chapel Hill: University of North Carolina Press, 2003).

2. Baker and Cooke, "Bronx Slave Market," 330, 340. Cf. Patricia Hill Collins, *Black Feminist Thought: Knowledge, Consciousness, and the Politics of Empowerment* (New York: Routledge, 2000).

3. Patricia McFadden, "Becoming Postcolonial: African Women Changing the Meaning of Citizenship," *Meridians: Feminism, Race, Transnationalism* 6 (2005): 1–18, 4–5; W. E. B. Du Bois, *Black Reconstruction: An Essay toward a History of the Part which Black Folk Played in the Attempt to Reconstruct Democracy in America, 1860–1880* (1935; reprint, New York: Atheneum, 1985), 15–16; Baker and Cooke, "Bronx Slave Market," 340. On Du Bois and gender, see Shirley Moody-Taylor, "'Dear Doctor Du Bois': Anna Julia Cooper, W. E. B. Du Bois, and the Gender Politics of Black Publishing," *MELUS: Multi-Ethnic Literature of the U.S.* 40 (Fall 2015): 47–68. On Pan-Africanism and gender, see Carol Boyce Davies, "Gender/Class Intersections and African Women's Rights," *Meridians: Feminism, Race, Transnationalism* 13 (2015): 1–25; Patricia McFadden, "African Feminist Perspectives of Post-Coloniality," *Black Scholar* 37 (2007): 36–42; Selina Makana, "Motherhood as Activism in the Angolan People's War, 1961–1975," *Meridians: Feminism, Race, Transnationalism* 15 (2017): 353–81.

4. Kimberlé Crenshaw, *On Intersectionality: Essential Writings* (New York: New Press, 2019); Kimberle Crenshaw, "Beyond Racism and Misogyny: Black Feminism and 2 Live Crew," in *Words that Wound: Critical Race Theory, Assaultive Speech and the First Amendment*, ed. Mari Matsuda et al. (Boulder, CO: Westview Press, 1993), 112–13; Sumi Cho, Kimberle Crenshaw, and Leslie McCall, "Toward a Field of Intersectionality Studies: Theory, Applications, and Praxis," *Signs: Journal of Women in Culture and Society* 38, no. 4 (2013): 785–810; Patricia Hill Collins, *Intersectionality as Critical Social Theory* (Durham, NC: Duke University Press, 2019); Patricia Hill Collins and Sirma Bilge, *Intersectionality* (New York: Wiley, 2016).

5. Fredrick Douglass, *Narrative of the Life of Frederick Douglass* (London: Collins, 1851), 37; Ira Berlin, *Many Thousands Gone: The First Two Centuries of Slavery in North America* (Cambridge, MA: Belknap Press of Harvard University Press, 1998), 56; Jacqueline Jones, *Labor of Love, Labor of Sorrow: Black Women, Work and the Family, from Slavery to the Present* (New York: Basic Books, 2010), 21; B. W. Higman, *Slave Populations of the British Caribbean, 1807–1834* (Baltimore: Johns Hopkins University Press, 1984), 172–73; Laird W. Bergad, *The Comparative Histories of Slavery in Brazil, Cuba, and the United States* (Cambridge: Cambridge University Press, 2007), 195; Elizabeth Fox-

Genovese, *Within the Plantation Household: Black and White Women of the Old South* (Chapel Hill: University of North Carolina Press, 1988); Lorena Madrigal, *Human Biology of Afro-Caribbean Populations* (Cambridge: Cambridge University Press, 2006), 28–31; Marli Frances Weiner, *Mistresses and Slaves: Plantation Women in South Carolina, 1830–80* (Urbana: University of Illinois Press, 1997), 13–22; John Michael Vlach, *Back of the Big House: The Architecture of Plantation Slavery* (Chapel Hill: University of North Carolina Press, 1993), especially chap. 2.

6. Jones, *Labor of Love*, 18; Berlin, *Many Thousands Gone*, 158; Mary Karasch, "Slave Women on the Brazilian Frontier on the 19th Century," in *More than Chattel: Black Women and Slavery in the Americas*, ed. David Barry Gaspar and Darlene Clark Hine (Bloomington: Indiana University Press, 1996), 88; Higman, *Slave Populations of the British Caribbean*, 231–32; E. Susan Barber, "Depraved and Abandoned Women: Prostitution in Richmond, Virginia, across the Civil War," in *Neither Lady nor Slave: Working Women of the Old South*, ed. Susanna Delfino and Michele Gillespie (Chapel Hill: University of North Carolina Press, 2002), 155–73; Judith Kelleher Schafer, *Brothels, Depravity, and Abandoned Women: Illegal Sex in Antebellum New Orleans* (Baton Rouge: Louisiana State University Press, 2009).

7. Du Bois, *Black Reconstruction*, 8; Deborah White, "Female Slaves: Sex Roles and Status in the Antebellum Plantation South," *Journal of Family History* 8, no. 3 (1983): 251; Hilary Beckles, *Natural Rebels: A Social History of Enslaved Black Women in Barbados* (New Brunswick, NJ: Rutgers University Press, 1989), 90–91; Higman, *Slave Populations of the British Caribbean*, 348–54; Jones, *Labor of Love*, 32; Orlando Patterson, *Slavery and Social Death: A Comparative Study* (Cambridge, MA: Harvard University Press, 1982), 134–47.

8. Abayomi Azikiwe, "Pan Africanism, Women's Emancipation and the Meaning of Socialist Development," *Pambazuka News*, September 6, 2016, www.pambazuka.org/gender-minorities/pan-africanism-women's-emancipation-and-meaning-socialist-development.

9. Kwame Nkrumah, *Selected Speeches of Dr. Kwame Nkrumah* (Accra, Ghana: S. Obeng, 1973), 116; Azikiwe, "Pan Africanism"; Gerald Horne, *Race Woman: The Lives of Shirley Graham Du Bois* (New York: New York University Press, 2000).

10. Ula Yvette Taylor, *The Veiled Garvey: The Life and Times of Amy Jacques Garvey* (Chapel Hill: University of North Carolina Press, 2003); Lionel M. Yard, *Biography of Amy Ashwood Garvey, 1897–1969* (New York: Associated Publishers, 1988); Toyin Falola and Adam Paddock, *The Women's War of 1929: A History of Anti-Colonial Resistance in Eastern Nigeria* (n.p.: Carolina Academic Press, 2011); Shireen Hassim, *Women's Organizations and Democracy in South Africa* (Madison: University of Wisconsin Press, 2006).

11. Baker and Cooke, "Bronx Slave Market," 329–30, 340; David Killingray, "Significant Black South Africans in Britain before 1912: Pan-African Organisations and the Emergence of South Africa's First Black Lawyers," *South African Historical Journal* 64, no. 3 (2012): 393–417.

12. H. R. Fox Bourne, *Forced Labour in British South Africa: Notes on the Condition and Prospects of South African Natives under British Control* (London: P. S. King and Son, [1903]), 21; "Native Questions in South Africa," *Aborigines' Friend,* January 1902, 127.

13. Henry Fox Bourne, *Forced Labour in British South Africa* (London: Aborigines Protection Society, 1903), 21–24.

14. Fox Bourne; Frederick Douglass, "What the Black Man Wants: An Address Delivered in Boston, Massachusetts, on 26 January 1865," in *The Frederick Douglass Papers: Series One, Speeches, Debates, and Interviews*, ed. John W. Blassingame and John R. McKivigan, 5 vols. (New Haven, CT: Yale University Press, 1979), 4:59–69.

15. John Harris, *Africa: Slave or Free?* (New York: Negro Universities Press, 1969), 61, 178.

16. [Sir Donald Cameron], "Federation," London, May 22, 1927, Colonial Office (hereafter CO) 822/4/19, National Archives, London; "Correspondence Relating to the Welfare of Women in Tropical Africa," 1935–1937, 11, CO 879/139; "Original Draft," Passfield circular to colonial governors, March 8, 1930, CO 822/27/10; P. E. Mitchell, "Female Circumcision and the Status of Women in Tanganyika Territory," 22, enclosure 2 in Donald Cameron to Lord Passfield, May 22, 1930, CO 323/1067/2; "Report on Customs of the Gambia," enclosure in C. R. M. Workman to Lord Passfield, July 26, 1930, 2, CO 323/1067/5.

17. Orlando Patterson, "Trafficking, Gender and Slavery: Past and Present," in *The Legal Understanding of Slavery: From the Historical to the Contemporary*, ed. Jean Allain, 1st ed. (Oxford: Oxford University Press, 2012), 334, 50. Cf. Joseph Miller, "Women as Slaves and Owners of Slaves," in Gwyn Campbell, Suzanne Miers, and Joseph Calder Miller, *Women and Slavery: Africa, the Indian Ocean World, and the Medieval North Atlantic*, 2 vols. (Athens: Ohio University Press, 2007), 1:1–3.

18. Note on "An Essay on the Economics of De-Tribalisation in Northern Rhodesia by the Director of the Rhode-Livingstone Institute," [1941], CO 795/122/19; "Labour Report: Note of Government's Preliminary Conclusions on the Recommendations Pending Receipt of Observations from Interested Parties," [1939], 1–2, CO 536/203/11; note by Granville St. John Orde-Browne, September 18, 1942, CO 795/122/17; Northern Rhodesia Native Reserves Commission, "Report," 1926, vol. 1, 102, CO 795/17/1. On patterns of migration, see Alan Mabin, "Limits of Urban Transition Models in Under-

standing South African Urbanisation," *Development Southern Africa* 7, no. 3 (1990): 311–22; Christopher McDowell and Arjan De Haan, *Migration and Sustainable Livelihoods: A Critical Review of the Literature*, IDS Working Paper 65 (Brighton, UK: Institute of Development Studies, 1997), 11; Dorrit Posel, "Moving On: Patterns of Labour Migration in Post-Apartheid South Africa," in *Africa on the Move: African Migration and Urbanisation in Comparative Perspective*, ed. Marta Tienda (Johannesburg: Wits University Press, 2006), 217.

19. Teresa Barnes, "'Am I a Man?' Gender and the Pass Laws in Urban Colonial Zimbabwe, 1930–1980," *African Studies Review* 40, no. 1 (1995): 59–81. On the role of women in migration processes, see, e.g., Caroline S. Archambault, "Women Left Behind? Migration, Spousal Separation, and the Autonomy of Rural Women in Ugweno, Tanzania," *Signs* 35, no. 4 (2010): 919–42; Teresa Barnes, "Virgin Territory? Travel and Migration by African Women in Twentieth-Century Southern Africa," in *Women in African Colonial Histories*, ed. Jean Marie Allman, Susan Geiger, and Nakanyike Musisi (Bloomington: Indiana University Press, 2002), 164–90; Camilla M. Cockerton, "'Running Away' from 'The Land of the Desert': Women's Migration from Colonial Botswana to South Africa, c. 1895–1966" (PhD thesis, Queen's University, 1995); Miranda Miles, "Missing Women: Reflections on the Experiences of Swazi Migrant Women on the Rand, 1920–1970," *GeoJournal* 30, no. 1 (1993): 85–92; Hamilton Sipho Simelane, "The State, Chiefs and the Control of Female Migration in Colonial Swaziland, c. 1930's–1950's," *Journal of African History* 45, no. 1 (2004): 103–24.

20. Northern Rhodesia Native Reserves Commission, "Report," 1926, vol. 1, 70, 75, 81–82; McFadden, "Becoming Postcolonial"; Barnes, "'Am I a Man?'"

21. Baker and Cooke, "Bronx Slave Market," 329–30, 340.

22. Baker and Cooke; Keith P. Griffler, *What Price Alliance? Black Radicals Confront White Labor, 1918–1938* (New York: Garland, 1995), 165–90.

23. Ida B. Wells, *Crusade for Justice: The Autobiography of Ida B. Wells* (Chicago: University of Chicago Press, 2020), 86; Ida B. Wells, *Lynching: Our National Crime* (New York: Springer, 2020).

24. See Suzanne Mackenzie and Damaris Rose, "Industrial Change, the Domestic Economy and Home Life," in *Redundant Spaces in Cities and Regions? Studies in Industrial Decline and Social Change*, ed. James Anderson, S. Duncan, and Ray Hudson (London: Academic Press, 1983), 155–200; Linda McDowell, "City and Home: Urban Housing and the Sexual Division of Space," in *Sexual Divisions: Patterns and Processes*, ed. Mary Evans and Clare Ungerson (London: Tavistock Publications, 1983), 142–63; Leslie Weisman, *Discrimination by Design: A Feminist Critique of the Man-Made Environment* (Urbana: University of Illinois Press, 1992); Elizabeth Wilson, *The Sphinx in the City: Urban Life, the Control of Disorder, and Women* (London: Virago Press, 1991).

25. [East Africa Royal Commission], "The Development of Towns in East Africa," [1955], 9, CO 892/4/11; memo from Office of the District Commissioner, Mufulira Province, Northern Rhodesia, November 12, 1947, 2, CO/1018/54; Godfrey Wilson, *An Essay on the Economics of Detribalization in Northern Rhodesia*, 2 vols. (Livingstone, Northern Rhodesia: Rhodes-Livingstone Institute, 1941), 1:70–71; memo from Office of the District Commissioner, Chingola Province, Northern Rhodesia, November 12, 1947, 1, CO/1018/54; [East Africa Royal Commission], "Development of Towns in East Africa," 15; International Labour Office, "The Employment of Conditions of Work of African Women," 1964, 9, 101, CO 859/1781; Gustavo Anríquez and Libor Stloukal, "Rural Population Change in Developing Countries: Lessons for Policymaking" (ESA working paper 08-09, UN Food and Agriculture Organization, 2008), 6; Carmen Diana Deere, "The Feminization of Agriculture? Economic Restructuring in Rural Latin America" (UN Research Institute for Social Development, 2005); Tamara Jacka, *Women's Work in Rural China: Change and Continuity in an Era of Reform* (Cambridge: Cambridge University Press, 1997), 127–37; Susana Lastarria-Cornhiel, *Feminization of Agriculture: Trends and Driving Forces* (Washington, DC: World Bank, 2008); World Bank, Food and Agriculture Organization of the United Nations, and International Fund for Agricultural Development, *Gender in Agriculture Sourcebook* (Washington, DC: World Bank, 2009), 523.

26. Northern Rhodesia Native Reserves Commission, "Report," 1926, vol. 1, 126. Teresa Barnes takes exception to the notion that women were simply "left behind" in rural areas, which renders them passive and dismisses their agency. Barnes, "Virgin Territory?" 167. However, Barnes insists on the gendered nature of the political economy of colonialism's migrant labor system. This corresponds to the notion of "enforced" used in the text, which is also consistent with McFadden's notion of "postcolonial citizenship." Barnes, "'Am I a Man?'" 59–81; McFadden, "Becoming Postcolonial."

27. Minute by J. J. Paskin, July 16, 1938, CO 533/497/6; minute by J. A. Calder, August 12, 1938, CO 533/497/6; R. Brooke-Popham, Governor of Kenya, to Malcolm MacDonald, Secretary of State for the Colonies, November 26, 1938, 3, CO 533/497/6; minute by J. J. Paskin, June 9, 1938, CO 533/497/6; minute by Paskin, July 16, 1938; minute by Calder, August 12, 1938; A. de V. Wade, Governor of Kenya, "Memorandum on Certain Questions in the 'Red Report,'" November 2, 1938; minute by Malcolm MacDonald, October 3, 1938, CO 533/497/6; W. Harragin [for governor of Kenya] to Malcolm MacDonald, Secretary of State for the Colonies, August 1, 1939, CO 859/11/3.

28. Northern Rhodesia Native Reserves Commission, "Report," 1926, vol. 1, 126; Stefan Kieniewicz, *The Emancipation of the Polish Peasantry* (Chicago:

University of Chicago Press, 1969), 4, 15; Wojciech Szczygielski, "Dzieje spoleczne chlopow w okresie od XVI do XVIII w.," in *Z Dziejów Chlopow Polskich: Od Wczesnego Feudalismu Do 1939 R*, ed. Stanisław Szczotka (Warsaw, Poland: Ludowa Społdzielnia Wydawnicza, 1948), 71, 75.

29. Labour Research Department, "British Imperialism in East Africa," Colonial Series no. 1, 1926, 16, CO 323/954/39; J. C. Maxwell, Governor, Northern Rhodesia, to Lord Passfield, Colonial Office, January 10, 1930, CO 795/32/15; minute by H. F. Downie to Mr. Green, July 1, 1931, CO 525/142/1; Native Welfare Committee, memorandum on native policy in Nyasaland, January 1939, 15, CO 525/183/10; minute by E. L. Scott to Mr. Rogers, July 20, 1950; minute by A. B. C. [Cohen] to Sir T. Lloyd, July 21, 1950, CO 691/208/9; Busoga Land Policy [unsigned and undated, ca. 1928], CO 536/149/16; minute by Downie to Green, July 1, 1931; Zbigniew Stankiewicz, "Okres reform uwlaszczeniowych," in *Z Dziejów Chlopow Polskich*, 172; Wladyslaw Roczniak, "The Polish 'Gromada' Peasant Collectives in the Era of Re-Feudalization," *Polish Review* 49, no. 4 (2004): 1090. On the role of property rights, see, e.g., Gareth Austin, *Labour, Land, and Capital in Ghana: From Slavery to Free Labour in Asante, 1807–1956* (Rochester, NY: University of Rochester Press, 2005).

30. Deborah Gaitskell, "Housewives, Maids or Mothers: Some Contradictions of Domesticity for Christian Women in Johannesburg, 1903–39," *Journal of African History* 24, no. 2 (1983): 88; "Native Education on Mines," notes of meeting held in the Office of the Senior Provincial Commissioner, May 31, 1938, CO 795/109/2; minute by O. G. R. Williams, October 13, 1942, CO 859/60/7. On prostitution in East Africa, see Luise White, *The Comforts of Home: Prostitution in Colonial Nairobi* (Chicago: University of Chicago Press, 1990). On the twentieth-century transition from male to female domestic labor, see Jose C. Moya, "Domestic Service in a Global Perspective: Gender, Migration, and Ethnic Niches," *Journal of Ethnic and Migration Studies* 33, no. 4 (2007): 562–63. See also Catherine Coquery-Vidrovitch, *African Women: A Modern History* (Boulder, CO: Westview Press, 1997), 76; Raka Ray, "Masculinity, Femininity, and Servitude: Domestic Workers in Calcutta in the Late Twentieth Century," *Feminist Studies* 26, no. 3 (2000): 693; Victoria Haskins and Claire Lowrie, *Colonization and Domestic Service: Historical and Contemporary Perspectives* (New York: Routledge, 2014); Dirk Hoerder, Elise van Nederveen Meerkerk, and Silke Neunsinger, eds., *Towards a Global History of Domestic and Caregiving Workers* (Boston: Brill, 2015).

31. Baker and Cooke, "Bronx Slave Market," 330, 340.

32. "Extract from 'West Africa' dated Saturday, April 17, 1943"; Henry Ormston, "The Social Question: A Startling Disclosure," *West Africa*, March 15, 1941, clipping; R. W. Floyer, "Letter to the Editor: The Nigerian Social Question," *West Africa*, June 6, 1942, clipping, CO 859/60/7; Carina Ray, "Sex

Trafficking, Prostitution, and the Law in Colonial British West Africa, 1911–43," in *Trafficking in Slavery's Wake: Law and the Experience of Women and Children*, ed. Benjamin N. Lawrance and Richard L. Roberts (Athens: Ohio University Press, 2012), 108. Ormston concluded that the eighty girls in question had "probably" arrived on different boats, but Ray (109) cites a Gold Coast police report that confirms the "trafficking" of a "boatload of women and girls from Nigeria" at around that time. Minute by O. G. R. Williams, March 16, 1942; B. H. Bourdillon to Lord Moyne, August 21, 1941, CO 859/60/7; Stephanie A. Limoncelli, *The Politics of Trafficking: The First International Movement to Combat the Sexual Exploitation of Women* (Stanford, CA: Stanford University Press, 2010), 22. On the continuities of earlier slave markets as an element of the larger market for girls, see Lawrance and Roberts, *Trafficking in Slavery's Wake*.

33. Baker and Cooke, "Bronx Slave Market," 330; P. W. Perryman, Acting Governor (Uganda), to the Secretary of State for the Colonies, September 30, 1930, 14, CO 323/1067/4; "Correspondence Relating to the Welfare of Women in Tropical Africa," 1935–1937, 16, CO 879/139; Margaret Wrong, "The Education of African Women in a Changing World," written for 1940 edition of *Year Book of Education*, August 1939, 3, CO 859/1/9. Cf. Saheed Aderinto, "Prostitution and Urban Social Relations," in *Nigeria's Urban History: Past and Present*, ed. Hakeem Ibikunle Tijani (Lanham, MD: University Press of America, 2006), 75–98; minute by Williams, March 16, 1942; Bourdillon to Moyne, August 21, 1941; Limoncelli, *Politics of Trafficking*, 22. Cf. Lawrance and Roberts, *Trafficking in Slavery's Wake*; "Extract from 'West Africa,' April 17, 1943"; Ormston, "Social Question"; Floyer, "Letter to the Editor"; Ray, "Sex Trafficking, Prostitution, and the Law," 108; Elizabeth Elbourne, introduction to Gwyn Campbell and Elizabeth Elbourne, *Sex, Power and Slavery* (Athens: Ohio University Press, 2014), 19.

34. Minutes by F. Eastwood, June 5 and July 6, 1931; minute by A. C. Parkinson, July 7, 1931; minute by S. Wilson, April 13, 1932, CO 822/37/9.

35. Barnes, "Virgin Territory?" 167. See also Teresa Barnes, *"We Women Worked So Hard": Gender, Urbanization, and Social Reproduction in Colonial Harare, Zimbabwe, 1930–1956* (Portsmouth, NH: Heinemann, 1999); Belinda Bozzoli, *Women of Phokeng: Consciousness, Life Strategy, and Migrancy in South Africa, 1900–1983* (Portsmouth, NH: Heinemann, 1991); Cockerton, "Running Away.'"

36. Cockerton, "Running Away,'" 112, 125, 226. On African women's resistance, see Judith van Allen, "'Sitting on a Man': Colonialism and the Lost Political Institutions of Igbo Women," *Canadian Journal of African Studies* 6, no. 2 (1972): 165–78; Nancy Rose Hunt, "Placing African Women's History and Locating Gender," *Social History* 14, no. 3 (1989): 362–65.

37. Keith Griffler, *Front Line of Freedom: African Americans and the Forging of the Underground Railroad in the Ohio Valley* (Lexington: University Press of Kentucky, 2004); Du Bois, *Black Reconstruction*.

38. "Details of Proposed Lorry Service to and from Southern Rhodesia," n.d. [ca. 1937], CO 525/166/6; memo from Office of the District Commissioner, Ndola Province, Northern Rhodesia, November 11, 1947, 2–6, CO/1018/54; Women: Orders, Ushi-Ngumbo Fort Rosebery under Section 8 (o), of Ordinance 9/36, CO 1018/54; [East Africa Royal Commission], "Development of Towns in East Africa"; A. Cox, "Uganda: Township Ordinance," CO 1018/79; Municipal Council of Nairobi, notes of proceedings and evidence submitted to the meetings of the Committee of Inquiry, January 1946, 30, CO 533/564/6. Cf. Cockerton, "'Running Away'"; Nina Boyle, *What Is Slavery? An Appeal to Women?* copy in CO 323/1320/4.

39. Advisory Committee on Social Development in Colonial Territories, Reports Sub-Committee, Extract of Draft Minutes, CO 822/1139.

40. [East Africa Royal Commission], "Development of Towns in East Africa," 15; White, *Comforts of Home*; William Beinart, *The Political Economy of Pondoland 1860–1930* (New York: Cambridge University Press, 2009), 150.

41. Baker and Cooke, "Bronx Slave Market," 330. On the organization of slavery in the Americas, see, e.g., Ira Berlin and Philip D. Morgan, eds., *Cultivation and Culture: Labor and the Shaping of Slave Life in the Americas* (Charlottesville: University Press of Virginia, 1993), pt. 3, 203–302; B. W. Higman, *Slave Populations of the British Caribbean, 1807–1834* (Kingston, Jamaica: University of the West Indies Press, 1995), 210–15, 38–42; Mary Turner, *From Chattel Slaves to Wage Slaves: The Dynamics of Labour Bargaining in the Americas* (Bloomington: Indiana University Press, 1995).

42. Ray, "Sex Trafficking, Prostitution, and the Law," 103; [East Africa Royal Commission], "Development of Towns in East Africa," 15; P. W. Perryman to Lord Passfield, September 30, 1930, 13, CO 323/1067/4; note by J. E. King, December 30, 1953, CO 859/436; Note by [signature illegible], January 1, 1954, CO 859/436; Wrong, "Education of African Women in a Changing World," 3.

43. Municipal Council of Nairobi, notes of proceedings and evidence, January 1946, 8–10; White, *Comforts of Home*; Ray, "Sex Trafficking, Prostitution, and the Law," 103.

44. Limoncelli, *Politics of Trafficking*, 44, 69, 76, cf. 73–97; Anne Gallagher, *The International Law of Human Trafficking* (New York: Cambridge University Press, 2010); Jean Allain, "Trafficking and Human Exploitation in International Law, with Special Reference to Women and Children in Africa," in Lawrance and Roberts, *Trafficking in Slavery's Wake*.

45. Memorandum prepared by the department in connection with the debate in the House of Commons on the report of the commission appointed to

inquire into the disturbances on the Copper Belt, [1941], CO 795/122/18; A. Lynn Saffery, *A Report on Some Aspects of African Living Conditions on the Copper Belt of Northern Rhodesia* (Lusaka: Government Printer, 1943), 51, CO 795/128/12; John Weddington to Lord Moyne, Secretary of State for the Colonies, October 31, 1941, CO 795/122/19. On urbanization, see George Chauncey, "The Locus of Reproduction: Women's Labour in the Zambian Copperbelt, 1927–1953," *Journal of Southern African Studies* 7, no. 2 (1981): 135–64; Philip Daniel, *Africanisation, Nationalisation, and Inequality: Mining Labour and the Copperbelt in Zambian Development* (Cambridge: Cambridge University Press, 1979), 65–66; James Ferguson, "Mobile Workers, Modernist Narratives: A Critique of the Historiography of Transition on the Zambian Copperbelt [Part One]," *Journal of Southern African Studies* 16, no. 3 (1990): 400–401; Kenneth Lindsay Little, *African Women in Towns: An Aspect of Africa's Social Revolution* (London: Cambridge University Press, 1973), 17; Jane L. Parpart, "The Household and the Mine Shaft: Gender and Class Struggles on the Zambian Copperbelt, 1926–64," *Journal of Southern African Studies* 13, no. 1 (1986): 36–56; Jane Parpart, "'Where Is Your Mother?' Gender, Urban Marriage, and Colonial Discourse on the Zambian Copperbelt, 1924–1945," *International Journal of African Historical Studies* 27, no. 2 (1994): 241–71; H. J. Simons, "Zambia's Urban Situation," in *Development in Zambia*, ed. Ben Turok (London: Zed Press, 1979), 11; Helmuth Heisler, *Urbanisation and the Government of Migration: The Inter-Relation of Urban and Rural Life in Zambia* (London: C. Hurst, 1974).

46. See Amy Lind, "Gender, Development and Urban Social Change: Women's Community Action in Global Cities," *World Development* 25, no. 8 (1997): 1205–23; Diane Rothbard Margolis, "Women's Movements around the World: Cross-Cultural Comparisons," *Gender and Society* 7, no. 3 (1993): 379–99; Raka Ray and Anna C. Korteweg, "Women's Movements in the Third World: Identity, Mobilization, and Autonomy," *Annual Review of Sociology* 25, no. 1 (1999): 47–71; Lilia Rodriguez, "Barrio Women: Between the Urban and the Feminist Movement," *Latin American Perspectives* 21, no. 3 (1994): 32–48.

47. Dispatch from Passfield, March 8, 1930, CO 323/1071/8; International Labour Organisation, *Second African Regional Conference, 1964: The Employment and Conditions of Work of African Women* (Geneva: ILO, 1964), 4, 100–101, CO 859/1781. Cf. McFadden, "Becoming Postcolonial"; Iris Berger, *Women in Twentieth Century Africa* (New York: Cambridge University Press, 2016); Jean Parpart, ed., *Women and Development in Africa: Comparative Perspectives* (Charlottesville: University of Virginia Press, 1989).

48. Women to Kilimanjaro, "Charter of Demands: Actualizing Women's Land Rights in Africa," https://tgnp.org/wp-content/uploads/2017/04/The-Kilimanjaro-Rural-Womens-Final-charter-of-demands-.pdf (accessed October 10, 2020), 1; McFadden, "Becoming Postcolonial," 2–3.

49. Women to Kilimanjaro, "Charter of Demands," 2–4.

6. Black Abolitionism and the New Slavery in the Twenty-First Century

1. "Pre-strike Statement from Jailhouse Lawyers Speak," August 12, 2018, https://itsgoingdown.org/pre-strike-statement-from-jailhouse-lawyers-speak/; Bennu Hannibal Ra-Sun, "Boycott, Defund, Bankrupt," *San Francisco Bay View*, December 30, 2017, http://sfbayview.com/2017/12/boycott-defund-bankrupt-say-no-to-canteen-incentive-packages-collect-phone-calls-and-visitation-during-february-april-june-black-august-october-and-december-in-2018/; Ed Pilkington, "US Inmates Stage Nationwide Prison Labor Strike over 'Modern Slavery,'" *Guardian*, August 21, 2018, https://www.theguardian.com/us-news/2018/aug/20/prison-labor-protest-america-jailhouse-lawyers-speak. Cf. Adelle Blackett and Alice Duquesnoy, "Slavery Is Not a Metaphor: U.S. Prison Labor and Racial Subordination through the Lens of the ILO's Abolition of Forced Labor Convention," *UCLA Law Review* 67, no. 6 (2021): 1504–35; Mary Rose Whitehouse, "Modern Prison Labor: A Reemergence of Convict Leasing under the Guise of Rehabilitation and Private Enterprises," *Loyola Journal of Public Interest Law* 18 (2017): 89; Neveen Hammad, "Shackled to Economic Appeal: How Prison Labor Facilitates Modern Slavery while Perpetuating Poverty in Black Communities," *Virginia Journal of Social Policy and the Law* 26, no. 2 (2019): 65–90; Jaron Brown, "Rooted in Slavery: Prison Labor Exploitation," *Race, Poverty and the Environment* 14, no. 1 (2007): 42–44.

2. Swift Justice, "This 'Modern-Day' Slavery Isn't All that Modern," *San Francisco Bay View*, March 29, 2018, https://sfbayview.com/2018/03/this-modern-day-slavery-isnt-all-that-modern/.

3. Kevin Rashid Johnson, "Prison Labor Is Modern Slavery," *Guardian*, August 23, 2018, https://www.theguardian.com/commentisfree/2018/aug/23/prisoner-speak-out-american-slave-labor-strike; Swift Justice, "This 'Modern-Day' Slavery"; Pilkington, "US Inmates Stage Nationwide Prison Labor Strike."

4. Tom Philips, "Brazil's Ethanol Slaves: 200,000 Migrant Sugar Cutters Who Prop up Renewable Energy Boom," *Guardian*, March 8, 2007, 21. See also Ricardo Resende Figueira, "Contemporary Slavery in Brazil: 1985 to 2009," in *Human Rights in Brazil*, ed. Evanize Sydow and Maria Luisa Mendonça (Network for Social Justice and Human Rights, 2009), 65–74; Maria Luisa Mendonça, "Monocropping of Sugarcane and Counter-Agrarian Reform," in *Human Rights in Brazil*, 47–54; Terry-Ann Jones, "Migration Theory in the Domestic Context: North-South Labor Movement in Brazil," *Human Architecture: Journal of the Sociology of Self-Knowledge* 7, no. 4 (2009): 5–14; Siobhan McGrath, "Fuelling Global Production Networks with Slave Labour? Migrant Sugar Cane Workers in Brazilian Ethanol GPS," *Geoforum* 44 (2013): 32–43. See also Rodrigo Baptista et al., "The Invisibility of the Black Population in

Modern Slavery: Evidence Based on Conditions of Social Vulnerability," *Revista Organizações & Sociedade* 24, no. 87 (2017): 676–703. The authors conclude that for Brazil as a whole, "slave labor has a definite race/color identity" (689). They also quote Brazil's Ministry of Foreign Affairs: "It needs to be recognized that slaves in Brazil are mostly black. Denying this fact is to fly in the face of reality" (694).

   5. CNN Freedom Project, "Child Slavery and Chocolate: All Too Easy to Find," January 19, 2012, http://thecnnfreedomproject.blogs.cnn.com/2012/01 /19/child-slavery-and-chocolate-all-too-easy-to-find/; International Labor Organization, *Rooting out Child Labour from Cocoa Farms: Paper no. 1: A Synthesis Report of Five Rapid Assessments* (Geneva: ILO, 2007), 16–17; "Oversight of Public and Private Initiatives to Eliminate the Worst Forms of Child Labor in the Cocoa Sector in Cote d'Ivoire and Ghana" (Tulane University, Payson Center for International Development and Technology Transfer, March 31, 2011), 28; Norimitsu Onishi, "The Bondage of Poverty that Produces Chocolate," *New York Times*, July 29, 2001. On children in slavery today, see Gary Craig, *Child Slavery Now: A Contemporary Reader* (Portland, OR: Policy Press, 2010).

   6. ILO, *Rooting out Child Labour from Cocoa Farms*, 3.

   7. Mark Pendergrast, *Uncommon Grounds: The History of Coffee and How It Transformed Our World*, rev. ed. (New York: Basic Books, 2010), xvi. See also Antony Wild, *Coffee: A Dark History* (New York: W. W. Norton, 2005).

   8. Kevin Bales, *Disposable People: New Slavery in the Global Economy* (Berkeley: University of California Press, 1999); Paul Lovejoy, *Transformations in Slavery: A History of Slavery in Africa*, 2nd ed. (New York: Cambridge University Press, 2000). On Indian Ocean world slavery, see Joseph Inikori, introduction to *Forced Migration: The Impact of the Export Slave Trade on African Societies* (London: Hutchinson University Library for Africa, 1982). On slavery in the Indian Ocean world, see Gwyn Campbell, ed., *The Structure of Slavery in Indian Ocean Africa and Asia* (London: Frank Cass, 2004); Deryck Scarr, *Slaving and Slavery in the Indian Ocean* (New York: St. Martin's, 1998); John Wright, *The Trans-Saharan Slave Trade* (New York: Routledge, 2007); Paul Lovejoy, ed., *Slavery on Frontiers of Islam* (Princeton, NJ: Markus Wiener, 2004); Suzanne Miers and Igor Kopytoff, *Slavery in Africa: Historical and Anthropological Perspectives* (Madison: University of Wisconsin Press, 1977); Allan Fisher and Humphrey Fisher, *Slavery in Muslim Society in Africa* (New York: Doubleday, 1971).

   9. Bales, *Disposable People*, 10.

   10. George Steinmetz, *Sociology and Empire: The Imperial Entanglements of a Discipline* (Durham, NC: Duke University Press, 2013), 375; Jean Allain, *The Legal Understanding of Slavery: From the Historical to the Contemporary*, 1st ed. (Oxford: Oxford University Press, 2012), 99.

11. According to World Bank data, no more than 2.2 percent of the population of Europe and Central Asia fall at the standard poverty threshold of $2 per day. Most of this population is in Central Asia, with the exceptions of Romania, Moldova, Georgia, Armenia, and some of the Balkans (although the World Bank uses the higher figure of $2.50 per day for this region). At the other end of the spectrum, in both South Asia and sub-Saharan Africa, 70 percent of the total population of 2.5 billion lives on $2 a day or less. Both the United Nations and the International Labor Organization base their research on the same standard poverty thresholds as the World Bank: $1.25 a day for "extreme poverty" and $2 for "poverty." A report by the International Labor Organization notes that while the number of "working poor" living on less than $1.25 a day has decreased significantly since 2000 (predominantly in East Asia), the number of individuals living below $2 a day was higher in 2011 than projected by experts at the beginning of the 2000s. Moreover, the number of workers engaged in "vulnerable employment" (estimated at 1.52 billion globally) increased, mostly in sub-Saharan Africa and South Asia but also in Southeast Asia, Latin America, and the Caribbean. International Labour Office, *Global Employment Trends 2012: Preventing a Deeper Job Crisis* (Geneva: ILO, 2012), 10–11, http://www.ilo.org/global/publications/books/global-employment-trends/WCMS_171571/lang-en/index.htm. World Bank data are available at http://data.worldbank.org/topic/poverty. United Nations data are available at http://data.un.org/Default.aspx.

12. *By the Sweat & Toil of Children: The Use of Child Labor in U.S. Agricultural Imports & Forced and Bonded Child Labor* (Washington, DC: US Department of Labor, Bureau of International Affairs, 1995), 85–92; Human Rights Watch, "Toxic Toil: Child Labor and Mercury Exposure in Tanzania's Small-Scale Gold Mines," 2013, 36. Unfree child labor in industry is better studied in South Asia. See, e.g., Augendra Bhukuth, "Child Labour and Debt Bondage: A Case Study of Brick Kiln Workers in Southeast India," *Journal of Asian and African Studies* 40, no. 4 (2005): 287–302; Yogesh Dube and Godsen Mohandoss, *A Study on Child Labour in Indian Beedi Industry* (New Delhi: National Commission for Protection of Child Rights, 2013); International Labour Office, *Eliminating Child Labour in Mining and Quarrying: Background Document* (Geneva: ILO, 2005); Human Rights Watch, "The Small Hands of Slavery: Bonded Child Labor in India," 1996, 87; Human Rights Watch, "Toxic Tanneries: The Health Repercussions of Bangladesh's Hazaribagh Leather," 2012, 61–62; Human Rights Watch, "Small Change: Bonded Child Labor in India's Silk Industry," 2003; Chandra Korgaokar and Geir Myrstad, "Child Labour in the Diamond and Gemstone Industry in India," in *Protecting Children in the World of Work* (ILO, Bureau for Workers' Activities, 1997); Prayas Centre for Labor Research and Action, "Investigating Incidence of Child Labor in Cotton Ginning Factories of Gujarat," 2012. On global production

networks, see McGrath, "Fuelling Global Production Networks with Slave Labour." On racial capitalism, see Cedric Robinson, *On Racial Capitalism, Black Internationalism, and Cultures of Resistance* (London: Pluto, 2019).

13. US Department of Labor, Bureau of International Labor Affairs, "Findings on the Worst Forms of Child Labor," 2012, 171; Human Rights Watch, "Mali: A Poisonous Mix; Child Labor, Mercury, and Artisanal Gold Mining in Mali," 2011, 20; International Labor Organization, "Uganda: Child Labour in Tea Plantations," May 30, 2006, http://www.ilo.org/global/about-the-ilo/multimedia/video/video-news-releases/WCMS_083361/lang-en/index. htm; Kristin Palitza, "Child Labour: The Tobacco Industry's Smoking Gun," *Guardian*, September 14, 2011, http://www.theguardian.com/global-development/2011/sep/14/malawi-child-labour-tobacco-industry; International Labor Organization, *Investigating the Worst Forms of Child Labour, No. 9: Tanzania—Child Labour in Commercial Agriculture, Tobacco: A Rapid Assessment* (Geneva: ILO, 2001), 43–47; M. G. Otanez et al., "Eliminating Child Labour in Malawi: A British American Tobacco Corporate Responsibility Project to Sidestep Tobacco Labour Exploitation," *Tobacco Control* 15, no. 3 (2006): 225.

14. Palitza, "Child Labour"; Plan International (Plan Malawi), *Hard Work, Long Hours and Little Pay: Research with Children Working on Tobacco Farms in Malawi* (Auckland Park: Plan International, 2009), 14–15; ILO, *Investigating the Worst Forms of Child Labour, No. 9: Tanzania*, 48; *By the Sweat & Toil of Children*, 38.

15. ILO, *Rooting out Child Labour from Cocoa Farms*, 3; Plan International (Plan Malawi), *Hard Work*, 12. See also ILO, *Investigating the Worst Forms of Child Labour, No. 9: Tanzania*, 43–47; Robert H. McKnight and Henry A. Spiller, "Green Tobacco Sickness in Children and Adolescents," *Public Health Reports* 120, no. 6 (2005): 603.

16. ILO, *Investigating the Worst Forms of Child Labour, No. 9: Tanzania*, 50–52; Plan International (Plan Malawi), *Hard Work*, 31–48; Human Rights Watch, "Toxic Toil," 39; Human Rights Watch, "Mali: Poisonous Mix," 36; International Labour Office, "The Burden of Gold: Child Labour in Small-Scale Mines and Quarries," *World of Work* 54 (August 2005): 17. The conditions children face in East African tobacco production emerge more clearly in the better-studied cotton industry of India. Children, especially girls, are put to work cross-pollinating cotton plants, described as "very labour intensive." Ashok Khandelwal, Sudhir Katiyar, and Madan Vaishnav, "Child Labour in Cottonseed Production: A Case Study of Cottonseed Farms in North Gujarat," Dakshini Rajasthan Mazdoor Union, 2008, 23, http://www.clra.in/files/documents/Child-Labor-in-Cottonseed-Production.pdf. UNICEF describes the typical day of a child laborer thus employed: waking at 4:00 a.m., going to work without being fed, working for fourteen hours, preparing his own meals

with only a bag of flour provided, sitting in front of a television to pass the evening, and sleeping next to fourteen other children on the floor of a shed. Elliot Hannon, "Communities Mobilize to Stop Child Labour in India," UNICEF, accessed October 8, 2018, http://www.unicef.org/infobycountry/ india_58844 .html. Many children must find shelter in spaces where fertilizer is stored, but this is not their only exposure to agricultural hazards. Unlike plantation agriculture, the work of cotton pollination is continuous, including during and after the spraying of pesticides. The children are thus prone to the health effects of this exposure, ranging from finger and joint pain to respiratory problems. As in the case of virtually all child agrarian servitude, there has been little, if any, attempt to document the long-term effects. Other threats include snakebites in the fields and sexual and physical abuse from employers and hangers-on outside of them. The workers, especially the children, can expect no help or redress from authorities. Khandelwal, Katiyar, and Vaishnav, "Child Labour in Cottonseed Production," 38–39, 51, 54–55. See also Diana Coulter, "In Rural India's 'Cotton Corridor,' UNICEF and IKEA Partner to Tackle Child Labour," August 5, 2010, http://www.unicef.org/infobycountry/india_55444 .html; Humphrey Hawksley, "India's Exploited Child Cotton Workers," BBC, January 19, 2012, http://www.bbc.co.uk/news/world-asia-16639391; Davuluri Venkateswarlu, "Seeds of Bondage: Female Child Bonded Labour in Hybrid Cottonseed Production in Andhra Pradesh" (Business and Community Foundation and Plan International, India Chapter, 2001).

17. *By the Sweat & Toil of Children*, 88; International Labour Organization, "Girls in Mining: Research Findings from Ghana, Niger, Peru and the United Republic of Tanzania," 2007, 5. See also Human Rights Watch, "Toxic Toil," 10, 40–41; Human Rights Watch, "Mali: Poisonous Mix," 51; US Department of Labor, "Findings on the Worst Forms of Child Labor," 171. Cf. Korgaokar and Myrstad, "Child Labour in the Diamond and Gemstone Industry," 52.

18. Frank Laczko and Elżbieta M. Goździak, *Data and Research on Human Trafficking: A Global Survey* (Geneva: International Organization for Migration, 2005), 76, 77, 82. On trafficking in Africa, see Benjamin N. Lawrance and Richard L. Roberts, eds., *Trafficking in Slavery's Wake: Law and the Experience of Women and Children* (Athens: Ohio University Press, 2012). See also UNICEF India, *The Situation of Children in India: A Profile* (New Delhi: UNICEF, 2011), 29.

19. Human Rights Watch, "Bottom of the Ladder: Exploitation and Abuse of Girl Domestic Workers in Guinea," 2007, 41, 53; Dzodzi Tsikata, "Domestic Work and Domestic Workers in Ghana: An Overview of the Legal Regime and Practice" (International Labor Office, 2009), 29. See also International Labor Organization, *Working Hours in Domestic Work: Policy Brief No. 2* (Geneva: ILO, 2011). Cf. Therese M. Hesketh et al., "The Psychosocial Impact of Child Domestic Work: A Study from India and the Philippines," *Archives of Disease in Childhood* 97, no. 9 (2012): 53.

20. Annamarie K. Kiaga and Vicky Kanyoka, *Decent Work for Domestic Workers: Opportunities and Challenges for East Africa; a Consolidated Report of Tripartite Consultative Workshops in Kenya, Uganda and Tanzania* (Dar es Salaam: International Labor Organization, 2011), 14; Nicola Jones et al., "Stemming Girls' Chronic Poverty: Catalysing Development Change by Building Just Social Institutions," working paper (Chronic Poverty Research Centre, 2010), 40; Human Rights Watch, "Bottom of the Ladder," 43. Cf. Ayesha Shahid, "Silent Voices, Untold Stories: Women Domestic Workers in Pakistan and Their Struggle for Empowerment" (PhD diss., University of Warwick, 2007); Krishna Upadhyaya, "Bonded Labour in South Asia: India, Nepal and Pakistan," in *The Political Economy of New Slavery*, ed. Christien van den Anker (New York: Palgrave Macmillan, 2004), 131.

21. Laczko and Goździak, *Data and Research on Human Trafficking*, 77, 82, 279; Ifeyinwa Annastasia Mbakogu, "Exploring the Forms of Child Abuse in Nigeria: Efforts at Seeking Appropriate Preventive Strategies," *Journal of Social Sciences* 8, no. 1 (2004): 26; Sonja Fransen and Kate Kuschminder, "Migration in Ethiopia: History, Current Trends and Future Prospects," (Maastricht Graduate School of Governance, 2009), 16; Jens Chr. Andvig, Sudharshan Canagarajah, and Anne Kielland, "Issues in Child Labor in Africa," working paper 26701 (World Bank, Human Development Sector, Africa Region, 2001), 16; Dorte Thorsen, "Child Domestic Workers: Evidence from West and Central Africa" (UNICEF, 2012), 6; N. A. Apt, "A Study of Child Domestic Work in Northern and Upper East Regions of Ghana" (Centre for Social Policy Studies, University of Ghana, August 2005). Cf. Rajni Palriwala and N. Neetha, "Care Arrangements and Bargains: Anganwadi and Paid Domestic Workers in India," *International Labour Review* 149, no. 4 (2010): 520; N. Neetha, "Closely Woven: Domestic Work and Internal Migration of Women in India," in *Migration, Identity, and Conflict: India Migration Report*, ed. S. Irudaya Rajan (New Delhi: Routledge, 2011), 221–24.

22. Tsikata, "Domestic Work and Domestic Workers in Ghana," 32, 28; Kathleen Fitzgibbon, "Modern-Day Slavery? The Scope of Trafficking in Persons in Africa," *African Security Studies* 12, no. 1 (2003): 84; International Labor Organization, *Domestic Workers across the World: Global and Regional Statistics and the Extent of Legal Protection* (Geneva: ILO, 2013), 2; Kiaga and Kanyoka, *Decent Work for Domestic Workers*, 17. Bonded labor is more common, or at least better studied, in South Asia, where it renders children "virtual slaves," according to Human Rights Watch; it cites a figure in the millions for India alone. The renowned organization concludes, "The child is, in a sense, a commodity, exchanged between his or her parents and the employer." Human Rights Watch, "Small Change: Bonded Child Labor in India's Silk Industry," 2003, 6, 16. See also Mustafa Nazir Ahmad, *South Asian Review of the Commercial Exploitation of Children: Pakistan Study Report* (Lahore: South Asia Partnership-Pakistan,

2001), 6; E. Kamala et al., *Tanzania—Children in Prostitution: A Rapid Assessment* (Geneva: ILO, International Program on the Elimination of Child Labor, 2001), 19; Aaron Sachs, "The Last Commodity: Child Prostitution in the Developing World," *World Watch* 7, no. 4 (1994): 24–31.

23. Plan International (Plan Malawi), *Hard Work*, 14; Palitza, "Child Labour"; Jonathan Blagbrough, "Child Domestic Labour: A Modern Form of Slavery," *Children and Society* 22, no. 3 (2008): 179–90. See also Kiaga and Kanyoka, *Decent Work for Domestic Workers*; Andvig, Canagarajah, and Kielland, "Issues in Child Labor in Africa"; N. A. Apt, "A Study of Child Domestic Work in Northern and Upper East Regions of Ghana" (UNICEF and the Centre for Social Policy Studies, University of Ghana, 2005); International Labor Organization, *Ending Child Labour in Domestic Work and Protecting Young Workers from Abusive Working Conditions* (Geneva: ILO, 2013); ILO, *Working Hours in Domestic Work: Policy Brief No. 2*; Thorsen, "Child Domestic Workers"; Tsikata, "Domestic Work and Domestic Workers in Ghana"; UNICEF, "Child Domestic Work," *Innocenti Digest* 5 (1999): 2–13; Anti-Slavery International, "Domestic Slavery," https://www.antislavery.org/slavery-today/domestic-work-and-slavery/. For a comparative South Asian perspective, see Karachi Collective for Social Science Research, *A Rapid Assessment of Bonded Labour in Domestic Work and Begging in Pakistan* (Geneva: ILO, 2004); West Bengal Save the Children, *Abuse among Child Domestic Workers: A Research Study in West Bengal* (Calcutta: Save the Children, 2006).

24. Jean Allain, *The Slavery Conventions: The Travaux Préparatoires of the 1926 League of Nations Convention and the 1956 United Nations Convention* (Leiden, the Netherlands: Martinus Nijhoff, 2008), 785–86; Andvig, Canagarajah, and Kielland, "Issues in Child Labor in Africa," 16.

25. Kiaga and Kanyoka, *Decent Work for Domestic Workers*, 20; Fitzgibbon, "Modern-Day Slavery," 83; Joint United Nations Programme on HIV/AIDS (UNAIDS), *Report on the Global AIDS Epidemic* (Geneva: United Nations, 2000), 48; Nora Ellen Groce and Reshma Trasi, "Rape of Individuals with Disability: AIDS and the Folk Belief of Virgin Cleansing," *Lancet* 363, no. 9422 (2004): 1663–64; Kevin Lalor, "Child Sexual Abuse in Sub-Saharan Africa: A Literature Review," *Child Abuse and Neglect* 28, no. 4 (2004): 451; S. N. Madu and Karl Peltzer, "Risk Factors and Child Sexual Abuse among Secondary School Students in the Northern Province (South Africa)," *Child Abuse and Neglect* 24, no. 2 (2000): 264; B. L. Meel, "The Myth of Child Rape as a Cure for HIV/AIDS in Transkei," *Medicine, Science and the Law* 43, no. 1 (2003): 85–88; Karla Meursing, Theo Vos, Odette Coutinho, Michael Moyo, Sipho Mpofu, Olola Oneko, Verity Mundy, Simukai Dube, Thembeni Mahlangu, and Flora Sibindi, "Child Sexual Abuse in Matabeleland, Zimbabwe," *Social Science and Medicine* 41, no. 12 (1995): 1697.

26. Ifeyinwa Annastasia Mbakogu, "Exploring the Forms of Child Abuse in Nigeria: Efforts at Seeking Appropriate Preventive Strategies," *Journal of*

Social Science 8, no. 1 (2004): 23–27; Human Rights Watch, "Bottom of the Ladder," 25; Karachi Collective for Social Science Research, *Rapid Assessment of Bonded Labour*, 12, 14; International Labour Organization, "Girls in Mining," 5. See also Human Rights Watch, "Toxic Toil," 10, 40–41; US Department of Labor, "Findings on the Worst Forms of Child Labor," 171; Human Rights Watch, "Mali: Poisonous Mix," 51; *By the Sweat & Toil of Children*, 88. Cf. A. Dharmalingam, "Female Beedi Workers in a South Indian Village," *Economic and Political Weekly* 28, no. 27/28 (1993): 1461; G. Karunanithi, "Plight of Pledged Children in Beedi Works," *Economic and Political Weekly* 33, no. 9 (1998): 451.

27. In addition to prostitution and domestic servitude, there are India's beedi and cotton sectors. Surendra Pratap, *Current Trends in Child Labour: A Case Study of Beedi Industry in Tikamgarh* (New Delhi: Center for Education and Communication, 2001), 6; Dube and Mohandoss, *Study on Child Labour in Indian Beedi Industry*, 15. See also Dharmalingam, "Female Beedi Workers"; Karunanithi, "Plight of Pledged Children in Beedi Works." For other South Asian countries, see Omar Farrukh, *Report on Child Labour in Bidi Industry in Rangpur District* (Geneva: ILO, 2001); Govind Subedi, Bhim Prasad Subedi, and Prabha Kumari Hamal, *Child Labour in Bidi Industry in Nepal* (Kathmandu: Child Workers in Nepal Concerned Centre/Plan International, 2001); Coulter, "In Rural India's 'Cotton Corridor'"; Venkateswarlu, "Seeds of Bondage."

28. Laczko and Goździak, *Data and Research on Human Trafficking*, 244; West Bengal Save the Children, *Abuse among Child Domestic Workers*, 2. See also ECPAT International, "Global Report on the Status of Action against Commercial Sexual Exploitation of Children" (India2006), 12–13.

29. Kamala Kempadoo, "'Bound Coolies' and Other Indentured Workers in the Caribbean: Implications for Debates about Human Trafficking and Modern Slavery," *Anti-Trafficking Review* 9 (2017): 48. On the diversity within slavery, see, e.g., Gwyn Campbell, *The Structure of Slavery in Indian Ocean Africa and Asia* (London: Frank Cass, 2004).

30. Kiaga and Kanyoka, *Decent Work for Domestic Workers*, 15, 19–20; Human Rights Watch, "Bottom of the Ladder," 28; United Nations Human Settlement Programme, *The Challenge of Slums: Global Report on Human Settlements* (London: UN-HABITAT, 2003), 46. The situation is similar for girls and women in South Asia. A 2016 report on India filed jointly by Anti-Slavery International, Jan Jagriti Kendra, the National Domestic Workers' Movement, and Volunteers for Social Justice finds that "the vast majority of domestic workers in India migrate internally from rural or tribal areas," and "the majority" belong to scheduled or other disadvantaged castes. Anti-Slavery International et al., "Joint Submission for the Universal Periodic Review of India—3rd Cycle, 27th Session (May 2017)," 2016, 6.

31. Joseph Miller, preface to Gwyn Campbell, Suzanne Miers, and Joseph Calder Miller, *Women and Slavery: Africa, the Indian Ocean World, and the Medieval North Atlantic*, 2 vols. (Athens: Ohio University Press, 2007), 1:xx; Orlando Patterson, "Trafficking, Gender and Slavery: Past and Present," in Allain, *Legal Understanding of Slavery*, 350, 334; Kevin Bales, "Afterword: The End of Child Slavery?" in Craig, *Child Slavery Now*, 319. See also Lawrance and Roberts, *Trafficking in Slavery's Wake*; Craig, *Child Slavery Now*; Gwyn Campbell, Suzanne Miers, and Joseph Calder Miller, *Child Slaves in the Modern World* (Athens: Ohio University Press, 2011). On the female majority within slavery historically, see Joseph Miller, "Women as Slaves and Owners of Slaves," in Campbell, Miers, and Miller, *Women and Slavery*, 1:1–3.

32. International Labor Organization, *Report of the Committee of Experts on the Application of Conventions and Recommendations (Articles 19, 22 and 35 of the Constitution): General Report and Observations Concerning Particular Countries* (Geneva: ILO, 1998), 102; Orlando Patterson, *Slavery and Social Death: A Comparative Study* (Cambridge, MA: Harvard University Press, 1982).

33. West Bengal Save the Children, *Abuse among Child Domestic Workers*, 11–12. HRW reports that Nepalese girls in India "are raped and subjected to other forms of torture, to severe beatings, . . . and arbitrary imprisonment," including "the near total confinement of the women and girls to the brothel premises." Sections of brothels are set aside "for torturing newly-procured women" and plying them with drugs and alcohol. Human Rights Watch/Asia, "Rape for Profit: Trafficking of Nepali Girls and Women to India's Brothels," 1995, 1, 49, 43. See also ECPAT International, "Global Report on the Status of Action," 12; Fitzgibbon, "Modern-Day Slavery," 85; Kamala et al., *Tanzania—Children in Prostitution*, 29–30; Human Rights Watch, "Breaking the Silence: Child Sexual Abuse in India," 2013, 15; UNICEF Nepal, *Commercial Sexual Exploitation and Sexual Abuse of Children in South Asia* (Kathmandu: UNICEF, 2001), 18.

34. ILO, Worst Forms of Child Labour Convention, 1999 (No. 182), http://www.ilo.org/dyn/normlex/en/f?p=NORMLEXPUB:12100:0::NO::P12100_ILO_CODE:C182. On the connection between ending poverty and ending slavery, see Kevin Bales, *Ending Slavery: How We Free Today's Slaves* (Berkeley: University of California Press, 2007), 213–28.

35. Fredrick Douglass, *Narrative of the Life of Frederick Douglass, an American Slave* (London: Collins, 1851), 68. On UNESCO's vision of education, see Goal 6 of Millennium Development Goal 2, Universal Education for All, http://www.un.org/millenniumgoals/bkgd.shtml.

36. David Walker, *David Walker's Appeal to the Coloured Citizens of the World* (University Park: Pennsylvania State University Press, 2000), 41.

Index

abolitionism, antebellum, vii, 5, 7, 14; and abolition of the slave trade, 32, 43–44; and antiracism, 203; and emancipation, 19, 22, 25, 67, 100, 115, 119; and gender, 9, 159; and white slavery, 9–10; in Great Britain, 30–31, 44, 49, 56, 86; of African Americans, 44–51; role of enslaved within, 60, 176, 203–4; transatlantic, 58, 70, 84, 190

Aborigines Protection Society: antislavery work, 54–67; founding, 54; merger with Anti-Slavery Society, 54, 57, 94; official organ *Aborigines' Friend*, 55; on new slavery as racial, 62–65; relations with Pan-Africanism, 54–56, 60, 62, 79–80, 83

African Association, 39–40, 52, 54–56, 58

African Blood Brotherhood, 118–21

African independence movement, 20, 40, 127, 152–56, 162; and women, 158–59, 178

Anti-Slavery and Aborigines Protection Society (Great Britain), 78, 80, 82, 90; and Forced Labour Convention, 104–6, 116; founding, 94; leading organizational force in new antislavery, 94–96; official organ *Anti-Slavery Reporter*, 71, 83, 97; on the new slavery, 115–16, 136; position on new slavery in US, 96–97; racism within, 97, 152, 165; relations with Black abolitionism, 84–85, 96–104; relations with British Colonial Office, 94–96

antislavery, present-day, vii, 18, 154, 202; and prison activists, 2, 5, 7, 185–89

antislavery, twentieth century, vii, 6–7, 17, 35, 135; alliance with antiracism, 52–67, 190; in Great Britain, 52–67, 119; legacy, 5, 204; relation to antitrafficking movement, 10, 181–82. *See also* Black abolitionism; new antislavery; Pan-Africanism

Baker, Ella, 14; intersectional Black abolitionism of, 15–16, 18, 157–58, 179, 182; on the "slave market," 161, 163, 167–70, 175

Banks, Nathaniel, 21–25, 28, 33, 39, 88

Belgian Congo, 65, 69, 82, 89, 95

Black abolitionism, vii, viii, 14; and Black freedom movement, 2–6, 14–15, 47,

285

Index

Index

Labour Party (Great Britain), 80–82, 84, 91; and Forced Labour Convention, 104, 112–13; policy on the new slavery, 112–13, 116, 122, 143–45; relations with W. E. B. Du Bois, 99–104, 119

land policy: and African women, 166–67, 169–76, 183–84; and settler colonialism, 143–50, 173; in American South, 23; in colonial Africa, 121–22, 164–66, 169–76

Langston, Charles, 26

League of Nations, 80; and antislavery conventions, 8, 104–5, 118, 136, 181; on new slavery, 63, 92, 111; Permanent Mandates Commission, 101–5, 110

Liberal Party (Great Britain), 54, 89, 116, 163

Lincoln, Abraham, 44, 69, 120; and Civil War, 21; and emancipation, 2, 20, 49, 61–62, 86

Locke, Alain, 74–75, 122–23

Lugard, Frederick, 16, 18, 150; and definition of slavery in international law, 84–87, 92; authors Slavery Convention, 104; on abolition of slavery in Africa, 85–87, 115; opposition to colonial land policy, 144; representative to Permanent Mandates Commission, 101–4, 110

lynching, 24, 30, 48, 67; after World War I, 70; and slavery, 19–20, 34, 121–22, 168–69

MacDonald, Ramsay, 82, 99, 143–45

March on Washington (1963), 2, 3, 14

Marx, Karl, 88, 123, 127, 151–52

Marxism, 118, 128; and African Americans, 118–28, 151–52

McKay, Claude, 76, 119, 122

migrant labor: and African women, 163–67, 171; and colonial land policy, 146–50; and depopulation of Africa, 101–4; and new antislavery, 95; and new slavery, 35–41, 63–66; and skilled labor, 140–42; in twenty-first century, 188, 191–92, 195–202

NAACP, 44, 75, 119, 124; and antislavery, 67–71, 78, 120; founding, 18, 53

National Negro Congress, 123, 126–27, 167–68

new antislavery: alliance with colonialism, 6, 12, 84–97; and colorblind racism, 119, 152, 189–90, 200, 203; and women, 164–65, 170; approves of new slavery, 6–7, 12–13, 84, 92, 100–1; breaks antislavery-antiracism alliance, 6, 83–85, 97–104, 112, 116; countenances racism, 100; defined, 6; defines position on new slavery, 94–97, 151–52; John Harris as leader, 16; legacy 153, 184, 189–91, 203; origins, 17–18, 84–90, 133

New Negro, 73–75

new slavery, viii, 4, 6–7, 14–16, 135; and civil rights, 167–76, 182, 198, 200, 204–5; and compounds, 35–40, 56, 65–66, 122, 188; and contract labor, 66, 95, 107–8, 113, 131–33; and domestic labor, 126–27, 157–58, 161, 167–70, 194–99; and gender, 157–84, 194–202, 204; and global value chain, 191, 200; and health, mortality and nutrition, 63–67, 92, 101–4, 142, 158, 188–95; and indentured labor, 39–40, 56, 95–96, 131, 150; and labor taxation, 58–59, 87–88, 109–13, 122, 166; and payment of wages, 66, 138–39, 186–87, 192, 195–98; and penal sanctions, 108–9, 113; and porterage, 87, 91, 165; and railroads, 91–92, 150; and reproductive labor, 161; and sex work, 170, 174–82, 193–98; and skilled labor, 139–42, 194; and women's resistance, 176–84; as colonial, 108; as racial, 62–65, 114, 137, 142, 187–94, 200; bonded labor, 196–97; dangerous work conditions, 188, 192–95, 202; effects on all Black

Index